RESEARCH AND EVALUATION IN EDUCATION AND THE SOCIAL SCIENCES

RESEARCH AND EVALUATION IN EDUCATION AND THE SOCIAL SCIENCES

MARY LEE SMITH

GENE V GLASS

College of Education
Arizona State University

ALLYN and BACON
BOSTON LONDON TORONTO SYDNEY TOKYO SINGAPORE

Library of Congress Cataloging-in-Publication Data

Smith, Mary Lee.
  Research and evaluation in education and the
social sciences.

  Bibliography: p. 306
  Includes index.
  1. Social sciences—Research. 2. Education—
Research. 3. Evaluation research (Social action
programs) 4. Social sciences—Statistical methods.
5. Education—Statistical methods. I. Glass, Gene V,
1940–   . II. Title.
H62.S587   1987   300′.72   86-15163
  ISBN 0-13-774050-6

Copyright © 1987 by Allyn and Bacon
A Division of Simon & Schuster, Inc.
160 Gould Street
Needham Heights, Massachusetts 02194

Printed in the United States of America

10 9 8 7   95 94

ISBN 0-13-774050-6 01

CONTENTS

PREFACE

According to custom, the preface is the place where authors stake a claim for their own textbook in the landscape of competing books and state their reasons for writing a new one. Thus a context is established for professors and reviewers to judge whether the purposes of the book are realized. The expectations of students are set by this initial encounter with the authors' thoughts.

As recently as 1960 the dominant scholarly approaches in education and the social sciences were quantitative and theoretical. Now the field is larger and broader. The quantitative and theoretical approaches are still strong, but applied research or, as some call it, evaluation research has grown to a position of equal importance; more recently, qualitative methods are beginning to be recognized for their potential contribution. Some textbooks seem scarcely to have been touched by the developments of the last 30 years; some are uncomfortable with the notion of evaluation research, and others are hostile toward qualitative methods. We have attempted to deal fully with both new developments, and in so doing write a text that will do justice to an evolving field.

Some teachers and students may judge this book to be demanding. Its level of difficulty was chosen deliberately. We examined the contents of leading empirical journals in education and the social sciences (for example, *American Educational Research Journal, Journal of Educational Psychology, Journal of Counseling Psychology, Journal of Crime and Delinquency*). These journals publish some of the most important research in social science. Yet when we examined the contents of textbooks in research methodology, we found that few provide the knowledge and skills necessary to comprehend the technical sophistication represented in the leading journals.

Spanning the gap between the typical entry-level knowledge of masters and doctoral students in education and the social science and the knowledge needed to grasp the material in leading journals is difficult. But our own experiences with students in introductory classes at the University of Colorado convince us that the task can be done. Our tack is to proceed in a spiraling fashion. For example, a term such as the *null hypothesis* is introduced in the initial chapter. Although a definition is given and the role of the null hypothesis is presented, we do not expect the student to master the idea at first encounter. The null hypothesis again appears in the context of statistical tests in Chapter 3 and in the context of experimental research in Chapter 6. Following the principles of cognitive psychology, we believe that the initial presentation provides a kind of scaffolding or structure that supports the later presentation. In similar fashion, ideas such as construct validity, randomization, and generalization are introduced early and in later chapters grow more concrete, more elaborate, and more understandable. We hope that the student will be comfortable with an initial partial understanding that will grow and deepen from the first chapter to the last, and then continue to grow as the ideas presented here are used in life outside the classroom.

This book is intentionally designed for consumers of research and evaluation. It is not a "how-to" book, a fact which explains the absence of chapters on writing proposals, designing studies, or selecting which methods fit particular research questions. Indeed, we believe it is a rare student who can design a study at the completion of an introductory course. At best, the student can make an intelligent choice as to which advanced and specialized course (that is, a course in experimental design or survey research) should be taken next. Design and production of a research study such as a dissertation would occur *after* the advanced course. Yet the principles that enable one to read and critique studies—the meat of this book—are fundamental to the eventual production of one's own studies. Understanding the principles of internal validity, for example, will allow the student to understand existing studies now and to design his or her own study later.

Few people, even few professionals, actually do research; many people read research or read about it; virtually everyone is touched by what research has uncovered. This book was written for the professionals and scholars-in-training who must learn to read research and evaluation intelligently and critically and for those who may also be laying the foundation for doing research in the future. More thorough technical training in advanced courses will be needed by those who aspire to contribute to the research and evaluation literature. When finished with this text, the practicing professional should be able to read a reasonably large proportion of the research literature with critical understanding.

In summary, three purposes guided the writing of this book: to provide substance that is broader in scope and more eclectic in philosophy than that included in most existing textbooks, to match the level of technical sophistication typical of prominent educational and social science journals, and to focus on research and evaluation connoisseurship as both more general than and prerequisite to the skills related to the production of studies.

ACKNOWLEDGMENTS

Many colleagues contributed to the development of this book, and we wish to thank them. Among those who read and reacted to some or all of the chapters of the manuscript were Royce Sadler, Ernie House, Harold Levine, Bobbie Flexer, Lorrie Shepard, Elizabeth Heublin, Emily Healy, Greg Camilli, and Mary Catherine Ellwein. Faculty and students of the Laboratory of Educational Research at the University of Colorado–Boulder have given us intellectual stimulation and companionship over the years, and no doubt will recognize many of their ideas pilfered for this book. Richard Turner, Dean of the School of Education at University of Colorado–Boulder, supported the project. For the physical production of the manuscript, we have no secretaries to thank, for it was composed, edited, revised, and reedited entirely by ourselves. Our multitalented and patient friends, Abe and Bobbie Flexer, guided us through the intricacies of Osborne I and Wordstar, and we owe them. We also wish to thank Susan Willig and Jane Bower of Prentice-Hall, who gave us more support and encouragement than we had a right to expect from a publisher.

Finally, we dedicate the book to Robert E. Stake of the University of Illinois. Bob was responsible, in different eras and quite different ways, for bringing both of us into the field of research and evaluation methodology. We wish to express our appreciation in this way.

MLS
GVG

RESEARCH AND EVALUATION IN EDUCATION AND THE SOCIAL SCIENCES

1

INTRODUCTION TO RESEARCH

RESEARCH AND THE PROFESSIONAL

Understanding the work of social institutions, whether schools, hospitals, clinics, correctional facilities, or public service agencies, presents special problems both to those who conduct research and those who read the finished research studies. Researchers attempt (often with imperfect results, as we shall see) to apply techniques that work well in the controlled environment of the laboratory to the flux and variety of the social world and thus arrive at some truth about how and how well the institutions are working. Readers of the reports struggle to understand and apply the results of these studies to social and political actions and policy.

Should the citizen decide, for example, that the decline in achievement test scores warrants a change in the school board membership? Does the published relationship between teenage drinking and traffic accidents mean that the minimum age for obtaining a driver's license should be raised? Does the director of the County Mental Health Center respond to studies of the superiority of behavioral counseling methods by requiring therapists to adopt those methods? Should the superintendent raise the average class size because research shows no relationship between class size and academic achievement? Should the state government mandate driver education because studies show that its graduates have fewer accidents?

Research results are not the sole basis for making decisions or forming policies. Yet in each of these cases professionals in schools and social institutions are called upon to read the research reports and judge their worth and applicability. They must decide what the studies mean. Were the studies rigorously conducted, so that their findings are worth consideration? Was achievement measured in a sensible way? Could some other variable such as socioeconomic status account for the relationship observed between drinking and accidents?

Part of what it takes to be an intelligent reader and consumer of research reports is an understanding of the ideas and principles collected in this book. Although they require some intensive study, they are not so technical that they cannot be learned by any graduate student or professional. The other part of what it takes is commonly accessible—the application of critical thinking to the studies you read.

Chapter 1 has three main sections. The first introduces you to the principles of reading research studies and judging their merits. The second presents the sequence of steps that make up the research process and unveils important terms and concepts. The last section gives some preliminary ideas about the nature of the research endeavor.

JUDGING THE MERIT OF RESEARCH STUDIES

We offer four tools, or criteria, for interpreting and judging the merits of studies: logical validity, construct validity, internal validity, and external validity. To see how these criteria might be applied, assume, for a moment, that you are the director of a University Counseling Center who is confronting the decision to add biofeedback as a treatment available to clients of the center. Among other things, you have a research study on the effectiveness of biofeedback to help you make your decision. You also have the four criteria to help judge whether the study is good enough and applicable to your own circumstances. Read the **abstract**—summary of the study—in Figure 1–1. Afterward, consider these four tools for interpreting and judging its merits.

Logical validity Notice that the abstract was organized into six elements or pieces (e.g., research problem, research hypothesis, and so on). In every research study there is a logical argument that strings the elements together. If the study has **logical validity**, the reader should be able to follow the argument and assess whether the hypothesis follows logically from the problem, whether the methods follow logically and consistently from the hypothesis, the findings from the methods, and the conclusions from the findings. Given the hypothesis of the study, do the methods and procedures follow sensibly from that hypothesis? If the findings are acceptable, do the conclusions logically follow? Looking at the abstract, one can use common sense to judge that the procedures (giving some patients

---

"THE SUPERIORITY OF BIOFEEDBACK ON ANXIETY"

Research Problem: Is biofeedback training more effective than psychotherapy in reducing anxiety?

Hypothesis: Anxiety will be lower among subjects who have had biofeedback than among those who have had psychotherapy.

Definition of Variables: *Anxiety* is defined as the standard score on the State-Trait Anxiety Inventory (STAI)
Biofeedback training is defined as two hours per week for four consecutive weeks spent with a biofeedback therapist.
Psychotherapy is defined as two hours per week for four consecutive weeks spent with a state-certified psychotherapist who administers client-centered techniques.

Design and Procedures: Subjects were chosen from the list of adults who sought outpatient psychological services at the Feelgood Clinic during September. Subjects were pretested on the STAI and randomly assigned to either the biofeedback group or the psychotherapy group. After one month in treatment, all 50 subjects were posttested on the STAI. The averages of the two groups were compared and a test of statistical significance applied.

Findings: The average STAI score of the biofeedback group was significantly lower than the average of the psychotherapy group. (A lower score is indicative of less anxiety.)

Conclusion: Biofeedback training is superior to psychotherapy in reducing anxiety and therefore is the best choice among available treatments.

FIGURE 1–1 Abstract of Hypothetical Study

biofeedback and some others psychotherapy and then assessing which group had lower anxiety after the end of treatment) are plausible and relevant to the hypothesis as stated. However, if the procedures had specified that one group of subjects received biofeedback and another group no treatment, one would judge that the methods were *inconsistent* with the hypothesis (i.e., the hypothesis specified a comparison between two treatments but the procedures involved one treatment group compared to an untreated control group). The reader should always attempt to judge whether the methods of the study were capable of answering the questions and testing the hypothesis the researcher had stated.

Here is an example of poor logical validity. The hypothesis is this: "Young boys suffer academically when raised without a male role model." The procedures involve comparing the academic achievement of two groups of boys; one group is from intact families and the other from homes where the parents are divorced. Since male role models may be available even in homes where the mother is a single parent, the methods chosen to examine the hypothesis are not logical in this case.

Does the study as illustrated in the abstract have good logical validity? Notice that each step follows logically and consistently from the one before *until* the last part of the conclusions. The first statement ("Biofeedback training is superior to psychotherapy in reducing anxiety") logically follows the findings (assuming that the findings themselves are true). But biofeedback was not compared with all plausible treatments for anxiety in this experiment. Perhaps drug therapy would have reduced anxiety better than either biofeedback or psychotherapy. The argument that biofeedback is "the best choice among alternative treatments" is true only if the range of alternative treatments was limited to these two. Because we know of other treatments for anxiety, we can judge by common sense that the logical validity of this study slips a bit in the end.

Construct validity   The study must also be judged according to its **construct validity**—that is, how well the measures the researchers chose (the STAI, in this case) corresponded to the "construct" of anxiety. In the social sciences a **construct** is a mental, abstract idea about some quality of individuals such as intelligence, self-concept, or anxiety. Anxiety is not something that can be seen, touched, heard, or counted, but we can think about it as "something a person has" or as "a part (or element) of a person"; it is also called a **trait**. It is a characteristic that some people have more of than others (one can say, for example, that Bob is "more anxious" than Tom), and some situations are thought of as provoking more or less anxiety (such as speaking before a large crowd or facing the first day before a new class). The dictionary defines *anxiety* as "distress or uneasiness of mind caused by apprehension of danger or misfortune." The construct of anxiety is the subject of much theory in psychology. Although we cannot observe the construct of anxiety directly, we can observe some **indicators** of anxiety—rapid heart rate, sweaty palms, and the like. People can also report their own awareness of their anxiety, this "self-report" being another observable indicator of an unobservable construct.

When researchers conduct studies about the construct of anxiety, they have to define it in such a way that it can be observed and measured. In our example, the researcher selected the State-Trait Anxiety Inventory as the procedure by which anxiety would be defined and measured. But does this test correspond closely to the construct as we think about it? This evaluation of the construct validity of the test depends on first examining test items to see if there is a close connection between the items and the construct. The methods for a more technical evaluation of the test are presented in chapters 4 and 5. Suffice it to say for the present that technical evaluations of this test have already been made and are reported in a resource entitled *Mental Measurements Yearbook*. The summary on the STAI is that it is one of the best standardized measures of anxiety available, but that all measures that rely on the subjects' reporting their own psychological status are subject to some distortion (Dreger, 1978, p. 1095).

Internal validity   A **causal claim** is made when someone says that one construct influences another, such as "poverty causes crime." When the researchers make a causal claim such as "biofeedback reduces anxiety" based on the outcome of their study, the reader of the study must assess whether all alternative causes have been ruled out. The relative absence of reasonable alternative explanations is what gives a study **internal validity**. Suppose, for example, a researcher selected a group of children with articulation problems, recorded the number of articulation errors the children made, administered speech therapy for six months, then recorded the children's articulation errors again. Observing a marked decrease in the number of such errors between the first and second testing, the researcher concluded that speech therapy has a beneficial effect on articulation. The causal claim is reflected in the conclusion, "Speech therapy decreases articulation errors." But what are some alternative explanations for the researcher's conclusion? You can use common sense to generate them. The most obvious alternative explanation is that children simply grow out of their articulation problems naturally and would have lost them whether or not they had had speech therapy. In this example, then, internal validity is weak, because the alternative explanation ("children grow out of their articulation problems") has not been ruled out, or **controlled**. The latter explanation is a plausible alternative to the researcher's hypothesis ("speech therapy reduces articulation problems") in this particular design. Chapters 6, 7, and 8 deal extensively with the question of internal validity and how it is influenced by the design and procedures of studies.

In the abstract of our biofeedback study, the researcher concluded that biofeedback (the cause) decreased anxiety (the effect). Furthermore, the psychotherapy group acted as a comparison group that was used to determine whether people lose their anxiety naturally, without biofeedback, rather like children grow out of articulation problems. The reader might also wonder whether the individuals who received biofeedback were less anxious to begin with or were more motivated than the individuals who received psychotherapy (two plausible alternative explanations to the researcher's causal claim). But note in the procedures that the researcher used **random assignment** as a way of choosing which anxious subjects received biofeedback and which received psychotherapy. By use of this method it is possible to rule out the alternative explanation that the biofeedback group started out less anxious and therefore ended up less anxious than the psychotherapy group. For this study, therefore, the internal validity seems sound. In many cases the methods and procedures used by the researcher will provide the key to the reader's assessment of the internal validity of the study.

External validity   The reader next must evaluate the **external validity**, or generalizability, of the study. One asks, "To what individuals, *other than those in this particular study*, might we generalize these results? Or are they true only for the people directly involved?" In research, the people involved directly, the **sample**, are only of interest to the extent to which they inform us about similar groups of people not directly involved in the study. The larger group to which the researcher wants to generalize is called the **population**. Other questions related to external validity are these: Would another researcher in another setting find biofeedback superior to psychotherapy in reducing anxiety? Would an ordinary psychotherapist—that is, a psychotherapist who is not engaged in a research study—find effects similar to those found in the report? Are adult outpatients sufficiently similar to college clients to warrant generalization to the latter group? Would the same effects be demonstrated if biofeedback were compared to psychodynamic or behavioral therapy? What do other studies on this topic conclude? Judging external validity, as will be seen in Chapter 6, rests on the reader's assessments of the similarities and differences between the persons directly involved in the study (the sample) and some other, larger group, and between the treatment and conditions in the study and outside the study. Without making the vague complaint that "People are all different! You can't generalize!" the reader can make an intelligent assessment of the external validity of the research study. Chapter 6 includes a discussion of the methods that help with this assessment.

Four tools have been introduced for use by research consumers— logical validity, construct validity, internal validity, and external validity. The next section takes the reader one more step in understanding finished research by retracing the researchers' steps as they produced the study. As we have stated, the researcher's choice of methods influences the reader's assessment of, for example, the internal validity of the finished product. Therefore, research consumers need to know about processes and methods even if they never apply the processes themselves.

PROCESSES OF RESEARCH

Research may be defined as the disciplined search for knowledge. Like many searches, a variety of paths may be followed. To appreciate the finished studies, the reader must have some understanding of typical processes that a researcher may undertake. Although a variety exists, the "most typical" set of procedures, known as the **hypothetico-deductive paradigm**, or **scientific method**, will be presented first. We have used this section on the scientific method to introduce some important terms and ideas, all of which will reappear in greater elaboration in later chapters. The reader should be content with an awareness and partial understanding until the ideas are encountered again.

The scientific method is a sequence of steps to be followed in the course of a research study. The steps are:

Step 1: A *theory* about the phenomenon exists.

Step 2: The researcher detects a *research problem* within the theory and selects from it a research question to investigate.

Step 3: A *research hypothesis* is deduced from the propositions in the theory. The research hypothesis is a statement about the relationship between constructs.

Step 4: The researcher determines the *operations* (specific procedures or methods) by which the constructs will be defined and states an hypothesis that can be tested statistically. This hypothesis is called a *null hypothesis*. A **research design** is developed as a plan for implementing the operations and testing the null hypothesis. These operations, the null hypothesis, and the design make up the guidelines for the study.

Step 5: The researcher conducts the study according to the guidelines.

Step 6: The null hypothesis is tested based on the data from the study.

Step 7: The original theory is revised or supported based on the results of the hypothesis testing.

Already there are terms and ideas that require definition. This will be done below in the context of an imaginary research study on delinquency.

Research Processes Applied to an Example

Step 1: Theory The scientific method presumes that a particular theory of the phenomenon already exists. That theory is the intellectual source of guidance and direction for the study. A **theory** is a set of related, abstract propositional statements that define and explain the phenomenon. Theories can be small (for example, a theory about how students choose their seats in graduate classes) or grand (like the unified field theory in physics, which purports to explain the whole universe). Theories can be better or worse depending on the internal consistency of their propositional statements (like statements A through F below, about delinquency) and how well they explain the phenomenon.

Consider for now the phenomenon of delinquency. Several theories of delinquency exist. (For a description of these, see Elliot, Ageton, and Canter, 1979.) For the purposes of demonstrating the scientific method, we present the Contrived Theory of Delinquency, which draws heavily on, but oversimplifies, the work of Elliot, Ageton, and Canter (1979) and of Simons, Miller, and Aigner (1980). The Contrived Theory consists of six propositional statements:

> Statement A. *Delinquency* is defined as an individual's habitual engagement in any one of the following acts: sale or use of drugs or alcohol, theft, property damage, fighting, and running away from home.
>
> Statement B. Delinquency is unrelated to socioeconomic status.
>
> Statement C. Delinquency has its root cause in the failure of family socialization and the resulting alienation from conventional norms and values of society.
>
> Statement D. Among youth at risk for delinquency (see Statement C), the belief that one lacks legitimate paths to obtain success in society (anomie) causes delinquency.
>
> Statement E. Among individuals at risk for delinquency (see Statements C and D), association with delinquent peers is a cause of delinquency.
>
> Statement F. Individuals are delinquent because of the labels placed on them by society.

Several things should be apparent from this theory. Note carefully that delinquency is a construct, an abstract quality that represents a characteristic or trait of some youngsters. The theory elaborates on the overarching construct of delinquency by specifying its component parts. In other words, delinquency is made up of behaviors such as theft and drug use. The theory excludes sexual conduct from its definition of delinquency. Thus, the theory defines and draws boundaries around the phenomenon and tells what is and is not part of the construct, delinquency (Statement A). Next, note that the propositional statements propose the "relationship" between the construct of delinquency and other constructs. Particularly, the statements set out the "causes" of delinquency. For example, Statement B of the theory proposes that youth from middle and high socioeconomic groups are just as likely to be delinquent as those from low socioeconomic groups. In other words, according to this theory, poverty (another construct) is *not* the cause of delinquency. In Statement C, delinquency is said to be caused by a failure of family socialization (another construct). In other words, separation from the family unit, for example, might prevent a child from acquiring the patterns of behavior that society values, thus making it more likely that he or she will later engage in delinquent behavior. In this theory there are several "causes" of delinquency. Taken together, the six statements constitute a theory—an abstract explanation for a phenomenon, in this example, delinquency.

Step 2: Problem detection The researcher detects a problem in the theory. Problems are indicated when the constructs or propositions included in the theory are not well supported with empirical data. For example, good evidence may not exist in the research literature to support the proposition that delinquent behavior is more probable in a youth if his or her friends are delinquent. Problems are indicated when available data conflict, such as the evidence about the relationship between delinquency and socioeconomic status. In other words, some studies may show that delinquency is more prevalent in economically deprived classes while other studies show that delinquency is equally prevalent in all economic classes. Another indication of a problem is two propositional statements within a theory that logically contradict each other. Careful analysis shows that Statement F contradicts Statements C, D, and E. Statement F represents the "deviance" school of sociology, which contends that problems such as delinquency, mental illness, and the like are not traits and do not reside independently in the characters of individuals. Instead, acts such as running away from home are only considered "criminal," "delinquent," or "sick" because society labels them so. This theoretical position is not consistent with Statement D, for example, which suggests that certain perceptions and beliefs of individuals are causally linked to delinquent tendencies. That is, some youths hold the belief that they have few prospects for success in society, and these individuals are also likely to commit delinquent acts. Thus, the possible contradiction between Statements D and G presents another fruitful opportunity for an empirical study. For the purpose of carrying through this extended example, we will restrict the research problem to the following, "Is delinquency caused by anomie?" This is the **research problem**, or *research question*, to which the researcher wishes to supply a conclusive answer. The researcher's interest and discretion determines which part of the theory he or she will choose to explore. Each research study contributes only a small piece to the overall puzzle presented by the theory.

Step 3: Hypothesis deduction The researcher deduces a research hypothesis from the theory. A **research hypothesis** is a statement about the relationship between two or more constructs in the theory. You will remember from an earlier section of this chapter that a *construct* is an abstract idea about a property, or a characteristic of an individual. In our theory of delinquency, some of the constructs are delinquency, socialization, socioeconomic status, anomie, alienation, association, and labeling. Research hypotheses are deduced from the propositional statements of the theory. For example, the researcher reasons (deductively), "If it is true that 'the belief that one lacks legitimate means to obtain success in society causes delinquency,' then it is likely that a potential delinquent's pessimistic assessment of his or her chances of obtaining a decent job will be associated with such behaviors as theft, property damage, use of drugs and alcohol, and running away from home." If individuals who have committed more of these delinquent acts are also those who believe that their prospects for suitable employment are poor, then the theory would be supported. Conversely, if those who have committed few or no delinquent acts are also those who believe they have good prospects of employment, this would also be supporting evidence for the theory.

This deduction from one or more of the propositional statements of the theory is the gist of the *research hypothesis*. Its formal statement in this example is as follows: "Among youth at risk for delinquency, commitment of delinquent acts is caused by beliefs that one is unlikely to obtain employment." In general, a research hypothesis expresses the *direction* of the relationship between constructs that the researcher (based on deductions from the theory) expects to discover when the facts are gathered in subsequent stages of the study. The research hypothesis serves as a guide for the investigator's design and procedures, and as a touchstone to which the empirical data can be compared.

Other examples of research hypotheses are presented in Figure 1–2.

Step 4: Operationalization   Up to this point in the research process, all activity has been abstract, theoretical, and mental. Having thought carefully about the subject of delinquency, the researcher must decide on a set of methods, or operations, that will translate what was thought about and conceptualized into something that can be seen, heard, counted, and otherwise measured. In other words, the researcher must seek empirical data to confirm or disconfirm the abstract theory. In the example, the indicator,

FIGURE 1–2   Examples of Research Hypotheses

a. Positive reinforcement of grooming behaviors increases the incidence of such behaviors among hospitalized psychotics.

b. Urban density causes alienation.

c. Comprehension of text is enhanced by the number of words that are familiar to second graders.

d. Frequency of television viewing is positively related to passivity among adolescents.

e. Anxiety decreases performance on complex psychomotor tasks.

f. A child's intellectual capacity decreases as the number of siblings in the family increases.

g. Delinquency and gender are related; males are more likely than females to become delinquent.

"beliefs about one's likelihood of employment" was selected to indicate a more concrete realization of the abstract construct, anomie. This indicator in turn must be reformulated into something that can be measured in a relevant and accurate way. This is the process of providing an **operational definition** for a construct. An operational definition is a very specific definition, one that specifies the **operations**, or procedures, by which the construct will be recognized and measured—*in this particular study.* (Other researchers may define the constructs with different indicators altogether.)

The first objective of operationalizing is to define the indicator so that each person studied can be assigned a number that represents either whether the indicator is present or absent in that person or "how much" of the indicator the person possesses. Anomie cannot be measured directly, but a person can respond to a series of questions in an interview about his or her job prospects. These questions constitute the chosen indicator for the construct, anomie. The responses a person makes can be summarized into a total score that represents, for example, the strength of that person's belief in his or her prospects for employment. That series of questions and the rules for summarizing responses into an "anomie score" make up an operationalization of the abstract construct, anomie.

For the purpose of this research example, the operational definitions are as follows:

Delinquency (D-op) is defined as the scale score on the Self-Reported Delinquency Instrument (Elliot, Ageton, Hunter, and Knowles, 1976). This instrument consists of 19 behaviors such as "Taken little things (worth $5 or less) that didn't belong to you," "Damaged public or private property just for fun." The questions are asked by a trained interviewer in a confidential and private interaction. The subject is asked to respond to each one by indicating the number of times in the last two months he has engaged in that behavior. The scale of responses consists of "never" (scored 0), "once or twice" (scored 2), or "often" (scored 3). A subject's overall score is the sum of the 19 item scores. This will be denoted D-op.

Beliefs About the Likelihood of Obtaining Employment (Anomie, An-op) is defined as the response to an interviewer's question, "How good are your chances of getting any job as an adult you felt was a good, steady, well-paid job? Good or poor?" (Elliot et al. 1976). Subjects who respond "good" are categorized as low on anomie. Those who respond "poor" are categorized high on anomie.

Youth at Risk for Delinquency (Y-op) is defined as those males between the ages of 9 and 12 who are nominated by the schools or juvenile justice system as potential delinquents.

Any abstraction like delinquency can be defined in several ways. The researcher must select an observable indicator that best represents the theoretical definition. Sometimes the choice is good and sometimes it is not; this will influence the *construct validity* of the study. For example, instead of defining *delinquency* as the "self-reported number of times the person committed theft," the researcher might have defined it as "the number of incidents of theft as reflected in official police records." Both are indicators of delinquency, and both are imperfect indicators of that construct. On the self-report questionnaire, some individuals might lie to make themselves look better to the researcher. The police records, on the other hand, might be incomplete as a measure of a person's delinquency, because not all such acts are discovered and reported by the officials. In addition, there is some evidence to suggest that members of lower socioeconomic groups are more likely than others to be adjudicated. Therefore, the choice of police records to indicate delinquency may limit the generalizability of the findings.

Just as one construct can have several indicators, an indicator can be chosen that reflects some *other* construct than the one intended by the researcher when framing the hypothesis. For example, beliefs about one's likelihood of obtaining employment might also indicate the underlying construct of economic climate rather than some aspect of a person's psychological make-up such as anomie. It is important to remember, therefore, that the selection of indicators and operational definitions usually cannot be as exact as one might wish. It involves both intelligent decision making by the researcher and "construct validation," or research that has established the connection between the indicator and the construct (chapters 4 and 5). Once the indicators and operational definitions are selected, the definitions are fixed for the duration of the research study and must not vary.

In addition to selecting and defining indicators, another objective of operationalization is to determine the "function" these defined indicators will serve in this particular study. The determination rests on reexamining the research hypothesis, which in this case states that delinquent acts are caused by a person's beliefs about job prospects. In other words, "beliefs about job prospects" is the presumed cause of "delinquency," the presumed effect. The terminology for these functions is the **independent variable** for the presumed cause and the **dependent variable** for the presumed effect. A **variable** is a defined characteristic that varies; it has at least two **values** and usually more. For example, the variable of sex has two values— male and female, and it should be possible with relatively little uncertainty to sort all our subjects into one or the other classification, or value. Depending on the study, the variable of socioeconomic status has three values—high, middle, and low, perhaps—and with a few rules the researcher could sort all available subjects into one of these three classifications. The variable of Scholastic Aptitude Test has a whole range of values, varying from 200 to 800. And in our hypothetical study, the variable of delinquent acts has values ranging from zero (indicating the subject had engaged in no delinquent acts) to 57 (indicating he had participated in all 19 acts "often" during the two months prior to the interview). Finally, the indicator for beliefs about future employment has only two values, high (optimistic) and low (pessimistic).

Variables serve different functions in research. In the research hypothesis of our imaginary study, the beliefs about job prospects (anomie) is considered the "cause" of delinquency. Thus, beliefs about job prospects is referred to as the *independent variable* (the presumed cause in a claim that one variable was responsible for a change, increase, or reduction in the value of the other variable). The presumed effect in such a causal claim is called the *dependent variable*, also referred to as the outcome, criterion, effect, or result. The dependent variable in this study is delinquent acts.

Independent variables can be either measured as they exist or manipulated by the researcher. Think back to the abstract of the study of the effect of biofeedback on anxiety. The research problem made the causal claim that biofeedback is more effective than psychotherapy in reducing anxiety. Thus "type of therapy" was the independent variable having two values (biofeedback and psychotherapy), and "anxiety" was the dependent variable. Therapy was the presumed cause and anxiety the presumed effect. In the biofeedback example, the independent variable was a *manipulated independent variable* because the researcher could control it by determining in advance which of the available subjects would receive which form of therapy. According to the abstract, the researcher used random assignment to determine which subjects were given biofeedback and which psychotherapy. Therefore, the independent variable was a specific treatment under the control of (i.e., "manipulated" by) the researcher.

Contrast the manipulated independent variable in the biofeedback study to the independent variable in the delinquent study—persons' beliefs about their job prospects—which cannot be manipulated or determined in advance by the researcher. She cannot control whether subject 1 will be designated high anomie and subject 2 designated low anomie—at least not in the same way she could determine by a coin flip that subject one will be given biofeedback and subject two will be given psychotherapy. The subjects come into the study with their own levels of anomie that are already determined by their upbringing and social circumstances rather than by a researcher. The most the researcher can do is to "measure" the beliefs of all her subjects and classify them into high or low anomie on the basis of their measured scores. The subjects' beliefs are not under the researcher's control and must simply be recorded as they exist. A person's prior beliefs, like his or her sex, ethnic group, handedness, birth order, or eye color are **subject characteristics**, also called organismic, *or* personological, characteristics. When a researcher uses subject characteristics in studies as presumed causes of other things (as in these hypotheses: "Handedness affects penmanship," or "birth order determines intelligence," or "smoking causes cancer in humans"), they are called *measured independent variables*. Studies of this type are referred to as causal-comparative or ex post facto studies (see Chapter 8). Research studies in which the independent variables are manipulated are referred to as **experiments** (Chapter 6). When the researcher introduces a treatment but has less control over which subjects receive which treatments, studies are labeled "quasi experiments" (Chapter 7).

Variables in studies do not always function in cause and effect ways. Take, for example, the hypothesis, "Birth order and intelligence are positively related." Two variables are defined, and the researcher expects to observe that first- or second-born children will have higher IQs than third- or fourth-born children. But this researcher makes no cause-and-effect claim—only that the two variables will show a statistical relationship or pattern. The variables are **symmetric**—neither is claimed to be the cause of the other *in this study*. Here is another example of a hypothesis involving symmetrical variables: "Boys are more likely to engage in delinquent acts than girls." It proposes no cause-and-effect link, only a statistical pattern or relationship between the variables. Research involving hypotheses about the relationships among variables and in which no causal claims are made is called correlational research (Chapter 9).

Yet another noncausal type of research is survey research, where the investigator is attempting to study the incidence of some construct in a population. For example, the research question might be "What is the degree of reading competence among young people who graduated from high school in 1984?" Another example of a survey research question is "What is the rate of birth defects in the population of infants, and has that incidence increased or decreased between 1970 and 1980?" Notice that only one construct is involved (reading competence in the first example and birth defects in the second). The researcher aims to describe the magnitude, prevalence, trends, status, or degree of that construct in some specifically defined population. The purposes and methods of survey research are described in Chapter 10.

So far we have presented the simplest case of research that looks for symmetrical or cause-and-effect relationships between two constructs. In actual studies encountered in professional journals and theses, the researcher typically tests research hypotheses about relationships between two constructs that depend on some other construct. For example, it is probably an oversimplification to hypothesize, "delinquency is caused by anomie." It is more precise to assert, "delinquency is caused by anomie *among youth from broken homes*." The phrase, "among youth from broken homes" is a kind of contingency clause indicating that the cause-and-effect relationship between anomie and delinquency *depends on* a particular characteristic of subjects—the intactness of their families. In other words, the researcher predicts that if the population of young people is classified into two groups—one group from intact families and one from broken families, that the relationship between anomie and delinquency will be observed in the second group only, the one from broken homes. Delinquency is not universally caused by anomie, according to the more precise hypothesis, but only in a particular segment of the population.

Here is another example. A researcher considers the theory that computer-assisted instruction (CAI) is more effective in raising math achievement than traditional lecture-recitation instruction. The problem with that theory, according to the researcher, is that children with greater aptitude in math grow bored with the pace and repetition of CAI whereas children with lower math aptitude benefit from these same features. The researcher hypothesizes that the cause-and-effect relationship between type of instruction (CAI vs. traditional) and math achievement will only be true among subjects of relatively lower math aptitude. Subjects of higher math aptitude will perform equally well under either type of instruction. In this example the hypothesized relationship between type of instruction (independent variable) and math achievement (dependent variable) depends on (i.e., is influenced or moderated by) a subject characteristic—math aptitude.

Subject characteristics such as math aptitude, age, sex, socioeconomic status, family intactness, and the like have a substantial bearing on the findings of studies. Suppose that the effect of CAI in fact depended on the math aptitude of subjects, but no researcher was wise enough to suspect it. Researchers would continue to conduct studies with subjects of unknown or mixed levels of aptitude. The math achievement of high-aptitude subjects (showing no difference between those who had been given CAI and those who had been given traditional instruction) would be mixed up mathematically with the findings of the low-aptitude subjects (whose scores were raised by CAI). No clear pattern of results would emerge.

Researchers have several options for dealing with ("controlling" the effects of) subject characteristics. First, they can define the population so that only subjects with certain specified characteristics are included. In the delinquency example, only males aged nine to twelve who are nominated by school or juvenile justice officials were considered the population for the study. Thus three subject characteristics—age, sex, and nomination by school officials—were defined. These researchers may have hypothesized that the relationship between anomie and delinquency depends on the subject's gender, age, and whatever trait brings young people to the attention of the authorities. Perhaps the researchers felt that delinquency among girls or among older juveniles is caused by something else—child abuse, perhaps. By using these three subject selection variables the researchers chose to restrict their population and the generalization of their findings accordingly (the findings would only hold true for youth with the characteristics as defined).

The second option a researcher has for dealing with a potentially influential subject characteristic is to define that characteristic as a **moderator variable**. The researcher operationally defines and measures that characteristic in a sample of subjects, divides the sample into two or more groups with respect to their classification on the moderator variable, and examines the effect of the independent variable in each group. Figure 1–3 shows a graph of the hypothesized outcome of a study with type of

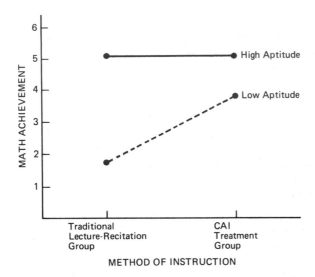

FIGURE 1–3   Factorial Experiment Testing the Hypothesis of the Effect of
CAI on Math Achievement Dependent on Math Aptitude

instruction (CAI vs. traditional) as the independent variable, math achievement as the dependent variable, and math aptitude as the subject moderator variable. Math aptitude would be measured in the sample, the members of the sample would be classified into either a high-aptitude or a low-aptitude group according to their aptitude score. The low-aptitude group would then be randomly divided into either a CAI group or a group receiving traditional instruction. The high-aptitude group would be likewise allocated at random to CAI or traditional groups. The researcher, in effect, is conducting two simultaneous and interlocking experiments on two groups known to differ on an important subject characteristic—math aptitude. This design is known as a factorial experiment. If the researcher indeed finds that the effect of the independent variable differs according to the two classifications of math aptitude, that finding is referred to as an **interaction**.

Figure 1–3 can be understood as follows: The subjects have been divided into two groups based on their math aptitude. The two groups are represented by the two separate lines (one solid, one dashed) on the graph. In the left half of the graph are the data from the traditional group, and on the right are the data from the CAI group. The degree of the dependent variable, math achievement, is plotted on the vertical axis; the higher up the scale, the higher the math achievement score. The dots represent the average achievement for the group. For example, the dot in the lower left-hand quadrant of the graph is the average score on the math achievement test attained by the low-aptitude group assigned to receive traditional instruction.

Note that the dots for the high-aptitude group are level between the two treatment groups. But within the low aptitude group the dot representing the average achievement of the CAI group is higher than the dot for the traditional group. This indicates that, for the low-aptitude group, there was an effect on achievement caused by the type of instruction received. No effect was observed for the high-aptitude group. The figure represents an interaction between type of instruction and aptitude.

In the delinquency example, the researcher could have introduced a moderator variable into the design as a way of discounting a part of the theory that seemed logically inconsistent. The construct in question was labeling, defined in this instance as a prior arrest record. She expects that the same relationship between anomie and delinquency will be observed whether or not the subjects have been labeled delinquent. In other words, she expects *no interaction*, no moderation by labeling of the effect of anomie on delinquency. To keep the example simple, however, we have chosen not to include labeling as a moderator variable in this design.

A third method for dealing with subject characteristics is to *control* their effects through research design or statistics. Suppose a researcher tests this hypothesis: "The phonics method is more effective than the language experience method in teaching children to read." She wants to test the hypothesis by forming two groups of first graders, one of which would be taught by the phonics method and the other taught by the language experience method. She knows, however, that many subject characteristics such as age and IQ are correlated with reading comprehension (the dependent variable). She wants to make sure that any difference between the two groups on the dependent variable is caused by the treatments *and not by the fact that one group started out systematically brighter or older.* Therefore, the researcher uses random assignment, a research design procedure, or statistical controls to make the two groups comparable to each other with respect to any subject characteristics (see chapters 3 and 6). Random assignment was the procedure used by the biofeedback researcher to make sure that the two groups were equal at the beginning of the study.

It is not subject characteristics alone that influence the outcome of studies. Task characteristics, setting characteristics, and method characteristics also need to be considered in formulating research hypotheses and rules to test them. Examples of **task characteristics** in the CAI research are the particular software program used, the level of difficulty of the exercises, the quantity and kind of teacher supervision that accompanies the computer work, and the like. Think of these as having the same potential effects on experiments that subject characteristics do. The results of CAI on math achievement may depend on, for example, the enthusiasm

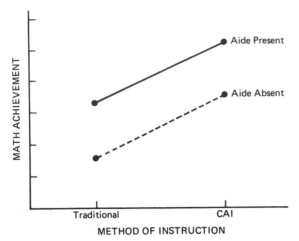

FIGURE 1-4   Factorial Experiment Testing the Hypothesis, "CAI Affects Math Achievement," with "Presence of Teacher Aides" as Moderator Variable

and experience of the teacher who administered the program. The researcher could use a factorial design with two different teachers to see if the effect on math achievement was due to CAI per se or to the qualities of a particular teacher. Or the researcher could randomly assign several teachers to each treatment group, thereby controlling for the differential effects of teachers' enthusiasm. Or the researcher could take special care to document the characteristics of the teacher in charge so that the conclusions of the study would be limited to CAI as implemented by teachers of the type described. Figure 1-4 presents the results of an experiment that tested the hypothesis, "CAI increases math achievement," and includes a task characteristic, "presence of teacher aide," as a moderator variable. The researcher randomly divided available elementary classrooms into two groups, one group to receive CAI and the other group to receive traditional instruction. The researcher noticed that teacher aides worked with the pupils during math instruction in certain classes but not others. He categorized the classes according to whether the aides helped or did not help with math. He measured the dependent variable separately within the two categories. He found (see Figure 1-4) that the groups given CAI were better off (their posttreatment averages were higher) than the groups given traditional instruction, regardless of whether or not an aide was present. In this example there is *no interaction* between the independent variable, type of instruction, and the task characteristic functioning as a moderator variable, presence of teacher aides.

Setting characteristics consist of those features of the environment in which the study takes place. The researcher must assess whether the effect of the independent variable depends on the characteristics of the school, clinic, classroom, or community in which the study takes place. In the delinquency study, it might be hypothesized that the relationship between anomie and delinquency depends on the type of community; that one would observe the relationship in small towns but not large cities. If so, then the research would have to cope with this contingency in the design or in the limitations placed on the conclusions of the study.

Methods characteristics have to do with the techniques or procedures that the researcher chooses to conduct the study. Methods encompass the means by which the subjects are selected and allocated to treatment groups, the variables are measured, and the data are analyzed. There is no one correct and definitive set of procedures, and the ones chosen may have an impact on the results of the study. For example, the effect of CAI may be demonstrated if the method of measurement of math achievement consisted of multiple choice questions but not if the dependent variable was measured by math problems that required the subject to supply the answer. If this is the case, one would say that the hypothesized effect of CAI was dependent on or moderated by the method of measurement. In the delinquency example it might be true that the method of obtaining subjects by nomination from school or court officials yields quite a different picture of the relationship of anomie and delinquency than if the subjects were obtained through a large-scale survey of the general population of youth. Figure 1–5 shows this interaction between the independent variable, anomie, and the method characteristic used as a moderator variable, selection

FIGURE 1–5 Interaction between Anomie and Selection Method on Deliquency

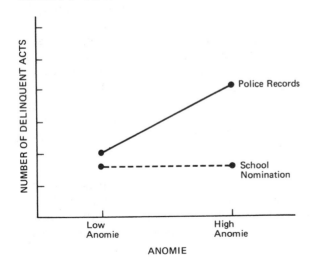

method. The figure shows that the effect of anomie on delinquency depends on the method by which the subjects were selected.

The foregoing few pages represent the kind of planning and thinking that the researcher must go through in translating the abstract conceptualizations of theory into the material, concrete reality of an empirical study. The parts of step four, operationalization, can be summarized as follows: The researcher provides an operational definition for the constructs and determines the roles that the variables in the study (independent, dependent, symmetric) should play and considers what characteristics of subjects, task, and setting might influence the outcome of the study. These are incorporated into a **research design**, which sets the guidelines for the study itself by specifying procedures for selection of subjects, setting the schedule for measuring the variables, and the like. Once the design is set, the researcher is obliged to follow it and to justify any later deviations from it. In our delinquency example the design calls for a random sample of 100 drawn from the population of nominees (males, ages 9–12). The design specifies that each subject will be interviewed individually during a specified time period and anomie and delinquent acts measured as specified in the operational definitions. The data from the measurements will be divided into two groups, high anomie and low anomie. Then the average score on delinquent acts will be calculated within the two groups, and the two averages compared.

The last part of this step in the scientific method calls for the researcher to set the rules and standards by which the data will be evaluated. In other words, the researcher must make a commitment, in advance, about what kind of data are necessary to conclude that anomie causes delinquency. This is done by specifying the statistical procedure that will be used and a **null hypothesis** that can be tested statistically. The null hypothesis in this example is this: "There will be no difference in the number of delinquent acts (D-op) committed by subjects of low versus high anomie (An-op). This will be tested by a t test at the 0.05 level of probability." What the null hypothesis does is to specify that, if the average score on delinquent acts is the same or nearly the same for those both high and low on anomie, the research hypothesis ("anomie causes delinquency") is not a good explanation for delinquency. If the scores of the two groups on the dependent variable differ by a prespecified amount, then the research hypothesis merits consideration.

Notice the differences in form between research hypotheses and null hypotheses. The latter deals with specific variables rather than abstract constructs, states that there will be no difference on the dependent variable between two groups, and is tested statistically (statistical procedures are covered in Chapter 3).

Step 5: Data collection   Based on the design already specified, the study is conducted. The data are gathered as detailed in the design. The sample of subjects is chosen, and the variables are measured for the subjects (these are the data). Descriptive statistics that summarize the measured scores of individuals are computed into averages. Graphs (such as the one in Figure 1–3) are drawn to help the researcher understand the data and eventually communicate the data to others. In this example, the average number of delinquent acts is compared across two categories of anomie. The researcher finds that subjects who reported a large number of delinquent acts were also high on anomie (had poor expectations for obtaining employment). Subjects with optimistic expectations for employment reported fewer delinquent acts.

Step 6: Test of hypothesis   The null hypothesis is tested, based on the size of the difference in delinquent acts reported by groups high and low on anomie. According to the value of the t test, the chances of the null hypothesis being true are small, less than five in one hundred. Therefore, the null hypothesis (that predicted *no* difference in number of delinquent acts between subjects high and low on anomie) is rejected. The researcher can say that the difference between the two groups who differed in their beliefs about future employment (An-op) on the number of delinquent acts they reported (De-op) was big enough to be **statistically significant** or "unlikely due to chance."

Step 7: Statement of conclusions and refinement of theory   Conclusions are stated, but they are once again in the language of the abstract constructs with which the study began: "Among young males at risk for delinquency, belief about one's prospects for employment (anomie) is a cause of delinquency." The assumption is made that what was true for the measured variables is also true of the constructs they indicate. A rejection of the null hypothesis gives support for the research hypothesis. Based on the conclusions, the original theory is supported or revised. Through successive repetitions the theory is further refined, eventually becoming a law about the phenomenon. By this progressive refinement, science is thought of as cumulative and self-correcting. The scientific method, or hypothetico-deductive paradigm, is an ideal that is not often realized in the studies encountered in the literature. For example, no research hypothesis is explicitly stated in some studies. Other studies show no signs of having been derived from theory, relying more on the results of previous studies. Yet the steps of the scientific method are implied in most extant studies.

Table 1–1 summarizes the sequence of steps in the scientific method and illustrates them with the example of a research study on delinquency.

TABLE 1–1   Scientific Method Summarized and Illustrated

SEQUENCE	EXAMPLE
Step One: Theory, made up of constructs and propositions that link them, already exists.	"Contrived Theory" proposes that delinquency (D) is caused by anomie (An), associalization (As), delinquent association (DA), and labeling (L).
Step Two: Propositions that are contradictory or lack empirical support are chosen as research problem.	"Is anomie the cause of delinquency?" is chosen as the research problem.
Step Three: Research hypothesis is deduced from theory.	"High anomie is a cause of delinquency" is deduced as research hypothesis.
Step Four: Constructs are operationally defined and assigned functions. Procedures for conducting study and rules for evaluating evidence are stated.	Anomie is defined as self-reported beliefs about job prospects (independent variable An-op); Delinquency is defined as self-reported acts (dependent variable, D-op); Sampling, measurement, and analysis procedures specified. The null hypothesis is, "There are no differences in number of delinquent acts reported by groups high and low on An-op." ($p < 0.05$)
Step Five: Study is conducted according to specifications in Step Four.	Data show an appreciable difference in average number of acts committed by the two groups. Subjects high in anomie reported more acts than those low in anomie.
Step Six: Null hypothesis is tested.	Null hypothesis is rejected based on the difference between the two groups.
Step Seven: Research hypothesis is supported or disconfirmed. The original theory engenders stronger belief or is revised accordingly.	Research hypothesis, "anomie causes delinquency," is supported. "Contrived Theory" is supported and yields further research hypotheses.

ALTERNATIVE THEORIES OF RESEARCH

The hypothetico-deductive paradigm is only a theory about how research happens. Scholars such as Kaplan (1964) have argued that scientists do not actually follow the sequence of steps described in the so-called scientific method. Yet the hypothetico-deductive paradigm carries with it the weight of authority in the minds of many researchers, editors of research journals, and dissertation advisors. They assume that those who seem to follow the prescribed sequence and employ the correct methods will produce credible findings. However, sophisticated consumers of research should be aware that this paradigm is only one of several alternative theories about research. Two such theories are briefly presented here.

The Inductive Paradigm

The **inductive paradigm** (sometimes associated with ethnographic or naturalistic research, described in Chapter 11) does not presume that a theory of the phenomenon exists prior to the collection of data. Indeed, the belief is that no social and educational theory is adequate as a source of research hypotheses. Instead, the researcher defines a research problem along with some loosely defined "working hypotheses." A case is found— that is, a classroom, school, clinic, ward, or other "bounded system" or environmental niche. The researcher gains access to this social system, gains rapport with the people in it, and spends an extended period collecting large amounts of data using a variety of methods. The researcher begins to discern patterns or regularities in the data, to define and interpret the construct in this setting. Thus, definitions and hypotheses are teased out of the data (rather than specified prior to data collection, as in the hypothetico-deductive paradigm). Hypotheses are explanations about the phenomenon (rather than prespecified predictions). These explanations are continuously compared to the data to make sure they are consistent with them. New data are gathered to test the explanations derived. The resulting theory about the phenomenon is "grounded" in the data and is considered credible as long as it accounts for the available data. Alternative hypotheses are tested to see if they provide better fits with the data.

Unlike the adherents of the hypothetico-deductive paradigm, which searches for universal explanations for phenomena, adherents of the inductive paradigm stress that a proposition like "anomie causes delinquency" depends on the immediate context in which people find themselves.

If an inductive researcher were to study delinquency, he might attach himself to a particular site, such as a youth center or neighborhood where delinquent acts are likely to occur. He would probably have many ideas about delinquency but no one fixed hypothesis. Nor would he have a predetermined design and set of procedures for conducting the study. He would spend a year or two gaining the trust of the people there, attempting to understand what life is like from their viewpoint and what acts such as petty theft or vandalism mean to them. He might interview authorities who come into contact with delinquent youths, examine court records and other documents, and directly observe their behavior over an extended period of time. Because he believes that social life is context-dependent, he would record as many features of the social, economic, and physical environment as possible, attempting to understand the various influences on the lives of these particular youths. He would record data carefully and fully and search the data for categories (constructs) and patterns (relationships among constructs), saving specific definitions for relatively late in the sequence.

Perhaps the researcher discerns that, in this particular site, he can find no link between family characteristics and delinquent behavior, but he does observe strong elements of peer pressure to fill time by engaging in illegal activities. He might then prepare more standardized methods for examining this tentative hypothesis relating delinquency to peer association. He might develop a model that defines what delinquency means in this setting and how it may relate to peer pressure, being careful to tie his developing ideas to the descriptive information in his records. He would try out alternative hypotheses to see if they might explain his data better than his model. He would not necessarily presume that his explanation also accounts for delinquency in other sites, but would treat his developing theory as tentative and revise it as new data emerge.

As he wrote the report of the study he would evaluate the methods he used and assess what impact the choice of settings, subjects, and methods, as well as the prolonged contact he had with his subjects, might have had on the results. The final report would represent an attempt to communicate his understanding of delinquency in that site and what the discovered categories mean to the people directly involved.

Those who support the inductive paradigm note that it requires fewer assumptions than does the hypothetico-deductive paradigm. For example, the latter model tacitly assumes that the theoretical construct corresponds closely to the operational definition. But one might ask of the delinquency study, for example, "Is anomie, the belief that one lacks legitimate access to success in society, the same as an interview question about one's beliefs about employment prospects?" "Can we assume that what we found in measuring the indicator is also true of the theoretical construct?" On the other hand, the inductive paradigm is criticized for its lack of predetermined rules for analyzing data and testing hypotheses and its vulnerability to subjectivity and bias due to the extensive personal contact between researchers and subjects.

The Multioperations Paradigm

The **multioperations paradigm**, advocated by Campbell and others (Brewer and Collins, 1981), works on the idea that all research methods have some error built into them, each operationalization of a construct is incomplete and only partly valid, and each perspective a researcher assumes with respect to research subjects (e.g., intimate participant observer or detached laboratory experimentalist) has a particular kind of bias associated with it. Yet each method, perspective, and operation has a degree of truth about the phenomenon. Only by examining data generated by different researchers, employing different methods and alternative operationalizations of the construct can a person accumulate truly scientific evidence about a phenomenon. In other words, a multioperationalist would say that a response to an interview question is not the same as anomie, but represents a partial view of that construct. If the findings of other studies that employed different indicators and different methods (some ethnographic, some experimental perhaps) begin to converge on a particular conclusion, the reader can attribute validity to that conclusion.

The three paradigms for how to do research and produce scientific knowledge are presented here to convince the reader that there exists no single, infallible method or sequence of methods that inevitably leads to truth. Methodology should not be viewed as dogma, in our view. All three paradigms are respectable and fall into a more general category termed **disciplined inquiry** by Cronbach and Suppes (1969). Research studies that differ dramatically from each other in *form* (e.g., the biofeedback experiment in the first section and the naturalistic study of delinquency in the third section of this chapter follow different sequences and use different methods) nevertheless fall together under the rubric of disciplined inquiry. They share the following characteristics: meaningful topics are addressed; the researchers employ systematic, clearly described procedures so that the reader can closely follow the logic of the study and assess the validity of the conclusions; the researchers are sensitive to the errors that are associated with their methods and seek to control them or consider how the errors influence the results; empirical verification and sound logic are valued; and plausible alternative explanations for results are sought.

SUGGESTED READINGS

BREWER, M.B., and COLLINS, B.E. *Scientific inquiry and the social sciences.* San Francisco: Jossey-Bass, 1981.

BRODBECK, M. *Readings in the philosophy of social science.* New York: Macmillan, 1968.

CRONBACH, L.J. Beyond the two disciplines of scientific psychology. *American Psychologist,* 1975, *30,* 116–127.

CRONBACH, L.J., and SUPPES, P. *Research for tomorrow's schools.* New York: Macmillan, 1969.

DEWEY, J. *How we think.* Boston: Heath, 1933.

KAPLAN, A. *The conduct of inquiry.* San Francisco: Chandler, 1964.

KUHN, T.S. *The structure of scientific revolution.* Chicago: University of Chicago Press, 1962.

MEEHL, P.E. Theoretical risks and tabular asterisks: Sir Karl, Sir Ronald, and the slow progress of soft psychology. *Journal of Consulting and Clinical Psychology,* 1978, *46,* 806–834.

MEEHAN, E.J. *Reasoned argument in social science.* Westport, Conn.: Greenwood Press, 1981.

SKINNER, B.F. The operational analysis of psychological terms. In H. Feigl and M. Brodbeck (Eds.), *Readings in the philosophy of science.* New York: Appleton, 1953.

TERMS INTRODUCED IN THIS CHAPTER

abstract
logical validity
construct validity
construct
trait
causal claim
indicator
internal validity
control
random assignment
external validity
sample
population
hypothetico-deductive paradigm
scientific method
theory
research problem
research hypothesis
operational definition
operations

independent variable
dependent variable
variable
value
subject characteristic
experiment
symmetric variable
moderator variable
interaction
task characteristic
setting characteristic
methods characteristic
research design
null hypothesis
statistical significance
conclusions
inductive paradigm
multioperations paradigm
disciplined inquiry

QUESTIONS AND ACTIVITIES FOR FURTHER STUDY

1. In your opinion, what should be the relationship between educational and social research on the one hand, and educational and social policy making on the other?

2. In 1985 the national news service reported a research study that had been published in the journal *Social Forces*. The study concluded that there is little relationship between the number of hours spent studying and the grades attained by college students. Therefore, students can expect little decline in their grade point average if they decrease their study time. What are some issues you might raise about the credibility of such a study?

3. During the next month, clip and save newspaper and magazine articles that report the results of research studies in education and social science. Keep a tally of the methods used, the conclusions reached, and the possible implications they have for policy.

4. The hypothetical delinquency study reported in Chapter 1 concluded that "anomie is a cause of delinquency." What are some alternative explanations for the observed difference in the number of delinquent acts reported by boys who were high and low on anomie? When alternative explanations are not controlled in research studies that make causal claims, what kind of validity (logical, construct, internal, or external) is weakened?

5. In the delinquency study, to what people do you feel the results may be generalized? What kind of validity do we refer to when generalization is discussed?

6. Would you judge that the methods chosen by the researcher in the delinquency study are reasonable given the research problem and hypothesis? Are the conclusions of the study reasonable given the findings? What kind of validity is this?

7. Discuss the construct validity of the delinquency study. Suggest an alternative indicator for the construct delinquency.

8. Identify the *function* served by the construct anxiety in each of the following research hypotheses:
   a. Meditation decreases anxiety among adolescents with mild mental retardation.
   b. Level of anxiety influences performance on rote memory tasks.
   c. There is a negative relationship between anxiety and psychological adjustment among college freshmen.
   d. Meditation increases feelings of life satisfaction among college students with low initial levels of anxiety but decreases feelings of life satisfaction among college students with high initial levels of anxiety.

9. Indicate, for each of the hypotheses in question 8, whether the independent variable is likely to be measured or manipulated. Explain the reasons you indicated as you did.

10. In the delinquency study, the construct labeling could have been used for what function? How might such use have strengthened the study?

11. Of the following, which might be considered a construct and which an operationally defined variable? Match the pairs.
   a. Assignment of 1 to subjects who have an arrest record at the police precinct nearest their residence and 2 to other subjects.
   b. Intelligence
   c. Distance in meters between the 12-foot boa constrictor and the nearest spot the subject can approach.
   d. Rating, from 1 to 5, by a trained counseling supervisor, of the understanding demonstrated by the counselor to the client.
   e. Labeling
   f. Snake anxiety
   g. Standard score on the Wechsler Intelligence Test for Children (Revised Form) as administered by a certified school psychologist under controlled conditions.
   h. Empathy

12. Choose one of the six research hypotheses in Figure 1–2. Write operational definitions for the constructs. Determine the function to be served by each variable as you define it. Suggest some methods by which the study could be conducted. State a null hypothesis that might be used to evaluate the data.

13. Following the model of Figure 1–3, and assuming the research hypothesis in question 8d was supported, draw a graph of the outcome, indicating all the variables.

14. Look at the seven research hypotheses in Figure 1–2. Which ones imply causal claims? What are the clues you might use to make such a determination? For those with causal claims, which will involve measured independent variables and which manipulated independent variables?

15. Find a research study by Rosenfeld, Lambert, and Black (1985) entitled "Desk Arrangement Effects on Pupil Classroom Behavior." It is published in the *Journal of Educational Psychology*, Volume 77, Number 1, pages 101–108. This journal should be available in the periodical room or education or psychology library at your university. Read the study and identify its parts. What is the research problem addressed? From what theory or body of existing research was the problem derived? What were the research hypotheses tested? Were causal claims made? Identify the independent and dependent variables. What moderator variable was used? Identify the sample that was chosen for study. How did the researchers deal with subject characteristics and task characteristics (e.g., position of teacher)? Locate the operational definitions used. Make sure you can recognize the procedures used by the researchers to select the sample and measure the variables. What statistics were used to describe the data? Was a null hypothesis explicitly stated? Identify the findings. Identify the conclusions. From what you know now, what issues would you raise about the logical, construct, internal, and external validity of the study?

2

EVALUATION

Evaluation is an important part of professional and social life. At the culmination of most graduate classes, students complete a questionnaire to evaluate the professor. Pupils are given standardized tests each year to see if they have made progress on basic academic skills. In clinics records are maintained to show accountability for public funds expended. In this chapter definitions of evaluation are presented along with descriptions of what kinds of things are evaluated and some ways evaluations are conducted. Evaluation is contrasted with research. Because there are so many different ideas about what evaluation is and should be, we present four evaluation paradigms and describe several currently accepted approaches or models of evaluation.

DEFINITIONS OF EVALUATION

What is evaluation? The dictionary defines the verb *to evaluate* as "to ascertain the value or amount of . . . ; to appraise carefully," so that one knows right away that values are involved in evaluation. Informal evaluation goes on constantly. For example, the reader might "carefully appraise" this textbook. Is it a good or a bad text? Is it better or worse than competing books? The words *good*, *bad*, *better*, and *worse* connote value or worth. But perhaps the words are too general. The criteria of value by which the book should be judged must also be specified. Some criteria that might be applied are readability, content coverage, correctness, cost, and aesthetic appeal. Is the book good or bad on each of these standards? Are each of these standards equally important to you as a reader, or is readability perhaps more important than aesthetics? Are you able to make an informed judgment alone, or do you rely on professional book reviewers? Perhaps the judgments might be different if the "evaluator" is a student rather than an instructor (instructors perhaps being less interested than students in cost, for example).

As the questions and issues grow more complicated, personal and informal evaluation must give way to formal evaluation—that is, to planned and disciplined procedures for appraising the object of evaluation and applying standards of value to it. In fact, data collection methods for formal evaluation resemble those of research in that both might include experimental studies, surveys, case studies, or other techniques that are used in research studies. Although there are several theories about what evaluation is, it is our position in this book that evaluation is a form of disciplined inquiry having both similarities to and differences from research. Evaluation and research use similar methods but have different purposes.

The definition of *evaluation* to be used in this chapter is this: *Evaluation is the process of establishing value judgments based on evidence about a program or product.* First, consider what things might be evaluated (referred to as **evaluation objects**). The possible objects considered here are either programs or products. A program is any organized set of activities for performing some service. Here are some examples:

The reading program at Washington Elementary School

The mayor's drive to reduce delinquency by sending adolescents to a wilderness survival camp

The state law to reduce accidents and save energy by setting the speed limit at 55 miles per hour

The national "Right to Read" program

The city's paper recycling program

The university plan to provide a microcomputer for each member of the faculty

The World Health Organization's drive to decrease infant mortality

The school district's math curriculum

Despite the obvious diversity in this list, about each item we can ask, "What is the value in this program? What social problem does it address? What does the program do? What are some ways it could be improved? What are the effects of this program? What does it cost? Should it exist in a different form or should it exist at all?"

Examples of products which are also the objects of evaluations are textbooks, curriculum packages, computer software, drugs, and educational or psychological tests. This chapter does not include notions of evaluation where the objects of evaluation are individual teachers (e.g., personnel evaluation) or pupils (e.g., clinical diagnosis), though some of what is said here will also apply to the evaluation of teacher performance or pupil learning.

Evaluation is the process of establishing value judgments based on evidence. By *evidence* we mean the result of design, measurement, and analysis, and the reporting of data pertaining to the features of the program and its effects. Many evaluation techniques are the same as those used in research. For example, one might conduct *attitude surveys* of parents whose children are involved in the gifted and talented program. The opinions of the parents about the quality of their children's program can be one source of information about its effectiveness. *Surveys of achievement* might be conducted as part of an appraisal of a school district's reading program. *Experiments or quasi experiments* might be conducted to determine the effect of a delinquency prevention program. For example, the evaluator might assign some children to the program and some to a control group and count the number of delinquent acts committed by the two groups five years later. An evaluator might perform *systematic observations* of the interactions between social workers and welfare clients to determine whether the services provided are beneficial and fair. *Naturalistic case studies* can be conducted that describe the features of a training program for parole officers; specialists in training can read this portrayal and appraise its adequacy relative to prevailing professional practices.

The process of applying judgments to data is neither simple nor straightforward. Evidence must be gathered and reported in such a way as to influence social thought, according to Cronbach and associates (1980), and so that dimensions of quality can be applied. Several **evaluation criteria** must be applied. The *effectiveness* of the program or product is the first and most obvious criterion. The evaluator asks, "How well does this program accomplish what was intended?" and looks to data that demonstrate achievement of objectives.

For programs with stated goals and objectives, the evaluator might determine the proportion of the participants who mastered the objectives. In an adult literacy program, for example, one objective might be that the participants will be able to read the directions on an aspirin bottle with complete understanding. The evaluator might devise a test of this objective and report the percentage of participants at the end of the program who met that standard. Someone must determine the standard at the outset, and someone must decide what percentage of participants who meet the cutoff constitutes a successful program. These are evaluative acts, judgments that precede or emerge from the data, and they are *absolute* rather than comparative.

Comparative evaluations, on the other hand, are those that assess the effectiveness of a program or product by pitting it against an alternative program or product that is designed to meet the same ends. The evaluator's responsibility is to collect comparable data from participants in the two programs and determine which is better in accomplishing their common purpose. The evaluative act or judgment involves someone's determining what amount of difference in the outcomes of the two programs constitutes relative merit. In addition to looking for data on accomplishment of program objectives, the evaluator would cast about for unanticipated and unplanned-for effects. In **non-comparative**, or absolute, **evaluations**, effects are measured in one group only, and the results compared to an absolute criterion. For example, the standard of success of a job placement program might be decided in advance to be 80 percent. Programs with actual placement rates of less than 80 percent would then be judged unsuccessful.

The second criterion by which programs or products may be judged is *efficiency*. The evaluator collects data to answer the question, "What is the cost of this program in relation to what it achieves?" The evaluation act involves using these financial and other data to make a judgment of efficiency. Standards of efficiency, like those of effectiveness, may be either absolute or comparative.

The third criterion is one of *fairness* or justice. The evaluator collects data to answer the question, "How does society in general benefit because of the existence of this program? Or are some segments of society harmed while others benefit?" House (1980, p. 131) addressed this issue using the example of the evaluation of the Illinois Gifted Program. The program might have accomplished its objectives for the children participating in it (i.e., satisfied the "effectiveness" standard). But there might have been deleterious effects on the nongifted, nonparticipating children who were denied the chance to affiliate with the gifted children. To the extent this happened, the program failed to satisfy the criterion of fairness.

The fourth criterion is that of *acceptability*. The evaluator collects data that reflect on the satisfaction of participants with the program or product. The fifth criterion is *aesthetics*, the qualities of unity, harmony, and coherence of the program or product.

These are five common criteria or dimensions of value by which judgments are made. But who makes the judgments? Who performs the evaluation? Evaluation theorists differ on this question. Some assert that the evaluator, being most familiar with the evidence, is in the best position to make the judgment. Others assert that the evaluator is simply an objective, neutral technician who gives the evidence to a "decision maker" who then makes the judgment. Still other theorists hold that the evidence should be made available to all parties who are affected by the program so that judgments of value are made by a variety of groups, each acting according to its own self-interest and according to the standards each feels is most important.

DIFFERENCES BETWEEN RESEARCH AND EVALUATION

So far little reason has been given to distinguish research from evaluation. Sometimes, confronted with the report of a study, even a careful reader cannot decide if it is the result of research or evaluation. Evaluators often (but not always) pose questions or hypotheses, select samples, manipulate and measure variables, compute statistics, and state conclusions, as researchers do. But they perform these activities for different reasons. *The distinction between research and evaluation lies in the intent and purpose of the investigator.* In the remainder of this section we will expand on this distinction by describing a hypothetical study.

Imagine a study in which the investigator is testing the effects of a computer-assisted math program on the achievement of math skills. The investigator hypothesizes that fourth graders who are given 30 minutes per day working with a computer math drill (in this case the program is Compucount) will exhibit higher scores on a standardized math test than comparable children without the program. Fourth-grade pupils are sampled and assigned at random to the experimental and control groups. The experiment is conducted, posttest data collected, and the hypothesis tested. A statistically significant advantage of treated over control pupils leads the investigator to conclude that the program in question does bring about better math achievement. Was the investigator a researcher or an evaluator?

A researcher conducts these activities ostensibly to advance the frontiers of knowledge, to gain general understanding about the phenomenon being studied. The researcher wants to contribute to theory. In this example the theory might be an educational theory of instructional technology, a psychological theory about information processing, or a social theory about the dehumanizing effects of machines. The theory or body of knowledge to which this "research" study is meant to contribute is a universal one, to put the aspiration somewhat pretentiously. The researcher seeks propositional knowledge about these constructs that will transcend the particular place where this experiment occurred. The children involved as subjects in the study are merely proxies for the population of schoolchildren whose learning or social interactions might be affected by technology. The conclusion reached in the study is meant to apply everywhere. Compucount, the software package employed here, is only an exemplar of a class of such programs. Thus, it can be said that the concerns and interests of the researcher are general, not parochial.

What, in contrast, might be the concerns of an evaluator? The evaluator's purpose is to use the experiment as a source of information for judging the merits of using Compucount in the particular way it was implemented by the teachers and administrators of this particular school Did the program accomplish its objectives, and was it efficient? The evaluator is less interested in contributing to any theory or general body of knowledge. Thus, it can be said that evaluation interests are parochial rather than universal. By *parochial* we do not imply local, for evaluations are sometimes national in scope. The evaluation of Project Follow-Through, described by House (1979), is an example of a study that was carried out simultaneously in 40 sites around the United States. The purpose was not to contribute to a general theory of education for the disadvantaged but to judge the value of this one particular federally funded program for disadvantaged pupils in terms of whether it should continue, cease, or change.

The second important distinction between research and evaluation is that evaluation studies are typically more comprehensive in the number and variety of aspects of a program that are studied. If the computer-assisted math study is intended to be an evaluation study, the investigator would not stop after conducting an experiment to determine if the program resulted in greater math achievement. The experiment would be only one means to the end of arriving at value judgments about the program. The evaluator would also collect data about the cost of the program, data that describe the extent and quality of participation of the pupils in the program (e.g., did the machines gather dust or attract only videogame fanatics?), data that could be used to compare the CAI program with other programs, such as cross-aged tutors, that can accomplish the same objectives. The evaluator would also look for side effects—negative and positive—of the implementation. For example, the program might increase performance on test items that measure rote memory of math facts but not affect performance on problem solving. Or the 30 minutes each day that the children spend on the computer might mean the equivalent amount of time lost to the arts or to programs for the gifted and talented. The evaluator must describe the program and place it in a broader context—that is, show how the people and places of this school might have an impact on the program. Each of these examples of further data that the evaluator would collect is also an example of a value standard that can be used to judge the program.

The third distinction between research and evaluation concerns the origins of the study. The origins and motivation for conducting research are rooted in curiosity and the researcher's need to know. The researcher—wanting to test and expand the theory of instructional technology, say—designs the study and approaches the administrators of a school district for permission to conduct it. The school administrators are concerned with whether the study will impose too heavy a burden on school time, with the proper and ethical treatment of the pupils, and with having a copy of the final report, but usually no more than that. The researcher is ideally answerable to his or her colleagues and to "science" for how the study is conducted and reported.

In contrast, when doing an evaluation, an investigator cannot simply approach a school and announce, "I want to evaluate your computer-assisted math program." Instead, an evaluator is normally commissioned by a "client" to conduct a study. The evaluator may be an employee of the agency that administers the program (in which case, the evaluation is referred to as an **internal evaluation**). For example, a superintendent, school board member, or director of curriculum directs the school district's testing and evaluation department to evaluate the math program of one elementary school or that of the district as a whole. In this case, one part of the organization seeks to appraise the activities of another part.

In an **external evaluation** the evaluator is hired from outside the agency; for example, the school district might hire a university professor or private evaluation consultant to conduct the study of the math program. Several large profit and nonprofit firms have sprung up since the late 1960s for the purpose of seeking evaluation contracts. These include American Institutes for Research, Research Triangle Institute, Apt Associates, RAND, and the National Opinion Research Center.

Evaluation may also be sought by a reference group outside the agency to be evaluated. For example, a teacher's union might commission an evaluation of the computer-assisted math program. The hospital patients' association might commission an evaluation of a hospital department. A state department of social services could hire an evaluator to determine whether welfare payments are being efficiently distributed in a county office. The local Association of Children with Learning Disabilities might commission an evaluation of availability of services for the handicapped. These examples show how evaluations are commissioned. One might suspect that the act of commissioning an investigator to perform a study might affect the investigator's autonomy. Members of the district's testing and evaluation department (internal evaluators) might feel somewhat obliged to confirm the favorite ideas of the superintendent because they are employees of the school district and hence responsible to the superintendent. In the jargon of evaluation, the superintendent is a partisan of the program.

On the other hand, internal evaluators have the offsetting advantage of being more familiar with the programs and personnel than any outsider could be. Employees of a private evaluation contracting firm (external evaluators) are not immune to the same pressure to produce positive results, since they need future contracts from school districts to stay in business. This is not to imply that all evaluations are suspect or that their results are produced primarily to accommodate the people who commissioned them. Nevertheless, one would be naive to disregard the climate of potential influences and the push-and-shove of competing interest groups that shadow the evaluation enterprise.

Several theorists have tackled the issue of the bias that can intrude based on the role and independence of the evaluator (Scriven, 1976). One general caution of Cronbach's should be noted here: the fair-minded evaluator frames questions "to expose both the facts useful to partisans of the program and the facts useful to its critics" (Cronbach et al., 1980).

Researchers, in contrast to evaluators, are supposed to be independent of these potential pressures. Ideally, researchers are dispassionate and impartial about the direction the results take. Evaluators, unlike researchers, have **clients**. These are the persons or agencies who hire them and commission the study. The only "client" for the researcher is the scientific community and perhaps the funding agency.

Evaluations also have **stakeholders**—reference groups or constituencies, individuals, and groups who have an interest in the program being evaluated and in the evaluation results. In the computer-assisted math program, the stakeholders include teachers, pupils, parents, administrators, math curriculum experts, taxpayers, software developers, and computer manufacturers. Other stakeholders are not so obvious—for example, parents whose wish for instrumental music programs is thwarted because the school does not have money to support both computer tutorials and instrumental music programs. Understandably, each of these groups cares about the program in a different way and hopes for a particular outcome of the study. The instrumental music parents group hopes that the evaluation will show Compucount to be ineffective, as do representatives for DigitalMath, the competing software company. Teachers in the math department hope for a positive result, which they can present to the superintendent along with their request for more money for hardware and software.

Each of these stakeholding groups makes up an "audience," or readership, for the evaluation report. An evaluation should consider the information needs of each audience. A highly technical report of the experimental results of the program, for example, would be inappropriate for the audience of taxpayers. Each stakeholding group has reason to contribute to the design of the evaluation and to the process of applying value standards to the results of the study. For example, competing software developers might wish the evaluation to include data that compare Compucount with other software to see which one produces better math achievement. The instrumental music parents group might want the evaluation to include an assessment of opportunity costs, that is, the costs of those programs that *could have been* funded with the money now used to fund the tutorial program. The political interests of clients, stakeholders, and audiences all figure in the theory of evaluation in ways quite different from the theory of research.

One might legitimately question the circumstances under which an evaluation is instigated. Some evaluations are periodic, such as the five-year cycle of evaluations linked to accreditation of secondary schools. No particular political motives can be attributed to the initiation of a particular cycle of these evaluations, because they are routine. Other evaluations are termed **formative**, for they occur while a program or product is being developed and for the express purpose of improving the program or product before it is disseminated. **Summative evaluations**, in contrast, focus on the finished program or product.

Other instigations of evaluation are more political in nature. By *political*, we do not mean Democrats and Republicans, but the dynamic struggle of people for resources and authority. For example, an evaluation can be launched to defend a program that its administrators believe is performing well. A community Mental Health Center with efficient programs and a well-qualified staff might commission an evaluation study to get out the good word, as part of a public relations drive, or perhaps in anticipation of future cutbacks in the state mental health center budget. Evaluations are also sometimes commissioned when a program is in trouble (as perceived by another part of the organization or by an affected reference group). A university president might begin an evaluation of the physics department because that department is believed to be staffed by too much "dead wood." A blue-ribbon panel is called in from prestigious physics departments across the country to collect facts about the department's effectiveness in teaching and obtaining research grants, its standing in the scholarly community, and the like. The judgments reached by these evaluators can then be used by the president to allocate money away from or toward the physics department.

These examples suggest the fourth distinction between research and evaluation: Evaluation is in many cases conducted when some problem becomes apparent or when a decision about the program or product must be made. The board of directors of a public health clinic needs to decide whether to put more of their resources into a screening and prevention program or into salaries for additional visiting nurses. Hence, an evaluation of the two programs is conducted to determine their relative cost effectiveness. A school board in a rapidly growing district is confronted with the choice of building a new school or putting another school on a year-round schedule. An evaluation study of schools in the system already operating under a year-round schedule will provide data (perhaps on teacher morale, pupil achievement, wear on the buildings, and so on) to the board so that it can make an informed decision. An evaluation of the computer-assisted math program could provide information to the school board in its deliberation on the decision to purchase more computers for the math department.

The importance of evaluation to decision making is evident. In fact, one theorist defined evaluation as the process of supplying information to decision makers (Stufflebeam et al., 1971). Another theorist argued that an evaluation report was good only to the extent that its recommendations were actually put into effect by decision makers (Patton, 1978). Because of its connection with decisions and problems, evaluation must be "timely," that is, it must produce results in time to be useful to those making decisions.

In summary, the differences between research and evaluation are several. First, research seeks general explanations. Its purpose is to contribute to theory and general knowledge. In comparison, evaluation is parochial. Its purpose is to appraise specific programs and determine their worth. Second, research aspires to (though never attains) value neutrality. Evaluations, however, must represent multiple sets of values and include data that address these values. Third, research is motivated by the search for knowledge. Evaluation is motivated by the need to solve problems, allocate resources, and make decisions. Fourth, researchers are autonomous and answerable to the scientific community. Evaluators are commissioned and are answerable to clients, audiences, and stakeholders.

The alert reader will have noticed that the word *ideal* has been used to describe researchers and evaluators. This modifier is necessary to distinguish the practice from the theory of the two endeavors. Distinctions between research and evaluation can become blurred in several ways. First, the norm in the scientific community for value-free research is often violated, particularly in the social sciences. Researchers have political affiliations and interests and purely personal motivations that sometimes enter into the choice of research problem, the methods chosen to address the problem, and the interpretation of data (Habermas, 1971).

In addition, an evaluation study may contribute to general knowledge (despite its original motivation) because of the way the report is used after the fact. Although the evaluator's concerns were parochial to the program evaluated, the reader of the report may be interested in the class of such programs and see applications to populations beyond the one directly affected by the particular program evaluated.

EVALUATION PARADIGMS AND APPROACHES

In Chapter 1 the idea was presented that researchers were governed by alternative paradigms, and that these paradigms give rise to different approaches to doing the work. Remember that a paradigm is a kind of organizing framework (a set of beliefs and assumptions), or lens, through which a person views the world. So, too, evaluators are governed by one of several paradigms. In this section we describe four alternative paradigms that can be distinguished from each other primarily by their different conceptions of what evaluation is. For example, one theoretical position conceives of evaluation as applied research. Another group of evaluation theorists believe that evaluation is part of systems analysis, to aid managers in the administration of their programs. A third paradigm considers evaluation as a matter of informed, professional judgment. The fourth emphasizes the political nature of evaluation.

Other distinguishing features of these paradigms (which follow logically from the varying conceptions of what evaluation is) are these: the relationship between evaluator, client, and stakeholder; the question of who should actually make the judgment of the worth of the program or product; and the criteria by which evaluation studies themselves should be judged. Naturally enough, evaluators who follow these different paradigms will design quite different studies. Many models or approaches have been developed, and some of these will be described.

Evaluation As Applied Research

Many evaluators began their careers as research scientists, trained in the academic disciplines of psychology, sociology, economics, and applied statistics. When they are called upon to perform evaluative studies, they tend to draw on the methods, procedures, and habits of researchers in the disciplines in which they were trained. These standards call for the most rigorous application of scientific theory and method. Likewise, recognized scholars (e.g., Boruch and Cordray, 1980) advise legislators and government administrators that only rigorously designed and executed *comparative* studies can provide unequivocal answers to questions such as "Are the compensatory education programs doing the job?" or "What has been the effect of the lead reduction program on ghetto children's health?"

Under the influence of this paradigm the terms *research* and *evaluation* are closely intertwined. One of the two major professional associations of evaluators is named the Evaluation Research Society, and a prominent evaluation journal is entitled *Evaluation Review: A Journal of Applied Social Research.*

The evaluation-as-applied-research paradigm is based on the idea that because of imperfect program design or implementation, many educational and social innovations are bound to fail. Therefore, it is in the best interests of society to weed out systematically the ineffective from the promising innovations. A program such as merit pay for teachers, for example, should be tried out on a small scale and subjected to rigorous testing before it is implemented nationwide. The rigorous test would be a true field experiment in which the program is the independent variable and the goal of the program (e.g., pupil achievement) is the dependent variable. Teachers and pupils would be assigned at random to two conditions: a merit pay treatment and a comparison group that works under a standard salary schedule. After a two-year trial, pupil achievement would be measured for the two groups and then compared. Statistical significance tests would be applied, and a significant difference would provide a quantitative estimate of the effect of merit pay on pupil achievement. This evaluation is primarily *summative* as opposed to formative. It is comparative; it is quantitative. As one set of authors described it, "The problem of discerning the effectiveness of a program is identical with the problem of establishing causality" (Rossi, Freeman, and Wright, 1979, p. 161).

Several assumptions of this paradigm can be identified in the writing of its proponents. The audience for evaluation is assumed to be official policy makers (who speak indirectly for the citizenry). Policy makers, when provided with experimental data, will act rationally to implement those programs shown to be effective. Program goals are assumed to be few in number and agreed upon by all parties. Only clearly specified goals can be the focus of experimental designs. With regard to the audience for evaluation, Raizen and Rossi wrote the following:

> Responding to the myriad, often conflicting expectations of all the audiences is likely to diminish the integrity of an evaluation and limit its usefulness to any one audience ... Defining the [primary] audience and targeting the message will reduce the frustration that often accompanies the more eclectic attempts to speak simultaneously with many tongues to many groups. (1981, p. 39)

The most important assumption is the belief that the experimentally controlled comparison is the most valid way to produce evidence that the program produced results. According to Riecken:

> Perhaps the most important feature of an experimental trial, however, is that it puts the question of effectiveness where it belongs, in a comparative context. For an experiment always asks whether the proposed program is effective *compared* to something else. The "something else" may be doing nothing at all or it may be instituting some rival treatment, purported to be as effective in achieving the same ends. The need for a comparative context is clear. Without comparing a given treatment to "something else" in a systematic way, we cannot be sure that it is the treatment *per se* which is responsible for an observed change or difference. Sometimes problems disappear even if nothing is done deliberately to resolve them; sick persons recover their health without medical treatment, unemployed do find jobs, some children learn to read by themselves, and incipient stuttering will often disappear if only parents and teachers will ignore it. (1975, pp. 2–3)

The methods for evaluation are experimental and (when experiments are impossible to implement) quasi-experimental. The criteria for judging evaluations are methodological rigor—primarily internal validity—and utility for policy makers.

Evaluation as Part of Systems Management

The paradigm of evaluation as part of systems management is followed by those who think of an organization such as a school or clinic as closed system of inputs, operations, and outputs (as the computer people would describe it). The evaluator's task in the system is to describe the inputs, operations, and outputs, relate them to each other, and provide this information to the manager who can then make decisions that regulate and improve the functions of the system.

The history of evaluation thus conceived mirrors the history of centralization of social functions in federal and state governments during the Great Society of the 1960s. The **planning, programming, and budgeting system (PPBS)**, first used in the Defense Department by Robert McNamara, was applied to the other departments in the executive branch as a means of assessing the efficiency of the social programs administered by them (House, 1980). Ralph Tyler, one of the founders of evaluation in education, influenced Congress to require evaluations of the educational programs instituted under the Elementary and Secondary Education Act of 1965 (Glass and Ellett, 1980). In both cases, the conception of evaluation was comparing outcomes with inputs.

There are several approaches or models that can be characterized as systems management. They share the basic idea that, to evaluate a program, one must measure the products of the system on the basis of stated goals. In schools the goals include cognitive development of pupils, achievement of basic skills of reading, writing, and calculating, as well as social development. The evaluator asks, "Given these goals, what is the level of attainment on performance indicators of these goals?" "Are there discrepancies between the stated objectives and what was actually produced?" "Are some parts of the system more effective than others in reaching the desired outcomes?"

The methods of evaluators who work in this paradigm are likely to be surveys of educational achievement, surveys of satisfaction with services provided by the program to its clients, surveys of decision makers to determine what their goals, needs, and priorities are, analyses of the costs of programs, and (in some approaches) monitoring of the processes of the program. Formative evaluation would be used to provide interim feedback to managers so that the program can be improved.

In this paradigm the primary audience of the evaluation is thought to be the managers themselves. The role of other stakeholders is to provide information and apply pressure to managers to improve outcomes. The goals are taken as given by the evaluator (in some other paradigms, the goals themselves are evaluated). The manager is assumed to be rational and will maximize the efficiency and effectiveness of the program if provided with the right information. For example, a mastery testing program that requires high school seniors to take a test of basic literacy is one example of the evaluation-as-system-management paradigm. The goal of the system (public schools) is basic literacy. The method of evaluation is the test. The assumption is that poor performance on the test will expose the poor schooling received and that school administrators will change the system so that basic literacy will be reemphasized.

Evaluation reports themselves are judged according to their usefulness for managers, their timeliness and credibility, and their technical adequacy. Within the evaluation-as-systems-management paradigm there is a variety of evaluation models or approaches. Three of them are described here.

Tylerian model   Ralph Tyler (1950) thought of evaluation as a recurring sequence of steps. **The Tylerian model** consists of: (1) establishing broad goals and more specific objectives; (2) classifying these objectives according to curricular content and the kinds of behavior expected of pupils who meet the objectives; (3) developing tests or other performance assessments; (4) collecting the achievement and performance data; (5) comparing performance with goals and objectives; and (6) studying these data to see where the curriculum can be improved. These steps and this conception of evaluation underlie other movements in education and social services. The National Assessment of Educational Progress was heavily influenced by Tyler. The accountability movement, the behavioral objectives movement, and the mastery testing and mastery education movement are all basically Tylerian. The goal attainment scaling procedures used in mental health centers is also Tylerian.

PPBS   The planning, programming, and budgeting system (PPBS) is another approach to evaluation subsumed under the system management paradigm. According to Hartley, (1969, p. 66), "PPBS seeks to relate inputs to the programs of an organization in a way that enhances a rational means-ends calculus." The goals and specific objectives of a system are identified. The programs are analyzed or broken down into component subprograms and activities. These subprograms are each logically related to system objectives, and they are analyzed according to their costs—the personnel, supplies, and other resources they consume. Alternative subprograms (i.e., interchangeable activities that would likely accomplish the same objectives) are proposed, and each one is subjected to cost analysis. This PPBS process then helps the manager make better decisions about the program. Evaluation takes place at the end of a program cycle and is a comparison of actual accomplishments with programmatic objectives.

Consider the example of a private vocational training school. This school operates as a system. Its objectives are: (1) pupil attendance; (2) satisfactory completion of a training program leading to a certificate; (3) life skills literacy (skills in balancing a check book, filing a correct tax return, etc.); (4) job skills relevant to the training program completed; and (5) employment in a job related to training. Each of these objectives has a performance indicator and a desired level of performance. The managers target a 90 percent daily attendance rate as desirable for the first objective. The school has three training programs that lead to certificates: secretarial, court stenographer, and data processing. Each program also has subprogram components. In the secretarial program, for example, the subprogram components include classes in typing, dictation, records management, and office deportment. In addition, there are subprograms in resume preparation and job interviewing skills. Other program activities include an attendance check, a job placement service, and a graduate follow-up research service.

The PPBS evaluator would graphically relate each subprogram activity to the objective it is likely to meet. Then the resources that each activity consumes would be assessed. For example, the attendance check contributes to the objective of maintaining pupil attendance. It costs the salary of two person-hours per day, space allocated for that person, plus costs of the telephone and on the average one auto trip per week tracking down an absent pupil. Several alternative means of maintaining attendance would be proposed, and their costs estimated. The same process occurs for all the subprograms included in the system. Having these data, the manager of the school is in a better position to judge which alternatives are most likely to be efficient and effective. The evaluator comes in later to measure outcomes on the performance indicators. An actual pupil attendance rate of 70 percent would lead the manager to look back at those subprograms linked to that objective and tighten the connection, allocate more resources to it, or whatever. Then the PPBS cycle continues.

CIPP model   Goal-attainment models such as those of Tyler have been elaborated and extended by authors such as Alkin (1969), Provus (1971), and Stufflebeam and associates (1971). The proposed models included examination of the goals of a system (Tylerian models asked the evaluator to consider the goals as "given" and not to judge whether they were worth attaining). In addition, the models considered a study of the actual day-to-day activities of the program (PPBS examines planned and projected activities but not the activities as they exist). Only one of these models, the **CIPP model**, will be considered here.

Stufflebeam defined evaluation as a continuing, cyclical process of assisting decision makers by delineating what information is needed to clarify decision alternatives, then obtaining that information and interpreting it in such a way that the decision maker can best put it to use. There are four components to evaluation: context, input, process, and product (hence the acronym CIPP). In *context evaluation*, the problems of the system are diagnosed, and the needs and unmet opportunities are identified. The setting, history, and social environment in which the program exists are analyzed. This contextual information then serves as a basis for developing goals and objectives that will result in improvement of the system. The purpose of input evaluation is to provide information concerning the ways to use resources to achieve project goals by identifying (1) relevant capabilities of the responsible agency, (2) strategies for achieving project objectives, and (3) designs for implementing the strategy chosen (Stufflebeam et al., 1971). The potential of these strategies to meet program objectives is then assessed.

Process evaluation occurs once the program is put into operation. The activities are closely monitored to provide feedback to decision makers, who can then make modifications and improve program functioning. It is interesting to contrast this notion of process (also known as formative) evaluation with the evaluation-as-applied-research paradigm. In the latter, you will remember, experiments are the method of choice. To run an experiment correctly, the independent variable must be held constant; tinkering with it would be discouraged. In contrast, process evaluation provides corrective feedback which can be implemented during the evaluation program.

In *product evaluation*, the program objectives are given operational definitions. The indicators are measured, either before and after a program cycle or only at the end. The resulting data help the managers decide whether to change, terminate, or continue the program.

Evaluation as Professional Judgment

The professional judgment paradigm of evaluation emphasizes the notion that judgments about the quality of a program are best made by those with the most expertise. Thus, movies are best reviewed by those with extensive experience and knowledge of cinematic art. Social studies programs are most validly judged by master social studies teachers and professors in that field. Community mental health centers are best judged by peer review. In each case the expert judges the program or product against established standards in the field. Any deficiencies in the program or product are brought to the attention of program administrators and the profession generally.

The methods used in this paradigm are direct observation and interviews of participants by the expert judges. Checklists based on the criteria established in the field (client-supervisor ratio, equipment and supplies, etc.) may be used. The assumption is made that peer review provides objective, reliable, and valid judgments. In other words, one assumes that the important features of the program will be revealed to the expert by whatever methods are used, and that one expert's judgments will not be seriously dissimilar to those of other expert judges.

The audience for the evaluation consists of program administrators and the relevant professional associations. Other groups with a stake in the outcome are not considered. The criteria by which an evaluation report is judged under this approach are comprehensiveness, credibility, and adoption of the recommendations of the expert judges.

Accreditation model   One of the most pervasive evaluation models, the **accreditation model**, is familiar to professionals in education, social work, law, medicine, and mental health; it follows the paradigm of professional judgment. Many secondary schools, for example, belong to accrediting organizations such as the North Central Association. Member schools must undergo periodic assessment and accreditation, the first step of which is a self-study. The schools establish committees to gather data on school functioning on various criteria. The programs are described, as are physical facilities, personnel, equipment, and the like. After the self-study is completed, a team of experts visits the school for several days, observing and interviewing. The team uses standard checklists. For example, the guidelines for school guidance services include the following:

> Every school counselor holds a master's degree with a major in counseling and guidance.
>
> Every counselor has a background of successful teaching or work experience.
>
> The administrators of the school and the school system support the guidance program by providing the physical facilities, supplies, and equipment needed for effective guidance services. (Adapted from *Evaluative Criteria*, 1969)

The team then prepares an evaluation report that points out the strong points and deficiencies of the program. On the basis of that report, the agency decides whether to accredit the school. In some cases accreditation is deferred until the deficiencies uncovered by the visiting team are corrected. The threat of removing accreditation pressures the program administrators to bring the program up to the established standards in the profession.

Connoisseurship model   In the work of Eisner (1979) one finds the **connoisseurship model** to evaluation. The connoisseur of wine can detect more characteristics of a glass of wine than can an ordinary person. Likewise, a connoisseur of, say, math programs is aware of many more characteristics on which math programs can be judged than is a layperson or educational generalist. The expert in math instruction will be attuned to more, will know exactly what to look for when observing a first-grade math lesson. Frequently, a nonexpert will see only confusion where a connoisseur will recognize order and quality.

Not only can connoisseurs perceive and make more distinctions, but they also are able to recall their experiences with hundreds of similar programs, so that comparisons can be made with the one currently being studied. Therefore, the best person to evaluate a program is the connoisseur, and the best method is the critical review. The evaluator as connoisseur studies the qualities of a single case. When these qualities are understood, a public declaration is made of the evaluator's understanding and judgment. According to Eisner, "Criticism is the art of disclosing the qualities of events or objects that connoisseurship perceives" (1979, p. 197). The public declaration is a narrative description of the features of the case and comparison of that case with similar cases. The evaluator makes a judgment about the program based on this personal critical review. The intent of the review is to make the audience more perceptive about this class of program.

Evaluation as Politics

Many evaluators have expressed dissatisfaction that evaluation studies have had so little impact on the decisions of policy makers. And many reasons have been advanced in the evaluation literature for this perceived failure. Those who believe that evaluation is applied research usually blame poor research methods. Others note that the assumptions imbedded in the paradigms are seldom met. One assumption is that managers are rational and will make the best decision once the data are available to them. To cite only one of many examples, several early evaluations of Title I (the federal program for compensatory education for the disadvantaged) showed that program to have negligible impact. Yet, in spite of these negative evaluations, Title I was not eliminated; now it is called Chapter I of the Educational Consolidation and Improvement Act of 1981. (This saga is documented in McLaughlin, 1975). For its constituents Title I had value that was unrelated to any documented gain on achievement tests of those children who participated. Its constituents, in turn, exercised political power to maintain the program.

Why did this happen? Some would say that the evaluation results were overshadowed by politics. There were special interest groups that backed Title I, the negative evaluation results notwithstanding. These groups lobbied Congress, making sure that funding was not eliminated. In fact, efforts were renewed to find evaluation designs that would show compensatory education to be effective.

A group of evaluation theorists have argued that, far from being an isolated instance of the intrusion of politics into evaluation, evaluation and politics are inextricably mixed (House, 1973; Cronbach et al., 1980, Cronbach, 1982). These theorists conceive of society as democratic and pluralistic. Policy making is the result of political compromise. The role played by evaluation in a democratic society was set out by Cronbach and associates as "a process by which society learns about itself" (1980, p. 2). "Its mission is to facilitate a democratic, pluralistic process by enlightening all the participants" (p. 1). This view of society and evaluation is in marked contrast to the view implicit in the evaluation-as-applied-research and evaluation-as-systems-management paradigms, where evaluation results are fed to a powerful decision maker who then commands that a program be instituted, altered, or terminated. Instead, this view sees society as made up of many layers and factions that compete with each other for goods and for a greater share of authority over social affairs. Programs, whether Chapter I, community extended care, or delinquency prevention, are always subject to the tugging among these factions. Each program has stakeholders and active partisans; some want to see the program succeed and others want to see it fail.

The evaluation itself becomes an object of the political give and take. For example, advocates of the Title I program solicited critical reviews of those evaluation studies that showed the program to be ineffective. Evaluators dare not overlook such struggles as they design, conduct, and report their studies.

Cronbach, among others, believes that in designing an evaluation, an evaluator should represent the concerns of as many factions as possible. Later, when the information is gathered and analyzed, it should be fed back to all concerned groups so that each can contribute to the formation of judgments and policy. In other words, knowledge is power; all parts of the democratic society should have access to knowledge. In this way, all have access to the political and policy-making process. In the words of MacDonald, "The basic value is an informed citizenry, and its evaluator acts as broker in exchanges of information between differing groups" (1974, p. 226).

The methods employed in the evaluation-as-politics paradigm are more various and eclectic than in other evaluation models. Experiments may occasionally be used, but they are not assumed to be the sole avenue to truth. Designs are more likely to be flexible and to accommodate shifting circumstances and needs of stakeholders for information. Evaluators uncover new questions as well as answer obvious ones. Evaluators concern themselves with transmitting information that is intelligible to the stakeholders.

A series of small designs using multiple methods and perspectives is seen as more likely to generate useful knowledge than one large, tightly controlled study. The way to judge the worth of an evaluation study is to ascertain the extent to which the stakeholding groups have been enlightened and can participate in the policy-making process. According to Cronbach and associates "Scientific quality is not the principal standard; an evaluation should aim to be comprehensible, correct, and complete, and credible to partisans on all sides" (1980, p.. 11).

Responsive evaluation model   The words of Robert Stake best describe the **responsive evaluation model**:

> An educational evaluation is responsive if it orients more directly to program activities than to program intents; responds to audience requirements for information; and if the different value perspectives present are referred to in reporting the success and failure of the program. To do a responsive evaluation, the evaluator conceives of a plan of observations and negotiations. He arranges for various persons to observe the program, and with their help prepares brief narratives, portrayals, product displays, graphs, etc. He finds

out what is of value to his audiences, and gathers expressions of worth from various individuals whose points of view differ. Of course, he checks the quality of his records; he gets program personnel to react to the accuracy of his portrayals; and audience members react to the relevance of his findings . . . . He chooses media accessible to his audiences to increase the likelihood and fidelity of communication" (Stake, 1975, p. 14).

The responsive evaluation approach assumes that any program has several groups of stakeholders and that each deserves to be given attention when deciding on the evaluation design. Each deserves to be informed by the results of the evaluation. By being better informed, each can contribute to the formation of judgments and the making of decisions.

The responsive evaluation approach is only one of several similar ones called qualitative (Patton, 1980), naturalistic (Guba and Lincoln, 1981), or transactional (Rippey, 1973). All share an emphasis on descriptive, qualitative data such as appears in case studies as well as a commitment to obtaining multiple perspectives and multiple value positions relative to the program.

Cronbach's approach   In *Designing Evaluations of Educational and Social Programs*, Cronbach (1982) laid out his approach. Each evaluation is a fresh undertaking; therefore, no single form (such as a randomized comparative design) is appropriate in all cases. He imagined an extensive period in which every issue and question would be considered as a possible focus for an evaluation study. In this approach questions are solicited from all stakeholding groups. Existing research and theory are used to generate lists of all possible effects of the program. From an analysis of program goals and activities the evaluator tries to speculate about what costs and benefits might reasonably follow. From this "divergent phase" in evaluation design, the evaluator and the client settle on a shorter list of questions that are worth studying. There is a trade-off: The evaluation can either have a short list that lends itself to rigorously and carefully controlled studies, or the same resources can be used to answer a longer list of questions with slightly less concern for rigor. Cronbach opts for the more comprehensive list, since the needs of more stakeholders can thereby be met and, at any rate, no one study is definitive. (Contrast this with the evaluation-as-applied-research paradigm that opts for large investment in a tightly controlled experimental study.) Cronbach would allocate resources to answer questions where "there is great prior uncertainty about the answer . . . the study promises great reduction of uncertainty . . . the inquiry costs comparatively little . . . and the information would have a high degree of leverage on policy choices or operating decisions" (Cronbach, 1982, pp. 226–227).

Once the list of questions has been decided, the evaluator (or preferably several evaluators working independently of each other) designs a study for each question. A variety of techniques can be used: case studies, survey data, experiments, and quasi experiments. Attempts are made to insure internal validity (ruling out alternative explanations to the claim that the program was responsible for producing the outcome) but not at the expense of generalization. Outcomes are measured by several methods. The program and the setting in which it occurs are carefully described. Cronbach emphasized that the reports of the investigations must be credible and understandable to the stakeholders and must provide the information they need.

Four paradigms for evaluation and several evaluation models or approaches have been described in this section. The purpose of the presentation is to show the reader the scope and variety of ideas about what evaluation is and how evaluation studies can best yield responsible and credible value judgments. There is no consensus among evaluation methodologists on a single, correct way to evaluate.

METAEVALUATION

Meta-evaluation is the evaluation of an evaluation. Theorists have studied the problem of meta-evaluation, particularly the question of which criteria to employ in judging whether a given evaluation study was good or bad. For an extensive account of meta-evaluation, the reader is referred to *Joint Committee on Standards for Educational Evaluation* (1981). This book reports the results of a project undertaken by professional groups such as the American Psychological Association and the American Educational Research Association to develop criteria for judging evaluation studies.

A reading of the previous section of this chapter, which pointed out how the different paradigms and approaches define evaluation, reveals that different criteria are valued depending on the paradigm to which one adheres. Nevertheless, one list of criteria will be provided here so that the student and reader of evaluation reports will be able to make an informed judgment while keeping in mind the diversity among the paradigms.

Criteria for meta-evaluation include:

1. *Technical adequacy.* Has the design yielded plausible statements about whether the program was responsible for the effects observed? Can the reader make reasonable inferences about whether the same program would be effective in other settings and on other individuals? Was the measurement of the outcomes reliable and valid?

2. *Descriptive adequacy.* How well was the program described? Were the context, setting, and sample well described?

3. *Scope.* Were all aspects of the program subjected to scrutiny? Were all possible costs and effects of the program considered? Were all points of view and the interests of all groups with a stake in the outcome made a part of the evaluation design?

4. *Timeliness.* Was the report finished in time to be used in decision making?

5. *Cost effectiveness.* Was the maximum of relevant information obtained for a reasonable amount of money?

6. *Communication.* Were the qualities of the report such that all audiences would find it intelligible, credible, and usable?

7. *Utility.* To what extent were the stakeholding groups enlightened by the report so that they could contribute more effectively to policy making?

SUGGESTED READINGS

CAMPBELL, D.T. Reforms as experiments. *American Psychologist*, 1969, *24*, 409–429.

CRONBACH, L.J. *Designing evaluations of educational and social programs.* San Francisco: Jossey-Bass, 1982.

CRONBACH, L.J. and others. *Toward reform of program evaluation: Aims, methods, and institutional arrangements.* San Francisco: Jossey-Bass, 1980.

HOUSE, E.R. *Evaluating with validity.* Beverly Hills, Calif. SAGE, 1980.

Joint Committee on the Standards for Educational Evaluation. *Standards for evaluations of educational programs, projects, and materials.* New York: McGraw-Hill, 1981.

LEVIN, H.L. *Cost-effectiveness: A primer.* Beverly Hills: Calif. SAGE, 1983.

MORRIS, L.L., Fitz-Gibbon C.T. and Henerson, M.E. *Program evaluation kit.* Beverly Hills, Calif. SAGE, 1978.

RAIZEN, S., and ROSSI, P.H. *Program evaluation in education: When? How? To what ends?* Washington, D.C.: National Academy Press, 1981.

STAKE, R.E. (Ed.). *Evaluating the arts in education: A responsive approach.* Columbus, Ohio: Charles E. Merrill, 1975.

WORTHEN, B.R., and SANDERS, J.R. *Educational evaluation: Theory and practice.* Worthington, Ohio: Charles A. Jones, 1973.

TERMS INTRODUCED IN THIS CHAPTER

evaluation
evaluation object
evaluation criteria
comparative evaluation
noncomparative evaluation
internal evaluation
external evaluation
evaluation clients
stakeholders
formative evaluation

summative evaluation
planning, programming, and
    budgeting system (PPBS)
Tylerian model
CIPP model
accreditation model
connoisseurship model
responsive evaluation model
meta-evaluation

QUESTIONS AND EXERCISES FOR FURTHER STUDY

1. List the evaluation activities that you have been involved in during the past several years (e.g., accreditation site visits, mastery testing programs, course evaluations, performance evaluations). What were the sources of evidence collected? What criteria of value (e.g., effectiveness, costs) applied to the

evidence? Who commissioned and conducted the evaluations? Who made the judgments? What political forces influenced the evaluations? What resulted from the evaluations?

2. Suppose someone were to commission you to evaluate your graduate program What sources of evidence would you employ (you would probably want to cover both the processes and the products of the program)? What are some relevant criteria that should be applied? What groups have a stake in this program and how should their needs for information be addressed?

3. Take the role of someone who believes that evaluation is applied research. What meta-evaluative criteria do you think should be applied to evaluation studies (they will probably be a subset of the list in this chapter)?

4. List the similarities and differences between research and evaluation. Why is it not always possible to classify a given study into one or the other category?

5. Contrast absolute and comparative criteria for evaluation. Consider a summative evaluation of a course in research methods and provide three examples each of absolute and comparative criteria in this evaluation.

6. In an evaluation of the ongoing career education program at University A, the components were surveys of students to determine if career education was needed, documentation of the qualifications of the staff, an assessment by an expert in career education of the quality of instructional materials and computer systems used in the program, an assessment of the ability of the teachers to communicate with participating students, and a cost analysis. The evaluation was commissioned by the chancellor of the university and conducted by a research associate employed by the Office of Institutional Studies at the university.
   a. Would this study be classified as formative or summative? Justify your answer.
   b. Would this study be classified as internal or external? Justify your answer.
   c. What are some groups that have a stake in this program?
   d. How might the criterion of fairness be applied to this program?

7. Find the evaluation study by Quinn, Von Mondfrans, and Worthen (1984) in *Educational Evaluation and Policy Analysis* (Vol. 6, No. 1, pp. 39–52). Read the study and respond to the following.
   a. What were the programs evaluated?
   b. How would you classify this evaluation study: formative, summative, or both formative and summative?
   c. What was the function of the "Level of Implementation" measure?
   d. How could you determine whether this was an internal or external evaluation?
   e. What paradigm does this evaluation likely represent?
   f. Besides program costs and program effectiveness as measured by math achievement tests, what measures and criteria could have been applied to this program to achieve comprehensiveness?
   g. What are some stakeholding groups and what issues of values and politics might be relevant to this program and its evaluation?
   h. What are the audiences for a study such as this?
   i. Think through the meta-evaluation standards and speculate on how they might be applied to this study.

3

STATISTICAL TOOLS IN RESEARCH AND EVALUATION

This chapter will not teach you how to compute statistics; rather, it will increase your understanding of how statistics are used in research and evaluation studies. Interpreting and critiquing studies requires some familiarity with commonly used statistical techniques. You need to know, for example, what the *mean* (average) represents, not necessarily how to calculate it. You need to know something about certain other descriptive statistics, but it is enough to understand the concepts underlying them rather than the mathematical procedures for producing them. Finally, you need to know the statistical methods (commonly known as inferential statistics) researchers use to judge the reliability of outcomes of studies. Again, it is enough to understand the underlying concepts rather than the mathematics needed to generate them. For the reader interested in how to calculate these various statistics, many appropriate texts are available, including those listed at the end of this chapter.

DESCRIPTIVE STATISTICS

The fundamental purpose of statistics is to simplify and reduce a large set of information to some smaller set without discarding the essential information in the process. **Descriptive statistics** are numbers that represent some characteristics of the set of scores. For example, suppose a physical education researcher is studying serving accuracy in tennis, which she defines as the number of times a novice player can serve a ball into a target set in the court. There are 50 10-year-olds in the researcher's sample. Each youngster has 20 chances to serve. The score for each youngster is the number of times out of 20 that the serve hits inside the target area (as recorded by a sharp-eyed observer). When all 50 have taken their serves and their scores have been recorded, the researcher has 50 pieces of information, probably too many to be thought about in any efficient or meaningful way. So the researcher reduces by mathematical formula the 50 items of information to two—a mean and a variance. This reduction does two things. First, it is easier and more economical for the researcher to deal with and think about two pieces than 50. Second, in many cases this reduction retains nearly all the important features of the 50 pieces of data; nothing essential is lost.

Measures of Central Tendency

The **mean** informs the researcher about the typical score, the average score, of the entire set or "distribution" of scores. In this example, the mean represents the typical number of times this group of 10-year-olds can serve into the target area. Look at the list of scores in Panel 1 of Table 3–1. You can see how difficult it would be to get an overall impression about how skillful these 10-year olds are by looking at the 50 scores individually. We get a better view of their skill if we line up the scores from the lowest score to the highest score (in Panel 2 of the table) and see that the members of the sample ranged from Bobbie, who never hit the target in 20 tries, to Rick, who hit the target all 20 times. This visual representation aids our understanding of the set of scores and shows where the bulk of the scores lies along the scale. Notice that the hump, or highest column of hits, is in the left region of the distribution, where the lowest scores are. By calculating the mean, which is done by adding all the individual scores and dividing by the number in the sample, one can see that the typical number of target hits in this group was 4.02:

$$\text{Mean} = (3 + 3 + 5 + \ldots + 1 + 11)/50 = 4.02$$

As you can see by looking back at the individual scores, no one person got a score equal to the mean. The mean is an abstraction, and thinking otherwise leads to confusion or amusement, as in the example of the average-sized family in the United States consisting of 1.8 children. Still, the mean has meaning. We can say that our sample of 50, considered as a group, has much room for improvement in their tennis serving skills (except for Rick, who looks discrepant from the rest). The procedure for calculating the mean (usually represented by the symbol $\overline{X}$) is illustrated in Formula 3–1.

TABLE 3–1   Hypothetical Data on the Serving Accuracy of 50 10-Year Olds

PANEL 1. INDIVIDUAL SCORES

(Numbers in parenthesis are the individual's posttreatment scores)

Jacqueline	3 (5)	Mary Ann	6	(6)
Josh	3 (2)	Jeff	2	(3)
Madeline	5 (6)	Darnall	0	(1)
Bobbie	0 (4)	Wendy	4	(3)
Steven	1 (9)	Eve	4	(5)
Matthew	0 (2)	Joey	2	(5)
Jean	6 (5)	Skip	3	(5)
Ernie	1 (6)	Kris	3	(4)
Marilyn	10 (14)	Ian	0	(0)
Jo	10 (9)	Ken	7	(6)
Stephanie	2 (6)	Henry	9	(10)
Leslie	3 (6)	Pat	6	(12)
Mindy	1 (6)	Federico	5	(13)
Ron	5 (6)	Alan	0	(5)
Tracy	2 (8)	Jamie	1	(10)
Nick	5 (9)	Clyde	12	(16)
Benjamin	0 (3)	Laurie	3	(3)
Louis	5 (6)	Craig	4	(3)
Jon	4 (3)	Brian	6	(5)
Nina	4 (4)	Elizabeth	1	(4)
Sammy	2 (3)	Sherylann	0	(0)
Rick	20 (20)	Bo	1	(6)
Bill	1 (5)	Andre	8	(12)
Juan	8 (9)	Kathleen	1	(8)
Becky	1 (6)	Emily	11	(14)

PANEL 2. FREQUENCY DISTRIBUTION OF PRETREATMENT SERVING ACCURACY

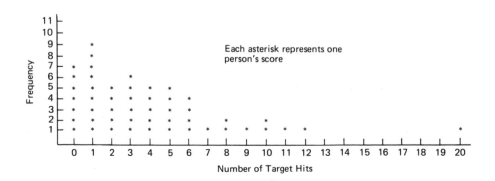

TABLE 3–1 **Continued**

PANEL 3. FREQUENCY DISTRIBUTION OF POSTTREATMENT SERVING ACCURACY

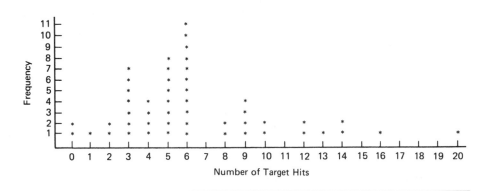

Number of Target Hits

Formula 3–1 $$\overline{X} = \frac{\Sigma X_i}{n}$$

where X_i, the individual observations, are summed (Σ) and divided by the sample size (n).

Two other descriptive statistics also represent the typical score in a distribution of scores. The **mode** is the most commonly occurring score in the sample. Among our tennis novices in Table 3–1, the mode, or most frequently obtained score, is a single hit of the target: Mode = 1. The **median** is the middle score in the distribution, one having half the scores above it and half below it (between 3 and 4 target hits in this sample). Although the mode and median are important descriptive statistics, the mean is by far the statistic most often used in social and educational research to represent the typical score in a distribution.

The mean has other purposes in research besides describing and typifying a set of scores. Suppose that the researcher wanted to try out a treatment or instructional technique for improving the accuracy of tennis serves. A logical way to do this would be to use the group of 50 10-year-olds and consider their number of target hits as a kind of baseline or pretreatment assessment. Having established the fact that their baseline as a group is 4.02 hits, she now implements her treatment, which consists of teaching them to meditate. They are taught that each time they begin to serve, they are to recite a mantra, or magical word, "Wimbledon." The training period lasts two weeks. At the end of that time they are tested again with the same target, the same number of trials, and the same observer. The second set of data is presented in parentheses in Panel 1 of Table 3–1. The second, or posttreatment, mean is calculated to be 6.42. Note that, as a group, the scores improved (although certain individuals did not). This is the logic of the experimental trial, to compare the means of the group before and after the treatment intervention to determine if, on the average, the scores changed. The impact of the treatment is gauged by comparing two means and assessing the difference between them. Just by comparing the initial mean number of hits with the mean number of hits after the group had been taught to meditate, one can get some, albeit an imperfect, grasp of the effectiveness of the treatment (just how "imperfect" will be the subject of Chapter 6).

Measures of Variability

Descriptive statistics are numbers that represent some characteristics of the set or distribution of scores. The mean represents the typical score or the central score in the sample. The **variance**, as one can guess from the commonsense meaning of the word, represents the degree of variability of the individual scores in the sample. The variance gives a measure of how different the scores of individuals are from each other and from the typical score. In other words, one number, the variance, reflects the amount of individual differences on a characteristic. One statistic contains the essential information about how the individual scores are dispersed or are spread out from one another in a sample. This concept can best be understood by comparing three samples against each other, one having little variability, another having a great deal of variability, and a third with an intermediate amount.

In the top part of Table 3–2 is a sample of the service target hit rates of 10 individuals. One might guess that this particular sample is made up of members of a college tennis team. Their performance as a group is high (mean = 19.6). More to the point for the present discussion, the scores of the 10 are quite close together. In fact, the only variability is between those who attained a score of 19 and those who attained a score of 20. Thus, *in this sample*, and *on this characteristic* (serving accuracy as measured by target hits), the variance is small. Keep in mind, though, that variance is always specific to a particular subject characteristic or variable. Sample 1 may be extremely homogeneous with respect to service accuracy, but very heterogeneous with respect to some other variable, such as writing ability.

In the center of Table 3–2 is a second sample made up of quite different individuals. The target hit rates vary from 0 to 20. This sample is much more heterogeneous with respect to serving accuracy than the first sample. Perhaps it is made up of members of a college fraternity who have quite different backgrounds and experience with tennis. At the bottom of Table 3–2 is a third sample of individuals along with their target hit rates.

TABLE 3–2   Hypothetical Data on the Serving Accuracy of Three Samples

---

SAMPLE 1 (VARIANCE = 0.267)

Mark (M) 19   Karen (K) 20
Sean (S) 19   Jennifer (J) 20
Terry (T) 19   Rob (R) 20
Lyn (L) 19   Gerri (G) 20
Victor (V) 20   Barb (B) 20

```
                                                                    R
                                                                    V
                                                       M            K
                                                       S            B
                                                       L            G
                                                       T            J
  |___|___|___|___|___|___|___|___|___|___|___|___|___|___|___|___|___|___|___|___|
  0   1   2   3   4   5   6   7   8   9  10  11  12  13  14  15  16  17  18  19  20
```

SAMPLE 2 (VARIANCE = 77.167)

Alan (A) 20   Steve (S) 1
Matt (M) 7   Conrad (C) 0
Dave (D) 19   Rick (R) 18
Patrick (P) 1   Jason (J) 0
Bob (B) 19   Edward (E) 10

```
  J   P                                                              B
  C   S                       M           E                     R    D    A
  |___|___|___|___|___|___|___|___|___|___|___|___|___|___|___|___|___|___|___|___|
  0   1   2   3   4   5   6   7   8   9  10  11  12  13  14  15  16  17  18  19  20
```

SAMPLE 3 (VARIANCE = 6.267)

Bill (B) 10   Zack (Z) 9
Eileen (E) 11   Dave (D) 15
Michael (M) 8   Kathy (K) 14
Jean (J) 10   Ted (T) 9
Natalie (N) 11   Peter (P) 7

```
                              Z   J
                              T   B   E
                      P   M       N            K   D
  |___|___|___|___|___|___|___|___|___|___|___|___|___|___|___|___|___|___|___|___|
  0   1   2   3   4   5   6   7   8   9  10  11  12  13  14  15  16  17  18  19  20
```

Number of Target Hits

The hit rates for these people range from a low of 7 to a high of 15. The scores tend to cluster around the mean of the group, which is 10.4. The third sample is less heterogeneous—its members are more alike on serving accuracy—than the second sample. The first sample is the most homogeneous of the three groups on serving accuracy. Notice that the numerical values of their respective variances reflect this same pattern. The lowest variance is in the first sample (0.267). The largest variance is in the second sample (77.167), with the third sample falling between (6.267). The square root of the variance is called the **standard deviation**, another commonly used statistic expressing the degree of heterogeneity in a sample. The standard deviation is easier to interpret than the variance because it uses the same scale as the measure itself. For example, the standard deviation of Sample 3 is 2.5. This implies that the typical "distance" between an individual score and the mean of the sample is two and a half hits of the target. The method of calculating the variance (usually represented by s^2) is given in Formula 3–2.

Formula 3–2 $$s^2 = \frac{\Sigma (X_i - \bar{X})^2}{n - 1}$$

Variance is more than simply a troublesome calculation that some students learn by rote. Understanding and explaining variability is at the heart of research. In fact, one could say that research would not exist if there were no variability among things. There are many reasons for persons to differ from each other on some trait or measure. All of these ways show up in the variance statistic. For example, there is so-called **natural variation**, which reflects differences among individuals in genetic endowment and the cumulative effects of varying psychological and social backgrounds. Individuals differ from each other genetically on characteristics such as height, bone structure, motor coordination, and eye color. Suppose that two persons, of the same age and sex, start out with approximately equivalent genes for eye-hand coordination; suppose they were identical twins. Yet one was raised in a home with a tennis court and the other was not. This difference in background introduces some variability in their subsequent serving accuracy. Or, one went to a high school with a competitive tennis team and the other did not. Or another had peers who preferred soccer to tennis (and claimed all tennis players were sissies). Or still another was raised by parents who gave plenty of praise and support, thereby developing the child's self-confidence; the other was not. Imagine a tree with many branches. Each source of variation creates a new division or branching. Different genetic endowments create differences that are compounded by (or compensate for) differences in nutrition, exercise, psychological environment, material resources, social and cultural opportunities, school and recreational opportunities, and experiences. At the end of this multitude of branches is a rich variety of individual differences in serving accuracy, critical thinking skills, feelings of marital satisfaction, or whatever. What this describes is a kind of natural variation—**true variance**—or the true extent of individual differences on the characteristics that interest researchers.

Natural or true variance is not the only source of differences on a measured variable. In selecting a sample, the researcher worries about whether that group of individuals selected has the same degree of natural variation that exists in the population as a whole (or in the population to which the researcher wants to generalize). For example, if she was unlucky enough to select the individuals in Sample 1 of Table 3–2, she would observe substantially greater average serving ability and less variability than would be typical in the population of college students as a whole. Sample 1 would provide a poor representation of the serving accuracy of the population as a whole. Thus **sampling error**, or the differences introduced by the sampling technique used, (say, the difference one sees in the mean and variance of Sample 1 compared to those of Sample 2) is part of overall variance. Sampling error is estimated and controlled if the researcher uses the technique of **random selection** of the sample from the population (See Chapters 6 and 10). By defining a population (say, all college students in the nation) and selecting a random sample from it, a researcher can be reasonably certain that the essential characteristics of the sample being measured are like those of the population from which the sample was drawn.

Similarly, if a researcher used more than one observer to record target hits, and the observers were dissimilar in their accuracy or visual acuity, **measurement error** would be added to overall variance. Measurement error is estimated by various checks on reliability of measurement, such as interobserver agreement rates (Chapter 5).

Lastly, a researcher can *create* a kind of variance in the following way. Suppose the researcher in our example wants to test the hypothesis that meditation improves service accuracy better than does practice alone. In this hypothesis, meditation is the independent variable, and serving accuracy is the dependent variable. She creates **systematic variance** in the independent variable by constructing two treatments, one including meditation during practice and the other consisting of practice alone. The independent variable has two values: either meditation plus practice or practice without meditation. Having constructed the two treatments, the researcher can assign half of the available persons to one treatment value and the other half to the second value. After exposing these two groups to the different values of the independent variable, she measures the dependent variable separately within the two groups. She computes the means and variances of serving accuracy within each group and examines the difference. Studying the means and variances of the two groups on the dependent variable of serving accuracy, she can determine the effects of the systematically varied (manipulated) independent variable. If the means of the two groups differ (a kind of variance between means), it is a sign that the treatement was effective, and the hypothesis is supported.

But what about all that natural variation, those subject characteristics that the subjects brought with them to the research study? How does the researcher know that the meditation was responsible for the difference in means between the groups? How does she know that the meditation group was not more athletic prior to receiving the treatment? Control over natural variation is achieved by the technique of **random assignment** of subjects to the two treatments. At the outset of the study, the researcher flips a coin for each available subject. If the coin comes up heads, that person is assigned to the meditation-plus-practice treatment. If the coin comes up tails, that person is assigned to the practice-alone treatment. By using this procedure the researcher protects against the circumstance that all the coordinated, self-confident children are assigned to the same treatment. These potentially biasing subject characteristics will be equally distributed in the long run between the two treatments if random assignment is used (Chapter 6).

To summarize, individuals differ from one another in several ways, by nature and by the cumulative effects of background. Researchers introduce more variability by the sampling and measurement procedures they use and by deliberately creating variability in experimental treatments to which they assign people. All these sources of variability contribute to the variance statistic.

Measures of Relationship

The third descriptive statistic that must be studied before published studies can be understood is the **correlation**. Unlike the mean and variance, which represent essential information about a sample on a single characteristic or variable, correlations describe the degree of correspondence of *two* characteristics of a sample. Correlations answer questions like these: "Is there a relationship between time on task (the productive time spent in reading instruction) and reading achievement?" "Do feelings of self-worth tend to go along with one's employment status?" "Can a person's college grade point average be predicted by his or her college entrance examination scores?" Each of these questions involves examining the relationship between two characteristics.

Consider this hypothesis: "There is a positive relationship between pupil's attitude about school and their reading achievement." Two variables are the focus of interest, attitude about school and reading achievement. To test this hypothesis, a researcher could take a sample of 10 sixth graders, measure their attitude about school, compute the mean and variance of this measure, then measure the pupil's reading achievement and compute the mean and variance of the latter. The resulting statistics tell us about the variables separately, but fail to test the hypothesis. To determine whether those pupils with positive attitudes about school also have high reading achievement and pupils with negative attitudes also have low achievement in reading, the researcher must examine the *pair* of scores for each individual. The pairs of scores appear in Table 3–3. Simply by looking at this

**TABLE 3-3 Hypothetical Data to Test the Hypothesis that Attitude about School is
Postively Related to Achievement**

PUPIL	ATTITUDE	ACHIEVEMENT
Bobbie	3	11
Hal	1	7
Rachel	2	8
Matt	3	12
Marti	1	5
Jackie	5	19
Tom	5	18
Geoff	4	15
Rob	2	7
Jane	4	16

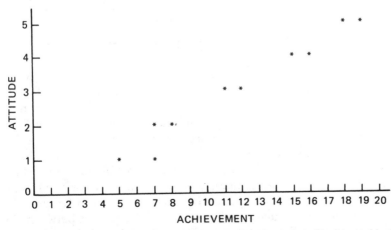

Scatterplot of the Relationship between Attitude and Achievement, with one subject illustrated.

Scatterplot of the Relationship between Attitude and Achievement with all ten subjects illustrated.
Each asterisk represents one subject's pair of scores.

small sample, you can get a sense that those pupils with relatively high attitude scores also have high reading scores (notice the pair of scores for Jackie). The converse is also true (notice the pair of scores for Marti). The graph at the bottom of the table provides a visual representation of the pairs of scores. The horizontal axis of the graph represents the scale of reading achievement, with higher achievement toward the right end of the axis. The vertical axis represents the scale of attitude about school, with more positive attitude toward the top. Each asterisk represents one individual in the sample and marks where that person's scores on the two variables intersect. This type of graph is called a **scatterplot**. The asterisk that marks the point both farthest to the right and highest up in the graph is that of Jackie, who had the highest score on each variable. Notice that if you were to draw a smooth figure to enclose the set of asterisks you would get a rather thin oval slanting upwards to the right. This indicates a linear, positive relationship between the two variables, such that persons with high scores on one variable tend to have high scores on the other. The hypothesis that attitude about school is positively related to achievement is therefore supported with this small sample.

With small sets of data like that in Table 3–3, we can assess the relationship between pairs of variables simply by looking at the *scatterplot* and at the pairs of scores on each individual in the sample. With larger data sets, however, just looking at pairs of scores may not reveal enough about their relationship. Therefore, **correlation coefficients** are computed. Although other coefficients are sometimes used (e.g., Spearman's rho, Kendall's tau, point biserial correlation), the Pearson product-moment coefficient is most prevalent in educational and social research. The correlation for the data in Table 3–3 is +0.98. Its symbol is r, and it can be calculated by Formula 3–3.

Formula 3–3 $$r = \frac{n\Sigma XY - \Sigma X \Sigma Y}{\sqrt{[n\Sigma X^2 - (\Sigma X)^2][n \Sigma Y^2 - (\Sigma Y)^2]}}$$

The correlation coefficient has two properties that describe the relationship between two variables—direction and size. *Direction* refers to whether the relationship between two variables is positive (direct) or negative (inverse). A positive relationship, such as that seen in Table 3–3, means that high scores on one variable are associated with high scores on the other variable; it is indicated by a plus sign (or no sign, which is always understood to be plus). A negative, or inverse, relationship is one in which high scores on the first variable are associated with low scores on the second variable and vice versa. This is indicated by a negative sign in front of the coefficient. An example of such a relationship might be that between the frequency of church attendance and commitment of delinquent acts. Young people who report high rates of church attendance also tend to report that they engage in few delinquent acts. Conversely, those who engage in more delinquent acts report that they attend church infrequently or not at all. Relationships between variables can also be *curvilinear*, like the relationship between age and motor ability over the life span. Motor ability is low in infancy, increases as the individual develops through early adulthood, and gradually declines in old age. Curvilinear relationships are best revealed in scatterplots and in coefficients other than the Pearson product-moment coefficient (see Glass and Hopkins, 1984, Chap. 7).

Size, or magnitude of relationship, is described by the numerical size of the correlation coefficient, which can vary from -1.00 to 1.00. Therefore, a correlation of $r = +1.00$ indicates a perfect, positive relationship between the two variables. A coefficient of $r = -1.00$ indicates a perfect, negative relationship between the two. When correlations are high, either in a positive or negative direction, it is possible to make a reasonably accurate prediction of a person's score on one variable just by knowing his or her position on the other. A correlation of $r = 0.00$ indicates the absence of a linear relationship between the two variables. In such a case, high scores on the first variable are no more likely to be paired with high scores on the second variable than they are likely to be paired with low scores on the second. One could not predict a person's score on variable 1 by knowing his score on variable 2 any better than one could predict the variable 1 score simply from the mean of variable 1.

Correlations are frequently found in matrices that represent the relationships between several pairs of variables simultaneously. For example, Table 3–4 shows a hypothetical **correlation matrix** depicting the interrelationships of the following variables, each measured by observing 45 first-grade classrooms: time on task, class size, pupil self-direction, and teacher control. The variables are listed both down the rows and across the columns. In the first cell, or box (first row and first column), is the correlation of time on task with time on task (in other words, with itself). The correlation

TABLE 3–4 Correlation Matrix

	TIME ON TASK	CLASS SIZE	PUPIL SELF-DIRECTION	TEACHER CONTROL
Time on Task	1.00	−0.31*	−0.47*	0.52*
Class Size	−0.31*	1.00	0.28	−0.19
Pupil Self-Direction	−0.47*	0.28	1.00	−0.56*
Teacher Control	0.52*	−0.19	−0.56*	1.00

$n = 45$
* $p < 0.05$

is $r = +1.00$. Moving one cell to the right is the correlation of time on task with class size: $r = -0.35$, which suggests that more time on task tends to be spent in classes that are smaller. In the fourth row of the first column is the correlation coefficient between time on task and teacher control,

TABLE 3–5 An Example of Hypothesis Testing Using Inferential Statistics

RESEARCH HYPOTHESIS: "Behavioral counseling increases the self-esteem of children"

DEFINITION OF CONSTRUCTS: Behavioral counseling will consist of 20 hours of individual counseling with a trained counselor who reinforces esteeming statements and extinguishes nonesteeming statements. Self-esteem will be measured by the Smith Self-Esteem Inventory.

DESIGN: Subjects will be selected from lists of 10-year-old pupils referred by their teachers as exhibiting nonesteeming characteristics. Twenty will be assigned at random to the behavioral counseling treatment and 20 to the control group (the latter will spend the equivalent time in the school library). Subjects will be pretested and posttested on the Smith Self-Esteem Inventory.

NULL HYPOTHESIS: "There will be no difference in the means of the self-esteem inventory of the group treated with behavioral counseling and the untreated control group, as assessed by a *t-test* at the 0.05 level of significance (alpha)."

STATISTICAL FINDINGS:

PRE-TEST DATA

Experimental group mean $= 28.1$
           Standard deviation $= 5.2$
           n (sample size) $= 25$
                     (obtained) $t = 0.667$ ($df = 48$)
                               $p = 0.50$
Control group mean $= 29.1$
           Standard deviation $= 5.4$
           $n = 25$

POST-TEST DATA

Experimental group mean $= 36.5$
           Standard deviation $= 6.5$
           $n = 25$
                     (obtained) $t = 2.3$ ($df = 48$)
                               $p < 0.05$
Control group mean $= 32.5$
           Standard deviation $= 5.5$
           $n = 25$

The *t-test* is significant at the 0.05 level. Therefore, the null hypothesis is rejected. Examination of the means shows that the experimental group had a higher mean self-esteem than the control group.

CONCLUSION: Behavioral counseling increases self-esteem.

which shows a positive relationship. The correlations in Table 3–5 are **bivariate**—that is, they describe the relationship of two variables at a time. Therefore, we can see one relationship between time on task and class size, another between time on task and pupil self-direction, a third between class size and pupil self-direction, and three other bivariate correlations. **Multiple correlations** depict simultaneously the relationships in the entire set of variables. Research that uses correlations is covered in Chapter 9.

INFERENTIAL STATISTICS

In the previous section we showed how statistics are used to describe and characterize, in an economical way, sets of scores on variables. A different purpose for statistical method is inference, which consists of a set of mathematical procedures for generalizing beyond the sample data. **Inferential statistics** involve a chain of reasoning that connects the observed data to populations of data too large to observe completely.

The problem of the link between sample and population was hinted at in Chapter 1 in the section on the scientific method. The researcher derives a research hypothesis from the relevant theory. This research hypothesis is stated in the abstract, as the predicted relationship between constructs. An example might be as follows: "Behavioral counseling increases the self-esteem of children." This research hypothesis is a conjecture about the cause-and-effect relationship of two constructs. Yet, in the abstract, the hypothesis cannot be tested directly. As the researcher begins to operationalize the constructs and set up the procedures of the study, he states a *null hypothesis*. The latter differs from the research hypothesis in the following ways. The null hypothesis is concrete rather than abstract— instead of dealing with constructs, the null hypothesis deals with operationally defined variables. The null hypothesis does not state a direction but merely states that no relationship between the two variables (or difference between the means of two groups on the dependent variable) will be observed. It can be tested directly by applying inferential statistical tests. It includes a probability value for these tests, with which the observed data will be compared, and which provides a criterion for rejection of the null hypothesis. Here is an example of a null hypothesis for the above research hypothesis:

"There will be no difference in the means of the measure of self-esteem (operationally defined) of the group treated with behavioral counseling (operationally defined) and the untreated group, as tested by a **t-test (alpha** = 0.05)."

A *t*-test is one method of testing the statistical significance of the difference in two means. Alpha (α) is the level of significance chosen in advance by the researcher. The logic of this procedure is that the null hypothesis is a kind of alternative to the research hypothesis. By rejecting the null hypothesis, one provides support for the research hypothesis (which cannot itself be tested directly or statistically). In an experimental trial, one assumes that if Treatment A is more effective than Treatment B (a research hypothesis), then one would observe that the mean of the group given Treatment A would be higher than the mean of the group given Treatment B. A null hypothesis, then, states that the mean of the group receiving Treatment A would be equal to the mean of the group receiving Treatment B. Cause-and-effect claims are examined by looking at the means of groups treated differently. Stated another way, if a researcher hypothesized that urban density was a cause of crime, he would state a null hypothesis such that the mean rates of crime would not differ in two groups, one exposed to high-density and one exposed to low-density living conditions.

The question for inferential statistical test is "How large does the difference between two means have to be in order to reject the null hypothesis?" Remember that the researcher *wants* to reject the null hypothesis, because rejecting the null hypothesis is the only way the researcher has of supporting the research hypothesis. The answer involves the comparison between the observed difference in the means of the two groups against a standard of *chance variation,* or the amount of variation to be expected in the differences resulting from sampling.

Take a look at Table 3–5, which contains an abstract of a study. Note that under Statistical Findings descriptive statistics are given to the left. The means, standard deviations, and sample sizes are listed for both the pretest measure and the posttest measure, for both the experimental and control groups. The inferential statistics—the *t*-test and the **probability level** (or **significance level**) are given on the right.

The first *t*-test provides an assessment of the difference between the experimental and control groups *on the pretest*. By computing a *t*-test, the researcher is asking, "How likely is it that the observed difference in the two means is due to chance fluctuations?" "How often would I observe a difference this large (the difference between 28.1 and 29.1) merely by the process of drawing two random samples from the same population?" "What are the chances of observing an average difference this great if the null hypothesis is true?"

A statistical test of significance, such as a *t*-test, provides a criterion for comparing the observed difference with the difference one would expect to encounter in the natural course of observing the variable. The expected difference takes into account all the ways individuals can differ from each other—natural variation, sampling error, and measurement error. The significance test indicates whether the observed difference between experimental and control groups is greater than the difference that would be expected due to these sources of variation.

Even though the experimental and control groups were constituted by random assignment, some difference in the means of the two groups would still be expected. When subjects are allocated to treatment and control groups by random assignment, the pretreatment differences between the groups will be the chance difference, the normally expected difference, the difference one would expect to encounter simply because assignment to the two groups was based on chance. The means of the groups would differ from each other by some amount just by chance alone. The *t*-test for the comparison of the experimental and control groups at the pretest was calculated to be 0.667. The degrees of freedom (*df*) were equal to 48 (degrees of freedom are related to the sample size in the two groups). These two numbers need not mean anything to you in order to read and critique research studies. The important number is the *significance level*, or *p* (probability) value. It refers to the magnitude of the *t*-test and assesses how likely it is that the observed difference in means is due to chance. In this case, the *p* value for a *t*-test at the stated magnitude is 0.50. This indicates that the chances of observing a mean difference of this size (i.e., between 28.1 and 29.1) are 50 out of 100. In other words, the likelihood is great that the difference on the pretest is simply due to chance or the normal variability one would expect from random assignment to the two groups.

Because it is known that groups that are randomly assigned will have small and usually nonsignificant mean differences on the pretest, experimenters rarely compute significance tests on pretreatment averages. Such calculation is unnecessary. The pretreatment *t*-test is presented here only for the purpose of explaining significance tests. In actual practice, researchers might calculate a *t*-test on the posttreatment averages only or compare the two groups on how much they gained from pretreatment to posttreatment.

Now look at the posttest data. The *t*-test ascertains whether the observed difference in mean self-esteem between experimental and control groups is likely to be due to chance. This is the direct test of the null hypothesis. A significant *t*-test will allow the researcher to reject the null hypothesis in favor of the research hypothesis.

The difference between the two means on the posttest is the difference between 36.5 and 32.5. Is that difference large enough to reject the null hypothesis, or is it also likely due to the chance fluctuation of random assignment? One cannot answer without the inferential test. The *t* statistic was calculated to be 2.3. Once again, the meaning of that number need not concern you. It is the *p* value associated with that magnitude of *t* that you should be able to understand and interpret. The *p* value is given as "*p* < 0.05." This figure indicates that the observed difference in the two means would be observed by chance less than 5 times out of 100 under the condition of no true difference in the means of the two populations. Since the obtained value of *t* has a probability value equal to or lower than the *p* value specified in the null hypothesis, the researcher can declare that the difference in the means was **statistically significant**, and the null hypothesis is rejected. By virtue of the rejection of the null hypothesis, the research hypothesis—"Behavioral counseling increases the self-esteem of children"—is supported. The observed difference in the posttest is too large to be accounted for by the fluctuations of random assignment; hence, the difference has other causes, namely the effect of the behavioral counseling.

If the researcher conducted the study 100 times, he would find this large a difference between the means only 5 times, even if the null hypothesis was true and the treatment completely ineffective. But, since 5 out of 100 represents a relatively unlikely occurrence, the researcher is willing to conclude that the difference was due to something else besides random fluctuation. The "something else" to which the researcher attributes the observed difference is *the treatment*. In other words, if it is unlikely that the difference between means of 36.5 and 32.5 can be attributed to chance (random assignment), then we can attribute it to the treatment.

Imagine an *alternative* set of scores for the posttest data. Imagine that the means are 34.5 and 35.5 (the standard deviations and sample sizes are the same). The resulting t-test would be calculated at $t = 1.68$ ($p = 0.10$). This p value indicates that the observed mean difference could occur by chance alone 10 times out of 100 experiments for which the null hypothesis was true. The obtained probability of $p = 0.10$ is larger than the p value stated in the null hypothesis, also called *alpha*. With this set of data, therefore, the statistical test is *not significant* (sometimes stated as n.s.), and the null hypothesis cannot be rejected.

The selection of a probability value for rejecting the null hypothesis (alpha) is partly a matter of convention and partly an assessment by the researcher about what risks he or she wants to take. The researcher might choose a conservative position, setting the probability level at 0.01 or 0.001. If so the researcher could be risking the chance that the treatment really did have an effect that he or she will be unable to report. Or the researcher might choose to be daring, set the probability at $p = 0.25$, and risk reporting an experimental effect that really was not there.

The test of statistical significance provides a standard for comparing observed difference to expected chance difference. The significance level, chosen in advance by the researcher, provides a standard for assessing how much variability between the means can be expected by chance alone. If the observed difference in means is larger than that chance difference, then the null hypothesis is rejected. In the example in Table 3–5, the null hypothesis would be rejected if the probability was less than 0.05. This means that a difference this large would be observed only 5 times out of 100 if the null hypothesis was true, indicative of the real, nonchance difference between the two groups.

The procedure for statistically testing hypotheses about differences between means can be outlined as follows:

1. The research hypothesis states that some treatment (called A) is the cause of some dependent variable, and maintains that individuals exposed to A will differ with respect to the dependent variable from individuals exposed to an alternative treatment (called B).

2. The null hypothesis states that there will be no difference in the means of the dependent variable between the two groups.

3. A statistical test (e.g., *t*-test) is chosen to test the null hypothesis, along with a significance level (alpha) for its rejection.

4. After the treatments are implemented, the measurements taken, and the means computed, the statistical test is calculated. The value of the statistical test is referenced to an obtained probability value (in a table of probabilities such as that of Hopkins and Glass, 1986, p. 408). In published studies the obtained probability value is printed in the table of statistics.

5. If the obtained significance level (*p*) is *less* than the probability value stated in the null hypothesis, the statistical test is "significant" or "reliable" or "exceeds chance," and the null hypothesis is rejected. The observed difference between the means is unlikely due to chance or naturally occurring variation. The research hypothesis is supported.

6. If the obtained probability value is *greater* than the probability (alpha) value stated in the null hypothesis, the null hypothesis cannot be rejected. The observed difference between the means is likely due to chance.

Conventional inferential statistical tests are variations on the above procedure. In spite of the rich variety of their forms (analysis of variance, analysis of covariance, chi square, multiple comparisons, and the like), the logic is the same. The statistically unsophisticated consumer of research can still go a long way toward interpreting the statistical results of studies simply by understanding this logic and the meaning of probability values. Nonexperimental studies also employ similar procedures with different types of conclusions. For example, studies of gender differences in spatial abilities compute statistical tests on the mean differences between boys and girls on measures of spatial ability. Although no causal claim can be made for differences found, the researchers may use statistical tests as a way of asserting that the differences are greater than what one would observe by chance sampling from two identical populations.

The subsequent section gives examples of inferential statistical tests selected to illustrate more sophisticated forms and to be typical of what one encounters in the research literature.

Analysis of variance   Analysis of variance is simply one step up from the *t*-test. The *t*-test, you will remember, was used to compare the means of the dependent variable in *two* groups in the behavioral counseling example in Table 3–5. The **analysis of variance (ANOVA)**, is analogous to the *t*-test, but is used to compare the means of *more than two groups*. Suppose that the research hypothesis is that the presence of advanced organizers (topic sentences placed at the beginning of a chapter in a textbook) will aid comprehension of a science text better than either a postorganizer (topic sentences at the end of a chapter) or no organizers. This is an example of a "single factor," or one-way, ANOVA. In this case there is one independent variable with three values or levels. The null hypothesis states that there will be no difference in the means of comprehension scores among the three groups receiving the three treatments. The significance level (alpha) for rejecting the null hypothesis is set in advance by the researcher at α = 0.01. The data are listed in Table 3–6.

The **F-test** is analogous to the *t*-test. Its value of 4.01 need not concern you, although its amount is a function of the differences among the means. The *p* value is interpreted the same way that a *p* value for a *t*-test is interpreted. Here the *p* value is equal to 0.05, indicating that differences in means as large as these for these three groups could have been found by chance 5 times out of 100. However, in this case, the *obtained probability value is greater than the probability value (alpha) stated in the null hypothesis.* Therefore, the results are not statistically significant at the $p = 0.01$ level, and the null hypothesis cannot be rejected. The research hypothesis is not supported by these data. Of course, a less cautious researcher—one willing to risk a false rejection of the null hypothesis with 0.05 probability—would have rejected the hypothesis of no differences.

Factorial analysis of variance   An *F*-test is also calculated for more complex designs having more than one independent variable or for designs with at least one independent variable and one moderator variable. As an example of a **factorial design**, consider the researcher who hypothesizes that mastery learning increases pupils' math achievement, but that pupils' quantitative aptitude (QA) may interact with or moderate the effect of the independent variable on the dependent variable. In other words, mastery learning may have a different pattern of results for pupils of high ability and pupils of low ability. The researcher measures the quantitative ability (the moderator variable) of a group of 80 pupils and divides them into a high-ability group and a low-ability group based on their scores. He divides

TABLE 3–6   Hypothetical Data on Advanced Organizer Example

Advanced Organizer Mean	= 5.6
Post-Organizer Mean	= 4.0
No Organizer Mean	= 3.9

$F(2,26) = 4.01$
$p = 0.05$

TABLE 3–7   Two-Factor "Treatment × Ability" ANOVA Design

		TREATMENT	
		MASTERY	TRADITIONAL
ABILITY	HIGH	Mastery, High Ability	Traditional, High Ability
	LOW	Mastery, Low Ability	Traditional, Low Ability

the high-ability group at random into a subgroup that will receive mastery learning and another that will receive traditional instruction. The low-ability group is similarly divided at random between mastery and traditional instruction. The null hypotheses are not stated (frequently the case in published research), but merely implied. The researcher chooses $\alpha = 0.05$ level to reject the implied null hypotheses that (1) the means of the groups receiving mastery learning and traditional instruction are equal; (2) the means of the ability groups are equal; and (3) the mean difference between mastery and traditional groups is equal for the two ability groups (i.e., no interaction). Table 3–7 displays the factorial design. Table 3–8 contains the means of all groups after treatment.

Table 3–9 is typical of factorial analysis of variance results. "Source" refers to the source of systematic variance, also called a *factor*. The researcher has created systematic variance in the independent, or treatment, variable. He has measured variance in the moderator variable of ability. "Treatment × ability" refers to the **interaction** of these two factors. A rejection of the third null hypothesis would mean that the ability factor interacts with the treatment, producing an alternative pattern of results than would be produced by the treatment alone. It might mean that mastery learning increased achievement more for one ability level than the other, for example. "Error," sometimes referred to as "residual" or "within groups," is naturally occurring variation, sampling, and measurement error; in other words, all variance beyond the systematic sources of variance listed above

TABLE 3–8   Means for "Treatment × Ability" ANOVA Design (Hypothetical Data)

		TREATMENT	
		MASTERY	TRADITIONAL
ABILITY	HIGH	29.8	35.2
	LOW	24.0	22.2

TABLE 3–9   ANOVA Table for "Treatment × Ability" Design

SOURCE OF VARIANCE	MEAN SQUARE	DEGREES OF FREEDOM	F	p
Treatment	18.17	1	0.90	>0.05
Ability	532.43	1	26.45	<0.001
Treatment × Ability	76.86	1	3.82	<0.10
Error	20.13	20		

it. The column headed mean square, or MS, is another term for variance, so that the quantity, 18.17, is the variance due to the treatment. Degrees of freedom, or *df*, is a number related to the number of ways the constituents of the source of variance are free to vary. *F* is the statistical test, and each source of systematic variance is tested. Therefore, there is an *F*-test for the treatment factor, the ability factor, and the treatment × ability interaction. The rightmost column is a column of the probability values associated with each *F*-test. Each specifies the chances of the mean differences associated with that factor being due to chance alone. The probability levels are interpreted in the same way as *p* values for *t*-tests and *F*-tests for single-factor ANOVAS. One can see that only the *F* test for the ability factor had a probability value smaller than the probability value (alpha) specified in the test of the null hypothesis. Only the second null hypothesis could therefore be rejected. The other differences in means did not exceed chance expectation. The research hypothesis that mastery learning increases achievement and interacts with pupil ability is not supported by these simulated data.

Analysis of convariance   A further elaboration of the statistical procedures of ANOVA is called **analysis of covariance**, or **ANCOVA**. The intent of the researcher is to reject the null hypothesis of no difference between means of treated and untreated groups. There may be a single factor or many. Each factor can have two or more levels. In these respects ANCOVA is like ANOVA. The difference is the statistical adjustment ANCOVA makes among the groups with respect to some other variable, called the *covariate*. Imagine a study in which the researcher has two independent, or treatment, variables: type of instruction (mastery learning vs. traditional instruction) and class size, and one moderator variable, gender. She divides her sample according to their gender. Among the boys, she randomly assigns her subjects to four possible treatment arrangements: mastery learning and small class, mastery learning and large class, traditional learning and small class, and traditional learning and large class. The girls are randomly assigned to the same four treatment arrangements. She now has a three-factor (type of instruction × class size × gender) ANCOVA. Each factor— also called **main effect**—has two levels, or values. Look at Tables 3–10 and 3–11 to get an idea of this design.

TABLE 3–10   Design for Three-Factor ANCOVA

SEX CLASS SIZE	BOYS LARGE	SMALL		GIRLS LARGE	SMALL
MASTERY	Mean for boys, in large classes, with mastery learning		MASTERY		
TYPE OF INSTRUCTION					
TRADITIONAL			TRADITIONAL		

The null hypotheses, all tested at the 0.05 level, include no difference in the means of the mastery learning versus traditional instruction groups (averaging across the other factors), no difference in the means of the small and large class size groups, no difference in the mean achievement of boys and girls, and no interactions among these factors. The covariate is IQ measured prior to the treatment. Its effect on the analysis is to reduce the amount of difference in IQ within the groups as well as between them. Even though the groups were constituted at random, they still reveal some natural variation that tends sometimes to obscure the treatment effects. Analysis of covariance reduces the natural variation and makes it easier to find statistically significant differences between the treatment groups. The statistical tables used for ANCOVA are similar to ANOVA tables and are interpreted the same way. There is an F-test for each factor, or main effect (in this case, type of instruction, class size, and gender); for each interaction

TABLE 3–11   Table for Three-Factor ANCOVA

SOURCE OF VARIANCE	MEAN SQUARE	DEGREES OF FREEDOM	F	p
1. Type of Instruction				
2. Class Size				
3. Sex				
4. Instruction × Class Size				
5. Instruction × Sex				
6. Class Size × Sex				
7. Instruction × Class Size × Sex				
8. Covariate Residual				

(instruction × class size, instruction × gender, class size × gender, and a three-way interaction among instruction, class size, and gender); and for the covariate itself.

Multivariate analysis of variance Another elaboration of the ANOVA design and statistical testing procedure **multivariate analysis of variance**, or **MANOVA**. This is equivalent in all respects to ANOVA except that more than one dependent variable is employed. Recall the example in Table 3–7 of the two-factor mastery learning × ability design. Suppose the researcher had hypothesized that mastery learning has both an immediate and a lasting effect on achievement. He administers the achievement test as soon as the treatment is completed and again six weeks later. Rather than conducting two parallel two-factor analyses, one on each set of measures, he employes a MANOVA design with measure as a factor, or systematic source of variance. This is virtually like a three-factor analysis, with a main effect for type of instruction (mastery and traditional), ability, and measure, plus interactions—instruction × measure, ability × measure, instruction × ability, and instruction × ability × measure. Each source of variance has a *F-test* of the difference between the relevant means as well as a probability value for each *F-test*. Once again, the probability values are interpreted in the way already presented.

Multiple comparisons In ANOVA designs, the null hypothesis usually states that the means of various groups are all equal. A rejection of the null hypothesis is unambiguous when there are only two groups. But recall the example in Table 3–6. There were three treatment groups whose means were compared: advanced organizers (mean = 5.6), post-organizers (mean = 4.0), and no organizers (mean = 3.9). The *F-test* of the difference among these three means was statistically significant, and the null hypothesis was rejected. One cannot really tell by looking which pairs of means are different from each other. Are advanced organizers better than post organizers? Are post organizers really no better than no organizers in enhancing comprehension? These questions can be answered by using the family of statistical techniques known as **multiple comparisons**. The particular names of these techniques are planned orthogonal contrasts, the Tukey method, and the Scheffe', Dunnett, Dunn, and Newman-Keuls methods. Some of these methods yield *t* statistics, others yield *F* statistics. In any case the statistics are accompanied by probability values that are interpreted in much the same way as you already know. (See Glass and Hopkins, 1984, Chap. 17 for more detailed explanation.)

Inferences about correlations In an earlier section of the chapter, correlation coefficients were shown to be descriptive statistics that summarize the relationship between two variables. Correlation coefficients of $r = 0.00$ indicate an absence of linear relationship between two variables. When $r = 1.00$, a perfect relationship is represented. However, correlations contain some element of chance just as differences in means do. Hence, there is a need for statistical tests of correlation coefficients just as there is a need for statistical tests of the difference in means of two groups. A correlation coefficient of $+0.35$ may merely reflect some fluke of covariability in a sample. Or the same coefficient may reflect some genuine, nonrandom relationship between the variables in the population sampled. To sort out which of these interpretations is true, a statistical test is applied. The test is based on the size of the sample. A null hypothesis is stated that there is no relationship between the variables in the population. A probability value (alpha) is selected as a criterion to reject the null hypothesis. Given the alpha, the sample size, and the value of r, one can access a table to determine whether the null hypothesis can be rejected (in published studies the obtained probability values are generally given as part of the table of statistics). Rejection indicates that the observed relationship is unlikely due to chance and is "significantly nonzero." Look back at Table 3–4 and note the asterisks beside the correlations that are significantly greater than chance ($p < 0.05$). Coefficients without asterisks may have arisen from sampling error in drawing samples from populations in which the two variables are unrelated.

Nonparametric statistics   All the statistical tests so far described are classified as *parametric*. A different class of inferential statistics is known as **nonparametric statistics** (Siegel, 1956). These are used for data that can be classified, ranked, or counted, that is, that cannot be measured along some scale. Variables such as gender, political affiliation, eye color, and religion are called *nominal* (see Chapter 4), and it is usually not sensible to compute means and variances for such data. Gender, for example, has two values: male and female. Members of a sample can be classified into one or the other of the categories. One could not meaningfully compute an "average gender" for a sample. The only way to represent typicality is to count the relative frequencies and percentages of each category. Consequently, the parametric inferential tests are not appropriate to data of this type. It is a controversy among methodologists whether parametric tests ought to be used with variables that are rank ordered (such as pupil's rank in class) or for small samples or samples with odd distributions. For those who believe that parametric tests are not appropriate, nonparametric tests are used. The latter include the Mann-Whitney U-test, median test, Wilcoxon signed rank test (all similar in purpose to a t-test), Kruskal-Wallis test, or Friedman test (similar to ANOVA), tetrachoric correlation, and chi square (explained below). All the nonparametric tests yield probability values similar to probability values of parametric inferential statistics.

Chi square   The **chi-square** test is a widely used nonparametric statistic. It is employed when the variables are nominal (or when the researcher dichotomizes a scale) and the research objective is to determine if there is a relationship or association between two such variables. Take as an example the research question, "What is the relationship between alcoholic recovery (as measured by subsequent hospitalizations) and marital status?" The null hypothesis predicts that no such association exists (the categories are independent) in the population (to be tested at alpha = 0.01 level). The researcher draws a sample of men who had been treated for alcoholism in a private hospital five years prior to the study. The recovery status variable is divided into three categories: more than two subsequent hospitalizations, one or two hospitalizations, and no subsequent hospitalization. The simulated data are summarized in a *contingency table*, shown in Table 3–12. The table shows, for example, that men with no hospitalizations are disproportionately represented in the "married" category. The chi-square value of 20.5 has a probability less than 0.001. There is less than 1 chance in 1,000 that these two variables are independent in the larger population sampled. This obtained probability is less than the alpha of 0.01 stated in the null hypothesis. Thus, a relationship in the population can be concluded.

Cautions on Inferential Statistics

Many researchers and consumers of research place more credence in significance testing than is warranted. They believe that a "statistically significant" result is important, meaningful, remarkable, or strong. These words, after all, are linguistically equivalent to the word "significant." Yet

TABLE 3–12   Hypothetical Data for Chi Square Analysis

MEN CLASSIFIED BY RECOVERY STATUS AND MARITAL STATUS

		RECOVERY SATUS (Subsequent Hospitalizations)		
		MORE THAN TWO HOSPITALIZA-TIONS	ONE OR TWO HOSPITALIZA-TIONS	NO HOSPITALIZA-TIONS
MARITAL STATUS	MARRIED	$n = 10$ 8.3%	$n = 12$ 10%	$n = 98$ 81.7%	$n = 120$
	NOT MARRIED	$n = 30$ 16.7%	$n = 48$ 26.7%	$n = 102$ 56.7%	$n = 180$
		$n = 40$	$n = 60$	$n = 200$	$n = 300$

Chi square (X^2) = 20.5 $p < 0.001$

this interpretation is incorrect. A statistical difference in means only refers to probability theory and the likelihood that a difference so large can be attributed to chance, or sampling fluctuation. A significant relationship is one that is unlikely due to chance. The difference between two means that is significant at the $p = 0.001$ level is not "more significant" than the difference between means that is significant at the 0.05 level (as is sometimes misinterpreted), unless the two differences are based on pairs of samples of the same sizes.

These misinterpretations can be avoided by understanding the components of a t-test (although the same logic holds for all the tests). The t-test is a function of the observed difference in means, the variance of the groups, and the size of the sample. The larger the difference between means, the larger the t and the greater the likelihood of finding statistical significance. The greater the variance within the groups, the smaller the t. With larger samples, the chances of reaching significance are greater, other things being equal. Due to the relationship between sample size and the chance of attaining significance in a statistical test, there is some controversy among methodologists. When a researcher has a large enough sample, statistical significance may be reached even though the mean difference between two groups is small. Thus, the distinction should be maintained between statistical significance and educational or practical significance.

On the other hand, powerful treatments sometimes fail to yield significant mean differences when the sample size is small or there is a large amount of measurement or sampling error or a large degree of individual differences within the sample.

A helpful supplement to the significance test is calculation of the **effect size** (Glass, McGaw, and Smith, 1981), which is a measure of the mean difference between two groups, divided by the standard deviation. This statistic indicates how large the effect or difference is without regard to the size of the sample. Other procedures for estimating the size of the effect are used by researchers. For example, the percent of the variance of the dependent variable that is explained by differences in the independent variable can be calculated as a way to judge the outcome of a study.

SUGGESTED READING

GLASS G.V, and HOPKINS, K.D. *Statistical methods in education and psychology* (2nd ed.). Englewood Cliffs, N.J.: Prentice-Hall, 1984.

HAYS, W.L. *Statistics for the social sciences*. New York: Holt, Rinehart & Winston, 1973.

HOPKINS, K.D., and GLASS, G.V. *Basic statistics for the behavorial sciences* (2nd ed.). Englewood Cliffs, N.J.: Prentice-Hall, 1986.

MARASCUILO, L.A., and McSWEENY, M. *Nonparametric and distribution-free methods for the social sciences*. Monterey, Calif.: Brooks/Cole, 1977.

SHAVELSON, R.J. *Statistical reasoning for the behavorial sciences*. Boston: Allyn & Bacon, 1981.

SIEGEL, S. *Nonparametric statistics for the behavioral sciences*. New York: McGraw-Hill, 1956.

TERMS INTRODUCED IN THIS CHAPTER

descriptive statistics
mean
mode
median
variance
standard deviation
natural variation
true variance
sampling error
random selection
measurement error
systematic variance
random assignment
correlation
scatterplot
correlation coefficient
correlation matrix
bivariate relationship
multiple correlation

inferential statistics
t-test
alpha
probability level
significance level
statistically significant
analysis of variance (ANOVA)
F-test
factorial design
interaction
analysis of covariance (ANCOVA)
main effect
multivariate analysis of variance
    (MANOVA)
multiple comparison
nonparametric statistics
chi-square
effect size

QUESTIONS AND EXERCISES FOR FURTHER STUDY

1. What are the two purposes for which statistics are used in research? Provide an example of each.

2. Match the statistic on the left with its purpose on the right.
    a. mean
    b. standard deviation
    c. correlation

    1. describes relationship between two variables
    2. describes the typical score of a variable in a sample
    3. describes the extent of variability in a sample

3. A college student wanted to study the relationship between religious denomination and dogmatism. His only available subjects were students in his psychology class, all of whom were Protestant. Discuss this issue as it relates to the concept of variance in research.

4. Examine the following set of data, which shows two groups (1 and 2) that have been randomly assigned to two kinds of kindergarten program (structured and open). Their scores on three variables (group membership, age, and school readiness) are reported. School readiness has been measured in age-equivalent scores so that a score of 4.5 indicates a level of school readiness equivalent to the average child at the chronological age of 4 years and 5 months.

GROUP MEMBERSHIP	AGE IN MONTHS	SCHOOL READINESS
1	49	4.5
1	52	3.8
1	54	4.0
1	52	5.0
1	61	4.5
1	68	5.5
1	70	5.6
1	73	6.5
1	73	6.8
1	74	6.5
2	55	5.0
2	61	4.5
2	61	5.5
2	63	4.0
2	63	4.8
2	65	5.8
2	66	5.8
2	67	6.2
2	68	7.0
2	74	7.5

Answer the following questions about the set of data above.
a. What kind of variance is represented in the variable, group membership?
b. Which group is more diverse in age?
c. Without doing any calculation, state which group is likely to have the smaller standard deviation.
d. How similar are the two groups in their typical age?
e. (Optional) Calculate the means and standard deviations of the two groups.

5. Take the data set in exercise 4 and plot the relationship between age (horizontal axis) and readiness (vertical axis). Refer to the scatterplot in Table 3–3 for a model. Disregard the group membership and plot all 20 pairs of scores in the same graph.
   a. Characterize the relationship between age and readiness as either (1) positive, (2) negative, or (3) near zero.
   b. Without actually plotting the data, characterize the relationship between age and group membership.
   c. (Optional) Calculate the Pearson product-moment correlation coefficient between age and school readiness.

6. An experimental study of the effects of a weight-lifting program on self-confidence yields the following results:

	TREATMENT GROUP	CONTROL GROUP
MEAN	3.75	2.75
STANDARD DEVIATION	1.25	1.35

$t = 2.5$ $p < 0.05$

Select the statement below which best represents an appropriate statement of findings.

a. The treatment had an educationally significant effect.
b. The difference between the means of the treatment and control groups is unlikely due to chance alone.
c. The findings are 95 percent accurate.
d. The statistics are 5 percent accurate.

7. A researcher selects an alpha of 0.05 to evaluate the mean difference on self-reported delinquency of two groups, one high on anomie and the other low on anomie. Which one or more of the following *obtained* probability values (p) would indicate that the results are statistically significant?

a. 0.01
b. 0.001
c. 0.10
d. 0.005

8. Consider this research hypothesis: "Immersion programs are superior to language lab training in second-language learning." A researcher designs a study to lend support to or disconfirm this research hypothesis by constructing two treatments (operationally defined), randomly assigning subjects to the two treatment groups, administering the treatments, and then comparing the average number of vocabulary words identified on a test. Write a null hypothesis that the researcher might use.

9. Suppose that the null hypothesis in question 8 is rejected at the chosen alpha probability level. Can the researcher state that the results are statistically significant? Is the research hypothesis supported or disconfirmed?

10. An industrial researcher explored the research question, "Does employee absenteeism relate to quality of work production?" He hypothesized that a relationship exists such that workers with high levels of absenteeism produce lower quality work. He operationally defined the variables as "number of days absent within a two-month period" and the "number of production errors made per day in a two-month period." The null hypothesis was as follows: "There is no relationship between number of days absent and number of production errors made." The probability value (alpha) for rejecting the hypothesis was set at 0.01. After collecting the data, the researcher computed a Pearson product-moment correlation coefficient. The value of this coefficient was $r = 0.40$, which is associated with a probability value of $p = 0.05$ for the number of subjects in this study ($n = 25$). Can the null hypothesis be rejected? Why or why not? Is the correlation statistically significant according to the significance level chosen by the researcher? Is the research hypothesis supported or not?

11. Shoham-Salomon and Jancourt (1985) conducted a factorial design comparing three treatments for reducing stress. They hypothesized: "Whereas paradoxical directives are more effective with less stress-prone subjects, non-paradoxical directives (e.g., 'try to relax') are more effective with less stress-prone subjects" (p. 449) The three treatments consisted of (1) paradoxical directives (i.e., instructions for the subjects to concentrate on and intensify the physical feelings related to their stress), (2) stress management (i.e., instructions to relax and concentrate on a calming scene), and (3) self-help. Subjects were classified into two groups based on their initial levels of stress and then randomly assigned to one of these three treatments. At the end of the treatment period, all subjects were tested on (1) a performance task (the

subject must find a "target digit" in a sequence of random numbers), and (2) heart rate during performance. Data were analyzed with a two-factor ANOVA. The authors reported the mean performance for the three treatment groups was not significantly different. The mean performance for the stress-prone and nonstress-prone groups was not significantly different. There was a significant ($p < 0.05$) interaction between treatment and stress proneness. The means (and standard deviations in parentheses) were as follows:

TREATMENT GROUP

	PARADOXICAL INTERVENTION	STRESS MANAGEMENT	SELF-HELP
Stress-prone	15.38 (4.81)	11.88 (1.55)	10.60 (2.88)
Nonstress-prone	11.43 (2.57)	12.14 (2.12)	12.38 (1.19)

   a. Assuming that a high score indicates better performance, was the research hypotheses disconfirmed or supported?

   b. In this study, although no null hypotheses were stated explicitly, three null hypotheses were actually tested in the ANOVA. State the three implicit null hypotheses and indicate whether they were rejected.

   c. What type of variable is stress proneness?

12. Find the article by Mevarech and Rich (1985) in the *Journal of Educational Research* (Vol. 79, No. 1, pp. 5–11). Read it and answer the following questions:

   a. What is the research problem addressed?

   b. What is the research hypothesis? Is it stated directly?

   c. The researchers called gender an "independent variable." This textbook refers to the way gender is used in this article as what kind of variable?

   d. The researchers compared two groups, one of which had experienced CATI and the other not. Was random assignment used to determine what pupils would be given CATI and which not?

   e. What descriptive statistics were calculated?

   f. What inferential statistics were calculated?

   g. Consider Table 2. How many main effects and how many interactions were tested?

   h. Interpret the asterisk next to the value of F associated with the main effect of "Instruction," (i.e., "the probability of observing a difference between the two groups due to chance alone is _____ ").

   i. Interpret the main effect due to sex, assuming the alpha level had been set at 0.05.

   j. Interpret the interaction between instruction and grade.

   k. Summarize the effect of CATI on all dependent variables (ignore moderator variables and interactions).

13. A large-scale evaluation of two competing eighth-grade math programs is conducted by a school district. There were approximately 1,000 eighth graders in math program A and about the same number in program B. A standardized achievement test serves as the dependent variable. At the end of the year, the test was administered to both groups and yielded means of 8.8 for those finishing program A and 8.9 for those finishing program B. The null hypothesis is rejected. The mean difference, however, reflects an advantage for program B of only two items on the test. Discuss this result in light of the distinction between statistical and practical significance—that is, should the district adopt program B for all eighth graders?

4

PRINCIPLES
OF MEASUREMENT
IN RESEARCH
AND EVALUATION

THE STUDY OF MEASUREMENT

In Chapter 1 we stated that the central problem in social and educational research is construct validity. When researchers set out to address the question, "What is the effect of psychoactive stimulants on hyperactivity?" a whole series of auxiliary questions lie in the background. What is the construct of hyperactivity? How does hyperactivity manifest itself in a child? By what procedures can a researcher obtain dependable observations of these things? Do the data obtained by these procedures really reflect what is meant by hyperactivity? These are problems of construct definition and measurement, a topic that is covered in scores of textbooks such as Cronbach (1970), Hopkins and Stanley (1981), Thorndike and Hagen (1977), and at a greater level of sophistication in Cronbach, Gleser, Nanda and Rajaratnam (1971), Fiske (1971), and Lord and Novick (1968). There is an elaborate professional literature consisting of theory and empirical work referred to as *psychometrics*.

Measurement is controversial. Tests are associated in the public mind with problems of labeling (low intelligence test scores tag youngsters with the label of "mentally retarded"), racism (some scientists have claimed inherited differences in intelligence among races based on test scores), and the failure of the educational system (allegedly revealed in declining achievement test scores). In the aftermath of these controversies some professional groups have publicly opposed all testing.

Although we in no way wish to minimize these controversies, the assertion must be made that research could not exist without measurement. The purpose of **measurement** is to describe differences among individuals with respect to constructs of interest—for example, dogmatism, ego strength, verbal fluency, motor development, and the like. Thus, Joseph has more ego strength but less muscle strength than Jennifer. Mark is dogmatic whereas Janice is not. Ron is both taller and balder than Don. If we are interested in answering the question, "What effect does an income maintenance program have on recipients' self-esteem?" we assume that persons differ among themselves in the level or amount of self-esteem that they possess, and we have to be able to describe differences in degree of self-esteem possessed by the population of people who receive or are eligible for income maintenance. Group differences—between experimental and control groups, say—are the accumulations and results of individual differences.

Measurement and testing are frequently used for purposes other than research and evaluation. For example, tests are given by psychologists to diagnose the intellectual abilities and achievements of schoolchildren to determine whether the children can best be served in special placements such as classes for the handicapped or programs for the gifted and talented. Tests are given to select the best candidates for exclusive schools and occupations or to determine who is most likely to profit from services like psychotherapy. These examples illustrate the classification and placement function that measurement can serve. Tests are also used in guidance, where they are given to clients by counselors who interpret the results so that the clients may make better choices of vocations. Still another function of measurement is to assess instruction. That is, the learning that takes place in schools and training facilities can be measured by administering tests of achievement. Although not all educators agree, tests seem to focus and motivate teaching and learning. Tests are also used for the purpose of certification; for example, when a lawyer passes the bar examination, the state organization that administers and scores the test certifies the competence of that lawyer to practice law.

These four uses and functions of measurement are listed here as a way of distinguishing them from the fifth and sixth purposes: *research* and *evaluation*. Why is this distinction necessary? A test or other measurement procedure may be perfectly fine for one function but not for the others. The bar exam may serve the purpose of certifying lawyers, yet not be adequate as an outcome variable in a study that compares passing rates among the state's law schools over several years. A test may be appropriate for deciding which children need special education but not for evaluating the effectiveness of the special education program they receive. Any measurement procedure must be understood and evaluated for a particular use. Only measurement in the context of research and evaluation is considered in this chapter.

CONCEPTUALIZATION AND QUANTIFICATION

All too often researchers and evaluators pay little attention to issues of measurement. They take for granted that the test, questionnaire, observation schedule, or other measurement procedure used to produce data corresponds well with what it claims to measure. We have even heard a doctoral candidate say, "I'm not sure what my research problem is, but I have this test of assertiveness I can use." This candidate was short-circuiting a complicated process of thinking about the construct of assertiveness and then selecting or constructing a measurement procedure that would reflect that thinking.

Conceptualization

Measurement consists of two stages: conceptualization and quantification. **Conceptualization** involves the definition and theoretical analysis of the construct to be measured and the selection of an indicator for that construct. **Quantification** refers to a set of measurement procedures that are applied to individuals so that a number can be assigned to them. Conceptualization deals with constructs. Remember that a construct is "some postulated attribute of people" (Cronbach and Meehl, 1955). A construct is an abstraction, an idea about some characteristic or property of individuals.

Let us take the example of the construct of hyperactivity. No one can observe hyperactivity directly because it is an abstraction, like freedom or tyranny; what one observes are reflections and instances of it. We assume that some children possess the trait or property that is called hyperactivity because these children seem to exhibit behaviors we have become accustomed to thinking of as hyperactive. That is, they fidget, tap their feet, leave their seats, play with their pencils, poke their neighbors, talk loudly, and the like. They bother their teachers and drive their mothers crazy. They engage in these behaviors with a frequency and intensity that sets them apart from other children. Because of this constellation of behaviors, we imagine that there is a trait of hyperactivity. This trait is a property of the child rather than the situation, according to conventional wisdom (though some psychologists disagree). In other words, hyperactivity exists in the psychological or physiological make-up of the child. Still, no one can see, hear, taste, or feel hyperactivity. There is no direct assessment of hyperactivity.

Instead, the researcher interested in the construct hyperactivity will have to analyze the construct theoretically and define it, then select an **indicator** of the construct. An indicator is any empirical manifestation of a construct, that is, some overt behavior that can be counted or rated, or perhaps a set of responses to a test or other standardized stimulus. For example, one indicator of hyperactivity might be the number of times the child leaves his or her seat in one classroom hour. Other indicators might be the decibel level of sounds the child emits or a score on the Connors Abbreviated Symptom Questionnaire (Connors, 1973), which consists of 10 scales including "cries easily and often," "mood changes quickly and often," each of which a teacher rates on a four-point scale from "not at all" to "very much." It is important to understand that each construct can have many indicators, and the researcher must select those that are relevant for a particular study. In this example, the researcher selects "number of seat-leavings" as the indicator. Unlike the construct hyperactivity, the number of seat-leavings is something that can be assessed directly. Of course, the researcher would have to establish standard procedures for how an observer would count seat-leavings (the actual measurement procedure). But once these procedures are set up, assessment of seat-leavings can be accomplished. However, our researcher can only infer, hypothetically and tentatively, that number of seat-leavings is a good proxy for, or reflection of, hyperactivity. It can only be *assumed* that the child with a large number of seat-leavings is also the one likely to be hyperactive. (For an extended analysis of the construct of hyperactivity, see Collins, 1981; Whalen and Denker, 1980.)

The researcher relies on a body of empirical and theoretical literature, called **construct validation literature**, that has established the connection between the construct—in this case, hyperactivity—and the indicator, number of seat-leavings. If such a body of literature did not already exist, it would be incumbent on the researcher to devise some theoretical conceptualization of the attribute to be measured. Based on critical thinking about the definition and meaning of the construct, research studies are conducted to verify the connection between the construct and the various indicators.

Conceptualization begins simply with dictionary definitions—in other words, with the meanings of the construct in everyday language. Next the researcher consults professional dictionaries, such as the one compiled by English and English (1958), for the meanings of the construct as used in the professional literature. Theories are used as well. (For a presentation of this kind of linguistic analysis, see Scriven, 1986. Refer to Fiske, 1971, for an excellent treatment of conceptualization in construct validation.) Out of this activity comes a working definition of the construct. The researcher begins to develop a series of hypotheses about the construct. For example, he or she may ask, "In what conditions would we expect this construct to manifest itself?" (Does hyperactivity show up only in schools, or does it manifest itself on the playground, in church, in unstructured as well as structured situations, only when the parents are present?) "How do individuals vary with respect to the construct? Do individuals possess it to different degrees?" (Are children either hyperactive or not, or can you say that person A is more hyperactive than person B?) "What are the presumed causes of hyperactivity?" (Does the presence of food additives and allergies lead to increased hyperactivity?) "Do genetics play a role in this construct?"

(Does hyperactivity run in families?) "Is the construct age- or gender-dependent?" (Do children grow out of hyperactivity? Do more boys than girls have it?) "Is this construct likely to be altered by an intervention?" (Will drugs or psychotherapy or family therapy lessen hyperactivity?) "How is this construct the same as or different from related constructs?" (Is hyperactivity the same entity as learning disabilities? Is hyperactivity unrelated to intellectual abilities?) "Can the construct be subdivided into more discrete units or subconstructs?" (Is hyperactivity really the sum of attentional deficits and emotional disturbance?)

Based on the best accumulation of thinking and research, the researcher states hypotheses about what is likely true. Such a series of hypotheses make up what Cronbach and Meehl (1955) referred to as the **nomological network**. A nomological network is like a theory in that it consists of abstract, interlocking definitions and statements about the relationships between the construct and its various indicators. From it one can deduce how the indicators ought to relate to each other in empirical trials. The network clarifies what the construct means and how it is likely to appear in nature.

The list that follows illustrates a rudimentary nomological network for the construct of hyperactivity. (This list is for purposes of teaching about construct validation, *not* about hyperactivity. For the best information on the substantive issues, refer to Collins, 1981; and Whalen and Denker, 1980.)

> H-1: Hyperactivity manifests itself in noise above the average level in a classroom; in excess small and large motor movements; in an excessive number of seat-leavings; in scores over 30 on the Connors Questionnaire.
>
> H-2: Since hyperactivity is a product of social learning, its severity will vary, depending on the social context. For example, it is more likely to manifest itself in structured situations (e.g., school, church, scouts) than unstructured situations.
>
> H-3: Hyperactivity will be reduced with the instigation of proper behavioral controls, reinforcement schedules, psychotherapy, and the like.
>
> H-4: Hyperactivity will show low heritability coefficients (it is not passed genetically from parents to children).
>
> H-5: Hyperactivity is unrelated to intelligence and to psychopathological symptoms such as depression and anxiety.

Each hypothesis is testable. As empirical trials are made, the construct becomes better understood and the links between constructs and indicators are forged more strongly. At the same time the network is elaborated by introducing hypotheses, such as the following, that contradict the theory.

> H-6: Since hyperactivity is a physiological condition, one would expect to find discontinuities at developmental transition points (e.g., puberty).
>
> H-7: Hyperactivity can be controlled by psychoactive stimulants.

The empirical part of construct validation consists of step-by-step testing of all these hypotheses as well as more detailed deductions from the nomological network, which itself evolves as a result of these trials. In testing Hypothesis 6, for example, the researcher might compare hyperactive individuals before and after puberty to see if indicators of excess movement and decibel level decrease. In testing Hypothesis 5, the researcher could measure intelligence in hyperactive children and control groups and expect no differences between the groups, or could correlate intelligence and teacher ratings of hyperactivity on the Connors Scale. If reliable differences in intelligence were found to exist between hyperactives and normals, and if the study were correctly done, then we would have to modify our theoretical hypotheses accordingly. If ratings on the Connors Scale did not correlate positively with decibel level (as Hypothesis 1 leads us to expect), then we would have to question the construct validity of one or both of these two indicators.

Correspondence between the two indicators would contribute a small piece to the puzzle of the meaning of the construct and these indicators. If, over many small studies, *all* the proposed indicators fail to confirm each other, we might begin to doubt our understanding of the construct itself. Hyperactivity might not exist as a physiological or psychological entity at all (see Schrag and Divoky, 1975, who called hyperactivity "a myth"), or we may have radically misunderstood what it is that some people mean by the term.

Consider some hypothetical data that might emerge from validation work on hyperactivity. Table 4–1 illustrates data supporting Hypothesis

TABLE 4–1   **Hypothetical Data Supporting the Deduction that Hyperactivity is Unrelated to Anxiety as Measured by Galvanic Skin Response (GSR): 110 Children Classified by Connors Score and Level of GSR**

ANXIETY

	HIGH GSR	LOW GSR
HIGH CONNORS SCORE	+ + + + + + + + + + 10	+ + + + + + + + + + + + 12
LOW CONNORS SCORE	+ + + + + + + + + + + + + + + + + + + + + + + + + + + + + + + + + + + + + + + + 40	+ + + + + + + + + + + + + + + + + + + + + + + + + + + + + + + + + + + + + + + + + + + + + + + + 48

5. Each "plus sign" represents an individual. The table shows no pattern of relationship between hyperactivity as measured by the Connors Scale and anxiety. Table 4–2 illustrates data that cast doubt on two selected indicators of hyperactivity. Children with high Connors Scale ratings are neither more nor less likely to emit excess noise than are children with low Connors ratings. Remember that these data are *hypothetical*, not real.

More about techniques of validation will be presented in a subsequent section. It will suffice to mention here that the process of construct validation never ends. By conducting these studies, however, we simultaneously learn about the meaning of the construct and about the indicators chosen to measure it.

Quantification

Conceptualization consists of delineating the meaning of the construct and selecting indicators or some observable manifestations of the construct. Quantification is specification of procedures, or **measurement operations**, by which the indicator can be observed, counted, or measured. The end result of these measurement operations is a numerical score or classification for each individual studied.

Consider the example of intelligence as a dependent variable in a study whose hypothesis is "Verbal stimulation of infants increases their subsequent intelligence." Intelligence is a construct, an abstract idea about a property of individuals. It cannot be observed directly. Based on a long history of conceptualization, indicators for intelligence have been developed and tested. One indicator is vocabulary knowledge, which can be

TABLE 4–2 Hypothetical Data Illustrating the Absence of Relationship between Two Proposed Indicators of Hyperactivity: 108 Children Classified by Connors Score and Noise Level

	HIGH NOISE	LOW NOISE
HIGH CONNORS SCORE	+ + + + + + + + + + + + + + + 15	+ + + + + + + + + + + + + 13
LOW CONNORS SCORE	+ + + + + + + + + + + + + + + + + + + + + + + + + + + + + + + + + 33	+ + + + + + + + + + + + + + + + + + + + + + + + + + + 27

measured directly. However, the procedures for measuring vocabulary knowledge have to be defined specifically. We would be remiss if we assessed vocabulary knowledge in one person at the age of 5 years and another person at the age of 2, or if we administered a paper-and-pencil test to one person and an oral test to another, or if the hardest word for one subject was *cat* but for another, it was *catty*. The resulting scores would result in unreliable and invalid assessments of the vocabulary knowledge of the subjects (whether or not vocabulary knowledge is, in fact, a good indicator for intelligence). Here is an example of a measurement operation or procedure for the indicator *vocabulary knowledge*:

> (1) the assessment is conducted by a certified school psychologist who is uninformed about the hypothesis of the study; (2) the assessment takes place in a quiet room with no distractions and no one else present; (3) the word list is from the revised form of the Wechsler Intelligence Scale for Children; (4) the test administrator reads the instructions as written; (5) the administrator reads each word, beginning from the first, reminds the subject to tell what it means, provides no prompts, records the response verbatim; (6) the administrator waits 60 seconds after which the next word is read; (7) the administrator discontinues the word list after four consecutive errors or refusals; (8) responses are judged right or wrong by comparing them to the scoring criteria in the test manual; (9) the score of the subject is the number of words answered correctly.

As you can tell from this example, measurement procedures or operations must be detailed and specific. They must also be standardized for all subjects, and they must be public. A good rule of thumb for measurement operations is that they be detailed enough that two different researchers could follow the specifications and arrive at nearly the same score. We will speak of this as *replication* and as *reliability* of measurement. Some measurement operations are tests plus the instructions on how to administer and score them. "Measurement operations" are broader than "tests"; the former include such methods as observation schedules, interview protocols, and the like.

Methods of measurement   Indicators and their attendant procedures of measurement may be categorized according to the type of **measurement method** used. There are six such categories (after Fiske, 1971):

1. **Self-report** by the subject. The individual responds to various stimuli such as adjectives, statements, rating scales, and questionnaire items that require the subject to report on the status of his or her own characteristics.

2. **Report by another** individual. The characteristics of the subject are described by another person, who responds to questions, rating scales, adjectives, and the like. The other person may be a family member, friend, coworker, or boss. Or the other person may be a professional clinician or diagnostician, such as the subject's psychotherapist or case worker who interprets the subject's responses to a clinical interview.

3. **Behavioral observation** of the subject. A trained observer records the quality, frequency, or intensity of the subject's behavior according to specified dimensions. The observation can occur in contrived or natural situations. For example, the empathic behaviors of a social worker may be rated in the context of a role-playing exercise set up by the researcher. Or the same behaviors can be observed through a two-way mirror in a clinical interview between the social worker and client.

4. **Psychophysiological measurement**. For some constructs that have physiological correlates, such as anxiety, direct measurement of the physiological states is possible. Such measures include galvanic skin responses, pulse rate, and the like.

5. **Tests of ability**. Standardized tasks are presented to subjects, who must perform as well as they can. Responses are either correct or incorrect, and an overall summated score (e.g., the number of items correct) is an indicator of some underlying construct related to ability, intelligence, perceptual acuity, or cognitive control.

6. **Indirect measurement**, also referred to as unobtrusive or nonreactive measurement (Webb, Campbell, Schwartz, Secrest, and Grove, 1981). Indirect measurement consists of analysis of archives, records, and documents for evidence that demonstrates the presence or absence or the degree of the indicator. The key idea is that the subjects do not know they are being "measured." A person who is aware could alter or distort the score he or she receives. If a teacher knows she is being observed for frequency of negative reinforcements, she can change those behaviors during the observation period, and the score assigned would not represent her true status on the construct. A patient in an experiment to decrease alcoholic symptoms by a milieu therapy program may fake a self-report of her symptoms. But examination of hospital or insurance records will reveal whether or not she was in fact able to maintain control over symptoms. Similarly, indirect measurement is used for indicators such as extent of vandalism of school buildings when the construct is community support for schools.

The choice of measurement method is an important one. Table 4−3 has within it the construct of test anxiety (Chambers, Hopkins, and Hopkins, 1972) and how it could be assessed using the six methods of measurement. This table shows what some of the implications for the researcher might be. If pulse rate was chosen to indicate test anxiety, might the scores reflect general health as well as anxiety? Would the subject be truthful in responding to items of the Taylor Manifest Anxiety Scale? Would the roommate have access to the subject's private thoughts and feelings? These issues are considered later in this chapter.

Being detailed, public, and specific about measurement operations helps researchers assign reliable numbers to individuals. Not only should the numbers be reliable, but they should reflect meaningfully on the "amount" of the characteristic being measured. In other words, we would like the individual in the sample with the "most" self-esteem to have the highest numerical score on the measure of self-esteem. This is what is meant by validity of measurement. Both reliability and validity are enhanced by the researcher's measurement operations.

TABLE 4–3 Indicators of the Construct of Test Anxiety Classified by "Methods of Measurement"

METHOD	EXAMPLES OF INDICATORS
1. Self-report	1a. Subject responds to 30 items on a scale of "very true of me" to "not at all true of me" (e.g., "On the night before an exam I have trouble sleeping"). b. Subject completes the Taylor Manifest Anxiety Scale one hour before taking an exam. c. Subject responds to 10 items (e.g., "Rate the degree of your anxiety about taking a pop quiz") on a scale from "Very High" to "Very Low."
2. Report by other	2a. Subject's roommate responds to items in 1a on a scale of "very true of roommate" to "not at all true of roommate." b. Expert clinician administers Thematic Appercep-tion Test to subject and scores the protocol for "instances of anxiety."
3. Observation of behavior	3a. Observer is located in classroom where subject is taking exam, recording frequency of the subject's limb movements (noncontrived). b. In a laboratory simulation of test-anxiety-provoking situation, an observer counts frequency of eye movements by the subject (contrived).
4. Psychophysiological measurement	4a. Pulse rate b. Galvanic skin response
5. Test of ability	5a. Score on the final exam of a course. b. Score on digit span test
6. Indirect measurement	6a. Incidence of requests for help from the University Mental Health Clinic evidenced in clinic records during exam week b. Increase in filled ash trays in classroom buildings during exam week.

Measurement scales   The **scale of measurement** is sometimes referred to as the assignment of numbers to individuals according to rules. There are good rules and bad rules. A bad rule for assigning self-esteem scores to individuals would be by flipping a coin. For each person, the researcher flips a coin. If it comes up heads, that person is given a self-esteem score of one. If it comes up tails, that person is assigned a self-esteem score of two. Obviously the resulting set of scores would have nothing to do with the construct of self-esteem. Contrast the coin-flip rule with the rule that assigns scores based on the number of items agreed to by the individual. If the items adequately cover the construct, the researcher has a better set of data because the rule specified that individuals with high self-esteem (the construct) were assigned the highest scores.

Good measurement rules allow us to capitalize on some meaningful properties of the number system. For example, the most elementary rule of a measurement operation is to divide the subjects into two (or more) exclusive categories that represent distinctions with respect to the indicator. Suppose that the construct is political affiliation. At the most fundamental level, we would want to recognize that in the U.S. at least two qualitatively distinct categories of political affiliation exist: Republicans and Democrats. We would also want rules that would permit a sorting of most persons into one of these two categories. By so doing, a *classification* of the persons is made. This classification is similar to that property of the number system that specifies that 1 is not 2.

Once all persons are sorted into the two categories, we could arbitrarily attach a number to each category, that is, assign all Democrats the number 1 and all Republicans the number 2. The numbers do not mean that Republicans are twice as good as Democrats or even that Republicans are "more" or "less" or "better" or "worse"—only that the two groups are different. The numbers are like names and serve only to distinguish the two groups from one another. This kind of measurement rule is called **nominal** or **categorical measurement** and the numerical scale it yields is called categorical or nominal data.

Other examples of nominal variables are gender (all subjects can be exclusively and exhaustively divided into groups of males and females), ethnicity, high school graduation status (yes or no), state of birth (note that there would be 50 categories for persons born in the U.S.), and marital status. About the most a researcher can do with categorical data is to tote the frequencies and percentages of individuals in the categories.

The next "level of measurement" is called *ordinal measurement*. This rule makes it possible to rank the individuals in the sample according to the degree to which they exhibit the indicator. Suppose we wish to measure the altruism of members of a sample of four men. We know that George is stingy, selfish, and not at all altruistic. Mike is mildly and sporadically altruistic, but more altruistic than George. Bill is more altruistic than either Mike or George, but is a piker compared to Andrew who does volunteer work 30 hours a week and donates half his salary to charity. We assign altruism scores to the foursome as follows: Andrew = 4; Bill = 3; Mike = 2; George = 1. In other words, the measurement procedure produces numerical scores along an **ordinal scale**. An ordinal scale offers some way to describe the quantitative differences among persons with respect to the indicator. Statistics can be applied to these data to obtain some idea about typical scores and about differences among individuals. Still, some information is lost with ordinal measurement. For example, the difference between the altruism of George and Mike may be very different from the difference between the altruism of Andrew and Bill. In addition, one could not say that Andrew was twice as altruistic as Mike even though 4 is twice 2. It is easy to be fooled because we know of the property of the number system that specifies that $4 - 3 = 2 - 1$. This property does not apply to ordinal measures. For ordinal measures the relevant property of the number system is that $4 > 3 > 2 > 1$. In this hypothetical example, the altruism of Andrew is greater than the altruism of Bill, and so on.

Most measurement procedures in the social sciences produce ordinal data. The object is to assign a number that represents where an individual falls along a continuum. For example, the California Preschool Social Competency Scale consists of 30 questions answered by a teacher who is familiar with the child being tested (an example of "Report by Other," in Table 4–3). One of the items is "He does not share equipment or toys." Each item has four possible answers that vary on a continuum from "very much like the child" to "not at all like the child." For the scale as a whole (the values of the individual items are summed) the range of possible scores is from 30 to 120. The overall score gives one an idea of how that person ranks in a hypothetical population of similar children. Anyone scoring 120 would be thought of as having the "most" social competence.

Derived scores are other examples of ordinal measurement. The form of the Scholastic Aptitude Test (SAT) is one kind of derived score wherein the answers to test questions are treated statistically so as to yield derived scores that range from 200 to 800 with an average of 500. The Graduate Record Examination (GRE) follows the same form. Thus, a person with a GRE score of 550 knows two things: first, that he or she possesses more of whatever construct the GRE measures than a person who scored 450; and second, the score of 550 is higher than the scores of more than half the test takers.

Grade-equivalent scores are one product of standardized tests of school achievement. An individual's performance is compared to that of a large standardization sample. The form, or metric, of the derived scores corresponds to the number of years and months of schooling achieved by the typical (median) pupil in the standardization sample. A grade equivalent score of 5.7, for example, indicates that the pupil has evidenced knowledge and skills on the test at the level of a typical child who has completed five years and seven months of school. Not only does this derived score indicate relative rank of achievement, but also can be compared to the student's actual grade placement. If a child had actually had only three years and three months of school and had a grade equivalent score of 5.9, one would be justified in saying that child was substantially outperforming other children of the same age.

Percentile ranks are also ordinal data. Raw scores on a test or other indicator are arranged in order of magnitude. The percentage of the sample that falls below any ranked score is calculated. Thus, in a 10-kilometer road race, the finishing times for all contestants are ranked. Percentiles are calculated so that an individual contestant can learn that her race time was better than 80 percent of all contestants. Position in high school graduating class is also calculated in percentiles.

Interval measurement is more highly refined than ordinal measurement. Not only do the numbers correspond to a continuum with higher numbers reflecting "more" of an indicator than lower numbers, but the distance between numbers has meaning. Numbers are assigned to individuals so that the difference in "amount" of the indicator possessed by two persons is the same as the difference between the numbers themselves. A person with a score of 5 and a person with an **interval scale** score of 10 are as different from each other in the "amount" of the indicator they possess as two persons with scores of 10 and 15.

There are few interval scales in social science. Some possibilities include the year A.D. and the time difference between any pair of swimmers in a race. The best example of an interval scale is in physical science. The difference between 50 and 60 degrees on the Celsius scale is the same difference as that between 60 degrees and 70 degrees. The zero point on the Celsius scale is arbitrary and does not have the meaning of "no heat." Nor is it safe to say that 100 degrees is twice as hot as 50 degrees.

Many instances of measurement in education and the social sciences use tests, questionnaires, or inventories composed of many distinct items. Scores are assigned by counting the number of math questions answered or the number of times a favorable attitude toward free enterprise was expressed. Researchers often wonder whether measurement of this type results in an ordinal or an interval scale. Suppose 100 words are drawn purposefully from a variety of intermediate-grade readers, and each word is used as the basis of an item in which it appears correctly spelled and misspelled in two ways. Students taking the spelling test must select the correct spelling; their score is the number of correct spellings picked out of 100. Will these measures of spelling performance have interval-scale or just ordinal-scale properties?

Measurement of this type clearly does not result in interval scales; this can be seen by recognizing the absence of a repeatable unit of measurement in the process (i.e., the lack of a second, meter, gram, calorie, and the like for a construct as complex as spelling achievement). Hence, one would certainly not maintain that Barb (score = 90) and Mitch (score = 80) differ in spelling performance exactly as much as Pete (score = 15) and Paul (score = 5). Ten words like "insincere" and "discernible" might represent the difference between Barb and Mitch, whereas Pete and Paul might be distinguishable by their relative success on "could," "rode," "eat," and the like. So one is confident that the very frequently used measures of this type do not produce interval scales. Must the scale be ordinal then? If it is, consider the consequences. If only Barb, Mitch, Pete, and Paul were given the spelling test, then their ranks would be 1, 2, 3, and 4. If the information in the numbers 90, 80, 15, and 5 is no greater than what ordinal measurement could produce, then the two sets of measurements below contain equal amounts of information.

STUDENT	SPELLING TEST SCORE	RANK
Barb	90	1
Mitch	80	2
Pete	15	3
Paul	5	4

But this reduction of the scores to ranks is too radical. No one really believes that Mitch, who is a little unsure of "-ible" versus "-able" as a suffix, and Pete, who forgets whether a synonym for a street is "rode" or "road," are really as close together as the ranks 2 and 3 seem to indicate.

Measurement of this general type is not so weak as implied by "ordinal" nor is it as exact as implied by "interval." Researchers have sometimes spoken of such measurement (i.e., via counting items on tests and inventories) as **quasi-interval measurement**, meaning that it is not strictly interval-level measurement, but that to treat it as ordinal (by ignoring the sizes of the gaps between scores) is claiming less for it than it deserves. Having once called such measurement quasi-interval, there is a tendency to treat it as though it is fully interval-scale measurement. The safest course seems to be to twist one's mind slightly and treat the measurement as more like interval in some instances and more like ordinal in others and to note for future reference that this point is just one of many on which the logic of methodology imperfectly reconstructs the complexity of real life (Kaplan, 1964).

Intelligence test scores form quasi-interval scales. Scores obtained from tests such as the Wechsler Adult Intelligence Scale or the Stanford-Binet, over tens of thousands of cases, seem to have more meaning than simple ranks. However, many professionals make the mistake of assuming that a person with an IQ of 120 is 20 percent smarter than a person with an IQ of 100 (a statement that would only be possible if somehow intelligence could be measured with a ratio scale).

The most refined measurement is called **ratio measurement**. Numbers are assigned to individuals in such a way that individuals are categorically distinct, are ordered according to the "amount" of the indicator they possess, and differ from each other on equal intervals; *in addition*, a zero score means absence of the indicator. Distance, time, and weight are examples of ratio scales as are, more specifically, age, the number of years a person has been employed, the number of minutes spent in completing a task, and the proximity (in meters) between the snake and the snake phobic (used as a measure of snake phobia).

Scales of measurement, methods of measurement, and the principles of conceptualization and quantification have been presented in this chapter as a foundation for material in Chapter 5. There you will encounter the means for examining and judging the measurement procedures used by researchers and evaluators in their studies.

SUGGESTED READINGS

BLALOCK, JR., H.M. *Conceptualization and measurement in the social sciences.* Beverly Hills, Calif.: SAGE, 1982.

CRONBACH, L.J. *Essentials of psychological testing (3rd ed.).* New York: Harper & Row, 1970.

CRONBACH, L.J., GLESER, G.C., NANDA, H., and RAJARATNAM, N. *The dependability of behavioral measurements: Theory of generalizability for scales and profiles.* New York: John Wiley, 1972.

FISKE, D.W. *Measuring the concepts of personality.* Chicago: Aldine, 1971.

HOPKINS, K.D., and STANLEY, J.C. *Educational and psychological measurement and evaluation* (6th ed.). Englewood Cliffs, N.J.: Prentice-Hall, 1981.

LINN, R.L. (Ed.). *Educational measurement* (3rd ed.). Washington, D.C.: American Council on Education and Macmillan, 1986.

LORD, F.M. and NOVICK, M.R. *Statistical theories of mental test scores.* Reading, Mass.: Addison-Wesley, 1968.

THORNDIKE, R.L., and HAGEN, E.P. *Measurement and evaluation in psychology and education* (4th ed.). New York: John Wiley, 1977.

WEBB, E.J., CAMPBELL, D.T., SCHWARTZ, R.D., SECREST, L., and GROVE, J. *Nonreactive measures in the social sciences.* Boston: Houghton Mifflin, 1981.

TERMS INTRODUCED IN THIS CHAPTER

measurement
conceptualization
quantification
indicator
construct validation literature
nomological network
measurement operations
measurement methods
self-report
report by other
behavioral observation

psychophysiological measure
tests of ability
indirect measurement
scale of measurement
categorical measurement
nominal scale
ordinal scale
derived score
quasi-interval measurement
ratio measurement

QUESTIONS AND ACTIVITIES FOR FURTHER STUDY

1. What are the four separate purposes of measurement? State the rationale for distinguishing tests according to their purpose.

2. State the reasons a construct cannot be observed directly in empirical research.

3. State the activities you would engage in if you were to conceptualize the construct of altruism. Identify three alternative indicators you might use. Suggest some ways in which each indicator would be imperfect.

4. Select one indicator for altruism and show how you would go about the process of quantification. How would you be able to assign to persons meaningful and consistent numbers that would reflect "how much" altruism they have?

5. Take one construct from the following list: sexism, locus of control, autonomy, dyslexia, social maturity, school readiness, criminality, depression, speech dysfunction, curriculum structure, open education, language dominance (English or Spanish).

    a. State some specific ways you would engage in conceptualization and add to the construct validation of this construct.

    b. Select several indicators of this construct, trying to cover as many methods of measurement as possible. Classify each indicator by its method of measurement.

    c. Suggest some ways each indicator might provide an imperfect picture of the construct as you have defined it.

6. Classify each item of the following list by the method of measurement it represents.

    a. Ratings on a five-point scale by trained judges of the degree of pupil-centeredness expressed by teachers.

    b. Counts of the number of sentences beginning with "You" stated by husband and wife during marital therapy (the construct is "blame").

    c. Test of recognition of missing body parts on a series of cards displayed by an examiner to a small child (the construct is cognitive-social maturity).

    d. Reported number of delinquent acts admitted to by the subject during a structured interview.

    e. Ratings of a subject's religiosity given by the subject's spouse.

    f. Sweat print of the subject taken prior to his making a speech (the construct is speech anxiety).

    g. Scores on a subject's level of pathology taken during a Rorschach inkblot test administered by a licensed clinical psychologist.

    h. Score on the Wide Range Achievement Test (see Table 5–6).

    i. Speed of finding a "target digit" in a string of random digits, under conditions of induced stress (the construct is performance anxiety).

    j. Subject's responses to a series of items such as, "I believe I can accomplish every task that comes my way" (the construct is self-confidence).

7. Classify each of the following according to the level of measurement it most likely represents.

    a. Scholastic Aptitude Test scores
    b. Eye color
    c. Salary
    d. High school rank
    e. Counselor's ratings of pupil's level of vocational interest
    f. Social class
    g. Birth order
    h. Class size
    i. Number of birth defects per 100,000 live births
    j. School readiness expressed in age-equivalent scores
    k. IQ

5

CHARACTERISTICS OF MEASUREMENT PROCEDURES IN RESEARCH AND EVALUATION

In the previous chapter, we saw how abstract constructs are translated into concrete measurement procedures and how numbers can be assigned to individuals. In this chapter we will examine the characteristics of measurement procedures and see how these characteristics can affect the quality of the research and evaluation studies in which they are used.

RELIABILITY

If an ordinary person were asked the meaning of the word *reliability*, he might answer "Coming to work on time every morning—being dependable." This common-sense meaning of the term is not far from the technical meaning of **reliability** in measurement. Think of the time a worker arrives at the workplace as an indicator of dependability. If someone kept track of the time Worker A punched in every day for a week, the data might look like this:

ARRIVAL TIMES OF WORKER A

Monday	7:59
Tuesday	8:00
Wednesday	8:00
Thursday	8:01
Friday	7:58

Think of these five arrival times as five numerical scores representing Worker A's dependability—her arrival time generally. The arrival times differ from each other—she did not come at exactly the same time each day. But they differ from each other by only a small amount, so we are willing to say that Worker A is reliable and dependable.

The reliability of a measurement procedure is analogous. The degree to which the procedure yields about the same numerical score each time and in each way we measure an individual with it is its reliability. The more consistent, dependable, precise, and stable the numerical scores are, based on several readings of a particular individual, the greater is the reliability of the measurement procedure. On the other hand, when a measurement procedure is repeatedly applied to the same individual, and the scores are widely discrepant from each other (so much so that individuals' rankings vary considerably), we can say that the procedure is unreliable, unpredictable, inconsistent, or unstable.

To understand reliability of measurement procedures, it is important to think of the discrepancy among repeated readings or testings as **errors**. If all readings or estimates or test administrations yielded the same numerical score for an individual, the measurement procedure would be perfectly reliable and error-free. The more variability among the scores, the greater is the amount of error, and correspondingly, the lower the reliability.

In any measurement procedure, one expects some error, something less than perfect reliability. Consider as an example a researcher studying the effect of cross-age tutoring on math achievement. To assess the reliability of the measurement procedure (that is, the administration of a standardized achievement test), the researcher selects a pilot sample of students like those in his experiment. He administers the math achievement test to his pilot sample on Monday and the same test to the same pupils again on Friday. Thus he has two math scores for each pilot subject (two readings or estimates of how much math each one knows). The data from these two administrations are in Table 5–1. The data are hypothetical and somewhat unrealistic because they assume no "practice effect" (i.e., on a second administration, subjects benefit from having taken the test before; see Chapter 6) and they assume that the pilot subjects had learned no math (i.e., their true level of math achievement had not changed) between Monday and Friday.

Notice in Table 5–1 that the pairs of scores are numerically close to each other, yet certainly not the same. Looking at the differences between the pairs of scores for the individuals, one can see that Pupil A's Friday score was slightly higher than her Monday score, Pupil B's score was quite a bit higher, and so on. Let us speculate about what might have happened. Pupil A was tired on Monday, owing to an active weekend, but was more herself on Friday. Pupil B hit a triple biorhythmic high on Friday. Pupil

TABLE 5–1   Test and Retest Data on Math Achievement

PUPIL	MONDAY SCORE	FRIDAY SCORE
A	5	6
B	7	9
C	8	6
D	8	7
E	4	5
F	7	7
G	7	5
H	9	9
I	10	12
J	10	6

C lost motivation by Friday, was bored by the test, and simply went through the motions. Pupil G had had a fight with his mother on Friday morning. Pupil I profited from the fact that an item on the Friday test was on a topic that she had discussed over the dinner table Thursday night. Pupil J's answer sheet revealed that he had marked the correct answers in the wrong column about half-way through the test; thus his Friday score was much lower than his Monday score, even though his "true" knowledge of math had not changed. For the most part, high scores on one administration are associated with high scores on the other. Low scores on the Friday test go along with low scores on the Monday test. By calculating a correlation coefficient between the two sets of scores, the researcher can assess the reliability of the measurement procedure. Knowledge of how high the reliability is will be used in thinking about the findings of the study.

This example demonstrates several kinds, or *sources*, of error that can creep into a measurement procedure and reduce its reliability. In general, four *sources of error* can decrease the reliability of the measurement procedure.

Sources of Error

Error due to nonstandardized test administration or scoring   Suppose that the measurement procedure consists of administering an intelligence test with a time limit. For some reason, the psychologist administering the test allows one student an extra 10 minutes beyond the time limit specified in the test manual. Another child, whose "true" intelligence is the same as that of the first, gets only the officially allowed time. This nonstandard measurement procedure would result in error variation between the children. One would get a higher score than the other, even though they did not differ in intelligence.

Likewise, when a subject is motivated to work uncharacteristically hard, just because the psychologist is charming and encouraging, error is introduced. If a different psychologist with a dull personality followed the same procedures without giving special encouragement, the intelligence score for that particular subject would not equal the first one. Tests given in less than ideal circumstances also contribute to unreliability. For example, giving the test in the school custodian's closet or in the hallway with other children passing by probably violates standard conditions for administering tests.

Any time that the test stimulus given to the subjects departs from standardization guidelines, or that the subjects for some reason do not understand the directions or the task they are asked to do, error is introduced and reliability suffers. Error can also be introduced in subjective, nonstandardized scoring of tests. Clerks can make mistakes in transfering test results onto computer cards, keypunchers misread and mispunch, readers of essay tests become tired and waver in their judgments and standards about what constitutes a quality essay, and the like. All of these circumstances lower reliability.

Observer error   When measurement procedures call for another person to observe or rate a subject's characteristics, there is always a danger that the observer may be counting, rating, or otherwise quantifying the indicator based on personal judgments that are not common to other observers. If this happens, the numbers assigned to the subjects are idiosyncratic to that particular observer. A second observer might have assigned a different number to that subject. This can happen if the two observers have vague or contradictory implicit definitions of the construct being measured. Disagreements or discrepancies between observers' ratings may also be due to differences in their abilities to perceive, remember, and maintain concentration, or to differences in their motivation. Some observers are more lenient and some more stringent in their ratings. The numerical difference between the ratings given to a subject by two or more observers is an estimate of the unreliability of the measurement procedure.

As an example of observer error, consider the assessment of the construct of hostility among patients in a psychiatric care program. The construct of hostility is operationalized for a research project as the frequency of physical assaults among patients, as recorded by the psychiatric technician during the afternoon recreation hour. The technician is given specific instructions about what behavior constitutes physical assault, how to quantify the data, and so on. In spite of these specifications, however, he counts one instance of severe verbal abuse, counts one physical assault against himself, is looking the other direction when one patient kicks another, and is too tired and bored by the end of the recreation hour to count a clear instance of assault that occurs at the far end of the grounds. The problem of inconsistency is obvious here; the observer has deviated from the prescribed operational definitions, has reinterpreted the indicator to suit his own implicit definition, and has failed to observe and record some instances of the behavior. Another observer might have made mistakes of other kinds, and the differences between the ratings of the two observers constitute error.

Temporary characteristics of the subjects   On the day that the measurement procedure takes place, an individual subject may be feeling atypically depressed or elated, well or ill, calm or anxious, fatigued or fresh. These temporary swings in emotional or physical states will affect performance on a test or other measurement procedure. On another day, that same subject's performance would be different, and the difference between scores or ratings assigned on the two days is a source of error and instability, provided that the "true" amount of the indicator possessed by individuals had not changed in the meantime. The math achievement testing described above and illustrated in Table 5–1 provides examples of this source of error.

Idiosyncracies of items and measurement components   Most measurement procedures are made up of component parts like items on a test or questions in a questionnaire. Each component or item can be thought of as a separate subindicator for the construct. Ideally, the researchers want a subject's responses to these subindicators to yield equivalent or consistent values. That is, they want each of these subindicators to be measuring the same thing. Measurement experts think of each item on a test as a sample from a hypothetical population ("universe") of similar items measuring the same construct. If this is the case, a subject's score would not depend on the particular items that happened to be chosen for that test but would be numerically close to his or her score on any other set of items from that same population. When the individual items are tapping different things — when they are acting in an idiosyncratic or inconsistent fashion — then the reliability suffers.

Take as an example the knowledge of general information as an indicator of intelligence. The specific questions in the test protocol of a test like the Wechsler scale are not so important in and of themselves. (A person with very little intelligence could memorize the correct answers by rote, and then the general information score would have little to do with the construct of intelligence as most people think of it.) Instead, these questions are merely proxies or exemplars of other bits of general information of similar conceptual difficulty and relative familiarity. It is the ability to answer questions *such as these* that serves as an indicator of intelligence. Occasionally, there is a fortuitous match between a specific question included as a test item and the background, recreational reading, or specialized vocational knowledge of a person taking the test. For example, the following question is typical of some items on the general information subtest of adult intelligence tests: "What is the central theme of the Book of Exodus?" The subject who happened to be the son of a minister might achieve a score on that item that would overestimate his "true" grasp of general information (hence his intelligence). This overestimation would not show up if he were given a different list of questions that did not include questions about the Bible. The difference between the scores on the two lists is a source of error and unreliability known as **nonequivalence.**

It is important at this point to relate these sources of error to the specific purpose of measurement considered by this text—research and evaluation. In research, particularly, one is interested in producing replicable, generalizable knowledge. In other words, when researchers produce a set of scores on their subjects and use these scores to test hypotheses and reach conclusions, they do not want these conclusions limited by idiosyncracies of observers and items, the temporary mood states that their subjects experienced on the day of the posttest, sloppy test administration, and the like. Unreliable measurement procedures lead to conclusions that will not replicate and are not generalizable. It is also true that the less reliable the measurement procedure, the harder it is to demonstrate the statistical significance of the results, for example, the difference in means of experimental and control groups or the correlation between two variables. Thus, it is critical that researchers and evaluators account for *each* source of error.

Techniques For Estimating Reliability

Retesting Repeating the measurement procedure on the same set of subjects is one way of estimating reliability. The source of error assessed here is that of fluctuating, temporary characteristics of the subjects. **Test-retest reliability** is the name given to this technique. It involves computing the correlation between the two sets of scores generated by repeated application of the measurement procedure to the same subjects under nearly identical conditions. Reliability coefficients range from $r = 0.00$ (indicating that all the variance in the measurement procedure is due to error) to $r = 1.00$ (indicating perfect reliability). The higher the correlation coefficient, the greater the reliability and the lower the amount of error that can be attributed to the temporary characteristics of the subjects.

Internal consistency When a test is administered, we would like to think that each item in a test is measuring the same property or quality. We would like to be able to say that our assessment of a construct is not limited by the particular items chosen to measure it, but is generalizable across a population of such items. We do not want the quantification of the indicator to be influenced by idiosyncracies of the items chosen. A set of procedures is available for determining whether all the items in a test are measuring the same thing (or conversely whether certain items are performing in ways unique from the rest of the items). These procedures are estimates of the **internal consistency** of a test. One such procedure assesses the **split-half reliability,** wherein the researcher divides the items in the test into two parts (such as the odd-numbered items and the even-numbered items), scores the two parts separately, calculates the coefficient of correlation between the two parts, and performs a statistical adjustment known as the Spearman-Brown correction formula. The result informs us of whether two sets of items are measuring the same thing. More elaborate procedures for estimating internal consistency are the *alpha coefficient* and the Kuder-Richardson Formulas (Cronbach, 1970, pp. 159–161), which report a reliability based on the average correlation of all pairs of items on the test.

The same principle of internal consistency holds true for measurement procedures other than tests. For example, the construct of speech anxiety can be operationalized as the score on the rating scale made up of 10 component parts. One component calls for the observer to record the frequency of the utterance of "uh" in a five-minute extemporaneous speech given by an anxious college student. A second component calls for the same observer to rate the degree of eye contact between the student and the audience. A third component is a rating (from inaudible to clearly audible) of the speaker's voice, and so on. The overall score achieved by the subject is a composite of the 10 components, each of which is purported to measure the same construct of speech anxiety. Estimates of the internal consistency of these components can be made by applying any of the aforementioned techniques.

Alternate forms   Another way of addressing the source of error attendant on the selection of a particular set of items or measurement components is to build parallel tests or test forms and administer them to the same sample of subjects. This provides a measure of **alternate forms reliability**. The correlation coefficient between the two sets of scores is a measure of item equivalence or, conversely, idiosyncracies. High values of the correlation indicate that the scores on individuals can be generalized beyond the particular items on that test to a population of similar items. Low correlations demonstrate how much an individual's scores are influenced by an idiosyncratic item or two on one or the other of the test forms.

Interjudge agreement   For those methods of measurement that require ratings, behavioral observations, or judgments of one individual by another, there are techniques for estimating the error associated with the observer. The procedure requires the same individual or event to be observed or rated by two or more judges. The ratings given by the judges are then correlated or the percentage of agreement calculated to provide a measure of **interjudge reliability**. The resultant statistics reflect the ability to generalize across potential judges or observers. A high value of the statistic indicates that the quantities assigned to the individuals are not limited by the personality and abilities of one judge.

Standardization of procedures   When the procedures for measuring indicators are not objective, public, and standardized, measurement error is likely. Although there is no one technique or statistical procedure for assessing this source of error, it can be judged. The reader of a study should look for evidence that the researcher did the following:

1. Conducted pilot tests to make sure that potential subjects could understand and make the desired responses to the measurement stimulus and test instructions

2. Controlled the environment in which the measurement took place (making sure that there were no distractions and the like)

3. Trained the observers, and if possible, kept them uninformed about the purposes and hypotheses of the study (i.e., "blinded" them)

4. Provided standardized, written instructions and observed the measurement situation to see that the test administrators or experimenters followed them

5. Provided guidelines to test administrators about specific methods of motivating and ensuring the cooperation of test takers, about whether to respond to questions from test takers, and about whether to encourage guessing

6. Cross-checked procedures for scoring, keypunching data, and the like.

No one researcher will do all of these. Some may do none of them and still do an adequate job of measuring. We present them as an ideal that should, perhaps, be aimed at more often.

Judging Reliability in Extant Studies

When examining an existing research or evaluation study, the critical reader should list each source of possible measurement error and determine how the investigator controlled it. Most investigators, unfortunately, control only one source. Internal consistency reliability is most easily assessed. However, internal consistency reliabilities provide information on only one source of error and ignore sources of error from observers, temporary states of the subjects, and nonstandardized procedures. Consider the example, earlier in this section, on the measurement of speech anxiety. Estimating the internal consistency of the component scores was a desirable thing to do, but was insufficient to determine whether the one observer was rating in a general or peculiar way, or whether the subjects were particularly up or down on the day they were measured. One reliability technique is simply not enough to estimate all sources of error.

When examining the statistics of reliability, look for correlations of $r = 0.50$ or higher. For research purposes, moderate reliability is often sufficient. Low reliabilities indicate that there is more error variance than "true variance" (that is, the "true" differences among individuals in the sample with respect to the amount of the indicator they possess). However, you should be very cautious about relaxing the reliability criterion for tests used for purposes other than research and evaluation. When using tests to make decisions about individuals, such as deciding whether a child should be placed in special education, one usually has a right to expect that reliabilities be much higher, perhaps on the order of $r = 0.90$ (Nunnally, 1978). And yet no simple generalizations can be made about how much reliability is enough.

Several conditions affect the degree of reliability of a measurement procedure. The longer the test, the higher the reliability will be (other things being equal). The greater the variance in a sample, the higher the reliability will be. (Samples made up of individuals who are all alike in the amount of the indicator they possess produce underestimates of reliability.) Internal consistency reliabilities will generally be higher than other kinds. Reliabilities will be artificially low if the test or procedure does not have a high enough "ceiling" (maximum score) or a low enough "floor" (minimum score) to accommodate the true range of differences among the members of the sample.

VALIDITY

A measurement procedure can be highly reliable—that is, produce the same score for an individual on several occasions or by several observers—yet have no validity. **Validity** has to do with the *meaning* of the score assigned and the inference from that score on that indicator to the construct the researcher intended to measure. The means by which that meaning and the relationship between the indicator and the construct are established is a long and complex process of construct validation best described by Cronbach:

> Construct validity is established through a long-continued interplay between observation, reasoning, and imagination. First, perhaps, imagination suggests that construct A accounts for the test performance. The investigator reasons, "If that is so, then people with a high score should have characteristic X." An experiment is performed, and if this expectation is confirmed, the interpretation is supported. But as various deductions are tested, some of them prove to be inaccurate. The proposed interpretation must be altered either by invoking a different concept, by introducing an additional concept, or by altering the theory of the concept itself. The process of construct validation is the same as that by which scientific theories are developed. (1970, p. 142)

Evidence that links an indicator to a construct accumulates gradually and is never final. One can never say with resolve, "This test is valid." The validity of a measurement procedure always depends on the context and on the purpose for which it is used. Therefore, a test such as the Scholastic Aptitude Test, which has a great deal of evidence for its validity to predict success in college, may be invalid and useless as a criterion variable in an experiment whose hypothesis is that an open campus high school organization is superior to a traditional organization for enhancing scholastic achievement. Furthermore, a measure may be valid for some kinds of individuals but not for others. For example, an intelligence test may be an adequate predictor of intellectual achievements for white persons of average socioeconomic status but be a poor predictor for ethnic minorities from poor backgrounds. In other words, the interpretation of the meaning of an IQ test depends on a body of evidence that connects the indicator to the construct for persons of the type involved in the research or evaluation study.

When researchers or evaluators set out to gather data, they cannot merely assume that the indicators they choose and the measurement procedures they establish have meaning. These investigators must tap into the construct validation literature of the tests and procedures they choose, so that the reader can make some independent judgments about how the scores should be interpreted. If the investigators are developing their own procedures rather than selecting from those already available, they themselves must produce evidence that the scores have meaning.

Evidence about the validity of measures falls roughly into four categories, which are presented here in the form of four questions (after Fiske, 1971). It is important to remember that all these forms of validity are part of the overarching category of construct validity.

1. *Is there logical consistency between the content of the test items, observation schedule, rating scale, and so on and the definition of the construct?* Researchers attempting to support the interpretation of the measurement and its connection to the construct will seek professional judgment that there is a plausible connection between the surface features of the measure's content and the construct as theoretically defined in its nomological network. This is sometimes referred to as establishing **face validity**. For measures such as achievement tests, evaluators are concerned with **content validity**. In other words, an assessment is made of the overlap of the curriculum and objectives of the instructional program with the content of the test items and the level of their difficulty. This is done to make sure that the test data can be interpreted as the evaluator intends, namely, as a true indication that the instructional program has been effective. If the test content did not match the instructional program, the scores would underestimate the true achievements of the pupils. Content validity is also a concern in ob-

servation studies of typical behavior, such as the study of what kinds of interaction occur between social workers and clients in a welfare office. The researcher would want to confirm that the interactions observed on certain occasions and circumstances were representative of interactions in other circumstances, such as at different times of day, when covering different topics, interactions in the field as well as in the office, and so on.

2. *Has an empirical connection been established between the performance on the chosen indicator and some other indicator that purports to measure the same construct?* **Validity coefficients** are correlation coefficients summarizing the relationship between the test or indicator used and some other indicator. For example, a researcher may want to use the Jones Vocabulary Test (JVT) as an indicator for the construct of intelligence. In order to have some evidence for validity (and a basis for interpreting the meaning of the scores of the JVT), the researcher gives a sample of subjects both the JVT test and the Stanford-Binet Intelligence Test. The correlation between the two sets of scores is the validity coefficient for JVT; it is referred to as an assessment of the **concurrent validity** of the vocabulary test. Researchers frequently use factor analytic techniques to intercorrelate many indicators of the same construct simultaneously (see Chapter 9).

Although concurrent validity is a way of substituting one measure for another or piggybacking on the validity of a more established instrument, it should be clear that the validity of the older instrument must already have been established independently. It so happens that the Stanford-Binet has a rich accumulation of construct validation behind it—which is not true for many other indicators.

The term **predictive validity** has been used to describe validity coefficients between the indicator and some criterion assessed later in time. For example, a measure of academic potential can be administered to a sample of high school pupils and correlated with the first-semester college grades for the same sample. A positive correlation provides some meaning to the scores on the academic potential test. Whatever construct it measures, it at least predicts college grades with some accuracy.

3. *Has an empirical connection been established between the indicator and other indicators of the same construct that use different measurement methods?* The researchers or evaluators should demonstrate, either with their own data or data in the construct validation literature, that the indicator correlates with some criterion that is measured with some different method. For example, a test of academic potential (using the method referred to in Table 4–3 as "Test of Ability") administered to high school seniors could be correlated with ratings of academic potential as judged by their high school counselors (this method of measurement was referred to as "Report by Other" in Table 4–3). A test of the trait of anxiety could be correlated with psychiatric ratings of anxiety made on the same subjects (Taylor, 1950).

A test of psychopathology could be related to whether or not an individual was a patient in a mental hospital.

Establishing a correlation between two indicators of the same construct when two indicators are measured with alternative methods is particularly strong evidence for validity. This is because each method of measurement seems to "share" certain kinds of error. By this we mean that self-report ratings, regardless of the construct they are supposed to refer to, tend to correlate with each other. Thus, an individual's assessment of her own self-esteem will often correlate more highly with her assessment of her own psychological adjustment than with a psychiatrist's rating of her self-esteem. This phenomenon is called **method variance** as a way of showing that indicators making use of the same method tend to overlap each other, even though they are measuring different constructs. Another example of method variance is observer ratings. Campbell and Fiske (1959) reported that a correlation between observer's ratings of teachers' IQ and voice quality was very high ($r = 0.63$), but that the correlation was a function of *halo effect* (an observer's tendency to rate all attributes of an individual as high or low) rather than evidence that the two constructs are actually related.

Thus, if indicators not sharing method variance correlate positively with each other, there is strong evidence for validity, known as **convergent validity**. A high correlation shows that the two indicators are measuring the same thing. Before one becomes too impressed by these validity coefficients, it is important to remember that the criterion must itself demonstrate adequate reliability and validity to be informative about the validity of the indicator. Suppose that anxiety was the construct a researcher wanted to measure in a study. He chooses as an indicator of anxiety the Taylor Manifest Anxiety Scale. To validate that indicator, he correlates it with psychiatrists' ratings of anxiety and finds a satisfactory correlation. However, it may be that psychiatrists' ratings of anxiety are not themselves a valid indicator (perhaps these ratings are unduly influenced by the patient's mannerisms and dress). The two indicators are measuring the same thing (as evidenced by the positive correlation), yet neither measures the construct of anxiety as the researcher understands it.

4. *Have successful efforts been made to establish that the indicator of a construct* does not correlate *with indicators of other constructs that are theoretically unrelated to the first?* According to Campbell and Fiske (1959), when a test correlates too highly with other tests from which it is intended to differ, its validity is suspect. Low correlation between a test and other indicators that are theoretically unrelated is evidence for the test's **discriminate validity**. Consider the example of creativity. As a construct, creativity is theoretically unrelated to intelligence. In other words, creativity is considered in theory to be equally distributed among more intelligent and less intelligent individuals. One might hypothesize that if the constructs do not

overlap, then measures of creativity and intelligence should not correlate. But if an empirical test of this hypothesis shows a correlation, then these indicators do not show discriminate validity. The empirical results would fail to confirm the expectations deduced from the nomological network (see McNemar, 1964).

Multitrait-Multimethod Analysis

Convergent and discriminate validity can be demonstrated simultaneously in a single analysis, called **multitrait-multimethod analysis**. The researcher includes two or more constructs in the analysis. Each construct is measured with three or more indicators. The indicators must encompass at least two methods of measurement. For example, the construct of creativity can be made manifest by three indicators—the Picasso Test of Divergent Production (PTDP), expert ratings of creative production in literary themes (creativity-expert), and teachers' ratings of creativity (creativity-teacher). Intelligence is also included, measured by test (IQ-test), by psychologists' ratings (IQ-expert), and by teachers' ratings (IQ-teacher). These measures are all administered to a likely sample of subjects, and the results are intercorrelated. Table 5–2 contains the hypothetical correlation matrix. Instead of the actual coefficients, however, their size is described as high, medium, or low. The hypothetical matrix shows the convergent validity of the creativity measures, because the different indicators of creativity (measured by different methods) correlated highly with each other. The matrix shows discriminate validity in that the relationships between indicators of creativity and indicators of intelligence are moderate, even though the same methods were used to measure them.

A multitrait-multimethod matrix like this is difficult to find and has not actually been demonstrated for the construct of creativity. More frequently we find that correlations are high between indicators of different

TABLE 5–2   Hypothetical Multitrait/Multimethod Matrix

	CREATIV-ITY-TEST	CREATIV-ITY-EXPERT	CREATIV-ITY-TEACHER	IQ-TEST	IQ-EXPERT	IQ-TEACHER
1. *CREATIVITY-TEST*	—	High	High	Low	Moderate	Low
2. *CREATIVITY-EXPERT*		—	High	Low	Low	Low
3. *CREATIVITY-TEACHER*			—	Low	High	Moderate
4. *IQ TEST*				—	High	High
5. *IQ-EXPERT*					—	Moderate
6. *IQ-TEACHER*						—

constructs when measured by the same method. For example, one is likely to see teacher ratings of intelligence correlating highly with teacher ratings of creativity, because the measures share the same method.

Characteristics of Measurement Procedures that Detract from Validity

Validity is the correspondence between the construct and the indicator and the ability of the measurement procedure to yield scores that represent the true amount of the indicator possessed by each individual. No indicator attains this ideal; the idea that there is even a "true amount" is disputed by some (see Suttcliffe, 1965). The many ways an indicator may fall short of the ideal have already been mentioned. In addition, there are characteristics of tests and other measurement procedures that detract further from validity. These include *reactivity, insensitivity, response sets*, and *group bias*.

Reactivity is the term for measurement procedures that allow the subjects to alter, distort, or misrepresent the true state of their characteristics. Consider, for example, an inventory of adjustment with the item, "I have trouble making friends." The persons responding to the inventory are meant to assess their own feelings and experiences. Researchers assume that the responses closely approximate the true (called *veridical* by some authors) status of the subjects with respect to the item, according to the scale of response from "very true of me" to "not at all true of me."

Instead of responding with veridicality, however, a subject may distort his true characteristics and respond "Not at all true of me," when in fact he does not have a friend in the world. Why would a person distort the truth this way? Perhaps he wishes to paint a more positive picture of himself than reality warrants. The subject can "fake good." Or, if the measurement was taken as an outcome of an experiment, the subject might guess how this item would help the researchers confirm their hypotheses. Orne (1969) and Rosenthal and Rosnow (1969), among others, have demonstrated the ability of research subjects to discern and confirm researchers' hypotheses. (Some people will do anything for Science!) Because the subject is able to alter and distort the score received, this measure has high reactivity.

Short-term observations of behavior are also highly reactive. Take the example of the Behavioral Approach Test, which in one form is a measure of snake anxiety expressed as the distance from a live snake a phobic person can tolerate (the best score is obtained by the subject who can pick up the reptile). This procedure seems objective on the surface. However, it takes only a little thought to spot a problem: some subjects can overcome their fear long enough to approach the snake closely (to "fake good" or reward the experimenter) without having their long-term phobia altered very much.

Contrast the measures above with one that is more difficult to distort.

It is impossible to fake good on a test of ability, to make it seem that one has greater mental ability or achievement than one has (although "faking bad" is possible and might be done if the subject wanted to punish the researcher). It is also impossible for most people to distort their finger temperature or blood pressure when these are used as indicators of anxiety. These measures have low reactivity as do indirect measures and classifications such as rates of employment, recidivism, rehospitalizations, and the like.

The influence of reactivity is illustrated in Table 5–3, which shows how estimates of the effect of psychotherapy differ reliably depending on the reactivity of the measure used in the study. The data are in the form of effect sizes (average standardized differences between groups treated by psychotherapy and control groups). Substantial differences in the estimates of outcomes of psychotherapy, aggregated from nearly 500 experimental studies, were produced by measures of high versus low reactivity (Smith, Glass, and Miller, 1980, p. 112).

Insensitivity is the term for indicators that do not reveal a statistical difference for an intervention when that intervention or treatment is truly effective. Standardized, norm-referenced achievement tests may not reveal statistical effects of short-term educational treatments, even when such treatments can be shown to be effective on other kinds of measures. For example, an intensive two-week remedial reading program that can be shown to be effective on measures that are closely coordinated to the objectives of the program may not yield significant effects on standardized tests. The achievement test is alleged to be insensitive. Likewise, intelligence

TABLE 5–3   Effect Sizes Associated with Different Levels of Reactivity of Outcome Measurement[a]

REACTIVITY SCALE VALUE	EXAMPLES OF "INSTRUMENTS"	AVERAGE EFFECT SIZE	STANDARD ERROR OF MEAN $\sigma_{\overline{ES}}$	NUMBER OF EFFECTS
1 (low)	Galvanic skin response, gradepoint average	0.55	0.06	222
2 (low average)	Blind ratings of adjustment	0.55	0.04	219
3 (average)	MMPI (Minnesota Multiphasic Personality Inventory)	0.60	0.04	213
4 (high average)	Client self-report to therapist, E-constructed questionnaire	0.92	0.03	704
5 (high)	Therapist ratings, behavior in presence of therapist	1.19	0.06	397

[a]Average reactivity for all cases: 3.46. Correlation of reactivity and effect size: linear, $r = 0.18$; curvilinear, $\eta = 0.28$

Source: Smith, Glass, and Miller, 1980.

tests and multifactorial personality tests do not produce statistical differences between pretreatment and posttreatment assessments or experimental and control comparisons. It is important to remember that validity is always linked to the specific purpose for which the measure is being used. A test such as the Wechsler Intelligence Scale for Children may be valid for predicting subsequent school performance but may be invalid as a measure of cognitive growth produced by a year of schooling, because it is insensitive to interventions of that sort.

Response sets include a variety of distortions associated with different methods of measurement. Fiske (1971, p. 214) listed five response sets associated with a subject's self-report of characteristics (e.g., on rating scales or checklists): *social desirability* (the tendency to respond in conventional rather than truthful ways), *acquiescence* (the tendency always to agree with statements or questions), *extremity* (the tendency to respond to the highest or lowest response alternative), *evasiveness* (the tendency to respond to the middle alternative or the "no opinion" response option), and *carelessness* (the tendency to respond randomly or thoughtlessly to statements or questions). Fiske noted three response sets of the observation method of measurement: *halo* ("allowing one's general impression of the subject to affect one's ratings of specific characteristics"), *leniency* (an observer's tendency to give overgenerous ratings to all individuals), and *position set* (tendency of observers to mark the same response category on each item, moving directly down the page of items).

Group bias refers to the fact that a measure may be valid for some groups but not for others. The Graduate Record Exam may accurately predict performance in graduate school for American students but not for students who learned English as a second language. Certain interest inventories may be valid for males (i.e., correlate with satisfaction and performance in chosen occupations) but not for females.

SOURCES OF INFORMATION ABOUT MEASUREMENT PROCEDURES

Now that you are more familiar with principles of measurement and desirable features of measurement procedures, it is important to be aware of sources of information about the measurement procedures used in the studies you read. Given that reliability and validity are important, how do you determine whether an investigator's procedures were adequate? The most important source of information is the research or evaluation report itself. Investigators are obliged to describe thoroughly the measurement procedures used. They must describe in detail the conditions and environment in which the measures are administered, the techniques for scoring, the training given to and control over observers and test proctors, and procedures of rating and scoring. In addition, they must report evidence on reliability and validity of measurement procedures. The reader should be able to determine how each source of measurement error was estimated and addressed and should have access to at least a summary of the construct validity evidence for the measures used.

Table 5–4 contains a reprint of portions of a study detailing measurement procedures (Owens and Barnes, 1982, pp. 184–188). Notice that the authors described the measures in terms of the content of the items and categories of response required, the procedures for combining responses into scale scores, statistics on internal consistency and test-retest reliability, the conditions under which the subjects were measured (e.g., promise of confidentiality), and the like. For evidence of validity the authors refer the reader to a separate journal article (i.e., Owens and Straton, 1980).

If the information necessary for reaching a judgment about the adequacy of measurement procedures is not included in the paper itself, the reader may locate information in test manuals, the *Mental Measurements Yearbooks*, or journals that regularly print reviews of tests—journals such as *Educational and Psychological Measurement, Measurement and Evaluation in Guidance*, and *Journal of Special Education*. If the requisite information cannot be located in these sources and is not a part of the research or evaluation

TABLE 5–4   Excerpts from L. Owens and J. Barnes, The Relationship between Cooperative, Competitive, and Individualized Learning Preferences and Students' Perceptions of Classroom Learning Atmosphere (1982)

INSTRUMENTS

Preferences for cooperative, competitive, and individualized learning modes were obtained by means of the *Learning Preference Scale—Students* (LPSS). Developmental work on an early version of the LPSS (Form B) has demonstrated factorial validity, internal consistency, and test-retest stability (Owens & Straton, 1980). The current version of the LPSS (Form C) is shorter than its predecessor with a number of changes in item phrasing (Barnes, Owens & Straton, 1978). There are 36 items, brief statements about a feature of learning by cooperating with others, by competing with others, or by working alone. Items referring to each of these learning modes are content-matched in 11 groups, and one additional group contains unmatched items. Each content group, therefore, contains 3 matched items, and each preference subscale in the LPSS, therefore, is composed of 12 items. Students respond to each item by indicating how "true" or how "false" the statement is for them. A 4-point answer scale is used, with the response categories "completely true," "more true than false," "more false than true," and "completely false." Three of the 12 items in each subscale are expressed in negative phrasing to counteract an acquiescence effect. Numerical values are assigned to the answers on a 4-3-2-1 basis, with 4 representing the strongest preference. Three main preference subscale scores (min. 12, max. 48) are calculated for each student, indicating strength of preference for cooperative, competitive, and individualized learning situations. In addition, two involvement scores are calculated. Combined Involvement is obtained by adding the cooperative and competitive subscale scores; this is an indication of desire for contact with others during the learning processes. Cooperative Involvement is obtained by subtracting the competitive subscale score from the cooperative score; this is an indication of the relative strength of the cooperative preference within the general desire for contact with others in learning.

Perceptions of learning atmosphere were obtained by the *Classroom Learning Atmosphere Scale—Secondary* (CLASS). Following developmental work on a trial version, the current scale (Form B) was prepared (Owens, Barnes, & Straton, 1978). There are 42 items, each a brief statement about a feature of the learning atmosphere or classroom climate in a designated class. Items, which were again balanced in direction of phrasing, were constructed on the basis of seven thematic concepts, six items referring to each. Three of these concepts refer to the perceived press for Interpersonal Relationships in the way classroom business is accomplished (Affiliation, Involvement, Spontaneity). Four of the concepts refer to the perceived press for Personal Development (Intellectuality, Autonomy, Practicality, and Self-Understanding). Students respond to each item in the same fashion as for the LPSS, indicating on a 4-point scale how true or how false they feel the statement is for that classroom. Answers are scored on a 4-3-2-1 basis, with a high score representing strong press perceived. Two perception scores are calculated for each student. Press for Interpersonal Relationships is obtained by adding the totals from the three component subscales (min. 18, max. 72). Press for Personal Development is obtained by adding the totals from the four component subscales (min. 24, max. 96). The Cronbach alpha for the two major scales administered in each subject was greater than .70. Mean intercorrelation among the seven subscales is .34, indicating that they measure distinct though somewhat related aspects of classroom social environments.

Administration of the scales was carried out by the authors and an assistant, with teachers being excluded from the room to ensure complete confidentiality. Absentees were followed up by return visits to the schools.

Testing was carried out in Term 2 of the school year, although the students had also been tested in Term 1 as part of the main investigation. Students from the selected classes answered both LPSS and CLASS with reference specifically to English and mathematics. Thus, it might be quite possible to answer "clearly true" to "Trying to be better than others makes me work well" regarding mathematics and "clearly false" to the same question regarding English. Similarly, a mathematics class might be described as high on press for relationships, whilst the same student describes his English class as low or average in press for relationships.

Using a balanced design so that half the classes in each year and school, as far as possible, began with LPSS and the other half began with CLASS, the students were asked to complete the paper for one subject and then the other subject.

The students answered the questions in English classes in School A and in mathematics classes in School B. They were required, therefore, to consider both the group they were in at that time and one other. For Grade 7 students, the only difference would be the classroom and the teacher with the students being the same, but the Grade 11 students answered one of their sets of questions with reference to a class which was different in student composition as well as in subject content, room, and teacher.

In all, each student completed 4 scales, a total of 156 questions, with little or no difficulty or resistance. In fact, students generally felt it was an interesting exercise, and it is worth noting that, although the strictest confidentiality was promised and ensured, a number of students expressed the view that their teachers should be made more aware of the students' feelings and attitudes in these matters. In addition to the student data, the teacher associated with each of the classes completed the teacher form of the LPSS (LPST) and the CLASS, referring specifically to that class group.

Once completed, the question papers were coded in order to match the four papers for each student and to identify the school and class for each subject, and then they were scanned. After editing to eliminate marking and coding errors and to exclude cases of incomplete data, a merged data file was raised containing 279 cases each with identification data and 7 subscale scores. Data were analysed by means of the procedures in the SPSS (Nie et al., 1975).

report itself, the reader should regard the adequacy of the measurement procedures as unproven.

Test manuals   Published tests are available from their publishers (e.g., Psychological Corporation, American Guidance Services). To find out the name of the publisher of a test, consult the book entitled, *Tests in Print*, Volume III (Buros, 1983). Persons with sufficient training or with sponsorship may purchase a specimen of the test itself as well as the test manual from the publisher. They can then examine the content of the test to reach a judgment about its appropriateness for use with the population to be sampled. The test manual should contain instructions for administering and scoring the measure and should describe the research activities used to standardize the test. For example, it is desirable for the test developer to administer the test to representative samples of individuals. The scores obtained from this standardization sample then serve as the basis for transforming raw scores to derived scores such as percentiles and age equivalents. Most important, the test manual should contain evidence for the reliability and validity of the measure. The reader can use this evidence as the basis for judging the merits of the measure for the research or evaluation study in which it was used.

So important is the test manual in determining the adequacy of measures that the three professional organizations most interested in educational measurement (the American Psychological Association, the American Educational Research Association, and the National Council for Measurement in Education) have developed standards for test manuals (*Standards for Educational and Psychological Testing*, 1985) as well as standards for those who administer tests and for the tests themselves.

Mental Measurements Yearbooks   The *Mental Measurements Yearbooks* (*MMY*) represent the single most valuable source of information available on published tests in psychology and education. Through eight editions, 1938–1978, Oscar K. Buros organized and edited these publications. Since his death, the work has been carried on by the Buros Institute of Mental Measurements at the University of Nebraska-Lincoln. In addition to *MMY*, Buros and later the Institute also published *Tests in Print*, Volumes I, II, and III (1961, 1974, and 1983), *Personality Tests and Reviews* (1970), and various monographs on tests in reading, intelligence, achievement, and vocations. Information on tests is kept current between publication of editions of the *MMY* and is available from the Buros Institute for a fee.

The *Eighth Mental Measurements Yearbook*, Volumes I and II (Buros, 1978) consists of a large section of test reviews, a section of reviews of books about testing, and an extensive cross-indexing section. The test review section covers nearly 1,200 tests, 900 of which are reviewed by experts in measurement methodology. This section also contains reprints of 150 test reviews originally appearing in various professional journals. References to research reports in which the tests were used are also included, making *MMY* a rich "secondary source" for researchers looking for extant studies (Chapter 12).

The tests are organized by category: achievement batteries, English, fine arts, foreign languages, intelligence, mathematics, miscellaneous (e.g., courtship and marriage, learning disabilities, socioeconomic status), multi-aptitude batteries, personality, reading, science, sensorimotor, social studies, speech and hearing, and vocations (e.g., careers and interests, mechanical ability). Within each category, tests are organized alphabetically by name of test. Tests have "entry numbers" that allow the reader to locate them from the index of test titles, index of names, or four other indexes. The *MMY* is rather formidable for the beginner, but a section on "How to Use this Yearbook" overcomes most difficulties.

Table 5–5 contains a reprint of the review of the Wide Range Achievement Test (WRAT), a test that is extensively used in public schools. This reprint comes from the seventh edition of *MMY* (Buros, 1972); it is test

TABLE 5–5. **Reprint of the Test and Review Section on the Wide Range Achievement Test in the *Mental Measurements Yearbook*, Seventh Edition, (Buros, 1972)**

[36]

Wide Range Achievement Test, Revised Edition.* Ages 5-0 to 11-11, 12-0 and over; 1940–65; WRAT; 3 scores: spelling, arithmetic, reading; individual; 1 form ('65, 4 pages); 2 levels; manual ('65, 63 pages); $3.75 per 50 tests; $2.60 per manual; $2.75 per specimen set; postpaid; (20–30) minutes; J. F. Jastak, S. R. Jastak, and S. W. Bijou (test); Guidance Associates.

REFERENCES

1–15. See 6:27.

16. REGER, ROGER. "Brief Tests of Intelligence and Academic Achievement." *Psychol Rep* 11:82 Ag '62.* (*PA* 37:5654)

17. BRICKER, AMY L.; SCHUELL, HILDRED; and JENKINS, JAMES J. "Effect of Word Frequency and Word Length on Aphasic Spelling Errors." *J Speech & Hearing Res* 7:183–91 Je '64.* (*PA* 39:5601)

18. MATTHEWS, CHARLES G., and FOLK, EARL D. "Finger Localization, Intelligence, and Arithmetic in Mentally Retarded Subjects." *Am J Mental Def* 69:107–13 Jl '64.* (*PA* 39:2525)

19. OLDRIDGE, O. A. "A Congruent Validity Study of the Wide Range Achievement Test at Grade Seven." *Ed & Psychol Meas* 24:415–7 su '64.* (*PA* 39:5084)

20. SEYBOLD, FRED R., and PEDRINI, DUILIO T. "The Relation Between Wechsler-Bellevue Subtests and Academic Achievement Using Institutionalized Retardates." *Psychiatric Q* 38:635–49 O '64.* (*PA* 39:12755)

21. STONE, F. BETH, and ROWLEY, VINTON N. "Educational Disability in Emotionally Disturbed Children." *Excep Children* 30:423–6 My '64. * (*PA* 39:5920)

22. DALY, WILLIAM C. "The Relationship Between Reading and Anxiety in a Group of Mental Retardates." *Training Sch B* 62:113–8 N '65.* (*PA* 40:3299)

. . . .

64. WASHINGTON, ERNEST D., and TESKA, JAMES A. "Relations Between the Wide Range Achievement Test, the California Achievement Tests, the Stanford-Binet, and the Illinois Test of Psycholinguistic Abilities." *Psychol Rep* 26(1):291–4 F '70.* (*PA* 45:4931)

JACK C. MERWIN, *Professor of Educational Psychology and Dean, College of Education, University of Minnesota, Minneapolis, Minnesota.*

In a review of this test the persisting problem of differentiation between "intelligence" and "achievement" is boldly brought to the fore. This issue, confusing as it is for many, is further complicated in regard to this particular test. The author reports a "general" factor from "a clinical factor analysis" which accounts for 28 percent of the variance of each of the three scores (reading, spelling and arithmetic) and five group factors which the authors say "may be conceived of as true *personality* [reviewer's emphasis] variables." For example, the Group Factor I, labeled the "Verbal," said to be a personality variable unrelated to intelligence, is reported to carry 30 percent of the variance of the reading score and 24 percent of the variance of the spelling score. Careful examination of the materials leads one to seriously question why these authors chose to label this an "achievement" test.

The latest edition, like earlier editions, provides scores in: reading, "recognizing and naming letters and pronouncing words"; spelling, "copying marks resembling letters, writing the name, and writing single words to dictation"; and, arithmetic, "counting, reading number symbols, solving oral problems, and performing written computations." The individual user must determine the extent to which these activities reflect "achievement" in his own situation.

The authors make little effort to describe how this revised edition differs from earlier versions or the reason for the 1965 revision. They do note that the 1965 edition, unlike the earlier editions, is divided into two levels: Level 1 for ages 5–11 and Level 2 for ages 12 and over. In personal correspondence the author reports that, "the new form differs in content only in minor ways."

Administration interestingly involves sequential procedures. For example, parts one and two of the spelling subtest are not given to a person over 7 years 11 months if he has six or more successes in the dictation portion of the third part of that test. Similarly complex, if not confusing, procedures of administration are followed in the other parts of the test. It is basically an individually administered test with provision for group administration of some parts under specified conditions.

The authors report that no attempt was made to obtain a representative national sampling for norming purposes. They note the seven states used in the administration for norming to arrive at sets of norms for six-month age groups from age five through adults for Level 1 and for age 9 through college student for Level 2. Sample size for the various sets of grade equivalents, standard scores, and percentile norms ranges from 86 to 691, half being based on 310 or fewer cases. In addition to number of cases, the only descriptive information regarding the norm group is a brief verbal description (no data provided) that an attempt was made to use IQ's available from a variety of tests to develop norms, "that would correspond to the achievement of mentally average groups with representative dispersions of scores above and below the mean." Thus a user can make comparisons with the norms provided, but with questionable meaning since the identity and nature of the groups serving as the basis for score interpretation is far from clear.

The authors report questionably high reliability coefficients by one-year age groupings. It is not possible to determine the extent to which the reported split-half coefficients based on "odd-even" scores are affected by the sequential administration and scoring procedures used for the test from the information provided. However, the procedures and the reported magnitude (e.g., low of .981 out of 14 coefficients on the reading test) make them suspect, at best.

There are several problems involved in assessing the value of the validity information provided in the manual. One of these relates to the above concern of what the potential user might consider achievement and the content validity of the items of this test for that individual user. While the authors provide several pages of "validity" data and discussion, it is not always clear when the data reported is based on results from the 1965 two-level edition.

The authors report that this test was designed as "an adjunct to tests of intelligence and behavior adjustment." They cite five ends which the method used in the test was devised to accomplish. The extent to which they have succeeded in attaining these ends is far from clear, as are some statements of the ends themselves, e.g., "to permit validity analyses by the method of internal consistency." The authors cite 11 ways in which the test reportedly "has been found of value" though no statistical evidence or research studies to support the statement are reported.

In summary, this "achievement" test is a unique, individually administered test. While possibly a potentially useful clinical tool for the psychologist working with specialized cases, for general school use it is impractical.

Robert L. Thorndike, *Professor of Psychology and Education, Teachers College, Columbia University, New York, New York.*

This is a brief test, in part individually administered, that provides a rough indication of three limited components of educational achievement. The components are spelling, decoding isolated printed words and pronouncing them correctly, and carrying out computational exercises in arithmetic and algebra. The adequacy with which these tasks represent the goals of education in today's schools is never questioned, and the content validity of the test is not considered by the authors at any point. This reviewer does not believe that it would be judged to be high.

. . . .

All parts of the test are timed, if not speeded, and in the word pronouncing test the task is stopped after a specified number of failures. Both of these features tend to inflate split-half reliabilities, and cause one to discount the rather startling values that the authors report. The correlations between Level 1 and Level 2, two separate forms differing in difficulty but printed in the same 4-page booklet, provide a more conservative estimate of reliability. The typical values for samples allegedly chosen to have a mean and standard deviation corresponding to the population of persons at that age run about .90 for the spelling and word reading and about .85 for arithmetic. No data are provided on truly parallel forms, with any time interval between testing, or where forms were given by different examiners. Since strictness in timing and in scoring could vary appreciably from examiner to examiner, such factors could attenuate appreciably the precision of scores.

However, it is in the domain of validity that the most serious questions about this test would seem to arise. Here, the authors appear to have some bizarre conceptions, and to engage in somewhat exotic procedures. They state, for example, "Validity can be determined only by the comparison of one test score with those which measure entirely different abilities." Again, "It is acceptable practice to use criteria of internal consistency in the validation of tests. Criteria of internal consistency, if properly interpreted, are usually more meaningful and more valid than are external criteria of comparison." One finds it hard to reconcile these statements with each other or with the usual concepts of test validation.

The authors report, with considerable verbal elaboration but with no presentation of any of the data on which the interpretations are presumably based, a "clinical factor analysis" of the WRAT together with the WISC and the WAIS. Clinical factor analysis is described only as "successive regressions and score transformations in such a way as to obtain individual scores for each factor as it is extracted from the test comparisons." The exact nature of the procedure is apparently known only to the authors and God, and He may have some uncertainty.

The uses that the authors propose for the test are many, but few of them seem justified. For example, hopefully one would hesitate to count on it for "the accurate diagnosis of reading, spelling, and arithmetic disabilities" or to use it for "the selection of students for specialized technical and professional schools." Overclaiming seems fairly general in the test manual. This test may have some value in a clinical or a research setting in which one is testing individually persons of such diverse ability or background that one cannot tell in advance what level of test would be appropriate, and needs to get a quick estimate of each person's general level of ability and educational background. One would hesitate to recommend it for other purposes.

For reviews by Paul Douglas Courtney, Verner M. Sims, and Louis P. Thorpe of the 1946 edition, see 3:21.

number 36 on pages 65–68. After the name of the test is a paragraph of descriptive information, including the fact that the test comes in two forms, one for children ages 5 years to 11 years, 11 months, and the second for persons aged 12 and over. There are three subtests for assessing achievement in spelling, arithmetic, and reading. It is an individually administered test. There is a manual available. Next is information about the costs of the tests, its authors, and publisher. A list of references to studies in which the WRAT was used follows (it is abridged here, but the actual review includes 48 references—15 references can be found in the sixth edition of *MMY*). Two critical reviews follow, one by Professor Jack C. Merwin and the other by Professor Robert L. Thorndike (both prominent experts in testing). Note that both describe the test, the manual, the procedures for standardizing the test, and the evidence about the test's reliability. At the end are references to reviews of this test that have appeared in earlier editions of *MMY*.

OTHER SOURCES OF INFORMATION AND TESTS

What follows is a bibliography of resources for finding tests and other instruments. Some of these sources also provide technical information about the measures.

BEERE, C.A. *Women and women's issues: A handbook of tests and measures.* San Francisco: Jossey-Bass, 1979.

BONJEAN, C.M., HILL, R.J., and McLEMORE, S.D. *Sociological measurement: An inventory of scales and indices.* San Francisco: Chandler, 1967.

BORICH, G.D., and MADDEN, S.K. *Evaluating classroom instruction: A sourcebook of instruments.* Reading, Mass.: Addison-Wesley, 1977.

CHUN, K.T., COBB, S. and FRENCH, J.R. *Measures for psychological assessment: A guide to 3,000 original sources and their application.* Ann Arbor: Institute for Social Research, University of Michigan, 1974.

COMREY, A.L., BACKER, T.E., and GLASER, E.M. *A sourcebook for mental health measures.* Los Angeles: Human Interaction Research Institute, 1973.

GOLDMAN, B.A., and BUSCH, J.C. *Directory of unpublished experimental mental measures,* Vol. II. New York: Human Sciences Press, 1978.

GOODWIN, W., and DRISCOLL, L. *Handbook for measurement and evaluation in early childhood education.* San Francisco: Jossey-Bass, 1980.

GUTHRIE, P.D. *Measures of social skills: An annotated bibliography.* Princeton, N.J.: Educational Testing Service, 1971 (ERIC Document No. ED 056 085).

HOEFNER, R., and others (Eds.). *CSE elementary school test evaluations.* Los Angeles: Center for the Study of Evaluation , University of California, 1976.

JOHNSON, O.G. *Tests and measurements in child development: Handbook II.* San Francisco: Jossey-Bass, 1976.

LAKE, D.G., MILES, M.B., and EARLE, R.B. *Measuring human behavior: Tools for the assessment of social functioning.* New York: Teachers College Press, 1973.

MILLER, D.C. *Handbook of research design and social measurement (4th ed.).* New York: Longman, 1983.

PRICE, J.L. *Handbook of organizational management* Lexington, Mass.: Heath, 1972.

REEDER, L.G., RAMACHER, L., and GORELNIK, S. *Handbook of scales and indices of health behavior.* Pacific Palisades, Calif.: Goodyear, 1976.

ROBINSON, J.P., ATHANASION, R., and HEAD, K.B. *Measures of occupational attitudes and occupational characteristics.* Ann Arbor: Institute for Social Research, University of Michigan, 1969.

ROBINSON, J.P., RUSK, J.G., and HEAD, K.P. *Measures of political attitudes.* Ann Arbor: Institute for Social Research, University of Michigan, 1968.

ROBINSON, J.P., and SHAVER, P.R. *Measures of social psychological attitudes.* Ann Arbor: Institute for Social Research, University of Michigan, 1973.

ROSEN, P. (Ed.). *Test collection bulletin.* Princeton, N.J.: Educational Testing Service (quarterly publication).

ROSEN, P. (Ed.). *Self-concept measures: Head Start collection.* Princeton, N.J.: Educational Testing Service, 1973 (ERIC Document Numbers ED 086 737, ED 083 320, ED 083 319).

ROUTH, D.K. *Bibliography on the psychological assessment of the child.* Washington, D.C.: American Psychological Association, 1976.

SHAW, M.E., and WRIGHT, J.M. *Scales for the measurement of attitudes.* New York: McGraw-Hill, 1967.

SIMON, A., and BOYER, E. *Mirrors for behavior III: An anthology of observation instruments.* Wyncote, Pa.: Communication Materials Center, 1974.

STRAUS, M.A., and BROWN, B.W. *Family measurement techniques: Abstracts of published instruments, 1935–1974.* Minneapolis: University of Minnesota Press, 1978.

SWEETLAND, R.C., and KEYSER, D.J. (Eds.). *Tests: A comprehensive reference for assessments in psychology, education, and business.* Kansas City, Mo.: Test Corporation of America, 1983.

WALKER, D.K. *Socioemotional measures for preschool and kindergarten children.* San Francisco: Jossey-Bass, 1973.

WARD, M.J., and FETLER, M.E. *Instruments for use in nursing education research.* Boulder, Colo.: Western Interstate Commission on Higher Education, 1979.

TERMS INTRODUCED IN THIS CHAPTER

reliability

error

nonequivalence

test-retest reliability

internal consistency

split-half reliability

alternate forms reliability

interjudge reliability

validity

face validity

content validity

validity coefficient

concurrent validity

predictive validity

method variance

convergent validity

discriminate validity

multitrait, multimethod analysis

reactivity

insensitivity

response sets

group bias

QUESTIONS AND ACTIVITIES FOR FURTHER STUDY

1. When a measurement procedure administered repeatedly or in similar form yields the same score on an individual, that measurement procedure is said to be _____ . List some synonyms for this characteristic.

2. The greater the measurement error in a measurement procedure or test, the _____ is the level of reliability.

3. Classify each of the following according to what source of error it represents:
    a. A psychologist administers an individual achievement test that serves as

the dependent variable in an experiment. She believes that certain of the subjects are learning disabled and she gives them hints and prompts if they give the incorrect answer the first time.

b. The lawnmower makes an excessive and unusual amount of noise that disturbs the back row of a class taking a group-administered achievement test.

c. Student A has the bad luck of having comprehensive exams on the same day as her midterm exam in research methods.

d. Student B is doing a content analysis of science textbooks on their inclusion of "creationism." Her advisor requires her to hire an independent researcher to code the same textbooks to verify her findings.

e. The pretest for an experiment is administered early Friday morning. Some subjects had come home late the previous night after a football game.

f. A research assistant is assigned the task of standing behind a two-way mirror and counting the number of assertive comments made by participants of an assertiveness training workshop. Although instructions of how to recognize assertive comments have been provided, this particular research assistant has his own ideas about what assertiveness means, and these do not correspond to those of the researcher.

g. The most knowledgeable and brightest students, who get the correct answers on nine of the ten items of a multiple choice achievement test, consistently picked choice c for the tenth item. Choice a was considered correct by the teacher.

h. Items 1 through 5 on an attitude scale yielded a different picture of a pupil's attitude than did items 6 through 10.

4. For each of the above cases, suggest a procedure that could be used to reduce the error of measurement.

5. Why must a test have greater reliability when it is used to make diagnostic or placement decisions than when it is used as an outcome variable in research?

6. Look at Table 5–4 and find the information on the reliability of the CLASS measure. What sources of error are addressed by the researchers? Which are not addressed, and which, if any, are irrelevant?

7. An evaluator compared children's ability to recognize letters before and after kindergarten by administering the same 20-item test. On the posttest, almost all of the children correctly answered all the items. Was the reliability of the posttest likely to be lower or higher than the reliability of the pretest?

8. A researcher wants to use grade point average as an outcome measure in a comparative study of various treatments of test anxiety. Discuss the characteristics of grade point average, both its reliability and its validity, when used for this purpose.

9. Students in the statistics class complain that the midterm exam was not valid because it covered knowledge and skills that the instructor had not yet taught. What kind of validity did the test lack?

10. A 25-item forced-choice questionnaire is developed by a researcher to measure depression. She defends the validity of this questionnaire on the basis of its positive correlation with the Depression Scale on the Minnesota Multiphasic Personality Inventory. What kind of validity is this? What, if any, other evidence could bolster the case for using this measure?

11. According to a critical review of Test A, it has "established validity for predicting performance in first-grade reading. The validity coefficients between Test A and reading achievement at the end of first grade are high." A researcher chooses Test A as the dependent variable in an experiment comparing two treatments for teaching letter recognition to kindergarteners. Can the researcher use the critical review as evidence for the validity of Test A in his experiment?

12. An ability test used to select candidates for the police academy correlates $r = 0.40$ with ratings of proficiency on the job. What is the term for this correlation? What type of validity is this? Why is this correlation more convincing than a correlation of $r = 0.40$ between this test and another test of ability?

13. A researcher who wants to contribute to the construct validation literature on a test of psychopathology compares inpatients and normal persons and finds significant differences between their average scores. What kind of validity is this?

14. A researcher of learning disabilities intercorrelates 10 different indicators of the construct. He finds that (1) the teachers' ratings of pupils' erratic performance on learning tasks correlate near zero with a consistency score derived from daily objective achievement tests; (2) teachers' ratings of pupils' erratic performance correlate positively with teachers' ratings of pupils' disruptive behavior; and (3) teachers' ratings of pupils' disruptive behavior correlate negatively with teachers' ratings of pupils' likability. Discuss these three items of evidence in light of types of validity.

15. Review the material on construct validation in this chapter and on conceptualization in Chapter 4. Defend the statement that all types of validity evidence (e.g., concurrent, convergent) are really subsets of construct validity.

16. Consider a self-esteem inventory made up of items such as "I like myself a lot." Relate it to the problem of reactivity in an experiment to test the effect of encounter groups on self-esteem.

17. Some textbook writers claim that *any* published instrument is superior to instruments developed by researchers for their studies. State arguments against this statement. What should researchers do to establish that the reliability and validity of their specially constructed instruments are sufficient?

18. An evaluator must select a personality test to assess outcomes of therapeutic programs at a mental health center. List four places this evaluator could look for information on the reliability and validity of possible tests.

19. Select a construct such as readiness, achievement, study habits, vocational interest, or some other. Find two measures of the same construct for which critical reviews are available (*Mental Measurements Yearbooks* are the best sources). As best you can from the information provided, compare the two measures on their evidence for reliability and validity. Make a comparative evaluation of the two measures of the same construct.

6

EXPERIMENTAL STUDIES

When researchers or evaluators ask "What is the effect of urban density on crime?" or "Does pupil cooperation improve when verbal reinforcement techniques are used?" or "Is unemployment a function of illiteracy?" or "Can reading comprehension be increased by allowing pupils to choose their own reading materials?" or "What is the cause of the decline in achievement test scores?" they are asking questions about cause-and-effect relationships. Each question implies the action of one phenomenon (the independent variable, or *cause*) on another (dependent variable, also referred to as the *criterion, effect, outcome,* or *consequence*). By changing the independent variable, the dependent variable is altered, changed, increased, decreased, improved, or negatively affected in some way when the two are causally related. In stating the hypothesis "Cognitive therapy decreases depression," the researcher is proposing that when one provides cognitive therapy to people, their depression will decrease *because of* the cognitive therapy.

Establishing cause-and-effect relationships, and indeed the whole idea of causation, has posed knotty problems for philosophers over the centuries. Review of the philosophical issues is beyond the scope of this book (see Brodbeck, 1968, for further information). The dominant position among research methodologists is that to establish the claim that one variable was the cause of another, three conditions have to be met. First, a statistical relationship between the two variables must be demonstrated. Second, the presumed cause must occur before the presumed effect. Third, all other possible causes of the presumed effect must be ruled out. These three conditions will be elaborated in the following section. They represent the canons of evidence necessary for establishing cause-and-effect claims in science. In realms other than science, canons of evidence differ. In law, for example, establishing cause is less strict, requiring the prosecuter to prove that the defendant had means, motive, and opportunity to commit the crime. In everyday life we attribute causality freely from our accumulated experience. We do not need a rigorous experiment to infer that the change of the traffic light from red to green was the "cause" of pedestrians crossing the street.

CONDITIONS FOR ESTABLISHING CAUSE AND EFFECT

Statistical relationship   The first condition that must be met concerns the determination that the independent variable and the dependent variable are related statistically. The answer lies in inferential statistical testing procedures such as those described in Chapter 3. Consider the example of the hypothesis, "Balance-beam training improves the coordination of young children." The researcher measures the degree of coordination in a group of 4-year-olds. She then conducts a program of eight hours of balance beam training over a two-week period. She then retests the degree of coordination in the children. She now has two averages—pretreatment mean and a posttreatment mean. By computing a particular kind of t-test and finding that the posttreatment mean was significantly higher than the pretreatment mean, the condition that there be a statistical relationship between independent (balance beam training) and dependent (coordination) variables has been met. In a different research design of the same hypothesis, the researcher might compare the posttreatment mean of a group of children who had received balance beam training with another group who had not. Finding a significant difference between the means of the two groups also satisfies the condition that there be a statistical relationship between the two variables.

Suppose, for a second example, that a hypothesis concerns the effect of urban density on crime. The researcher consults police reports and calculates the number of crimes committed in each residential block of a large city. He then determines the number of persons who occupy those blocks. He computes a chi square test (or some type of correlation) and finds a statistically significant association between these two indices, such that more crimes were committed in heavily populated blocks. The condition of statistical relationship has been met. The inferential statistical test makes chance an unlikely explanation for the association between the independent and the dependent variable.

Time sequence   The researcher must establish that the hypothesized cause, or independent variable, occurred prior to the hypothesized effect, or change in the dependent variable. A trivial example of this requirement is that World War II (circa 1939) cannot be considered a cause of the Great Depression (circa 1929). In causes like this one, meeting the condition is self-evident. If the researcher hypothesized that gender is the cause of differences in math achievement, it is obvious that the condition of temporal sequence is met, since a person acquires gender before going to school. But a researcher who argued that gender-role identity is the cause of self-esteem would have a difficult time proving that the independent variable came first and was thus the cause of the dependent variable. In hypothesizing that urban density causes crime, a researcher would find it difficult to establish the appropriate time sequence.

In certain research designs, such as the balance beam training example used earlier, the problem of time sequence is handled by defining the independent variable as a *treatment,* with specific components and lasting a specific amount of time. The treatment is deliberately introduced to a sample of subjects by the researcher, who then *controls* temporal sequence by measuring the dependent variable before and after treatment (or in treated and untreated groups).

Alternative causes ruled out   Suppose the researcher measured coordination in a group of 4-year olds, introduced the balance beam training treatment, then measured coordination again at the end of the treatment. She finds a significant improvement in coordination from pretreatment to posttreatment means. The significance test rules out chance as an explanation of the difference in means and meets the condition of statistical relationship between independent and dependent variables. The temporal sequence is controlled by the researcher's deliberate manipulation of the treatment and the measurements made before and after treatment. Can the researcher claim that the independent variable was responsible for the gains on the dependent variable? Not yet. She must also establish that no other variables, unnoticed or unmeasured in her design, could have been the cause of the observed improvement. In other words, alternative causes, also called **rival hypotheses**, must be discredited. The most obvious rival explanation to the researcher's hypothesis is that the children had grown more coordinated simply due to the passage of time and their own development or maturation, quite apart from balance-beam training. Another possibility is that the children performed better on the posttreatment measure because they were more familiar with it the second time it was given. Still another alternative explanation is that these particular children were taking a course in toddler gymnastics at the same time the study was being conducted. These rival hypotheses imply that the cause of the improved coordination was maturation, the practice effect, or the gymnastics rather than the balance-beam training. Each of these rival hypotheses limits the researcher's ability to establish a causal claim for the balance beam training. Each suggests that some **extraneous variable** other than the hypothesized cause was responsible for all or part of the statistical relationship between the independent and dependent variables. The extraneous variables in the balance beam experiment are (1) normal growth and development, (2) learning from practicing the test, and (3) learning from gymnastics.

INTERNAL VALIDITY

Methodologists Donald T. Campbell and Julian C. Stanley (1963) used the term **internal validity** to refer to the extent to which one could claim that the independent variable was responsible for or caused the dependent variable. The greater the internal validity of a particular study, the more credible is the causal claim. The term **threats to internal validity** stands for rival hypotheses or alternative explanations to the researcher's hypothesis that changes in the independent variable were the cause of changes in the dependent variable. Specific threats include *history, maturation, testing, instrumentation, nonequivalence, regression,* and *mortality.*

History   The claim that changes of the independent variable cause changes of the dependent variable can be invalidated by **history**—that is, by specific events that are not part of the independent variable but occur during the time period in which changes in the dependent variable are observed. For example, consider the case of a social worker who has implemented a program to encourage neighborhood reporting of instances of child abuse and neglect. The program consists of televised public service messages and distribution of leaflets throughout the target area. As a method of evaluating this program, the rate of reports is measured the week before the program starts and the week immediately after it ends. Results show a significant increase in reports of child abuse and neglect in the neighborhoods involved in the program. However, three days before the end of the program, network television aired the movie *Sybil*, which dramatizes the story of an abused child who develops multiple personalities. A strong case can be made that the increased reports of abuse were caused by the movie rather than the social worker's program. The movie is an example of an event to which the subjects are exposed, that is different from the independent variable, that occurs contemporaneously with the independent variable, and that may be responsible for the differences on the dependent variable. Keep in mind that the real cause of the change in reporting rates may still be the social worker's program. Just because a threat to internal validity exists in a study, we cannot assume that the research hypothesis is false. The correct interpretation is that either of these alternative hypotheses (and some other possible causes as well) must be considered plausible. We can say that the hypothesized cause (the program) and the alternative cause (the movie) are **confounded**, or mixed up inextricably; there is no way of choosing which "cause" is more credible than the other, and that the third condition for establishing cause and effect has not been met.

Maturation   The **maturation** threat to internal validity comes about when certain events *internal* to the research subjects may be responsible for the differences on the dependent variable. These internal events consist of physiological or psychological development that occurs naturally through the course of time, or as the subject grows older, more coordinated, fatigued, bored, and the like. These natural processes, occurring at the same time as the independent variable, pose rival claims for the cause of the dependent variable. Take as an example a speech pathologist who wants to test the hypothesis that tongue-thrust therapy has a beneficial effect on articulation disorders of young children. He designs a study using 3-year-old children. By objective means he measures the number of articulation errors they make when they first come to the clinic. Then he treats the children for one hour a week for one year. At the end of the year the children are tested again, and the statistical test shows a significant decrease in the number of articulation errors demonstrated by the children who received treatment. His ability to claim that the therapy was the cause of the decrease in articulation errors is hampered by the rival hypothesis that children at about this age lose many of their articulation errors naturally and developmentally without special treatment. Thus, maturation is a threat to the internal validity of this study.

Testing   One testing method commonly used in experimental studies (to establish the temporal sequence condition) is to measure the dependent variable before and after introducing the treatment to research subjects. A pretest is given, then the treatment, then the posttest. Considerable research (e.g., Willson and Putnam, 1982) shows, however, that subjects learn something merely from taking the pretest. Perhaps they learn test-taking skills or even the content of the test items. Perhaps their test anxiety decreases due to greater familiarity with the format or test examiners. Whatever the case, this *practice effect* results in higher posttest scores, even when the intervening treatment itself has no effect on the outcome variable. The practice effect can masquerade as the effect of the independent variable. Thus, in a pretest/treatment/posttest design, the practice effect is a rival hypothesis, or alternative explanation, to the research hypothesis that the treatment was the cause of the difference between pretest and posttest.

The likelihood that the practice effect was responsible for the posttest difference decreases as the length of time between the administration of the two tests increases. The testing threat can occur on tests of personality and adjustment as well as achievement and ability tests with the subjects' appearing better adjusted on the posttest, even if no true changes in their adjustment has occurred.

Instrumentation   The **instrumentation** threat occurs when the method of measuring the dependent variable changes from one group or time to the next. If the instrument itself changes from time to time, person to person, or group to group, then these changes in the instrument can be confused with changes in the subjects. Suppose, for example, that a researcher designed a study of the effects of psychotherapy on adjustment, with the subject's adjustment being rated by clinicians trained in psychological assessment. The subjects are volunteers who present themselves for therapy at the community mental health center. Subjects are randomly assigned to either a treatment group or a "wait-list control group" (meaning they will receive treatment as soon as the study is completed). The adjustment of subjects in both groups is rated as a pretest. The treatment group receives six months of therapy for an hour once each week; the control group is untreated. Then both groups are again rated for adjustment (posttest). A significant difference is found between the averages of the treated and control groups on the adjustment measure. However, the clinicians who did the rating knew which clients were in the treated group and which were in the control group. This knowledge may have influenced their ratings of adjustment (unconsciously, perhaps, because they believe strongly in the efficacy of psychotherapy). Thus, the significant difference between the two groups may have been due to slightly elevated ratings given to subjects who received treatment and slightly depressed ratings given to subjects who were not treated. In a "blind" study the clinicians would not know which subjects were in which groups, and instrumentation would not be a threat to internal validity. If a less subjective, pencil-and-paper measure had been used, then instrumentation would not threaten internal validity of the claim that the independent variable was responsible for the dependent variable.

Nonequivalence   Many research designs involve the comparison of two or more groups. Consider the hypothesis, "Instruction in rules of essay writing is more effective than use of essay models in promoting the ability to write essays." The evaluator picks three groups to serve as subjects: One group is taught by the rule-learning method, the second is taught by the model method, and the third is given no instruction. After the treatment period, the dependent variable is measured by having each essay scored for coherence and organization by "blind" raters. Significant differences among the three posttest means are found. Examination of the means shows that the essay quality of the group taught by the rule method was greater than that of the other two groups. One threat to the researcher's claim that the independent variable is responsible for the differences on the dependent variable is the nonequivalence of the groups prior to the study. The **nonequivalence** threat is any subject characteristic that makes the groups compared unequal in any respect other than the treatment. Perhaps in this case the subjects who were assigned to the rule-method group were brighter, older, more experienced writers, or more motivated at the start. In other words, there are subject characteristics that correlate with the dependent variable. Suppose one such subject characteristic is verbal ability. Suppose further that for some reason the group receiving the rule-method treatment happened to contain a greater number of subjects with high verbal ability. This bias in the composition of the groups and the higher levels of verbal ability in one group could be the true cause of the observed posttest differences. Those in the rule-method group wrote better essays than the other groups. So it would be the *nonequivalence of the subjects* assigned to the groups, rather than the *differences among treatments* that was responsible for the observed posttest differences in means.

The nonequivalence threat has much to do with how members of the sample come to be assigned to one treatment group rather than another. It is particularly a threat when one of the two groups that are compared consists of volunteers. For example, if the treatment is marital therapy and the treatment group is made up of volunteers who seek such therapy while the control group is made up of couples randomly selected from the community but not seeking therapy, then the two groups are probably very nonequivalent. Any posttest differences could be due either to the treatment or to subject characteristics that are related to the perceived need for therapy. The nonequivalence threat is also evident when intact groups like classrooms are used for comparisons. For example, consider a case in which a new reading method (the treatment) is compared to traditional instruction. The treatment group is Ms. Jackson's classroom and the control, Mr. Steven's class. Members of the two groups are likely to be nonequivalent since they were not assigned to the classes at random. Some bias usually exists. Perhaps, for example, Mr. Stevens is perceived by the principal as particularly adept at teaching troublesome pupils and is therefore assigned disproportionately more of them.

Regression   The threat to internal validity known as **regression** occurs only when the subjects in the study are chosen because of their extreme position on some variable. Disadvantaged children selected because they are in greatest need for remedial education are an example; mentally retarded adults are another; gifted individuals are a third. A statistical artifact of studies using such extreme groups makes it inevitable that individuals will appear *less extreme* on a second measure (not perfectly correlated with the first variable). This movement in the direction of the mean of the group may be mistaken for a treatment effect.

Suppose that a school wanted to establish and evaluate a remedial reading center where second-grade children with the lowest reading achievement scores can go for one-half hour per day to receive tutoring. The standardized achievement test of reading serves both as a selection device for identifying the children most in need of the center's services and as the pretest for the evaluation of the program. At the end of the academic year, the children served by the center are again given the standardized achievement test, this time as a posttest. The children show a gain of 0.50 standard deviations on the average. To attribute the gain to the center's program, however, one would have to rule out alternative explanations. Besides the maturation, history, and testing threats, the regression threat is another rival explanation of the evaluator's claim that the center improved reading. Because the subjects chosen represented an extreme group (their pretest scores were far below the mean for the whole second grade), there would be a tendency for their posttest scores to be closer to the mean and higher than their pretest scores. It would appear that the students had made gains in reading even if the center was a total failure and had no effect whatsoever.

For groups of subjects who are selected for the study because of their extremely high scores in a population (e.g., gifted children), studies may seem to show a deleterious effect simply because their scores will regress to the mean (be lower than their pretest scores) even if the program had some benefits. The interested student can refer to Campbell and Stanley (1963), or Cook and Campbell (1979) for further explanations of the regression effect. For most students it is enough to be able to recognize those situations and research designs in which regression poses a threat to internal validity (i.e., when the subjects are selected because of their extreme position on some variable).

Mortality   Even well-designed and carefully conducted studies usually have dropouts. That those subjects who complete the study may have different characteristics from those who drop out could threaten the internal validity of the study. This threat is known as **mortality**, or *attrition*. Imagine a recreation therapist's study of the effect of aerobic dancing on lung capacity of adult females. She designs a study in which volunteers solicited through newspaper advertising are randomly assigned to treatment and control groups. The lung capacity of both groups is measured by objective, mechanical apparatus. The treatment consists of one-hour aerobic conditioning classes that meet three times a week for eight weeks. The control group meets once a week for lectures on the value of fitness. At the end of eight weeks, lung capacity is again measured. A *t*-test of the difference in posttest means between the two groups shows that the group receiving the aerobics treatment had lung capacity significantly greater than the control group.

However, it was noted that of the 40 women who began the aerobics treatment, only 30 remained at the end to participate in the posttesting. All 40 members of the control group completed the posttest. Why does this threaten internal validity? One has to look at the subject characteristics of the women who dropped out and compare them to the characteristics of those who remained. Perhaps those who persisted were more physically fit to begin with, more motivated to improve, and the like. Those who dropped out might have been less fit, less motivated, or maybe even injured by the treatment. This latter subgroup did not contribute to the posttest mean of the treatment group, which was biased upward by the fact that only the persisters were measured. In the control group, by contrast, both subgroups—the more fit and motivated and the less fit and less well motivated were included in the posttest mean. The control group mean would be lower than the treatment group mean even if the treatment had had no effect whatsoever. This is true even if the groups started out equivalent, as they did because of the random assignment of subjects to groups. The idea of "random equivalence," introduced in Chapter 3, means that pretest averages were only randomly different from each other because there were roughly equal numbers of more and less fit in the treated and control groups at the beginning. At the end there were disproportionately more of the fit subgroup in the treatment group than in the control group.

Interaction of nonequivalence and other sources of invalidity

A source of internal invalidity can confound many types of experimental design. It is relatively easy to see how regression or mortality can make it appear that averages are improving in a one-group pretest-posttest design. These same sources, and the others, can likewise confound a two-group design. Suppose, for example, that 100 students are pretested with the SAT and divided into two groups: the top 50 scorers serve as a control group and the bottom 50 are given practice on vocabulary building. The top group will drop and the bottom group will rise from the effect of regression to the mean, but the pattern of regression is different in the two groups, leading one to label the source of invalidity as **nonequivalence by regression interaction**. Other sources of invalidity can also interact with the nonequivalence of groups to produce bogus relationships between independent and dependent variables. **Nonequivalence by mortality interaction** could invalidate a two-group design if the drop-out rate in the experimental group was very much different from the drop-out rate in the control group.

It is also important to realize that certain methods of control, to be discussed in the next section, can neutralize the effect of a source of invalidity even when it is present. Suppose an experiment is performed on

1,000 students, all of whom scored below 300 on the SAT verbal exam. By random assignment, 500 are given vocabulary training and the other 500 are held as a control group. Even though both groups will regress upward toward the mean of the group from which they were selected, the regression will be the same in both groups and will not create an invalid difference between the two groups' posttest means. In this case there is no interaction of nonequivalence and regression. Even though regression is present in the pretest-to-posttest gains, it is equalized and still permits a valid comparison of posttest averages.

Methods of Control

Threats to internal validity, or alternative explanations, can be ruled out by several means. The first is by *logical argument*. Take the example of a study that includes a posttest given two years after the pretest. One can argue and accumulate evidence that the practice effect is substantially reduced if there is a lengthy interval between the administrations of the test. Therefore, the testing threat is not credible as an alternative explanation for the differences between pretests and posttests. Or, if a researcher conducts a short-term treatment in a laboratory setting, isolating subjects from outside events, then history is not a plausible rival hypothesis to a pretest-posttest difference. When the subjects are not chosen because of their extreme position, then regression is not plausible. If no subjects are lost, or if all the dropouts' pretest scores are eliminated, then mortality is obviously not a threat.

The second means of dealing with threats to internal validity is the use of *control groups*. To rule out the history threat, for example, the researcher would have an untreated control group, members of which are exposed to the external, "historical" events but not to the treatment. Table 6–1 shows a diagram of such a design. Two more or less comparable groups are selected. Both are measured at the same time (pretest). One group is given the treatment; the second is untreated. At the end of the treatment period, both are tested a second time. The difference between the pretest and the posttest means of the *control group* reflects the impact of any historical events (and some other influences) on the dependent variable. The difference between the pretest and the posttest of the *treated group* is made up of the same external, historical events *plus* the effects of the treatment. Thus, the difference between the posttest means of the treated group and control group "subtracts out" the effects of the historical events and leaves only the treatment effect. History is therefore controlled as a threat to the internal validity of this design.

Similarly, testing and maturation are eliminated as threats to the internal validity of a study when an untreated control group is included in the research design. The difference between the pretest and posttest means

TABLE 6–1 Control Group Design

CALENDAR OF A CONTROL GROUP STUDY

APRIL 1	APRIL 2	APRIL 3	APRIL 4	APRIL 5	APRIL 6	APRIL 7
Researcher selects sample.	Researcher divides the sample into two equal groups- Group A and Group B.	Group A gets pretest. Group B gets pretest.	Group A gets treatment. ⟶ Group B gets no treatment. ⟶			Group A gets posttest. Group B gets post-test.

"Historical" events affect both groups.
Both groups "mature" at same rate.
Both groups "regress" toward the mean.

of the control group is the consequence of the practice effect, the effect of normal maturation, historical events, and other possible influences. In the case of the maturation threat, however, it is important that the untreated control group be quite comparable to the treated group with respect to the stage of development of its members.

Nonequivalence is best controlled by *random assignment* of subjects to treatments. This will be more fully discussed in a later section of this chapter. However, it is important to understand that when the researcher decides by random assignment which subjects will receive the treatment and which the control condition, then the possibility that the groups are greatly unequal prior to the treatment is substantially reduced. If the decision is made on the basis of the researcher's convenience or professional judgment, or because certain subjects volunteered for a particular treatment, then the probability that the groups are nonequivalent may be greater, but in any case their nonequivalence is not calculable as it is with random assignment.

Researchers and evaluators sometimes use **matching** as a way of equating groups. For example, an evaluator of a compensatory education program might match pupils who had received the program with control pupils on verbal ability, then compare their achievement of the program objectives. Such a technique, although intuitively appealing, does not remove the nonequivalence threat to internal validity in this design. Only one extraneous variable (verbal ability) has been controlled by the matching technique. Other ones, such as socioeconomic status or parental interest in education, might correlate with the dependent variable and be disproportionately represented in the control group. Adding matching variables to the design helps to reduce the nonequivalence of the treated and control groups. However, someone can always suggest another extraneous variable that remains uncontrolled and might rival the evaluator's hypothesis that the program was responsible for the observed difference on the posttest.

Besides matching, there are two other procedures for dealing with nonequivalence. One is the statistical equating of two groups (i.e., using a statistical procedure such as analysis of covariance for reducing the systematic variance between the two groups on some extraneous variable). The second is designing the study so that each subject serves as his or her own control. Neither of these techniques is as satisfactory for removing the nonequivalence between groups as is random assignment. But since random assignment is impossible in many real-world evaluation studies, these techniques may be usefully employed. Both will be described more fully in the next chapter.

The internal validity threat of mortality is not controlled by random assignment. But certain procedures can sometimes reduce the threat when subjects are lost before the end of the study. First, the researcher can locate the dropouts and measure them on the dependent variable, so that the mean difference between treatment and control groups will more fairly represent the characteristics of those who were originally selected. Second, the researcher can match pairs of individuals, one from the experimental groups with one from the control group, based on their pretest scores. When one person drops out of the experimental group, that person's matched pair can be dropped from the control group. Still other steps can be taken to make sure that those who left the treatment had similar subject characteristics to those who persisted (Jurs and Glass, 1971).

Instrumentation is controlled by the use of paper-and-pencil tests rather than tests that call for some degree of examiner judgment. Or, if the examiners (those who administer the measure of the dependent variable) are "blind," that is, uninformed about which subjects are in which group or which condition, then instrumentation is controlled as a threat to internal validity.

Other Threats   The threats to internal validity thus far enumerated are alternative explanations for an observed and statistically significant difference between treated and control groups on the dependent variable. They pose puzzles about what actually caused the statistical difference— the treatment or some extraneous variable? Other threats concern the outcome of *nonsignificant differences* on the dependent variable. Was the failure to find significance explained by an ineffective treatment, a poor theory, or something else? Here are some alternative hypotheses to be considered:

1. The sample was too small. Remember from Chapter 3 that significance tests are affected by the size of the sample, and smaller samples have less chance of yielding significant results.

2. The dependent variable was poorly measured. Unreliable tests or inexact procedures may produce data that fail to yield significant findings.

3. The treatment was not fully implemented as the researcher intended. Perhaps the teachers who were supposed to administer an educational program as part of the study chose to modify it according to their own professional judgment. Thus, the failure to find significant effects was due to poor **treatment fidelity**. Many field studies are thus bolstered by observation to make sure that the treatments were actually administered as defined.

4. The treatment was not sufficiently long or intense to produce an effect. Readers of research often wonder how a researcher expected to find an effect on clients' performance anxiety from a treatment of one hour's duration or from reading a one-page pamphlet.

5. The **John Henry effect** can produce nonsignificance when the members of the control group work particularly hard in order to compete with the treatment group. The result of this extraordinary effort is to reduce the difference between the two groups on the posttest.

6. **Treatment diffusion** occurs when some important features and components of the treatment are leaked to and used by members of the control group. The diffusion reduces the difference between the two groups on the posttest.

THREE TYPES OF RESEARCH THAT ADDRESS CAUSE AND EFFECT

When a research hypothesis suggests a cause-and-effect relationship, the researcher commonly chooses among three varieties of design to test the hypothesis. **True experiments** are those in which the independent variable is a treatment that the researcher deliberately introduces and manipulates, *and* the researcher's control extends to the ability to assign subjects at random to the levels of the independent variable. **Quasi experiments**, covered in Chapter 7, are studies in which the researcher has only partial control over the independent variables employed as treatments. The researcher may control when and how the dependent variables are measured but cannot control the experimental setting sufficiently to employ random assignment of subjects to treatment groups. In **causal-comparative studies**, also called *ex post facto* studies, the researcher does not have control over independent variables. Either the independent variable has occurred in the past, prior to the study, or subjects have assigned themselves to the various "treatment conditions," (such as public or private schools), or the independent variable is some fixed characteristic of the subjects (as, for example, in the research question, "What is the effect of birth order on intelligence?"). Causal-comparative studies are covered in Chapter 8.

TRUE EXPERIMENTS

Experiments follow a prescribed sequence of steps. First, the researcher *selects subjects* from some population that is appropriate to the research hypothesis. Second, the *subjects are assigned* to two or more treatment conditions or groups. Third, the subjects are observed or measured on the dependent variable of the study. (This *pretesting* is an optional step.) Fourth, the *treatment conditions are implemented*. Fifth, at the conclusion of the treatment period, the *dependent variable is measured*. This sequence can be graphically depicted as follows, with the temporal order of steps moving from left to right:

STEP 1	STEP 2	STEP 3	STEP 4	STEP 5
Subject Selection	Subject Assignment	Pretest (Optional)	Treatment Period	Posttest

Step 1 Two types of procedures are used to select subjects for experiments—random selection (symbolized by "R-S") and nonrandom selection ("No R-S"). In random selection the population is carefully defined (e.g., "all first graders in the state of Missouri," or "all patients who are treated at emergency rooms in San Francisco hospitals during 1985"), and a probability sample from that population is selected to participate in the study. A specific technical procedure must be used to ensure random selection. All the members of the population must be listed and a table of random numbers used to select individuals from the population. These procedures almost always result in a representative and unbiased choice of subjects. In nonrandom selection the researcher may use volunteers or referrals or samples of convenience that are readily available to the researcher, such as pupils in the researcher's own class. The methods used to select a sample can determine whether the results of the experiment can be generalized from the subjects directly involved to some larger population.

Step 2 The essence of the true experiment is that two or more groups of individuals are formed, and each group experiences a different treatment condition. For example, in a study with two groups one might receive the treatment, and the other might be an untreated control group. Whether the two groups are equal prior to the treatment period is established by the method of assigning individual subjects to the two groups or treatment conditions. The method is either by random assignment (R-A) or nonrandom assignment ("No R-A").

Random assignment refers to a specific mechanical act performed by the researcher. Either a fair coin, a die, or a table of random numbers is used to make sure that the allocation of subjects to treatment conditions is determined by chance and not affected by the researcher's bias. In using a coin, for example, the researcher designates that when the coin comes up heads, the subject will be assigned to the treatment group, and when it comes up tails, the subject will be assigned to the untreated control group. For each available subject (whether selected by random or nonrandom methods), the researcher flips the coin and thus assigns that subject to either the treatment or the control group. The procedure results in an equitable distribution of subjects betweeen the two groups because the series of coin flips constitutes a series of independent events, governed by the laws of probability. The larger the sample is, the more likely the two groups will be comparable.

With random assignment a researcher can be fairly sure—*and can specify the probability*—that the two groups will be comparable. When the two groups are comparable at the outset of the experiment, any differences between them on the posttest larger than those expected by chance can be attributed to the independent variable (assuming no mortality or instrumentation threats exist). Random assignment of subjects to treatment conditions provides the utmost control over the independent variable and serves to discriminate true experiments from quasi experiments or causal-comparative studies.

Nonrandom assignment methods (No R-A) include matching, use of volunteers for treatment conditions, researcher judgment, and assignment of intact groups to treatment conditions. None of these methods insures that all subject characteristics that correlate with the dependent variable are distributed equally between the two groups. Each nonrandom method is subject to the nonequivalence threat to internal validity. For example, if the researchers assign subjects to treatment conditions based on personal judgment, there is no guarantee that they will not put the most favored ones into the treatment group and the least favored ones in the control group, thus biasing results in favor of the hypothesis. Or if a psychotherapy researcher assigns the first 25 volunteers to the treatment group and the next 25 to the control group, the two groups might be nonequivalent since the first to volunteer might be more motivated to seek treatment. Motivation for treatment is probably correlated with the dependent variable of mental health.

Step 3   The dependent variable is measured or observed before treatments are implemented. The act of pretesting can be denoted O_1. The pretest establishes a baseline for the status of the groups on the dependent variable prior to implementing the treatment. In studies where subjects are randomly assigned to groups, the pretest is unnecessary. The posttreatment measure of the dependent variable in the untreated group actually substitutes for a baseline or measure of where the treated group *would have* *been* if its members had not received the treatment. Moreover, the pretest may alert the subjects to the hypothesis of the study and therefore detract from the external validity of the study. On the other hand, the pretest may be a check on those rare occasions when random assignment fails to yield comparable groups. The pretest may also be used as a covariate to increase the statistical precision of the study or to control mortality as a threat to internal validity. In studies using nonrandom assignment, the pretest is extremely important as an indication (albeit imperfect) of the initial comparability of the two groups on the dependent variable.

Step 4 During the treatment period, the researcher introduces the treatment conditions to the groups formed in step two and makes sure that they are implemented as defined. The researcher controls the environment of the study so that every circumstance other than the treatment conditions is common to both groups ("held constant") and only the treatment conditions vary. For example, suppose that a researcher designs an experiment to determine the effects of study skills training on grade point average (GPA) of college freshmen. He has access to 50 students referred by their professors as needing remedial assistance (No R-S) and assigns 25 of them to a study skills training condition (X) and 25 to an untreated control group (No X). Assignment is by a random method (R-A), using a table of random numbers. The duration of the treatment is defined by the researcher (e.g., five hours per week for three weeks) as are the specific components of the study skills training. The researcher makes sure that each student in the treatment condition (X) experiences all components of the study skills training for the duration and intensity defined by the independent variable. Ideally, the subjects in the untreated control group (No X) are monitored to make sure they are given none of the components of the study skills training program. Thus systematic, experimental variance is maintained. Meanwhile, extraneous influences are avoided in so far as possible so that any subsequent difference between the two groups on the posttest can be attributed to the differences in treatment conditions.

The degree of control exercised over extraneous influences differs depending on whether the study is a **laboratory experiment** or **field experiment**. The study skills training experiment is an example of a field experiment, because the subjects carry on with their lives as usual except for the training they receive. Laboratory experiments involve short-term treatments that are implemented in isolated settings where the independent variable can be closely monitored and extraneous influences controlled. In field experiments, an aspect of the treatment may interact with some extraneous influence in the environment, producing unpredictable results. For example, a component of the study skills training program (teaching subjects to identify main points in textbooks) may confuse the subjects, and some of them may then seek additional help from a tutor during hours when they are not directly monitored by the researcher. The tutoring may serve as a catalyst for those students to improve their GPAs. Thus the change in GPA is falsely attributed by the researcher to the study skills package, when in fact a combination of study skills training plus tutoring was responsible for the change. In a laboratory experiment this contamination of the treatment effects with extraneous influences could be prevented. In laboratory experiments with animals, for example, researchers make sure that environmental circumstances such as the color of the maze, the temperature of the room, and the time of day the subjects are treated have no impact on the results of the study.

If a psychologist suspects that subjects in a paired-associate learning experiment perform better in the morning than the afternoon, she can do one of two things: (a) implement all treatments during mornings only, thus controlling this extraneous variable; or (b) randomly assign subjects to morning or afternoon treatments (thus creating systematic variance in the time of treatment) and testing the difference in learning between subjects in the two time periods.

Field experimenters need to be alert to the various extraneous influences that can intrude and should endeavor to approximate the kinds of control used in laboratory experiments. The longer the study, the greater are the chances for contamination. On the other side, the more tightly controlled a laboratory study is, the more artificial its conditions are, and the more difficult it is to generalize beyond the laboratory.

In the study skills training example just given, a single treatment condition (X) was contrasted with an untreated control condition (No X). Other comparisons among treatment conditions are possible, such as one treatment (X_1) compared to an alternative treatment (X_2). In an experiment testing the hypothesis that study skills training is more effective than test-anxiety reduction therapy in improving academic performance, a researcher might use three groups, one given study skills training (X_1), one given anxiety reduction therapy (X_2), and one placed in a wait list control group (No X). Other configurations of treatment conditions can be readily imagined.

Step 5   At the end of the treatment period, the dependent variable is measured on the posttest (O_2 or O if no other testing occasion is to occur) within each group. More than one variable can be measured at this time (in the study skills training experiment perhaps GPA, attitude about college, and dropout rate all constitute different measures of the effect of the treatment). Follow-up measures of one or more dependent measures may also extend the experiment and would be designated O_3, O_4, and so on, with the subscripts representing each subsequent occasion for measuring the effect of the treatment. Differences among the groups on the posttest (and follow-up measures) are subjected to inferential tests of statistical

TABLE 6–2   Representation of Steps in an Experiment

STEP 1	STEP 2	STEP 3	STEP 4	STEP 5
Subject Selection	Subject Assignment	Pretest	Treatment Period	Posttest
R-S (or No R-S)	R-A (or No R-A)	O_1 (or no pretest)	X_1 vs. X_2 (or) No-X	O_2

significance (see Chapter 3). Barring threats to internal validity, the significant differences in means can be attributed to differences in the treatment conditions experienced by the groups.

The steps in the experimental process are symbolically represented in Table 6–2.

In the study skills training experiment, the subjects were selected by referrals from professors, randomly assigned to two treatment conditions, received no pretest, and were treated and posttested as illustrated in Figure 6–1.

Consider another example, this time a laboratory experiment to determine the effect of the presence of a picture that illustrates some aspect of a story on the ability of children to remember the details of that story. The subjects are randomly selected from the population of first graders in Belleview School District. They are randomly assigned to one of two treatment conditions—picture present (X_1) or picture absent (X_2). They are pretested on vocabulary knowledge. Each subject is treated individually. The same story is presented to each subject in both conditions. Each subject is given the same instructions to read the story silently so that he or she can answer questions about it later. The amount of time allowed for reading the story is controlled. For subjects in X_1, the experimenter displays the picture with the story. Subjects in X_2 see only the written text of the story. After the reading period is over, the children go to another room where experimenters who are not informed about which treatment condition the children experienced administer the posttest. The test is administered orally and individually to each subject. No follow-up assessment is conducted. This design can be depicted graphically as in Figure 6–2.

FIGURE 6–1
Representation of Study Skills Experiment

$$\text{No R-S} \rightarrow \text{R-A} \begin{array}{cc} \nearrow X & O \\ \searrow \text{No } X & O \end{array}$$

FIGURE 6–2
Representation of Text-Embedded Picture Experiment

$$\text{R-S} \rightarrow \text{R-A} \begin{array}{ccc} \nearrow O_1 & X_1 & O_2 \\ \searrow O_1 & X_2 & O_2 \end{array}$$

Five Varieties of True Experiment

The most familiar case of the true experiment is the *randomized, pretest-posttest, control group design*. Subjects are selected by either random or non-random (volunteer, referral, convenience) methods. They are assigned at random to two or more treatment conditions and are pretested. The treatment is implemented and the dependent variable measured. The three conditions for establishing cause and effect are met if there is a significant difference between the means on the posttest. The researcher has controlled temporal sequence by testing, then introducing the treatment and holding everything else constant, then testing again. Alternative explanations are ruled out because of random assignment, assuming that few subjects drop out of the study and no instrumentation problems exist.

The second variety of true experiment is the same as the first except that the pretest is eliminated. This is called the *randomized, posttest only, control group design*.

The third variety is the *Solomon Four-Group Design*, which tests the effect of the pretest on the subject's subsequent performance on the posttest. Available subjects are randomly assigned to one of four groups, as represented in Figure 6–3. Two of the groups are pretested and two are not. By looking at the differences between pairs of means, one can assess the effect of treatment, the practice effect of testing, and the interaction of test and treatment (i.e., how the pretest may sensitize the subject to the coming treatment).

The fourth variety of true experiment is the *factorial experiment with more than one independent variable*. Consider an elaboration of the experiment on text-embedded pictures. The researcher hypothesizes that pictures enhance memory for story details and that reading silently as opposed to aloud also enhances such memory in children. A two-factor experiment is designed with two independent variables. The first factor is the picture factor, comparing the treatment conditions of picture present (X_1) and picture absent (X_2). The second factor is reading silently (Y_1) versus reading aloud (Y_2). The available subjects are randomly assigned to one of four groups: (1) picture present, reading silently (X_1Y_1); (2) picture present, reading aloud (X_1Y_2); (3) picture absent, reading silently (X_2Y_1); or (4) picture absent, reading aloud (X_2Y_2). All subjects are pretested on vocabulary knowledge, administered their assigned treatment condition individ-

$$\text{No R-S} \rightarrow \text{R-A} \begin{array}{ccc} \nearrow O_1 & X_1 & O_2 \\ \nearrow O_1 & \text{No-}X & O_2 \\ \searrow & X_1 & O_2 \\ \searrow & \text{No }X & O_2 \end{array}$$

FIGURE 6–3
Representation of the Solomon Four-Group Design

FIGURE 6–4
Representation of Factorial Experiment with Two
Independent Variables

$$R\text{-}S \to R\text{-}A \begin{array}{ccc} \nearrow O_1 & X_1Y_1 & O_2 \\ \nearrow O_1 & X_1Y_2 & O_2 \\ \searrow O_1 & X_2Y_1 & O_2 \\ \searrow O_1 & X_2Y_2 & O_2 \end{array}$$

ually, and posttested on memory for story details. This design is represented in Figure 6–4. By using a two-factor ANOVA, the researcher can test the separate *main effects* of the two independent variables as well as the interaction between them (whether certain combinations of treatment conditions aid or inhibit memory over and above the separate effects of the independent variables). Other statistical tests that could be used with this design are ANCOVA and repeated measures ANOVA).

The fifth variety of true experiment involves *one or more independent variables plus one or more moderator variables*. A moderator variable is a subject, task, or method characteristic that can be used as a factor in an experiment along with the independent variable of interest. The moderator variable is systematically varied to determine whether it interacts with the independent variable. For example, the researcher might hypothesize that text-embedded pictures aid the memory for story details of 6-year-olds but not 7-year-olds. Thus age (a subject characteristic) is used as a moderator variable. The 6- and 7-year-olds, drawn at random from a population, are first classified into two groups according to their age (represented as C-A, for "classified by age"). The 6-year-old group is then randomly assigned to either the picture present (X_1) or picture absent (X_2) treatment condition. The group of 7-year-olds are likewise randomly assigned to X_1 or X_2. The design is represented in Figure 6–5. An ANOVA can determine the main effect of the picture as well as the interaction of the picture with the age of the subjects. Task characteristics and method characteristics can also be used as moderator variables in this variety of experiment.

EXTERNAL VALIDITY

In an attempt to establish cause-and-effect relationships, the researcher is confronted with this task: to observe a statistical difference between two

FIGURE 6–5
Representation of Experiment with a
Moderator Variable

$$R\text{-}S \to C\text{-}A \begin{array}{c} \nearrow \\ \searrow \end{array}$$

$$\text{Age 1} \to R\text{-}A \begin{array}{ccc} \nearrow O_1 & X_1 & O_2 \\ \searrow O_1 & X_2 & O_2 \end{array}$$

$$\text{Age 2} \to R\text{-}A \begin{array}{ccc} \nearrow O_1 & X_1 & O_2 \\ \searrow O_1 & X_2 & O_2 \end{array}$$

or more groups on the dependent variable and to infer that that difference was caused by the independent variable. This is the issue of internal validity. However, having established that the difference is due to the treatment, the researcher is confronted with another task: to infer that the effect observed in the experiment would also be observed in broader contexts. Would the same effect be obtained with individuals other than those who participated directly as subjects in the experiment? Would the same effect be obtained in other settings, say, outside the laboratory or particular place where the study was done? Would other experimenters find the same effect? If another researcher defined the independent or dependent variable slightly differently, would the same effect be obtained, or is the experimental effect limited to the persons, settings, and operations that this particular researcher used? These are the issues of *external validity*. How far can the experimental effect be generalized? What are the limits on generalization of the study findings?

Population External Validity

The first consideration of external validity is whether the results of a study generalize to some population of individuals. Are the results true for just the sample of subjects who participated, or true for a broader group of persons? There are two ways this question can be addressed. First, if the researcher has employed the *random selection* method of drawing a sample from a defined population of individuals, then statistical and probability arguments can be used to infer that what was found in the sample is also likely to be true of the population from which the sample was drawn. If random methods were used, such as a table of random numbers, the selection would be an unbiased representation of the population. The subject characteristics of the sample would differ from the subject characteristics of the population only by the amount of statistical error specified in the sampling procedure. Therefore, the effect observed in the experiment—that is, the mean difference between experimental and control groups on the dependent variable—would likely have been found if a different random sample had been chosen or if the population as a whole had been directly involved in the experiment.

The method of random selection insures **population external validity** from the sample to the population from which the sample was chosen. The population from which the sample is drawn (by probability methods) has a special name, the **accessible population**, to distinguish it from the **target population**, which is an ideal group to which the researcher would like the findings to apply. If a researcher studied the effect of text-embedded pictures on the recall of stories by first graders, she might like her findings to apply to all first graders across the country. This is the target population of her study. Because she lacks the resources to list and draw at random from among all first graders, she gains access to the first graders of Belle-view School District. These constitute the accessible population (sometimes called the *sampled population*), from which she can select a random sample. After she has performed the experiment and found an effect in the sample, she may generalize the effect to the accessible population. Generalizing to the target population, however, is a different matter.

In experimental research, random selection is infrequently used to choose samples. More often samples are chosen because certain people volunteer or are volunteered by someone who controls their time, because they are referred to the experiment based on their perceived need for the treatment, or because they are readily accessible to the researcher. You have probably participated in psychological experiments because such participation is a required part of many undergraduate psychology classes. Members of university communities often volunteer for experiments because payment is promised. Or graduate students gain access to certain high schools to conduct their experiments because they know the principals of those schools and can convince them of the value of the studies. It should be clear that such samples are not strictly representative, in the statistical sense, of many target populations. Volunteers, whether paid or unpaid, may have characteristics that are different from nonvolunteers. If so, the effect observed in the experiment may not hold true for people more generally. Teachers and principals who permit pupils in their charge to be subjects of experiments may have the most advantaged children and be eager to display their advantage. The experimental effect observed in those advantaged classes may not be representative of typical classes that span the range of abilities and opportunities.

The second basis for population external validity involves description and judgment. Even though a sample in an experiment was not selected at random, it may still be typical of some larger group of individuals. But the researcher is obliged to describe the subject characteristics of the sample as completely as possible. What was their age, their intellectual ability, gender, socioeconomic level, motivation to participate in the study? If the researcher provides these data, along with any clues about how the sample might have been atypical, then the reader can make an informed judgment about similarities of the sample and the **target population**, or ideal group to which the experimental effect might generalize. Lacking a statistical basis for generalizing the result (as would have been available if random sample selection had been used), the reader of the study must make a different kind of inference, namely, that the findings of the study might generalize to individuals similar to the ones in the sample.

If the researcher has sampled at random from an accessible population, generalizing from the sample to the accessible population is based on probability and statistics. Generalizing from the accessible population to the target population, however, is based on careful description and judgment. In the earlier example the researcher must describe the characteristics of Belleview School District, so the reader can make a judgment of how similar its pupils and circumstances are to a wider group of districts, to see how far the results may be generalized. Judgments of similarity are just that—personal judgments. Some readers of a study will assert that the findings do not generalize beyond the sample (a very conservative and perhaps futile stance), while others will claim broad generalizability. Unlike internal validity, which can sometimes be established fairly well by techniques of experimentation, external validity can never be settled finally and objectively.

Noncomparability threat to external validity   Campbell and Stanley (1963) and Bracht and Glass (1968) enumerated threats to the external validity of studies. Threats limit the generalizability of the effects of a particular study. The first is the **noncomparability** threat—that is, a lack of comparability between the sample or the accessible population and the target population. For example, sophomore psychology students required to participate in faculty experiments on short-term memory may not be comparable to the target population of English-speaking adults. If the college selects students based on above-average admission test scores, and the abilities tapped by such admission tests correlate with short-term memory, then the possible limitation on generalization is apparent. We might judge that such findings generalize to sophomore college students of abilities and social class similar to those involved in the study (Rosenthal and Rosnow, 1975).

Interaction of subject characteristics and treatment   The second threat to population external validity comes about when the effect of the treatment is limited to individuals with certain subject characteristics. For example, Figure 6–5 illustrates such a set of circumstances, where the effect of text-embedded pictures was thought to be limited to 6-year-olds. The generalizability of the effect was not unconditional, but was confined to one age group. Thus, age is a subject characteristic that interacts with and limits the generalizability of the treatment effect of text-embedded pictures. Factorial experiments using moderator variables reveal such **interactions of subject characteristics and treatment**. When factorial experiments fail to yield significant interactions between independent variables and moderator variables, the generalizability of the study is said to be enhanced.

Ecological External Validity

Generalizing the experimental effect to broader groups of individuals is only one aspect of external validity. Even with comparability of sample and target population guaranteed, other features of the study may limit generalizations from it. A second broad class of threats to external validity has to do with the setting, or *ecology*, in which the study takes place, hence the term **ecological external validity**. Experimental studies have physical and social contexts that may restrict their generalization.

Noncomparability of research setting to natural setting   To gain better control over extraneous variables, researchers will often conduct their studies in special environments. In the experiment on text-embedded pictures, for example, the researcher employed experimenters who took the subjects individually to a quiet room, free from distractions such as pictures on the wall or announcements on the intercom; there the treatment was administered and the dependent variable measured. It is uncertain whether the effect obtained in this special environment would be obtained in the regular classroom. Would the advantage of the pictures (if such were found in the experiment) be sustained in the noise and bustle of the classroom? After all, educational researchers want their findings to make a difference in a natural setting, not in a laboratory or other special place. There are many sound reasons for conducting studies in antiseptic surroundings: to achieve control over the extraneous influences on the dependent variable of noise, temperature, distractions, and the like. Such control often enhances internal validity. However, external validity is thereby threatened. Perhaps after a particular treatment has been thoroughly investigated in the laboratory, the time comes for trying it out in natural settings.

Demand characteristics   Considerable evidence has accumulated to show that people in experiments alter their behavior to conform to perceived expectations about what is proper and appropriate behavior for subjects of scientific research studies (Orne, 1969; Rosnow and Davis, 1977). In other words, a social context for research exists, what some have called "the culture of the experiment." Instead of revealing their true and typical behavior, people often act like "good subjects," ascertain what the research hypothesis predicts, and behave accordingly. To guess the purpose of the research, the subject uses cues in the setting, as well as hearsay about the study, the content of pretests, clearance forms that establish informed consent, experimental procedures, and instructions given by the experimenter. Subjects may also guess the direction of the hypothesis and act in the opposite way. In either case, the results of the study will have been distorted. The cues in the environment to which subjects react are referred to as **demand characteristics**, or **reactive arrangements**, and include anything that alerts the subjects to the purposes of the study or to just being in a study (special rooms, experimenters in white coats, testing apparatus). Demand characteristics constitute a threat to external validity because the results of the study do not generalize beyond the culture of the experiment. Back in his natural habitat and no longer part of the scientific enterprise, the subject acts naturally and perhaps quite unlike how he acted in the study. Readers of research studies should be alert for indications that demand characteristics might have affected the results and limited their generalizability. Producers of research have been provided with suggestions (see Rosnow and Davis, 1977) for reducing demand characteristics (e.g., reduce chances of communication between subject and experimenter).

Hawthorne effect   As a threat to the ecological validity of a study, the **Hawthorne effect** is a special case of demand characteristics. It is named after the Hawthorne studies of worker productivity in the Western Electric Company. The investigators wanted to know whether raising the level of light in the workplace increased productivity. A relationship was found, but further study revealed that *any* subsequent intervention, including lowering the light, also increased productivity. The investigators concluded that the workers' productivity was increased not by the light, but by the knowledge that they were in a study and had been singled out for special attention. The improvement subjects show during an experiment may be caused by the feeling of special handling rather than by the independent variable itself. Hawthorne effects are easily mistaken for treatment effects. The problem for external validity is that the results of the study would not generalize to the natural setting where no study is being conducted and the clients or workers have no reason to feel specially treated.

Novelty and disruption effects   The introduction of new programs in schools and agencies is frequently accompanied by the demand that the program be evaluated. Students or clients are pretested, the new program is introduced, sometimes with the teachers or service providers learning the program as they go along. Then, at the end of the cycle, the posttest is given. Treated and control groups are compared and found to be different on the dependent variable. But the cause of the difference may be not so much the program itself but the enthusiasm and high morale that sometimes accompanies *new* programs. This is the **novelty effect**. Novelty threatens external validity because the results of the study are unlikely to replicate if the study were to be repeated in the second year of the program, after the novelty wears off. The generalizability of the treatment effect, therefore, is limited in that it was really due to the novelty of the program rather than to the program itself.

The opposite result comes from the **disruption effect**, which can occur when the service providers are unfamiliar with the material or equipment involved in the new program and use it ineffectively. The evaluator who conducts an experiment in the early stages of such a program is likely to find negative results, but the results may be due not to the program but to start-up problems. Conducting the study during the second or third year of the program might yield different results.

External Validity of Operations

Operations are the specific techniques used by the experimenter to conduct the study, define the independent and dependent variables, implement the experimental procedures, and measure the change in the dependent variable. Would the same pattern of results turn up if a different experimenter were conducting the study, using slightly different operations? This question concerns the **external validity of operations**.

Experimenter effects   The external validity of a study may be limited by **experimenter effects**. That is, some experimenters, by virtue of their charm and energy, may motivate their research subjects to perform particularly well (thus distorting the typical level of the subject's motivation). Experimenters (the persons who actually interact with the subjects) sometimes provide more help and encouragement than was prescribed by the researcher. In such a case the effect of the study may not generalize beyond the individual experimenter or beyond experimenters with similar characteristics. Experimenter effects are sometimes mistaken for treatment effects. Worse still, Rosenthal (1966) demonstrated that experimenters generate expectations about how research subjects should perform (i.e., those in the experimental groups will do better than those in the control group) and act so as to fulfill these expectations. If this happens, the results of the study will be biased toward confirmation of the hypothesis.

Task effects   Any experimental treatment is made up of many tasks, procedures, and materials. Consider again the study of text-embedded pictures. At a certain time of day an experimenter comes to the classroom of a pupil who is a subject, calls his name, and escorts him to the laboratory where the treatment will be administered. The experimenter provides him with instructions and urges him to do his best. The story is presented to him in the form of a printed booklet. Then there is the story itself: its content, structure, appeal, length, the length of its words and sentences, and the familiarity of its vocabulary. The picture used to illustrate the story—whether it is in color or black and white, a photograph or a drawing—is another task characteristic. Perhaps a tape recorder or camera is used to record the events. The experimenter presents specific probes for the subject to retell the story. There is a collection of components and any one of them may be responsible for the effect observed on the posttest. In other words, **task effects** may be influencing the results. Would the same posttest difference be found if any one of these tasks were varied? This is one pressing question about external validity. The most obvious task effect is that of the story. The researcher hypothesizes that text-embedded pictures enhance children's ability to recall stories, not just the particular story used as a task in this experiment, but *stories in general*. If the researcher only uses one story in the study and finds a significant effect of text-embedded pictures, one cannot be sure that this particular story (or this particular picture) was not responsible for the effect. The effect may not generalize to other stories but may have been due to some characteristics of the story used; some passages are simply more "visual" than others.

Another aspect of a task effect is paramount when teachers or therapists deliver the treatment. Suppose that clients seeking family counseling are randomly assigned to two treatment conditions, one to receive psychodynamic therapy from therapist A and the other to receive behavior modification from therapist B. A significant difference is found in favor of the behavior modification group. However, one cannot be sure it was the treatment itself that was responsible for the effect. Rather, the effect might have been due to the special charisma or skill of therapist B. In the language of experimentation, the therapist (a task characteristic) is *confounded* with the treatment. The problem for external validity is that one cannot generalize the results of this experiment to other instances of behavior modification for family therapy (unless Therapist B happened to be presiding).

Readers of research studies should look for indications that the investigator systematically varied task characteristics (e.g., using more than one service provider and making sure that the same effects were obtained from each) or carefully standardized and described the tasks and task characteristics of the study. Then the reader can estimate whether task effects limited the generalizability of the results.

Definition of the independent variable   An ambiguously or poorly defined independent variable is a threat to the external validity of the experiment. If the researcher defined the independent variable as "commitment to a residential facility," the reader cannot be sure exactly what the subjects actually experienced. Even simple independent variables should be described fully so that those who wish to apply the results have some chance of doing so successfully.

A related problem is whether the same effect would be obtained if the independent variable was altered slightly. Research is the search for general knowledge. The search is impeded if what is called "individualized instruction" works well in one manifestation and not in another (unless researchers can specify the characteristics of the manifestations that work well). One would like to know whether the same effect would be obtained if the treatment were of longer or shorter duration, of greater or lesser intensity, implemented by a graduate student rather than a teacher, and the like. If individual teachers alter the defined independent variable, perhaps by tailoring a packaged curriculum to their special circumstances, is the treatment robust enough to demonstrate an effect? The problem for external validity is whether the experimental effect would still be obtained if the operational definition of the independent variable were altered.

Placebo effects   A placebo is a treatment that, according to the theory of the phenomenon, should not have an effect on the dependent variable. In medical research, the placebo is a drug that is chemically inactive and therefore ought not to produce an effect like that of the drug. Placebos are used in medical or psychiatric experiments as a way of assessing the effect of receiving attention and concern from a service provider or the expectation of becoming better through chemical means. These are **placebo effects** and need to be separated out from true treatment effects in formulating generalizable knowledge about the treatment itself.

Experiments in educational and social research are also susceptible to placebo effects. Suppose that a researcher wanted to investigate the effect of training in cognitive self-monitoring on the impulsive behaviors of hyperactive boys. The training of a randomly constituted group shows a significant decrease in impulsive behaviors as compared to an untreated control group. The study is internally valid because the two groups were randomly constituted and one group received the treatment while the other did not (differential mortality, instrumentation problems, and other threats are also judged to be unlikely). However, members of the treated group benefited, in addition to the treatment, from adult attention and concern and by their and their mothers' expectation that they would get better. In other words, the treated group received both the training in self-monitoring and the placebo condition in combination. The responsibility for the effect lies not only with the treatment per se but with everything else that happened to the treatment group between the times of the pretest and posttest.

In a sense, the treatment is like a black box or package. Inside the box are the components of the treatment along with the events that happen to occur in conjunction with it, including the interactions between the subjects and the experimenter or service provider, and interactions among the subjects. It is the task of the researcher to open up the box to determine which elements are responsible for the observed effect. Providing a placebo condition in addition to an untreated control condition in an experiment is a useful step. Suppose that our researcher randomly assigned available subjects to three groups: self-monitoring training, placebo, and untreated control. Those in the placebo condition would be given attention, concern, and encouragement to improve, but no specific training. By comparing the means of the self-monitoring training group with the placebo group, the researcher has some better idea about the effect of the treatment over and above that of the attention and expectation for improvement. Two cautions must be mentioned, however. First, the experimenters who measure the dependent variable must be unable to guess which group each subject is in; that is, they must be "blinded." The subjects must not be aware that they are in a placebo group, otherwise they will generate negative expectations for improvement. Second, the researcher must make sure the placebo is plausible, that it instills feelings of potential benefit. Some researchers put up placebo conditions as straw men against which favorite treatments are sure to appear effective.

Definition of the dependent variable   The external validity of a study can be threatened by an ambiguously and poorly defined dependent variable. If the dependent variable is something like "therapist judgment of patient improvement" or "teacher estimate of pupil's working up to his potential," the possibility of replicating the effect is lessened. A second researcher would not recognize the outcome if he saw it, since it was so vague in the first instance. A careful operational definition and description of the operations and procedures used to measure the dependent variable are necessary for the external validity of the study.

A related problem is whether the same effect would be obtained if the measurement of the dependent variable was altered slightly. Suppose, for example, a researcher hypothesizes that biofeedback training decreases test anxiety and confirms this hypothesis when the dependent variable is measured by a self-report questionnaire. Would the same conclusions be reached if the researcher measured the dependent variable with galvanic skin response, by the client's performance on achievement tests given by the experimenter, or on actual tests taken in college courses? Each of these constitutes an alternative operation for defining and measuring the same construct, test anxiety. Good external validity would be demonstrated if the same effect was obtained on *each* measure of the dependent variable. External validity is threatened if some measures yield effects and others do not.

Interaction of treatment and time of measurement   Most experimenters measure the dependent variable immediately after the treatment period has ended. Finding an effect then, can the experimenter generalize that effect to subsequent times? Follow-up testing is needed to insure that the effect was lasting or to establish the rate or pattern of decay of the effect. If the researcher measures the effect twice, finds more of an effect at one time and less of an effect at the other, there is said to be an **interaction of treatment and time of measurement** that threatens external validity.

Pretest sensitization   Pretests, particularly of attitude or personality measures, can alert the subjects to the content of the treatment and possibly to the hypothesis of the study. For example, an inventory of self-esteem given to pupils who are about to engage in a values clarification program contains some indication about the goals of the program. When the group leaders begin to introduce topics such as, "How your image of yourself influences your decisions," the pupils have an awareness of the importance of the topic that they might not have had without the preliminary inventory. That is, **pretest sensitization occurs**. The pretest acts in combination with the treatment to produce an effect that might not have occurred with the treatment alone. The effect of the treatment cannot be generalized to values clarification programs in general unless such programs are preceded by a pretest. The pretest sensitization threat to external validity is different from the testing threat to internal validity. The latter refers to the situation where the test alone causes the gain on the posttest, independent of the treatment. The pretest sensitization threat means that the pretest and treatment acted in combination to produce an effect that cannot be generalized to similar, nonpretested treatments.

CRITERIA FOR JUDGING EXPERIMENTAL STUDIES

The following questions should be asked when judging the merits of an experimental study.

1. Were the methods for selecting the subjects clearly described? If random methods were not used, have the sample, accessible population, and target population been sufficiently described so that the reader can make judgments about population external validity?

2. Have the methods for assigning subjects to treatment conditions been described so that the reader can judge whether the methods were random, or if not, how serious the problem of nonequivalence is?

3. Have the treatment conditions been adequately described so that another researcher could replicate the study? This description should extend to the characteristics of setting, tasks, service deliverers, and procedures and operations of the study itself.

4. Is the treatment of sufficient intensity and duration that an effect can reasonably be expected? Is the sample size large enough to reveal statistically significant effects for theoretically significant treatments?

5. Is there indication of attrition of subjects from the study? If there is differential mortality from different groups, has there been any attempt to control for its effect?

6. Is there any indication that the independent variable has been diffused to the untreated or placebo groups?

7. Has there been any control over whether the independent variable has actually been implemented as the researcher specified?

8. Has the dependent variable been reliably and validity measured? Are instrumentation threats controlled? Has blinding been employed, if necessary? Have different measures of the dependent variable been used and have measurements been taken at any time other than immediately after the end of the treatment period?

9. Have demand characteristics, novelty, disruption, Hawthorne, experimenter, placebo, and task effects and pretest sensitization been controlled or adequately described so that the reader can judge the limitations on generalizability?

SUGGESTED READINGS

BARBER, T.X. Pitfalls in research: Nine investigator and experimenter effects. In R.M.W. Travers (Ed.), *Second handbook of research on teaching.* Chicago: Rand McNally, 1973.

CAMPBELL, D.T., and STANLEY, J.C. *Experimental and quasi-experimental designs for research on teaching.* In N.L. Gage (Ed.), *Handbook of research on teaching.* Chicago: Rand McNally, 1963.

COOK, T.D., and CAMPBELL, D.T. *Quasi-experimentation: Design and analysis issues for field studies.* Chicago: Rand McNally, 1979.

CRONBACH, L.J. *Designing evaluations of educational and social programs.* San Francisco: Jossey-Bass, 1982.

KEPPEL, G. *Design and analysis: A researcher's handbook* (2nd ed.). Englewood Cliffs, N.J.: Prentice-Hall, 1982.

ROSENTHAL, R., and ROSNOW, R.L. (Eds.) *Artifact in behavioral research.* New York: Academic Press, 1969.

TERMS INTRODUCED IN THIS CHAPTER

rival hypothesis
extraneous variable
internal validity
threat to internal validity
history
confound
maturation
testing
instrumentation
nonequivalence
regression
mortality
nonequivalence by maturation
   interaction
nonequivalence by regression
   interaction
matching
treatment fidelity
John Henry effect
treatment diffusion
true experiments
quasi experiments

causal-comparative study
laboratory experiment
field experiment
population external validity
accessible population
target population
noncomparability threat
interaction of subject characteristics
   and treatment
ecological external validity
demand characteristics
reactive arrangements
Hawthorne effect
novelty effect
disruption effect
external validity of operations
experimenter effects
task effects
placebo effects
interaction of treatment and time of
   measurement
pretest sensitization

QUESTIONS AND EXERCISES FOR FURTHER STUDY

1. Random selection is to _____ validity as random assignment is to _____ validity.

2. State in your own words the three conditions that must be demonstrated for a researcher to establish that a cause-and-effect relationship exists between two variables. Apply these three conditions specifically to the conclusion, "A child's intellectual aptitude is affected by the number of children in the family."

3. A researcher conducted a study of the relationship between stress and participation in aerobic exercise. She selected a sample of girls from a college freshman psychology class and administered a questionnaire to them. Among the items on the questionnaire was one concerning the degree of stress they felt at the present time and another that asked the number of times they participated in some forms of aerobic exercise in a typical week. The researcher found a significant difference in amount of stress perceived by girls who reported frequent aerobic exercise compared to girls who reported no aerobic exercise (t-test, $p < 0.05$). The researcher concluded that "aerobic exercise reduces stress." Identify the independent and dependent variables in this study. Is the causal claim warranted? Explain.

4. In 1976 the Colorado Legislature revoked a law that had required motorcycle riders to wear helmets. In 1977 motorcycle accidents with head injuries increased 25 percent. The Attorney General concluded that the increase in head injuries had been caused by the change in the helmet law. Is the causal claim warranted? Explain.

5. A rival hypothesis is the same as a _____ to internal validity.

6. Explain in your own words why random assignment of subjects to two treatments controls the nonequivalence threat to internal validity better than if the two groups were matched on some important variable.

7. Consider the following symbolic representation of a research design. The independent variable is reading instruction and the two treatments are phonics method and look-say method. Translate these symbols into a step-by-step description of the design.

$$\text{No R-S} \rightarrow \text{R-A} \nearrow \begin{array}{cccc} O_1 & X_1 & O_2 & O_3 \\ O_1 & X_2 & O_2 & O_3 \end{array}$$

8. Is the example in question 7 a true experiment, quasi experiment, or causal-comparative study? State how one can tell the difference between these three types of research.

9. What is the most effective way of controlling for the history or maturation threats to internal validity?

10. A study in which a standardized pencil-and-paper test was used to measure the dependent variable before and after the treatment is *unlikely* to be subject to the _____ threat to internal validity.

11. What threat(s) to internal validity cannot be controlled by random assignment?

12. An evaluator wants to study the effect of an enrichment program on the very brightest gifted children in a large school district. He administers an adult intelligence test to all ninth-graders and selects the 50 pupils with the highest scores. These 50 complete the six-month program and are retested. The evaluator announces that the program actually had a negative impact on the participants, for their scores on the posttest were lower than their initial scores. This conclusion fails to consider what threat to internal validity?

13. What procedures might the evaluator use to control for the obvious threat to internal validity in question 12?

14. Consider the following abstract of a study: To test the effect of microcomputer use on creativity, a researcher selected 50 pupils at random from all third graders enrolled in Kissinger Elementary School. He divided them into two equal groups based on their teachers' judgments of their academic ability. From within each group the researcher assigned, by a coin flip, half to a microcomputer use group and half to a control group. No pretest was given. At the end of six months time, the treatment was terminated and all subjects were given the Torrance Test of Divergent Thinking. Results showed that the microcomputer use group had significantly higher scores on the posttest, as compared to the control group. After an additional three months' time, all subjects were again tested. This time the means of the two groups were not significantly different. There was no interaction between the treatment and initial math ability at either time of testing.
    a. Provide the symbolic representation of this design.
    b. Describe the specific ways in which requirements for cause and effect were satisfied.
    c. What kind of variable is initial math ability?
    d. Identify the independent and dependent variables.
    e. Suggest a conclusion appropriate to the findings of the study.
    f. Identify the accessible population and the target population for the study.
    g. Discuss the purpose of random selection in the design.
    h. Discuss the purpose of random assignment in the design.
    i. List seven issues related to the external validity of the study.

15. Suppose the study above was reviewed by a panel of educational experts. Each of the following criticisms reflects a threat to the validity of the conclusion. Categorize each statement according to the threat it represents. Indicate whether the threat is external (population, ecological, operations) or internal and, if enough information is available, whether the criticism is warranted or not.
    a. "The same result would not have been observed if the researcher had used the Jones Creativity Test."
    b. "Creativity was enhanced, not because of the treatment, but because of the increased publicity given to microcomputers in our society."
    c. "Research shows that everybody's creativity increases naturally as they get older."
    d. "The treatment group was just more creative than the control group at the beginning of the study."
    e. "Boys may be more likely to increase their creativity by use of microcomputers, but girls' creativity is diminished by microcomputers."
    f. "The particular microcomputer program and system you chose are not powerful enough to make a lasting effect on creativity. If you had used a Plum System instead of a Pear System, the results would have been different."
    g. "The teachers and pupils knew they were in a special treatment, so the results were bound to be positive."
    h. "Everyone familiar with Kissinger Elementary School knows that it has unusually able pupils."
    i. "The researcher wanted to confirm his pet theory, so he probably gave the treatment group extra help and encouragement on the posttest. An impartial researcher would not have obtained the same results."
    j. "The sample size was too small to yield meaningful results."

k.   "The teacher who administered the treatment may have been a superior teacher who would get good results no matter what the experimental treatment was."

16. Find the article entitled, "Fieldwork in Geography and Long-term Memory Structures," by Mackenzie and White (*American Educational Research Journal*, 1982, Vol. 19, No. 4, pp. 623–632). Read it carefully and respond to the following.
   a.   How do you determine whether this study was looking for causes and effects?
   b.   What type of study is this and how can you tell?
   c.   There is one independent variable and two moderator variables in this study. Identify them.
   d.   Represent the design of the study in the symbolic notation introduced in this chapter.
   e.   Review the theory from which the hypothesis was deduced.
   f.   What was the method of data analysis used?
   g.   Interpret the finding that the difference on the achievement test due to the instructional treatment was significant. Look at Table I to see the means for each treatment group. Notice the authors' statements about the practical significance of some of the findings.
   h.   How would you respond to the criticism that the three groups were not equivalent at the outset of the study?
   i.   What do you make of the lack of pretest in this design in terms of both internal and external validity?
   j.   Discuss the population external validity of this study.
   k.   Is the interaction of treatment and time of testing a threat to external validity? Discuss this issue.
   l.   What are possible task effects in this study?
   m.   What do you make of the fact that "all teaching was done by the first author" (p. 628)?
   n.   How easy would it be to replicate the study?

7

QUASI-EXPERIMENTAL STUDIES

The term quasi experiment (*quasi* meaning "seemingly, but not genuinely") is used to describe studies in which the purpose is to established a cause-and-effect relationship between an independent variable and a dependent variable, but the assignment of subjects to treatment conditions is not at random (Cook and Campbell, 1979). Suppose, for example, the governor assigns a policy analyst in a state's department of education the task of determining the effect of a new program for the mentally retarded. According to federal law, any child who is handicapped must be served, and the educational program must be funded by the state. Confronted with these legal restrictions, the analyst would have no comparable group of retarded individuals who are unserved; hence, random assignment to "treatment and control" conditions would be impossible. Another example is the researcher who wants to study a new state law requiring motorcyclists to wear helmets to determine whether this law results in fewer head injuries in accidents. What is the relevant comparison? Using either the previous accident rate or the accident rate of the adjacent states exposes the causal hypothesis to threats of history and nonequivalence. Or take the case of a social program that provides rent subsidies to those welfare recipients with the greatest financial need. Finding comparable groups is difficult, and random assignment to treatment conditions is particularly unacceptable. Such is the case for most evaluation and field research studies. Indeed, many interesting and policy-relevant questions do not lend themselves to the use of random assignment to treatment conditions.

In Chapter 6, random assignment was presented as a general solution to most threats to the internal validity of a study seeking to establish causality. But despite the importance of random assignment, an investigator or reader of studies cannot afford the luxury of ignoring those studies in which random assignment was unethical, illegal, or unfeasible. The alternative in such circumstances is to unravel the observed effect of the treatment from extraneous influences such as the initial nonequivalence of subjects in the different treatment conditions, the effects of normal development, and contaminations in the field (communication between subjects and service providers in the different treatment conditions, poor treatment fidelity, and the like).

This chapter covers three varieties of quasi experiment: nonequivalent comparison group designs, interrupted time-series designs, and regression-discontinuity designs.

NONEQUIVALENT COMPARISON GROUP DESIGNS

When two groups are compared in a study and random assignment to the groups is not possible, we say that the design involves **nonequivalent comparison groups**. This design is like the situation described in Chapter 6 in discussions of the nonequivalence threat to internal validity.

Pretest/posttest nonequivalent comparison group design One of the most frequently used research designs in education and social science, the **pretest/posttest nonequivalent comparison group design**, is represented in Figure 7–1. Subjects are selected by either random or nonrandom methods (usually the latter), assigned to groups by nonrandom methods, and pretested; the treatment is implemented for the relevant group, then both groups are posttested.

As an example, imagine that a federally funded day-care facility is charged with demonstrating that children who attend its programs have better social maturity than their peers who do not attend the program. Unless many more parents request services from the facility than it can accept (in which case a lottery could determine who would and would not be served), random assignment to the treatment conditions is quite unlikely. More commonly, some parents hear about the facility and decide whether to send their children or keep them at home, employ a baby-sitter or grandmother to tend them, or send them to some alternative facility. The evaluator's task is to find a group of children who do not attend but are

FIGURE 7–1
Representation of Pretest/Posttest Nonequivalent Group Design

$$\text{R-S or} \atop \text{(No R-S)} \longrightarrow \text{No R-A} \begin{array}{l} \nearrow O_1 \quad X \quad O_2 \\ \searrow O_1 \quad \text{No } X \quad O_2 \\ \quad\quad\quad (\text{or } X_2) \end{array}$$

more or less comparable to those who do. Perhaps the evaluator canvasses the neighborhoods from which the day-care children are sent, looking for children of similar ages and social backgrounds. She might run an advertisement seeking subjects for a study or ask the day-care parents to nominate children who will not be attending. From the list of available subjects she discards those who are receiving some alternative day-care services, those who are handicapped, perhaps, and those who are particularly discrepant from the group of children to be served. From those remaining on the list, she forms a control group. She measures the level of social maturity in both groups (we can assume a reliable and valid measurement, using blinding procedures) and shows that the social maturity in each is approximately the same. Then the treatment conditions are implemented. The evaluator makes sure that all the day-care children remain in the program and that members of the comparison group do not obtain similar services from another agency (those who do are removed from the study). At the end of one year, both groups are assessed again and tests of significance (ANOVA or ANCOVA scores, see Chapter 3) are computed.

Can the observed advantage of the day-care children be attributed to the treatment? The criteria of statistical relationship and temporal order of independent and dependent variables have been met. History is probably not a threat to internal validity because both groups would have been influenced by episodic external events to about the same degree. Testing is not a threat because both groups would have had the chance to learn from the pretest. Maturation is not a threat, provided the evaluator selected individuals for the control group that were of the same age as those in the treated group. Four threats to the internal validity of the design are uncontrolled, however. The threat of nonequivalence cannot be ruled out. Parents who elect to send their children to day care may be different in many undetected ways from those who stay home with their children, bring in a baby-sitter, or send them to a private facility. Differences may be economic or psychological, and they may correlate with the dependent variable in such a way as to be responsible for the posttest difference between the two groups. These differences threaten the internal validity of the design, even though the two groups appear to be equal on social maturity as measured on the pretest. Establishing equivalence of the two groups *on the pretest* does not rule out the threat of nonequivalence.

The threat of regression is also uncontrolled in this design if the treated group was selected because of its extreme position on some variable. Identifying a control group that is matched with the treated group on some variable does not alleviate the threat and may result in the **matching fallacy** (Hopkins, 1969). It is common in evaluations of compensatory education programs like Chapter I of the Educational Consolidation and Improvement Act of 1981 to determine the impact of the program by matching children who receive the program with children who have similar pretest scores but who are not eligible for Chapter I services. Thus, the study includes two groups that appear to be equal on the pretest. But the two groups come from different populations with different income levels (one eligible for compensatory education, one not). On the posttest the scores of the treated children will have regressed nearer to their own population mean (i.e., scores will be lower on posttest than pretest) while the posttests of the untreated comparison group will have regressed toward the mean of their own population (i.e., scores on the posttest will be higher than on the pretest) despite any effects of the program.

Two other threats to the internal validity of the design were noted by Cook and Campbell (1979). An **interaction of nonequivalence and maturation** can occur when the two groups are developing at different rates— for example, one group may be slightly younger and developing at a faster rate. An **interaction of nonequivalence and history** threatens internal validity if something other than the treatment occurs to one group but not the other. For example, a fire at the day-care center shuts it down for a month and so frightens the children that their psychological development is actually impeded. No comparable event disturbs the comparison group.

Do these uncontrolled threats mean that day care had no effect, or that the study was worthless? Not at all. Some critics make the mistake of thinking that, without the ability to employ random assignment to treatment conditions, a researcher should not bother with the study. Many confuse the possiblity of threats to internal validity with false findings. The correct interpretation of the results of a study with uncontrolled threats is that each threat is an alternative explanation for the posttest differences. Each alternative explanation competes with the hypothesis that the treatment was the cause of the observed difference. In the above example, the day-care treatment may have been the cause of the difference, but those other four causes cannot be ruled out. The researcher or evaluator's job is to investigate as many of these alternative explanations as possible and judge the plausibility of each one. For example, she could keep logs of as many important events occurring in each setting (treatment and control) as she can observe and note. She could measure as many subject characteristics as possible to determine the extent of nonequivalence between the groups. Ingenuity is needed to minimize the inevitable threats to design such as this. In any case, this evaluation problem, like many of its ilk, simply does not lend itself to true experimentation, so an insistence on random assignment is both snobbish and inappropriate, however desirable it is when it can be achieved.

Static-group comparison The second form of nonequivalent control group design is the **static-group comparison**, as represented in Figure 7–2. Subjects are selected by either random or nonrandom methods and assigned to groups by nonrandom methods; no pretest is given, the treat-

R-S
  or $\longrightarrow$ No R-A $\overset{\nearrow X_1 \quad O}{\searrow \text{No } X \quad O}$
(No R-S)
                   (or X_2)

FIGURE 7–2

Representation of Static-Group Comparison Design

ment conditions are implemented, and posttests are administered to both groups. The groups have been formed for some purpose and by some method that is unrelated to the study. For example, a researcher wants to investigate the comparative effectiveness of token economy versus milieu therapy on the adjustment of patients in a mental hospital. The researcher lacks sufficient control to assign patients at random to treatments. However, he can designate that Ward A, as an intact, or static, group, will receive the token economy treatment, while Ward B, also as an intact group, will receive milieu therapy. The manner by which individual patients came to be in Ward A as opposed to Ward B is not only out of the researcher's control but is influenced by the policies and perceptions of the hospital administrator in ways that might cause the two groups to be nonequivalent. For example, the administrator might perceive that the staff of Ward A is particularly adept with paranoid schizophrenics while the staff of Ward B works better with character disorders, and he might disproportionately allocate patients according to this perception. Thus, the researcher faces threats to the internal validity of such a design due to nonequivalence, and threats to the external validity of the study due to the confounding of the treatments with all other features of the setting, staff, and interactions with other patients in the wards. An interaction of regression and nonequivalence can also threaten internal validity, even though no pretest was given. Regression can occur if the selection criteria for allocating subjects to groups differed and the groups came from two different populations. Despite the existence of several uncontrolled threats to internal validity, the static-group comparison design offers the only hope of studying certain research and evaluation problems. It is up to the investigator to uncover potential threats and to patch up the design so that some of them can be addressed.

INTERRUPTED TIME-SERIES DESIGN

In the **interrupted time-series design** a string of observations of the dependent variable is made prior to the introduction of the treatment, after which another string of observations is made. In its simplest form it can be represented as shown in Figure 7–3.

FIGURE 7–3 Representation of an Interrupted Time-Series Design

No R-S $\rightarrow O_1 O_2 O_3 O_4 O_5 O_6 O_7 O_8 O_9 O_{10} O_{11} O_{12} X O_{13} O_{14} O_{15} O_{16} O_{17}$
(or R-S)

Consider the graph in Figure 7–4 of data from a time-series design that investigated the effect of behavioral therapy on the depressed thoughts of a teenage boy. The number of depressed thoughts he had was recorded every day for two weeks to establish a baseline. About 70 depressed thoughts were recorded on the first day, slightly over 50 on the fourteenth day. Then the treatment was introduced (notice the first vertical line) and maintained for 21 days. Following the treatment (termination of treatment corresponds to the second vertical line), the series of measurements continued for another two weeks. Notice that the series is higher during the baseline period, drops off abruptly at the start of treatment, and remains low after the treatment is terminated.

The time-series design is particularly useful when all the individuals eligible for the treatment must be treated alike (thus making an untreated comparison group unfeasible) or when single individuals are to be treated. For example, an evaluation of an inservice training program for nurses might require that all eligible nurses participate and that all be treated alike. Or applied research on the effects of a new medical regimen on

FIGURE 7–4 Incidence of Depressed Thoughts for a Patient Receiving Behavior Therapy: Time-Series Design

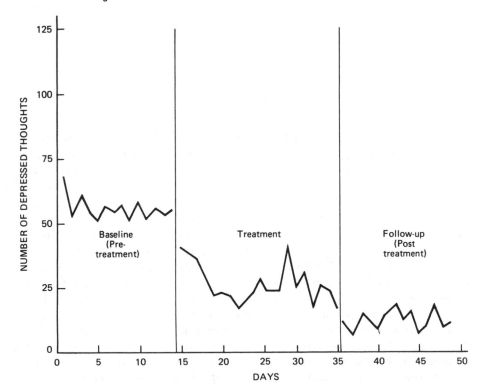

people with a rare illness constitutes a circumstance such that time series would be appropriate. In these instances, the researcher cannot assign subjects to an untreated control condition (indeed no comparable individuals exist) but can control how many times the dependent variable is measured and when it is measured in relation to the implementation of the treatment. The interrupted time-series design requires many measurements prior to the introduction of the treatment or intervention to establish a stable baseline of how the individual or individuals perform. After the intervention, many measurements of the dependent variable provide evidence of the effect and its duration.

As is the case with all quasi experiments, the problem faced by the researcher or evaluator is to attribute change in the dependent variable to the independent variable. The proper statistical procedures are too complicated to be covered here (see Glass, Willson, and Gottman, 1975), but suffice to say that demonstrating a statistical relationship between independent and dependent variables requires attention to what happens to the series of measures at precisely the point where the researcher intervened with the treatment. The temporal sequence is controlled by the researcher in the planned time-series quasi experiment (*archival time-series* studies are covered in Chapter 8).

What about alternative explanations or threats to internal validity? The reader should recognize that the time-series design represented in Figure 7–3 is an extension into the past and future of the one-group, pretest/posttest design, familiar in the physical sciences and represented as follows:

$$0_1 \; X \; 0_2$$

This design is subject to several threats to internal validity, including history, maturation, testing, instrumentation, and regression (leaving aside mortality for the time being). From the length of this list, one can surmise that establishing a causal claim with the one group, pretest/posttest control group design is a tall order. The principal problem is that one has little information about how this dependent variable behaves over time or what its natural course might have been if the individuals were left alone without a treatment. A single baseline, or pretreatment, assessment is inadequate and in fact may be misleading. Recall the example in Figure 7–4; reliable knowledge about the course of depression is not sufficient to allow us to know whether depressed thoughts follow a seasonal or cyclic trend, or how changeable such thoughts are. Taking many measures of the variable prior to intervening provides such information and allows one to judge whether the change of the series from just before treatment to just after is unique or merely part of a long-range pattern of change unrelated to treatment.

Suppose that, instead of the interrupted time-series design, the re-

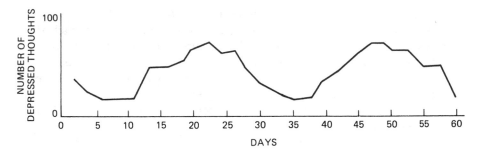

FIGURE 7–5 Hypothetical Series of the "Natural Course" of Depressed Thoughts in Person A

searcher had used the one-group (in this case, an individual), pretest/post-test control group design to assess the impact of behavior therapy on de-pressed thoughts. Suppose further that the real, unmanipulated course of development of depressed thoughts in this young man (Person A) is that depicted in Figure 7–5. This graph shows a sixty-day series of depressed thoughts such that depression is particularly apparent during some ten-day periods but much less a problem at other times, following a more or less regular cycle. Now imagine what would have happened if the researcher had intervened on Day 25. By happenstance the introduction of the treat-ment has coincided with the *natural* decline in depressed thoughts, but this decline is mistaken for a treatment effect. This is an obvious case of the maturation threat to internal validity.

Now look at Figure 7–6, which depicts a different hypothetical series of the natural course of depressed thoughts for Person B. His depressed thoughts are highly variable from day to day. If the researcher happened to begin his treatment on Day 20, and measured the outcome on Day 30, he might blame the increase of depressed thoughts on the intervention, rather than recognize that the increase was a natural spike in a spike-filled series.

To control for a variety of threats to internal validity in the interrupted time series, it is necessary to have a preintervention series long enough to

FIGURE 7–6 Hypothetical Series of Depressed Thoughts in Person B

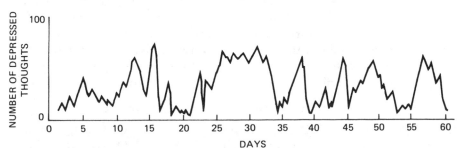

encompass whatever peaks and valleys are like to occur. Then treatment effects are not as likely to be falsely attributed to or masked by such fluctuations. Regression is unlikely to confound interpretation since the regression to the mean of extreme groups or individuals will be obvious in the initial series of measurements. The practice effect of testing can be estimated, if not ruled out, by the gains between pairs of points early in the series. It is likely that little additional practice effect occurs after the fourth or fifth test administration.

The instrumentation threat occurs in all those instances when it can occur in true experiments—that is, when the test has an element of judgment or subjectivity to it and the test administrator is aware of the status of subjects. In the example of recording depressed thoughts, instrumentation is particularly obvious as a threat since the individual is recording his own behavior and might become careless, bored, or complacent with the task or otherwise react to the fact that he is in an experiment. A historical event that occurred very near the introduction of the treatment would threaten internal validity, but it is impossible to generalize about the chance of this happening. Each application must be studied on a case-by-case basis to determine whether episodic, external events are plausible alternative hypotheses to the treatment effect.

More complicated variations of the interrupted time-series design provide more control. As depicted in Figure 7–7, the two-group, single intervention time-series design rules out history as a threat to internal validity in a particular application, because the untreated group (or individual) is subject to events external to the treatment but not to the treatment itself. Figure 7–8 adds an untreated individual to the design, also a mild depressive whose series would' have revealed the effect of any "historical" events on the dependent variable. None is evident in the graph. When the two groups to be compared are constituted by nonrandom methods, nonequivalence is a threat to internal validity; in this case it is evident in the initial difference in incidence of depressed thoughts between the two young men, but it may not be as serious a problem as with simpler designs like the single group, pretest/posttest design.

To what populations, settings, treatments, and outcomes can the findings of time-series designs be generalized? It is enough to say that whatever threatens the external validity of true experiments also threaten that of quasi experiments. The threat due to the interaction of treatment with time can often be mitigated by the use of time-series designs, since the duration of effect is one of the questions answered. Reactive arrangements are less likely to occur in field and applied research and in evaluation than in

FIGURE 7–7   Representation of the Two-Group, Single Intervention Time-Series Design

No R-S → No R-A ↗ $O_1O_2O_3O_4O_5O_6O_7O_8O_9O_{10}$ X $O_{11}O_{12}O_{13}O_{14}O_{15}O_{16}$
(or R-S)   ↘ $O_1O_2O_3O_4O_5O_6O_7O_8O_9O_{10}$ No X $O_{11}O_{12}O_{13}O_{14}O_{15}O_{16}$

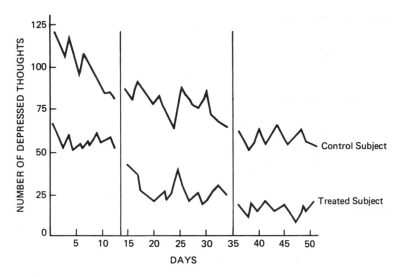

FIGURE 7–8 Incidence of Depressed Thoughts for a Subject Treated with Behavior Therapy and a Control Subject

laboratory studies. Time-series designs are often an excellent method of field research.

Figure 7–9 shows the versatility of time-series designs, with five variations that are appropriate for different evaluation and research questions and which control for extraneous influences in several ways.

So far we have discussed time-series designs as if the units of study were individuals (sometimes referred to as **single subject** or *n-of-one studies*) or intact groups, with each individual being assessed at each measurement time. It is also possible when studying a group to sample *different* individuals randomly from the group at each observation time. Each individual could be measured only once, and testing would not threaten internal validity. This method is illustrated by an evaluation of the effect of Outward Bound on the self-confidence of its participants (Smith, Gabriel, Schott, and Padia, 1975).

Two hundred male participants were assigned by the program administrators to one of three groups. The basis of assignment was nonrandom (self-selection or administrative convenience). All groups were scheduled to attend Outward Bound for 14 days, the first group in June, the second in July, and the third in August. The time period covered by the study extended from March 1 to October 1 and was divided into 26 measurement points. Individuals from all groups were randomly assigned to a measurement point, which would be the week the individual was to be measured. For some the measurement point would occur prior to the time they would attend Outward Bound and for others, measurement would occur afterwards. Measurement took place when the participant received

"Single Group/Multiple Intervention"

$$N_0 \ R\text{-}S \rightarrow O_1O_2O_3O_4X_1O_5O_6O_7O_8X_2O_9O_{10}O_{11}$$

"Multiple Group/Single Intervention"

$$N_0 \ R\text{-}S \rightarrow N_0 \ R\text{-}A \nearrow \begin{matrix} O_1O_2O_3X_1O_4O_5O_6 \\ O_1O_2O_3X_2O_4O_5O_6 \\ O_1O_2O_3X_3O_4O_5O_6 \end{matrix}$$

"Reversal Design"

$$N_0 \ R\text{-}S \rightarrow N_0 \ R\text{-}A \nearrow \begin{matrix} O_1O_2O_3X_1O_4O_5O_6X_2O_7O_8O_9 \\ O_1O_2O_3X_2O_4O_5O_6X_1O_7O_8O_9 \end{matrix}$$

"Sequential Multiple Group/Single Intervention"

$$\text{No } R\text{-}S \rightarrow \text{No } R\text{-}A \nearrow \begin{matrix} O_1O_2O_3X_1O_4O_5O_6 \\ \\ O_7O_8O_9X_1O_{10}O_{11}O_{12} \end{matrix}$$

FIGURE 7–9   Five Alternative Time-Series Designs

the self-confidence inventory in the mail (as determined by the measurement point to which they had been randomly assigned), filled it out, and returned it.

The design was a multiple group, single but sequential intervention time-series, which is represented in Figure 7–10. Statistical analysis showed an increase in the level of self-confidence coincident with the intervention. Maturation was controlled as a threat to internal validity because of the length of the baseline series (although one would wish for a greater number of pretreatment observations). Since the sample did not represent any extreme group, regression was not a threat; even if the subjects had been selected because they were extreme, regression would have been roughly equal between any two time points and its effects recognizable as distinct from an intervention effect. Testing was controlled because each individual was measured only once. No instrumentation threats were present since

FIGURE 7–10   Example of a Multiple-Group, Single but Sequential Time-Series Design in the Evaluation of "Outward Bound"

$$\text{No } R\text{-}S \rightarrow \text{No } R\text{-}A \begin{matrix} \nearrow O_1O_2O_3O_4O_5O_6O_7O_8O_9O_{10}O_{11}O_{12} \quad X \quad O_{15}O_{16}O_{17}O_{18}O_{19}O_{20}O_{21}O_{22}O_{23}O_{24}O_{25}O_{26} \\ \rightarrow O_1O_2O_3O_4O_5O_6O_7O_8O_9O_{10}O_{11}O_{12}O_{13}O_{14}O_{15}O_{16}O_{17}X_1 \quad O_{20}O_{21}O_{22}O_{23}O_{24}O_{25}O_{26} \\ \searrow O_1O_2O_3O_4O_5O_6O_7O_8O_9O_{10}O_{11}O_{12}O_{13}O_{14}O_{15}O_{16}O_{17}O_{18}O_{19}O_{20}X_1 \quad O_{22}O_{23}O_{24}O_{25}O_{26} \end{matrix}$$

the self-confidence inventory was a standard paper-and-pencil test. The threat of history was controlled because the posttreatment assessment of the June course group (measurement points 15, 16, and 17) coincided with pretreatment assessment points for the July and August course groups. Nonequivalence would have been uncontrolled had the three groups differed from each other in the impact of the treatment. In fact, the same positive effect of Outward Bound was observed for all three groups.

The effect of an intervention on an outcome variable can assume a variety of forms. Some of these are depicted in Figure 7–11. One important point should be made about these possibilities: The causal argument is stronger to the extent that the researcher correctly anticipates the precise form of the effect of the intervention. Having explicit and specific expectations about how the level, direction, or variability of a series should change as a result of the treatment is the best protection against being led astray by extraneous influences and chance events.

REGRESSION DISCONTINUITY DESIGN

In the nonequivalent comparison group design, the effect of a treatment is assessed by measuring the dependent variable of a treated group. The investigator finds a more or less comparable untreated group. Its performance provides an estimate of what the treated group would have been like if it had not been treated. In the interrupted time-series design, the in-

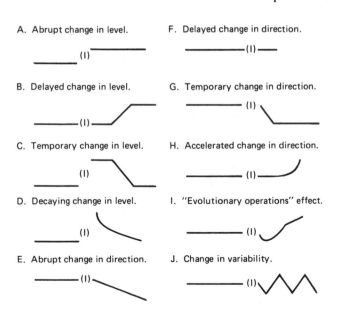

FIGURE 7–11   Varieties of Intervention Effects in the Time-Series Design

vestigator establishes a baseline of estimates of the status of individuals prior to treatment against which the posttreatment status is compared.

Regression discontinuity designs assess the impact of treatments in a different way. In the regression discontinuity design, all subjects are measured in advance on some variable related to the outcome variable of the quasi experiment. A point on the continuum is picked, and all subjects to one side of that point receive one treatment and all subjects on the other side receive the alternative treatment (or control). The regression discontinuity design is like a nonequivalent control group design, with the advantage that one knows precisely how the two groups differ on a relevant subject characteristic. Figure 7–12 illustrates the design. Subjects are assigned to the treatment because they need it or have earned it more than others. The performance of the treated group is compared to the performance that one would predict if treatment had not been given. The comparison group consists of the remaining individuals (those who did not need or earn the program).

Regression discontinuity designs are appropriate for evaluating those programs where allocation of services to individuals is based on the need for the program or on special merit. Consider some examples. A program to remediate difficulties first graders experience in learning to read requires one-to-one attention by a specialist. There is only one specialist available in each elementary school of the district. Therefore, a potentially

FIGURE 7–12 Regression Discontinuity Design

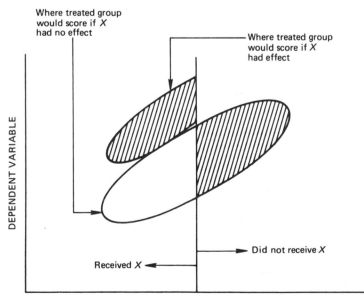

beneficial program exists, but it is in scarce supply—only 60 children can be served. How should the 60 children be selected? A lottery could be held, selecting children at random from the total group. But many of the 60 chosen would already be good readers. Both the time of these children and that of the specialists would be wasted. A second basis is self-selection; the first 60 children whose parents elect to send them will receive the program. A third basis is to ask teachers for referrals of children for extra help. Both the second and third bases may result in unfair allocations of the treatment. In other words, because parents vary in the extent to which they are informed about special programs and their assertiveness in obtaining them for their children, and because teachers vary in how and why they refer children for services, those children most in need are not always the ones served. A fourth basis for deciding which children should receive the reading program is by giving a test, such as a reading achievement test, to all first graders in the district. A cutoff score is established, and everyone who scores below that cutoff score is given the program. Anyone who scores at or above the cutoff score is not eligible for the program. Thus, the program is given to those who need it most, as determined by the selection pretest. Other examples of program assignment based on need are the following: an experimental and scarce drug, organ transplant, or medical procedure is given to the most seriously affected patients; child care subsidies are given to families in the worst economic predicaments; highway improvement funds are allocated to counties and cities with the worst highway hazards; diet programs are made available to the most obese.

Scarce resources can also be allocated to the individuals with the greatest merit. For example, medical schools establish cutoff scores on the Medical College Admissions Test. Those scoring above the cutoff are awarded positions in the school, or at least further consideration in the admissions process. Scholarships, nominations to the dean's list, and the like are awarded to those who score above a cutoff on achievement tests or grade point average.

How should programs such as these be evaluated? How is it possible to determine that the program had an effect on some valued goal? Finding comparable but untreated groups from the same population contradicts the social policy of serving the most needy or deserving. Examining pretreatment to posttreatment gains in such extreme groups is especially subject to the regression threat to internal validity. The regression discontinuity design (explained most fully in Trochim, 1984; also described in Cook and Campbell, 1979) is offered as a useful alternative.

The example to be used is an evaluation of a school district's policy to retain for a subsequent year in kindergarten all those pupils who score below a certain cutoff on a test of "developmental age," This is a hypothetical example; we know of no districts with this policy. The evaluation question is this: "What is the effect of retention in kindergarten on a pupil's

subsequent reading achievement?" The sample consisted of the entire cohort of children who began kindergarten in that district, were tested on
the Developmental Age Scale (DAS), were either passed or retained, and
remained in the district until the end of first grade when reading achievement is regularly tested.

The design rests on the relationship between the selection criterion
or pretest (DAS) and the outcome variable (reading achievement). On the
left-hand side of Figure 7–13, one sees a graphic representation of the
correlation of DAS (plotted along the horizontal axis) and reading achievement (plotted along the vertical axis). The plot shows a moderate positive
relationship in the cohort as a whole (not just the treated group). The
graph depicts the relationship between the two variables that would have
been obtained *if no treatment had been given*. The solid line is the regression
line, the line that best describes the relationship between the two variables.

On the right side of Figure 7–13 is an empty graph of the relationship
between the two variables with the cutoff score indicated perpendicular to
the horizontal axis. Any child who scores higher than eight on the DAS
will be passed on to first grade. Anyone who scores lower will be retained
in kindergarten for another year.

Figure 7–14 contains the hypothetical results of the study. Instead
of the single regression line, one sees two regression lines: one below the
cut-off score on DAS representing the treated (retained) group; the other
regression line, to the right of the cut-off score line represents the relationship of DAS and reading achievement for the untreated group. There
is a *discontinuity* between the two regression lines (hence the name of the
design). Such discontinuity indicates that the program had an effect. Whether
the effect was positive or negative depends on the position of the two lines
at the cut-off score point. At the cut-off score (the perpendicular line that
separates retained from nonretained children in the scatterplot) the regres-

FIGURE 7–13 Regression Discontinuity Design Features

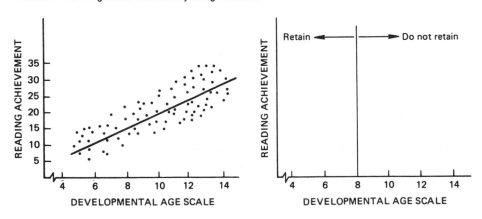

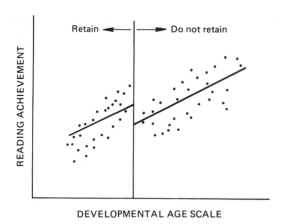

FIGURE 7–14 Regression Discontinuity with Positive Results

sion line is higher for retained than nonretained children. This indicates a benefit for those retained. Another way to see this is to look at the regression line for the untreated group. If this line were extended to the left of the cut-off score line into the area of the graph occupied by the treated group, one would have a line that represented the relationship between DAS and reading achievement that would be expected if the treatment had not been provided. This line of expectation-without-treatment is indicated by the dashed line in Figure 7–15. The solid lines are the obtained regression lines for the treated (on the left, below the cut-off score line) and untreated (on the right) individuals. As noted by Trochim (1984) in a similar example, the effect of the program is revealed by the difference between the two regression lines at the cut-off score. For any DAS score the obtained regression line has a higher achievement score than does the dashed line that projects the achievement score that would likely have been attained if those children had not been retained. In other words, the chil-

FIGURE 7–15 Regression Discontinuity with Positive Results, Another Look

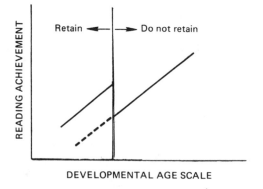

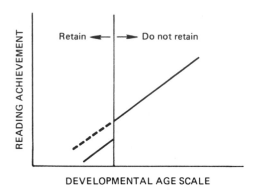

FIGURE 7-16 Regression Discontinuity with Negative Results

dren who were retained in kindergarten had better eventual first-grade reading achievement than they were predicted to have without retention.

Figure 7-16 shows the reverse side of the coin, a negative effect of treatment. The point at which the regression line for the retained group intersects the cut-off score line is lower than the point of intersection between the cut-off score line and the regression line for the nonretained group. Thus, the children retained had poorer achievement than what would have been predicted if they had not been retained. Retention was actually harmful. Figure 7-17 shows a graph of findings from a regression discontinuity design in which the program had no effects, either positive or negative. There is no discontinuity in the regression lines between the two groups.

Options for the analysis of the data from the regression discontinuity design range from the relatively simple (*t*-test of the difference between the intercepts of the treated and untreated groups' regression lines with the cut-off score) to the arcane, which are beyond the scope of this book. As for threats to the internal validity of this design, Cook and Campbell

FIGURE 7-17 Regression Discontinuity with No Effect

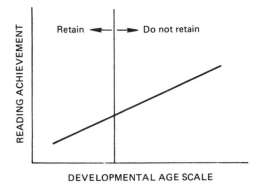

(1979) point out that the greatest threat is from the interaction between selection and maturation. The possibility exists that individuals at different points in the pretest or selection distribution develop at different rates, thereby creating discontinuities that can be mistaken for program effects.

CRITERIA FOR JUDGING QUASI EXPERIMENTS

The following list consists of questions that you, as a research consumer, should ask about the design and execution of quasi-experimental studies.

1. Were the methods for selecting the subjects clearly described? Have the sample, accessible population, and target population been fully described so that the reader can judge to what groups the findings apply?

2. For nonequivalent comparison group designs, were the methods of assigning subjects to treatment conditions fully described? Have enough subject characteristics been identified so that the reader can judge to what extent the groups were nonequivalent? Were matching or statistical adjustment procedures described and justified?

3. For interrupted time-series designs, were sufficient pretreatment measures taken to ensure a stable baseline of the dependent variable?

4. For regression discontinuity designs, were the assumptions of the design met? For example, was there a linear relationship between pretest and criterion? Was the cut-off selection procedure compromised in any way?

5. Have the treatment conditions (characteristics of setting, tasks, service deliverers, and procedures of the study) been adequately described so other people can thoroughly understand how to apply the treatment in their own settings?

6. Is the treatment of sufficient intensity and duration that an effect is reasonable to expect? Has the treatment actually been implemented as defined? Is the sample size large enough?

7. Has mortality been controlled?

8. Has the dependent variable been well measured? Are instrumentation threats controlled? If needed, have blinding procedures been used?

9. Have the limitations in design and execution been acknowledged by the investigator?

SUGGESTED READINGS

CAMPBELL, D.T., and STANLEY, J.C. *Experimental and quasi-experimental designs for research on teaching.* Chicago: Rand McNally, 1966.

COOK, T.D., and CAMPBELL, D.T. *Quasi-experimentation.* Chicago: Rand McNally, 1979.

GLASS, G.V., WILLSON, V.L., and GOTTMAN, J.M. *Design and analysis of time-series experiments.* Boulder: Colorado Associated University Press, 1975.

TROCHIM, W.M.K. *Research design for program evaluation: The regression discontinuity approach.* Beverly Hills, Calif.: SAGE, 1984.

TERMS INTRODUCED IN THIS CHAPTER

nonequivalent comparison group
  design
pretest/posttest nonequivalent
  comparison group design
matching fallacy
interaction of nonequivalence and
  maturation
interaction of nonequivalence and
  history

static-group comparison design
interrupted time-series design
single subject study
n-of-one study
regression discontinuity design

QUESTIONS AND EXERCISES FOR FURTHER STUDY

1. Explain in your own words the difference between true experiments and quasi experiments. What characteristics do they share?

2. A government agency commissions an evaluation to determine the differential effectiveness of public and private schools and their relative success in teaching math. The evaluators randomly selected a sample of schools of each type. From the schools selected, the evaluators selected samples of pupils whose IQs were in the average range, 95–105, to control for intellectual ability. In September they administered a pretest of math achievement and matched the two samples on their pretest scores so the groups would be similar on their levels of math achievement. At the end of the year they administered the math test again.
    a. Use the notation system presented in Chapter 6 to depict this design. What is the name given to a design such as this?
    b. Do the matching technique and the procedure for controlling for IQ remove the nonequivalence threat from this design? Why or why not?
    c. A hard-core experimentalist criticizes the study for its lack of random assignment. Discuss the ethics and feasibility of using random assignment to address this problem.

3. In Chapter 6 it was noted that pretesting is unnecessary when subjects are randomly assigned to treatment and control groups. Explain why pretests are unnecessary in true experiments and necessary in quasi experiments.

4. An evaluation of programs for the mentally retarded (MR) is commissioned. The average IQ of the MR group in the program is 80. From the MR group the evaluator selects a sample whose IQ averages 90 and matches them to a sample of non-MR pupils also with an average IQ of 90. A test of letter recognition, the dependent variable, shows that the non-MR group was better off. The evaluator concludes that the program for the mentally retarded is not effective.
    a. Explain how regression threatens internal validity of the study in this question but not of that in question 2.
    b. How can the regression threat be controlled when extreme groups are the individuals of interest?
    c. Redesign this study as a regression discontinuity design. State how that change represents an improvement.

5. Saracho (1982) in the *American Educational Research Journal* reported a non-equivalent comparison group design on the effect of computer-assisted instruction (CAI) on the achievement and attitudes of migrant children. The

treatment group and the comparison group were formed based on the discretion of principals in the schools studied. At the end of the study the treated group showed significantly more positive attitude scores than the control group. Because the groups were not randomly constituted, we can recognize a nonequivalence threat to internal validity. Does the presence of this threat mean that the CAI was *not* the cause of the observed difference in attitudes between the two groups? Explain your answer.

6. State in your own words why a single group, single intervention interrupted time-series design is more rigorous than a single group, pretest/posttest comparison group design.

7. A researcher wants to use an interrupted time-series design to study the effect of introducing rope jumping into an aerobic conditioning program. The dependent variable is average lung capacity in a sample of 20 participants. Examine the design notation below and state the most serious problem. State how you could redesign the study to correct the problem.

$$\text{No R-S} \rightarrow O_1 O_2 X O_3 O_4 O_5 O_6 O_7 O_8 O_9 O_{10} O_{11} O_{12} O_{13} O_{14} O_{15}$$

8. A researcher wants to know the effect of a cognitive stimulation program for infants at risk for developmental disabilities. The program is very expensive and requires that a physical therapist be present to deliver the treatment during all the infants' waking hours. Because of the expense of the treatment, the researcher decides that only the infants most at risk will receive the treatment. Under these conditions, what is the best design and why?

9. Suppose that in the situation described in question 8, an infant cognitive ability test administered at age 2 is to be used as a dependent variable. A neurological test with a range of 0–10 points is administered to the infants when they are 6 months old as a measure of "risk of developmental disabilities." What condition must be met for the regression discontinuity design to be appropriate?

10. Look at the following graph of the results of the study described in question 9.
    a. What variable does axis *A* represent?
    b. What variable does axis *B* represent?
    c. Identify lines *C, D,* and *E.*
    d. How do we know that the assumptions of the design are met?
    e. Interpret the result of the study.

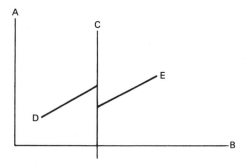

    f.   Discuss the threat due to the interaction of maturation and non-equivalence.

11.   Find the article by Van Houten, Malenfant, and Rolider entitled "Increasing Driver Yielding" in the *Journal of Applied Behavioral Analysis* (1985, Vol. 18, pp. 103–110). Read it carefully and respond to the following:

    a.   Use the notation to depict the design used (you will have to extrapolate from the designs in Figure 7–9).

    b.   Describe the type of effect produced by the treatments (Figure 7–11).

    c.   How was the threat of history controlled?

    d.   How was the threat of maturation controlled?

    e.   Was regression a threat? How do you know?

    f.   Was nonequivalence a threat?

    g.   What questions are answered by the "follow-up" series?

    h.   What are the elements of the study that would make it easy to replicate?

12.   Explain the following statement, "Even though the internal validity of quasi experiments may be less, their external validity may be greater than that of true experiments."

8

CAUSAL-COMPARATIVE STUDIES

Causal-comparative studies, also known as **ex post facto studies**, are the third type of study that can be used when the purpose of the investigation is to establish a cause-and-effect connection. In causal-comparative designs the researcher has less control over the independent variable than in true or quasi experiments. He or she is unable to establish a temporal sequence of independent variable changes preceding dependent variable changes. Extraneous influences are much more likely to be a problem because random assignment cannot be achieved in a causal-comparative study.

Faced with such a shortcoming, why would a researcher ever choose a causal-comparative design? Many interesting research questions lend themselves to this design and no others. Does smog cause emphysema? Do child-rearing practices affect personality characteristics? Did the community mental health movement improve mental health? Does attendance at "fundamental schools" lead to an authoritarian personality? Is intelligence the product of nature or nurture? Does increased mobility contribute to social estrangement? Randomized experiments cannot be used to answer these fascinating and important questions. Researchers cannot control where their subjects live, how they are raised, or where they went to school. Researchers cannot randomly assign communities to mental health center facilities as opposed to hospitals or hold environment constant while changing genetic endowment to study intelligence. Still, disciplined research methods can be used to search for answers to such questions.

In this chapter we cover the logic of the causal-comparative design and its pitfalls. We then introduce three types of causal-comparative design: the between-groups design, the path model, and archival time-series design.

LOGIC OF CAUSAL-COMPARATIVE DESIGNS

In experimental designs the researcher starts with the treatment, or independent variable, and after it has been implemented, observes its effects. In causal-comparative designs the researcher starts with the effect and works backwards in time to identify its cause. The independent variable has already occurred by the time the researcher begins the study; the researcher arrives "after the fact" of the treatment having been applied, thus the name *ex post facto*.

A study of the effect of cigarette smoking on lung cancer is an example of a causal-comparative study. The researcher selects a sample that is made up of individuals with and without lung cancer (the effect, or dependent variable). Then he examines the background of these subjects to see if they differ systematically in the extent to which they had smoked in the past. The sample is divided into two groups, not by random methods, but based on their measured status on the independent variable (prior smoking). A statistical connection is established between the two variables such that there is a statistically significant difference between the two groups (those with lung cancer versus those without it) on their prior record of smoking. The researcher then must *infer* that smoking is the cause of the observed condition. Note that the independent variable had already occurred and therefore could not be manipulated by the researcher. Extraneous influences could not be controlled. The urge and the decision to smoke is up to the individual, not the researcher, who can be only a passive observer and recorder of phenomena that have already taken place.

In this and most other instances of causal-comparative research, there is a large element of **self-selection** into groups. The researcher cannot control other subject characteristics that might influence the onset of cancer, such as emotional stress or exposure to environmental pollutants. These may also correlate with cancer and be unequally distributed between the two groups. Thus, many alternative explanations threaten the researcher's hypothesis that smoking causes cancer. These may be addressed with a program of research including the comparison of rates of lung cancer among those with greater and lesser stress, more or less exposure to pollutants of different kinds, and so on. As each alternative hypothesis is ruled out, the causal claim gains credibility. Animal studies, using randomized experiments, can also bolster the claim but still fail to prove it. With all these pitfalls, is it still possible that smoking cigarettes is the cause of lung cancer? Yes. Remember from the initial section of Chapter 7 that an uncontrolled extraneous influence or threat to internal validity must not be confused with a false finding. The hypothesized cause may be the real cause; alternative causes may still have to be entertained as plausible.

An experimenter with unlimited power and no ethical constraints would design a true experiment: subjects would be randomly assigned to treatment conditions, one smoking and the other not, and years later the difference in rates of cancer between the two groups would be observed. Contrasting these two methods, the true experiment and the causal-comparative, reveals the difference in the their respective logic and some of the difficulties of interpreting the results of the latter. The first of these is the **correlation-causation fallacy**, the mistake made when one observes a statistical relationship between two variables and infers that one variable is the cause of the other. In the smoking and cancer study it might be that anxiety causes both the tendency to smoke and lung cancer as well. This is known as **spuriousness**, or the **third-variable problem**, because a variable that was unmeasured by the researcher may be responsible for the observed relationship. The independent and dependent variable are only incidentally rather than causally related. Both variables may have a cause in common.

The **direction of causality problem** is the incorrect interpretation of which is the cause and which is the effect in a causal-comparative design. Take, for example, the studies of the effect of therapist empathy (emotional understanding) on successful outcome of therapy as measured by improved clients' self-esteem. Audiotape recordings of therapy sessions are rated by experts according to the degree of empathy expressed by the therapists. Ratings of empathy are correlated with self-esteem of clients after therapy, and a positive and statistically significant correlation is found. The researcher infers that high levels of empathy cause improvement in self-esteem. But perhaps that which the researcher assumes is the cause is really the effect, and vice versa. Is it possible that therapists respond with greater empathy to clients who are improving and with lesser empathy to clients who are remaining the same or deteriorating? If so, then the direction of effect has been misinterpreted. A third variable could also be responsible for the observed relationship; the level of experience of the therapists could have caused greater improvement and higher levels of empathy.

Another fallacy apparent in causal-comparative designs is known as the **post hoc fallacy**. This is the mistake made when an effect is observed, and an event that preceded it is claimed to be its cause. This fallacy is an abbreviation of the saying, *post hoc, ergo propter hoc* (after this, therefore because of this). It is a prevalent form of misinterpreted evidence because any social or human event can have many plausible explanations. If a person is diagnosed as schizophrenic, it is only natural to look back to previous events in his life to identify the cause of the illness. Was it because of his grandmother's schizophrenia, his father's absence, his controlling mother, the recent loss of his job, or some combination of these? All are plausible explanations, yet accepting any one of them is tantamount to committing the post hoc fallacy. There are always more explanations for the pattern observed in a set of data than there are data themselves. Such is the propensity of humans to try to explain events. If you doubt this, listen to the experts in the stock market as they attempt to account for daily fluctuations in the market index "caused by" national and global events. Social scientists are not immune to this human characteristic as they, for example, attribute the decline in literacy rates to such antecedents as the introduction of "new math," the abandonment of phonics as a method of teaching reading, to the Vietnam War, or television. Methods of controlling extraneous influences and avoiding the fallacies noted here differ among the three designs and are covered in subsequent sections of this chapter.

BETWEEN-GROUPS DESIGN

The smoking and cancer study described above is typical of a study employing a **between-groups design**. The researcher proceeds as follows: The scores of the sample on the dependent variable are classified or subdivided into two or more groups, which then represent the levels or values of the independent variable. Classification is based on some measured characteristic of the individual. The independent variable may be some enduring characteristic of the subjects—for example, sex, socioeconomic status, ethnic identification, eye color, handedness, intelligence, psychiatric diagnosis, or grade in school.

Then the scores of subjects within each of the subgroups or classifications are aggregated into a mean (or percentage, if the data are at the nominal level). The means of the two groups are compared. A statistically significant difference between the means of the two subgroups is evidence that the independent and dependent variables are related. As you will remember from the initial section of Chapter 6, this is the first criterion

TABLE 8–1 Between-Groups Design: Hypothetical Data Showing Mean Differences

MEANS ($\bar{X}$) AND STANDARD DEVIATIONS (s) FOR FIRST-, SECOND-, AND LATER-BORNS ON ACHIEVEMENT MOTIVATION

		BIRTH ORDER		
		FIRST BORN	SECOND BORN	LATER BORN
Achievement Motivation	$\bar{X}$	5.6	5.3	4.9
	s	1.5	1.2	1.7

$F = 0.90; p > 0.05$

TABLE 8–2   Between-Groups Design: Hypothetical Data Showing Frequency and Percents by Columns of Dyslexia and Impulse Control

		DYSLEXIA STATUS		
		DYSLEXIC	NORMAL	
IMPULSE CONTROL STATUS	HIGH	7 24%	53 65%	60
	LOW	22 76%	28 35%	50
		29	81	110

chi square = 14.69
$p < 0.05$

for determining cause and effect. Here are some examples of this type of between-groups design:

1. What is the effect of sex on spatial ability? The sample is classified into two groups—males and females. Spatial ability scores for the two subgroups are aggregated into a mean for males and a mean for females. A t-test is applied to the mean difference. A significant difference is attributed to the sex difference.

2. What is the effect of birth order on achievement motivation? The scores on an achievement motivation inventory are categorized into three subgroups of first-borns, second-borns, and later-borns. Analysis of variance is used to test the difference in the means of these three groups. Data are illustrated in Table 8–1. In this hypothetical example no significant differences are found.

3. What is the effect of dyslexia on impulse control? Table 8–2 shows that the dependent variable consists of only two levels: high and low impulse control. The statistics used are numbers of pupils within each level, subclassified by whether or not the subject has been identified as dyslexic. The significant chi square indicates that the two categories are related in the population.

4. Does an androgenous sex role identity lead to enhanced self-esteem? Two variables are measured in a sample. The sample is divided into two groups, based on whether the individual's sex role identity score was above or below the median (the middle score in the distribution). The means of these two subgroups on the self-esteem measure are then compared and a statistical test run.

The four examples above involve independent variables that are subject characteristics. The independent variable may also constitute some event or phenomenon that has already occurred to some of the subjects but not to others. The scores on the dependent variable are classified according to the status of the individual on that independent variable. For example, the researcher poses the question, "What is the effect of early father absence on a person's subsequent sex role identity? Information must exist to classify subjects according to whether their fathers had been present in or absent from the home during certain periods, such as while the subjects were between the ages of 1 through 5. Scores on a measure of sex role identity are then subclassified into those of a group whose fathers were present and another group whose fathers were absent at the designated times. The means of the two groups (or the percentages, if the data are in nominal form) are compared and a statistical test run. Significant differences are attributed to the presence or absence of the father.

Here are still other examples:

5. Does having had a mentor affect the career advancement of business executives?

6. Does college graduation increase lifetime earnings?

7. Does a "schizophrenogenic" mother (one who is simultaneously rejecting and clinging) cause her children's schizophrenia?

8. Does attendance at parochial school enhance critical thinking?

9. Are effective schools the product of principals and teachers who have high standards for academic performance?

Note the commonalities in these examples. The independent variables are not under the researcher's control. The subjects have found their way into the subgroups by choice (examples 6 and 8) or are classified by virtue of circumstance, opportunity, or perhaps accident of nature. The researcher takes advantage of differences that already exist and tries to establish that variation in the dependent variable is coincident with the existing differences in the independent variable.

Having documented a statistical relationship between independent and dependent variables, the researcher must also establish that the temporal sequence was such that the independent variable occurred before the dependent variable. This poses no difficulty when dealing with independent variables such as sex or birth order (examples 1 and 2) because people "become" male or female, first born or later born, before they develop spatial ability or achievement motivation. It is logical to assume that college graduation occurs before lifetime earnings, and illogical to assert that lifetime earnings could come before or cause graduation. But whether androgenous sex role identity develops before or after self-esteem or dyslexia before or after impulse control or "schizophrenogenic" mothering before or after schizophrenia in the child is merely a matter of conjecture. Because researchers cannot control temporal sequence, they must use plausible arguments to establish it.

As a way of inferring cause and effect, the between-groups design suffers most from an abundance of extraneous influences. Take the question of whether graduation from college increases lifetime income. The researcher finds a statistical relationship between the two variables and argues convincingly that income was produced following college (and that high income of the graduate could not logically have caused graduation). What alternative explanations are there? Most obvious is the probable relationship between lifetime income of the person and the socioeconomic status of the person's parents. Socioeconomic status is a third variable that correlates both with college graduation and income and may be the common cause of both. That is, greater economic advantages in the family may open up opportunities for higher-paying jobs (regardless of college) and make college tuition affordable. Or, perhaps level of intelligence may be positively associated with both variables. More intelligent people tend to graduate more often *and* tend to occupy higher-paying jobs, sometimes irrespective of what they learned in college. Thus college *per se* is not the cause of higher income but an incidental correlate.

A researcher using a causal-comparative design tests for spuriousness by adding a control variable or cross-classification variable such as family socioeconomic status. Table 8–3 displays some hypothetical results showing that with socioeconomic status (SES) held constant, the relationship between college graduation and income disappears. Such a finding is attained by comparing two analyses. In the top part of the table is the aggregate analysis showing that 68 percent of the graduates are in the high-income category, but only 60 percent of the nongraduates are in the high income category (a statistically significant relationship). But in the two constituent tables where the sample has been subcategorized by socioeconomic status, there is no relationship between graduation and income. That is, for the low socioeconomic status group, 30 percent of graduates are high income and the same percent of nongraduates are high income. For the high socioeconomic group, 76 percent of graduates and 75 percent of nongraduates have high incomes. The significant relationship between earnings and graduation disappears in the cross-classification table. If socioeconomic status was not a spurious third variable, then the same pattern of results would be obtained within each category of socioeconomic status and would be identical to the pattern revealed in the simple analysis between the two variables. Socioeconomic status and intelligence are only two of many "third variables" that threaten the hypothesized causal relationship between college graduation and earnings.

The cross classification of the independent and dependent variable with a third variable is one of the principal methods of control used in between-groups research. Another control is the use of **post hoc matching**. In very large sets of data it is possible to select subjects for a control group that are matched on plausible third variables. The two groups are then compared for differences on the dependent variable. To test the hypothesis, "Open-school arrangements promote short attention span among pupils," a large sample of elementary schools is chosen. Since the ratio of teachers

TABLE 8–3   Spuriousness Revealed in Hypothetical Between-Groups Design

*ADULTS CLASSIFIED BY COLLEGE GRADUATION STATUS AND INCOME WITH PER-
CENTAGES BY ROWS*

INCOME

GRADUATION STATUS	BELOW	ABOVE	
GRADUATED	19 32%	41 68%	60
NOT GRADUATED	24 40%	36 60%	60
	43	77	120

RELATIONSHIP OF COLLEGE GRADUATION AND INCOME WITH SES CONTROLLED

SES

	LOW				HIGH		
GRADUATION STATUS	INCOME				INCOME		
	BELOW	ABOVE			BELOW	ABOVE	
GRADUATED	7 70%	3 30%	10	GRADUATED	12 24%	38 76%	50
NOT GRADUATED	14 70%	6 30%	20	NOT GRADUATED	10 25%	30 75%	40
	21	9	30		22	68	90

to pupils is a third variable that might also influence attention span, the
researcher obtains information that allows her to sort all the schools into
four categories according to the pupil-teacher ratio in each. For each school
with open space arrangements selected for the study, a conventionally built
school with *the same pupil-teacher ratio* is also selected. Thus, the two groups
are equated on pupil-teacher ratio. Only schools that can be matched are
included in the analysis. Attention span is measured in each pupil who
attends the sampled schools (or in randomly selected pupils from the sample
of schools). The researcher averages attention span across all the pupils in
a school, then computes a mean of these means for the schools in the open
space group and a mean for the conventional schools. A significance test

(a *t-test for correlated means*) is computed on these means. The effect of the matching is to reduce the amount of extraneous variance in pupil attention span between the two groups of schools, and what is left can more safely be attributed to the differences in spatial arrangements. The researcher has the option of adding more matching variables, such as level of educational advantage (as measured by the average standardized achievement test scores obtained by each school) to further reduce extraneous variance and control for other third variables or spuriousness. Note, however, that each additional matching variable requires a larger population from which to select individuals. If the researcher decided to match subjects on, say, six or seven variables, it would prove difficult to find individuals who match on so many characteristics simultaneously.

The use of matching as a technique in between-groups studies does not remove the nonequivalence threat to internal validity. Even with seven variables controlled by matching, there remain an eighth, ninth, tenth . . . These latter extraneous influences may be the very ones that are causing the correlation between the independent and dependent variables. Nor is regression controlled as a threat to internal validity in those instances where the groups are selected because of their extreme position on some variable. Such is the case in **extreme-group studies**, which take the following form: The evaluator asks, "What is the effect of mental retardation on social adjustment?" A group of subjects judged to be retarded is selected and matched with a group of nonretarded individuals on a test of perceptual-motor speed. But to match these two groups, the evaluator must choose mentally retarded subjects who are bright relative to their own group and "normals" who are dull relative to their own group. Although the two groups seem to be equated on the matching variable, the regression effect renders them nonequivalent. Both groups will regress toward the means of their own populations (Hopkins, 1969).

Other methods of controlling third variables are used in between-groups studies as well. Analysis of covariance statistically removes the extraneous variance between two groups on a third variable. In the study of the effect of open-space arrangements on pupil attention span, pupil-teacher ratio could have been used as a covariate in an analysis of covariance on the attention span data. Or the researcher might have used pupil-teacher ratio as as **control variable** by selecting only those schools (both open space and traditional) that had a single, given level of pupil-teacher ratio. In other words, only those schools with, say, a high pupil-teacher ratio could be chosen in the sample. This technique reduces the variability between the two groups that is caused by pupil-teacher ratio, thus controlling for this third variable. The research question is altered somewhat to read, "Among elementary schools with high pupil-teacher ratios, what is the effect of open space on pupil attention span?" Findings of the study must be limited accordingly, to only those schools with similar characteristics.

Between-groups studies have much to offer social science and educational research. Yet as a reader you must beware of their hazards. Be particularly alert for third variables that are not accounted for by the researcher. In addition, watch for groups that are not internally homogeneous or that have dubious criteria for inclusion. Lumping private schools for the emotionally disturbed with elite prep schools will distort the findings of a study that set out to answer, "What are the comparative benefits of public and private schools on pupils' social maturity?" One must be cautious about questions such as "What is the effect of learning disabilities (or mental retardation, delinquency, speech pathology, language interference, dyslexia, schizophrenia, and the like) on a person's popularity (or adjustment, dichotic listening skill, lateralization, vocational development, and the like)?" The criteria for inclusion of individuals in these categories are not scientifically validated and are sometimes downright ambiguous. Great discrepancies among professionals exist in their tendency to diagnose, say, one person as schizophrenic and another as not schizophrenic. Enormous variability exists among individuals categorized as say, mentally retarded. Furthermore, the definition of categories is often socially determined, so that what passes for delinquency in some groups and eras is considered normal in others. Understand that establishing a statistical difference between the two groups is only the first step toward causality, not proof of it.

PATH MODELS

The purpose of **path models**—or **causal models**—is to test hypotheses about causal relationships among variables in those cases where the data are in the form of correlations. At least three variables are involved, and the starting point for the analysis is the correlation coefficients between all pairs of variables. To avoid the correlation-causation fallacy, some stringent conditions must be met. First of all, the researcher must begin with a theory that specifies the causal relationships among the collection of variables in the model.

Suppose, for example, that an exercise physiologist is studying the effect of aerobic exercise on cholesterol levels in the blood. For two reasons, he rejects the option of simply computing the correlation between these two variables and inferring causality. First, such an analysis fails to control for a plausible third variable—the amount of saturated fats (butter, egg yolks, and the like) ingested. Some physicians and nutritionists believe that a large amount of saturated fat in the diet is the fundamental cause of high blood cholesterol, exercise notwithstanding. Second, such a bivariate correlation oversimplifies the fact that there are at least two varieties of cholesterol: high-density and low-density lipoproteins, which may have different causal dynamics. The researcher proposes the following theory:

Aerobic exercise has a direct impact on low-density lipoproteins ('bad cholesterol' that clogs arteries and causes heart disease) as does eating saturated fats. Aerobic exercise also reduces high-density lipoproteins and changes the ratio of high-density to low-density lipoproteins. This change in ratio of concentration further reduces low-density lipoproteins because high-density lipoproteins are hypothesized to be carriers of low-density lipoproteins (i.e., high-density lipoproteins transport low-density lipoproteins to the liver where they are metabolized)."

Path analysts represent their theories with figures such as that in Figure 8–1. There are four variables in the model: saturated fats in the diet, aerobic exercise, and both high-density and low-density lipoproteins in the blood. The figure shows two independent variables, also called **exogenous variables**, on the left: aerobic exercise and eating saturated fats. The curved arrow with two points (*a*) that joins aerobic exercise and saturated fat signifies that the two variables are not causally related. They may or may not be correlated, but neither is the cause of the other. Neither are they caused by any other variable in the model. The arrow (*b*) from "eating saturated fats" to "low-density lipoproteins" suggests a **direct effect** of the exogenous, or independent, variable on the **endogenous**, or dependent, variable. Arrow *c* represents a direct effect of aerobic exercise on low density lipoproteins. Arrow (*d*) represents the **indirect effect** of aerobics on low-density lipoproteins through the **mediating variable**, high-density lipoproteins. In the model, saturated fats are assumed to have no influence on high-density lipoproteins.

After formulating this theory, each variable must be measured. Because of the constraints of path analysis, high levels of reliability and validity

FIGURE 8–1 Path Model for Hypothetical Study of Effects of Exercise on Cholesterol

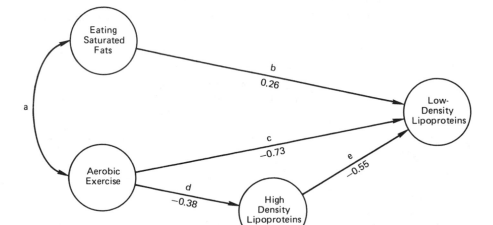

of measurement are critical to the accurate interpretation of results. The analysis of data is a complex form of multiple regression that is beyond the scope of this book (see Cohen and Cohen, 1983, for more information). The analysis yields **path coefficients** that correspond to each causal arrow in the model. Path coefficients are the same as correlation coefficients for those arrows that indicate direct effects of single causes (e.g., high-density lipoproteins are directly affected by aerobic exercise and no other variable in the model) or when the variable is caused by two or more exogenous variables that do not depend on each other. Otherwise, path coefficients are analogous to partial correlations, which reflect the relationship of two variables with the influence of a third variable controlled. Significance tests are applied to the coefficients to determine if the correlations are significantly different from zero, or chance, and thus reflect statistically stable relationships. In the example, the path coefficient between eating saturated fat and the level of low-density lipoproteins is 0.26. Between aerobic exercise and the level of low-density lipoproteins the coefficient is -0.73 (the more exercise, the lower the bad cholesterol). The coefficient between aerobic exercise and high-density lipoproteins is -0.38, and between high- and low-density lipoproteins is -0.55.

Having calculated the path coefficients, the researcher checks their fit with the original model. In many cases the researcher postulates alternative models (represented by different patterns and directions for causal arrows) to see if one is more accurate than another in accounting for the observed correlations. Table 8–4 shows the original correlation matrix from which the path coefficients are calculated.

Path models are currently enjoying the enthusiastic attention of causal-comparative researchers. They do, however, depend on the accurate measurement of variables in the model as well as the assumption that all plausible "causes" are included in the model. If there exists some variable that is the cause of both aerobic exercise and eating saturated fats (some genetic in-

TABLE 8–4 Correlation Coefficients from Which Path Coefficients are Calculated

	EATING SATURATED FATS	AEROBIC EXERCISE	HIGH-DENSITY LIPOPRO-TEINS	LOW-DENSITY LIPOPRO-TEINS
Eating Saturated Fats	1.00	0.10	0.07	0.15
Aerobic Exercise		1.00	-0.38	-0.50
High-Density Lipoproteins			1.00	-0.25
Low-Density Lipoproteins				1.00

fluence, perhaps), and the researcher fails to include it in the model and measure it, the resulting path coefficients are likely to be misleading. As you read such studies, keep in mind the assumptions of path models and be alert to whether the researchers satisfied the criteria for establishing cause and effect.

ARCHIVAL TIME-SERIES

The third variety of causal-comparative study is the **archival time-series design**. It is different from the time-series quasi experiment (Chapter 7) because the researcher cannot manipulate the independent variable in the archival time-series study. In the quasi experimental time-series design, the researcher introduces the treatment according to a planned schedule, after many observations of the dependent variable have been made. In the causal-comparative, or archival, time-series design, the independent variable occurs for nonresearch reasons; the researcher is a passive observer, not a manipulator of events. Measurements of the effect of the independent variable consist of historical records and archives routinely kept by governments and other agencies. The researcher quantifies and organizes these records so they provide a long string of data on the dependent variable prior to and following changes of the independent variable. Changes in the level, direction, or variability of the dependent variable that coincide with the change of the independent variable are evidence of its effect.

Archival time-series are useful for evaluating the impact of social policy decisions and government programs as well as one-time events such as natural disasters. Did the eruption of Mount St. Helens affect the economy of the region? Availability of sales tax figures for the preceding and subsequent months, adjusted for seasonal trends, can help answer the question. Did the city ordinance limiting the growth of the city to 2 percent each year contribute to higher housing prices? Again, if sales figures have been kept over several years prior to the time the ordinance went into effect, the impact can be analyzed through time-series studies. Complex statistical analyses (see Glass, Wilson, and Gottman, 1975) are needed to unravel seasonal trends, to remove long-range secular trends (such as inflation when working with costs), and to separate the effects of other events and policies that might have occurred during the series of measurements.

Figure 8–2 shows some results from a study of the effect of a program in Great Britain to reduce traffic accidents by keeping drunk drivers off the road (Ross, Campbell, and Glass, 1970). This evaluation depended on the existence of archival records of highway fatalities. The records were kept in standardized form for several years prior to the British Road Safety Act of 1967. Neither the maintenance of the records nor the passage of the legislation was under the researcher's control, so this is an archival,

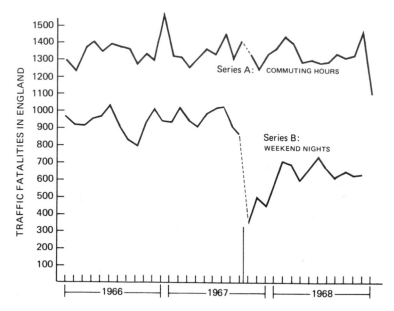

FIGURE 8–2   Time Series on the Effect of the British Road Safety Act   *(Source: Ross, Cambell, and Glass, 1970.)*

causal-comparative time-series study. The vertical axis represents the number of traffic fatalities per month. The horizontal axis represents date (1966–1968). There are two series of observations in the graph. Series A is the fatalities per month during commuting hours, and Series B is the fatalities during weekend nights. The vertical line marks the time at which the law went into effect, October 1967. Statistical analysis showed that the law had no effect on fatalities during commuting hours but did reduce fatalities on the weekends (when drunken driving is more apt to be a problem). It is interesting to speculate about the substantial immediate decline in Series B followed by a retreat in the direction of (but not equaling) the baseline rate of accidents during 1968. Perhaps the police enforced the law most vigorously when it was new but eased off later. This speculation, although interesting, is a good example of weak post hoc explanation, though it might be a lead worth tracking with additional data (e.g., numbers of arrests).

A third time-series graph in Figure 8–3 illustrates some principles of interpreting archival time-series studies. The policy question to be addressed is this: "Did the court order for desegregation contribute to the decline of enrollment in Denver public schools?" The horizontal axis of the graph represents the passage of time, marked off yearly from 1928 to 1975. On the vertical axis is pupil enrollment (yearly figures in thousands). The vertical line shows the point of intervention in 1969, the court order for desegregation that involved busing to achieve racial balance in the schools in 1969. Attributing the observed decline in enrollment to the court order is risky, however, without knowing whether any other policy or trend was likely to have affected the series (history threat to internal validity) or whether demographic trends such as the end of a "baby boom" was responsible for the decline. A control series showing pupil enrollment statewide would control for demographic trends. A control series showing pupil enrollment in suburban districts adjacent to Denver would likely show an increase in the same years as enrollment was decreasing in Denver public schools if the court order was causing or accelerating "white flight."

Other threats to internal validity of time-series studies have been mentioned in Chapter 7 and apply to archival time series as well. Some additional problems confront researchers with the archival design. The first is the problem of obtaining the necessary data. The British Road Safety Act series reveals how critical it is that the data in archives be sufficient and compatible with research objectives. If the records had not been kept separately for commuting hours and weekends, then the analysis would not have been sensitive enough to reveal the effect of the legislation. If the records had not been standardized or regularly recorded by the responsible government department, the analysis would not have been possible.

A second problem is the instrumentation threat to internal validity. Sometimes a policy change affects the form of record keeping more than it affects anything else. It might happen that the officials in the British government responded to the passage of the law by keeping closer track of fatalities. Police might respond to the law by filing a complaint whereas,

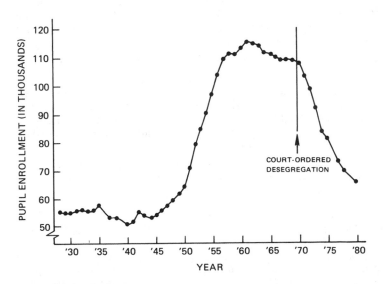

FIGURE 8-3 Archival Time-Series on the Effects of Desegregation on Pupil Enrollment in Denver Public Schools

before the law, they might have let a given offense pass without making a record of it. If that were true, then the series might show an effect of the intervention when nothing fundamental had changed, only the way the records were kept. Some archives are less sensitive to such influences than others, so the reader must make a judgment about the plausibility of the instrumentation threat in each individual study.

CRITERIA FOR JUDGING THE MERITS OF CAUSAL-COMPARATIVE STUDIES

1. Are the methods for selecting the sample adequate for establishing generalizability? Have the individuals and their environment been sufficiently well described so that the reader can judge to what populations and settings the findings apply?

2. In between-groups designs, is the basis for group membership well justified? Are the groups internally homogeneous?

3. If matching has been done, is regression a threat to internal validity? How closely have the groups been matched? Have appropriate statistics been chosen to depict the differences between groups?

4. In path models, was the theory developed prior to the analysis, or post hoc, based on the data? Is the theory complete or are there influential variables not specified in it? Are the variables measured with high levels of reliability?

5. In archival time-series designs, has there been any control over threats to internal validity due to history, maturation, and mortality? Is there any reason to suspect the presence of the instrumentation threat (a change in the measurement of the dependent variable as a reaction to the intervention)? Is the form, quantity, and standardization of the archival records sufficient and compatible with the purpose of the study?

6. For all three types of studies, are reliability and validity of measurement adequate?

7. Concerning the interpretation of the results of the study, are there third variables or events in the history of the phenomenon being studied that might explain the dependent variable better than the independent variable? In other words, are there indications of the correlation-causation fallacy or post hoc fallacy in the interpretation of findings?

8. Have limitations in the design and analysis of the study been acknowledged by the investigators, or do they overgeneralize and overinterpret their data?

SUGGESTED READINGS

BLALOCK, H.M., Jr. *Causal models in the social sciences.* Chicago: Aldine, 1971.
CAMPBELL, D.T., Reforms as experiments. *American Psychologist,* 1969, *24,* 409–429.
COHEN, J., and COHEN, P. *Applied multiple regression/correlation analysis for the behavioral sciences* (*2nd ed.*). Hillsdale, N.J.: Lawrence Erlbaum, 1983.
COOK, T.D., and CAMPBELL, D.T. *Quasi-experimentation.* Chicago: Rand McNally, 1979.

GLASS, G.V., WILLSON, V.L., and GOTTMAN, J.M. *Design and analysis of time-series experiments.* Boulder: Colorado Associated University Press, 1975.

JUDD, C.M. and KENNY, D.A. *Estimating the effects of social interventions.* Cambridge: Cambridge University Press, 1981.

KENNY, D.A. *Correlation and causality.* New York: Wiley-Interscience, 1979.

McCLEARY, R. and HAY, R.A. *Applied time series analysis.* Beverly Hills, Calif.: SAGE, 1980.

MERTON, R. *Social theory and social structure.* New York: Free Press, 1949.

TERMS INTRODUCED IN THIS CHAPTER

ex post facto study

self-selection

correlation-causation fallacy

spuriousness

third-variable problem

direction of causality problem

post hoc fallacy

between-groups design

post hoc matching

extreme-group study

control variable

path model

causal model

exogeneous variable

direct effect

endogeneous variable

indirect effect

mediating variable

path coefficient

archival time-series design

QUESTIONS AND EXERCISES FOR FURTHER STUDY

1. Suppose that in an observational study of a sample of classrooms a researcher found a positive relationship between teachers' use of praise and pupil attentiveness. What are the three possible interpretations of causality that can be drawn from this relationship?

2. Use a between-groups model to design a study that answers the question, "What is the effect of clients' socioeconomic status on therapists' judgments of clients' emotional adjustment?" Discuss the design in terms of criteria for establishing cause and effect.

3. Use a path model to redesign the study in question 2.

4. A researcher studies the effect of pupils' reading ability on their satisfaction with school. He tests a large sample of second-grade pupils on reading ability and uses their scores to establish groups of high- and low-ability readers. Specifically, he takes the 25 percent with the highest scores and the 25 percent with the lowest scores. Then he measures satisfaction with school in these two groups and finds a significant difference in their means. He concludes that reading ability influences satisfaction with school.
   a. Identify the type of design used.
   b. Identify a major difficulty with studies of this type.
   c. Name and discuss any fallacy that might exist in the causal conclusions.
   d. Discuss the regression effect in the context of this study.
   e. Is there any way to "patch up" this design?

5. A graduate student wants to study the influence of airport noise and pollution on the physical ailments of city residents. He has data from a large and

representative survey of the physical health of the residents. He forms two categories of physical ailments (no or minor ailments and moderate or severe ailments) and determines the number and percentages of individuals in each category. Then he uses the addresses of respondents to code the proximity of their residences to the airport. There are three categories of proximity (less than 5 miles from the airport, 5–10 miles, more than 10 miles). Finding a significant chi square on the relationship between these categories, he concludes that airport noise and pollution have a negative impact on physical health. A critic suggests that the relationship is spurious and that poverty is a plausible third variable. Show what a cross-classification analysis would look like if socioeconomic status was introduced as a control variable.

6. Suppose that the cross-classification analysis in question 5 showed that the original relationship was spurious. Describe what the table might look like and what the chi square would show.

7. Discuss the concept of self-selection as it relates to the study illustrated in question 5.

8. To understand the various influences on girls' choice of math-related college majors, a researcher proposed a path model using the theoretical model diagrammed below. The variables are defined as follows: "Ability" is the girls' academic aptitude for quantitative work. "Parental influences" consist of the level of support and encouragement of parents for their daughters' education. "School influences" consist of the opportunities and support of teachers and counselors for girls' pursuit of math-related courses and activities. "Self-perception" is the degree of self-esteem and self-confidence held by the girls. "Perceptions of math" are the girls' attitude about math as an appropriate pursuit for females. "Math course taking" is the number of elective math courses taken in high school. "Occupational motivation" is the girls' level of ambition for successful and challenging careers. "Math achievement" is the degree of success in high school math courses. "College major" is whether or not the girls' college major is related to math.
    a. Label the exogenous variables.
    b. Label the endogenous variables.
    c. Label the mediating variables.
    d. According to the theory illustrated in the path diagram, is any causal relationship assumed between ability and school influences?
    e. Describe in words the direct and indirect effects hypothesized in the model.

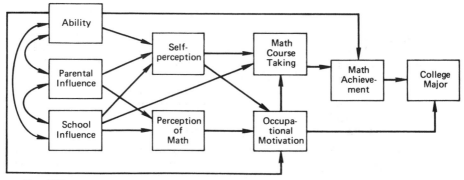

f. In a general way describe the measurement and analysis of variables that the researcher would use to test the model.
g. What two conditions must be met for the causal claims to have validity?
h. Discuss the implications of failure to meet these conditions.

9. Find the study by Robinson, Keith, and Page (1983) on "Now Who Aspires to Teach?" in the *Educational Researcher* (Vol. 12, pp. 13–21). After reading the article, respond to the following:
    a. What is the source of data for the study?
    b. To what population are the results generalizable?
    c. What is the research question addressed?
    d. What are the issues of reliability and validity that should be considered?
    e. Are there variables that might be a cause of a person's aspirations to become a teacher that are not included in the analysis? If so, what are they and how might their absence affect the conclusions of the study?
    f. Interpret the correlation between family orientation and parental influence in Table I. (It is significantly different from zero, $p < 0.05$.)
    g. What is the authors' rationale for doing the analysis separately for males and females, blacks and whites?

10. Look back to the time-series study by Van Houten et al. (1985) that you examined in question 11 of the exercises in Chapter 7. How do you know it is a quasi experiment rather than a causal-comparative design?

11. A large city police department had been keeping records of crime rates for the past 40 years. In 1980 a new police chief was hired. He inaugurated a package of reforms designed to reduce robberies and to improve the methods of reporting crimes. A plot of the yearly figures shows a slow but steady increase in robberies from 1940 to 1980, then a dramatic jump in the number of robberies at that point in the series. The rate of robberies has been about even from 1980 to 1985. The newspaper concluded that the new chief was responsible for the increase in robberies. What threat(s) to internal validity is (are) apparent?

12. In the same city, police who monitor the time-series of reported crimes on a weekly basis noticed that, in the current week, the rate of assaults on females was unusually and extremely high. The police chief immediately instituted a whistle-stop program, providing whistles to female workers throughout the city. The next week the rate of reported assaults was back to about the "normal" level, and the police chief attributed this to the whistle-stop program. What threat to internal validity is apparent?

13. Suggest some ways to add rigor to the designs presented in questions 11 and 12.

9

CORRELATIONAL
STUDIES

The previous three chapters covered studies with a common purpose: to investigate claims that one variable is the cause of another. Not all research and evaluation studies share that purpose. The goal of correlational studies is to understand the patterns of relationships among variables. The guiding questions take a form such as "What is the relationship between depression and learned helplessness?" rather than "Does learned helplessness cause depression?" Causal hypotheses are not examined in the correlational studies discussed here.

Correlational studies serve two broadly conceived purposes. The first is building theory about phenomena by better understanding the constructs, what they consist of, and how they relate to other constructs. For example, a researcher might ask these questions about the nature of creativity. Is it a composite of lower-order traits such as verbal fluency, flexibility, artistic productivity, and so on? Is creativity as currently defined and measured the same as or different from the construct of intelligence? Do creative people also tend to be eccentric and unbalanced? Does the creativity of children tend to be related to the creativity of their parents and grandparents? All of these questions serve to build and elaborate theory about this construct, and correlational studies are used to answer them.

The second purpose of correlational studies is to enable us to predict one variable from another (or several others). If two variables correlate with each other and the researcher knows an individual's status on one of them, then that person's status on the second variable can be forecast or predicted. Note that we differentiate *predict* from *cause*. The difference between a correlational study and a causal-comparative study is solely in the investigator's purpose: "to relate or predict" (correlational) as opposed to "to determine cause" (causal-comparative). Very often the methods used by the researchers are indistinguishable, both computing correlation coefficients, multiple regression analyses, chi square tests for independence of cross classifications, or mean differences between groups. Because the criteria for judging the merits of the two types of study differ, it is important for the reader to classify each study correctly. Internal validity is not a concern in a correlational study, because no causal claim is made. Although judgments of internal validity in correlational studies are irrelevant, in experiments, quasi experiments, and causal-comparative studies that judgment is central. On the other hand, correlational studies are more vulnerable to inadequate sampling and measurement and therefore must be judged more severely on these criteria than, say, experiments are. In correlational studies, the intent of the investigator to relate or predict, rather than establish cause, must be interpreted by the reader from the statements of questions, hypotheses, and conclusions.

In this chapter we deal first with the concept of correlation. In each subsequent section we examine some variety of correlational method: bivariate correlation, multiple regression, discriminant analysis, partial correlation, and factor analysis. Our aim in this chapter is to acquaint you with the principles and terminology you are likely to encounter in reading studies using these methods. To satisfy this aim, we have had to increase the technical level and use more complex statistics than found in the rest of the book. However, the increasing prevalence of correlational methods in the literature justifies the presentation. A review of the relevant sections of Chapter 3 may be useful if you encounter difficulties.

WHAT DOES IT MEAN WHEN WE SAY TWO VARIABLES ARE RELATED?

Correlational studies are a way to understand the variance of a variable. When two variables are related—that is, when they *covary* or are *concomitant* with each other—one "carries information" about the other. If, in a sample of individuals, height and weight are positively correlated, and we know that Alan's height is above average, then we can make a more or less accurate guess that his weight is also above average. If we know Wendy's weight and the extent of the relationship between height and weight, we know what her height is likely to be, even though her actual height is unknown to us. Of course, there is always some error involved in estimates such as these (Alan may be tall and extremely thin, thus defying the general pattern), because the relationships between variables are not perfect.

To determine how variables are related, we first look at the **direction of relationship**. A *positive*, or *direct*, *relationship* is one in which high scores on a scale or distribution of one variable are paired or associated with high scores on the other variable. Low scores on one are associated with low scores on the other, like height and weight. A *negative*, or *inverse*, *relationship* is one in which high scores on one variable go along with low scores on the other variable. Assume that a negative relationship exists between the number of school days absent and reading achievement. Pupils with a large number of absences are also likely to be the ones with poor reading achievement. Pupils with above-average reading achievement also tend to have fewer absences. One can predict achievement from absences, even when the relationship is inverse.

Variables may also be unrelated to each other, such as, perhaps, self-assertiveness and mathematics ability. If so, knowing that people are high on the dimension of self-assertiveness gives us no clue about whether their math ability is poor or excellent. In other words, there are likely to be as many math whizzes who are self-assertive as there are shy and timid math geniuses.

Beside the direction of the relationship between variables, relationships are of different **magnitude**; that is, they are either strong or weak. Furthermore, the relationships may be either **linear** or **curvilinear**. The shape of the relationship can best be determined by examining *scatterplots*, several of which are displayed in Figure 9–1. Figure 9–1a shows a positive, linear, and quite strong relationship between two variables: first-grade reading scores (plotted on the horizontal axis) and second-grade reading scores (plotted on the vertical axis of the graph). Note that high scores on one variable have a strong tendency to be paired with high scores on the other. Every person with a low score on first-grade reading also has a low score on second-grade reading. There are no individuals whose pair of scores departs very far from that pattern.

Figure 9–1b shows a positive, linear relationship of lesser magnitude, this time between the experience of therapists and the degree of success of their therapy. The points representing pairs of scores are not as closely packed as they are in the previous graph. Not only are they more spread out, but some individuals depart from the general pattern. Although the general trend is for more experienced therapists to have greater success, therapist M is inexperienced but successful. Such an individual is called an outlier and can be identified most readily by examining scatterplots. In spite of the outlier, the shape of the relationship of therapist experience and success is linear; not so with the relationship between age and psychomotor abilities depicted in Figure 9–1c. Low values of one variable are paired with either very high or very low values of the other. High values of the first variable are paired with middle-range values of the second. In other words, the relationship is curvilinear; very young people and very old people tend to have lower psychomotor abilities, while adolescents and young adults have the highest abilities. Figure 9–1d shows another sort of curvilinear relationship. Figure 9–1e shows a scatterplot of two variables that are unrelated. Figure 9–1f shows an inverse, or negative, linear relationship.

Relationships between variables are expressed in several ways. First, a researcher can compare the means of one variable of two or more groups that are differentiated on a second variable. For example, looking for a difference between right-handed and left-handed people on motor coordination is one way of examining the relationship between handedness and

FIGURE 9–1   Scatterplots that Reveal Relationships of Different Direction, Shape, and Magnitude

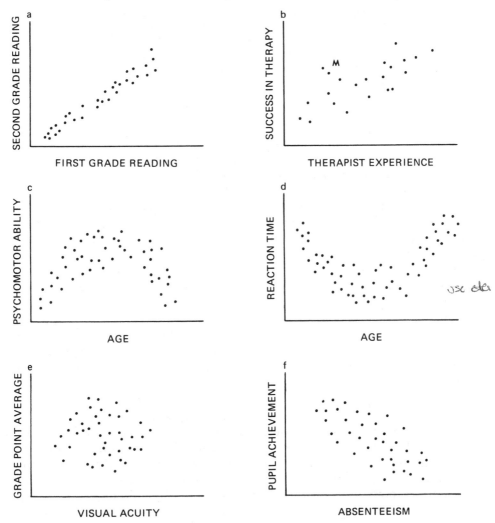

TABLE 9–1   Hypothetical Data Showing a Relationship between Television and Reading, Using a Cross-Classification Method

PUPILS CLASSIFIED BY NUMBER OF BOOKS READ AND AMOUNT OF TELEVISION VIEWED WITH PERCENTAGES BY ROWS

		NUMBER OF BOOKS READ		
		HIGH	LOW	
AMOUNT OF TELEVISION VIEWED	**HIGH**	$n = 2$ 10%	$n = 18$ 90%	20
	LOW	$n = 19$ 95%	$n = 1$ 1%	20
		21 52.5%	19 47.5%	$n = 40$

$X^2 = 28.97$; $df = 1$; $p < 0.01$

coordination. It is similar in method to the between-groups design in causal-comparative studies, *except* that no causal claim is made in correlational studies. The researcher is not claiming that left-handedness "causes" motor coordination. Instead, an attempt is being made to understand the pattern of relationship between the two variables.

The second way of expressing the relationship between variables employs the analysis of cross breaks, or the cross classification of variables. The researcher subcategorizes the sample according to two or more variables and looks for differences in relative frequency or percentages among the categories. Table 9–1 shows such a cross classification of amount of television viewing (the categories are high and low) and number of books read in a sample of 40 adults. The table shows an inverse relationship between the two categories (those who watch a lot of television are also those who read few books, and vice versa). A chi square statistic tests the null hypothesis that the categories are independent. A significant value of chi square indicates that the two variables are associated in the population. No causal claim is made.

The most prevalent way of expressing a relationship between variables is the correlation coefficient. The Pearson product-moment correlation coefficient is an index of the degree of relationship between two variables. It is used when the two variables are measured at least at the interval (or approximately interval) level of measurement. The symbol for the coefficient is *r*. It varies from − 1.00 (a perfect, inverse relationship) to + 1.00 (a perfect, direct relationship). Coefficients of 0.00 indicate an absence of a linear relationship between the two variables. Coefficients between 0.00

and 1.00 express relationships of lesser (nearer to zero) to greater (nearer to one) magnitude. An r of 0.50 is larger in an absolute sense than an r of 0.40. However, to conclude that a sample coefficient is large enough to permit a conclusion of nonzero relationship between the two variables in a population requires a test of statistical significance. The null hypothesis is that the relationship between the two variables is zero. A t-test is computed according to the following formula, which shows that the statistical significance of the correlation is a function of its magnitude (r) and the number of individuals in the sample (n):

Formula 9–1

$$t = \frac{r\sqrt{n - 2}}{\sqrt{1 - r^2}}$$

Most statistics books include table of r that correspond to different levels of significance and sample size. If the obtained r is greater than the tabled r at the sample size and chosen level of significance, then it is said to be "statistically significant," or "nonzero" in the population. For example, a researcher finds a correlation of $r = -0.38$ between recidivism and employment in a sample of 50 exconvicts. Assuming a previously chosen level of significance (alpha) of 0.05 and a sample size of 50, the standard table (Glass and Hopkins, 1984, p. 549) reveals that the magnitude of the correlation must be equal to or higher than 0.276 to be statistically significant, i.e., under -0.28 or over $+0.28$. The obtained r of 0.38 is larger in magnitude than the tabled value. Therefore, the researcher may conclude that the relationship between recidivism and employment "exceeds chance," is stable, or is "significantly nonzero."

The magnitude of a correlation in a sample is influenced by several features of the study. The level of reliability with which a variable is measured sets a limit on how high it can correlate with another variable. For example, the magnitude of the correlation between college aptitude tests and college grades may be "attenuated" by the low reliability of the grading procedure. To obtain a better idea on the actual relationship between two such variables, researchers sometimes perform what is known as **correction for attenuation**. This statistical procedure adjusts the obtained correlation upwards to account for error of measurement in either of the variables. Another restriction on the magnitude of the sample correlation is when the measurement of the variables has artificially "high floors" or "low ceilings." In other words, if the highest possible score that can be attained on a test is low enough to group several people together with perfect scores, then the correlation of that variable with any other will be artificially low (Glass and Hopkins, 1984, p. 84). Similarly, if the sample of individuals does not have sufficient variability with respect to the variable (e.g., if IQ and creativity are correlated in a class of gifted pupils), the correlation with other variables will be lower than it ought to be to reflect a better measured relationship between the variables. **Correction for range restriction** is a statistical procedure for better estimating the relationship between variables with less than sufficient variability in the sample (Hopkins and Stanley, 1981).

Pearson product-moment correlation coefficients will yield distorted results if the relationship between two variables is curvilinear. Figure 9–1c provides a good example. The product-moment correlation is about $r = 0.00$, which fails to convey the fact that the relationship between the two variables is not absent or random. This is one reason why the use of scatterplots is strongly recommended for correlational research. Although curvilinear relationships are relatively rare in social research, examination of scatterplots eliminates the criticism that linear correlation coefficients were inappropriately used. In those instances where curvilinear relationships are revealed in scatterplots, the researchers should use *eta*, the proper coefficient for relationships of that form (see Glass and Hopkins, 1984, pp. 141–144).

Both the product-moment correlation coefficient and the curvilinear correlation require that both variables have data in "continuous" form; that is, data that form scales at the interval or approximately interval level of measurement. For other forms of measurement, alternative indexes of relationship exist. Either the Spearman correlation (*rho*) or *Kendall's tau* is used when the data are in the form of ranks. *Biserial correlation* is used when one of the variables is measured in the form of a forced dichotomy and the other variable is in continuous form. Suppose that a researcher wanted to study the relationship between authoritarianism and religiosity. He measures both variables on a continuous scale but divides the religiosity scale at the median, creating a dichotomy of persons high and low on religiosity. The correct form of correlation is the biserial correlation because, although religiosity forms a dichotomy, there is a continuous variable underlying it (of course, there would be little point in translating continuous, fine-grain scales into dichotomies; the biserial *r* is generally used where a dichotomy is available that could have a continuous scale underneath it if more complex instruments were employed). Contrast this false or forced dichotomy with a true dichotomy. The researcher relates authoritarianism with Republican voting record. The first variable is continuous, the second is a true dichotomy (a person is classified into one of two categories—either he voted for the Republican presidential candidate in last election, or not). The *point biserial correlation* is used in such cases. The *phi coefficient* is used when both variables are true dichotomies, such as employment status (employed vs. unemployed) and high school graduation (yes or no). The *tetrachoric correlation* is used when the variables are both forced dichotomies. The *contingency coefficient* is used when the variables form two or more categories (employed, never employed, previously but not now employed). (For a presentation of details about these and other correlation coefficients, see Glass and Hopkins, 1984, Chap. 7.)

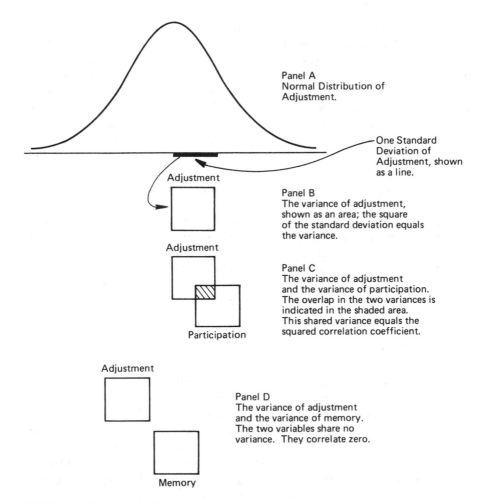

FIGURE 9–2   The Concept of Correlation as Shared Variance

When two variables are related to each other, they share **variance in common**. Look at Panel A of Figure 9–2. It represents the normal distribution of scores of former inpatients of a mental hospital in their self-ratings of adjustment. Notice that the double line on the horizontal axis of the distribution is the linear distance representing one standard deviation above the mean. The length of this line is a numerical index, or statistic, that tells how much variability there is on self-rated adjustment, or how much the individuals differ from each other on that variable. In Panel B of the figure, the double line has been squared to form an area that represents the variance of the variable. Both the standard deviation and the variance indicate the degree of individual differences. Panel C shows the variance of self-rated adjustment overlapping another variance, this one of a related variable, participation in aftercare programs. The fact that the two squares overlap tells us the two variables are related to each other. The area of overlap, indicated by the cross-hatched areas, is a measure of the extent of the variance that the two variables share. It is symbolized by r^2, the square of the correlation coefficient. If the correlation between these two variables is $r = 0.40$, the squared correlation is 0.16. It is interpreted as a percentage of the total variance that the variables hold in common—16 percent in this hypothetical example. The uncertainty about a person's participation in aftercare is reduced by knowing his self-rated adjustment. The remainder of the variance in participation is unknown; it is symbolized by τ^2, that is, the total variance minus the common variance equals the **unique variance**, or variance of adjustment, that is unexplained from knowledge of participation. Panel D shows the absence of shared variance in two other variables that do not correlate with each other: self-rated adjustment and memory. The correlation coefficient and the squared correlation are zero. The unique variance is near one. The two areas, representing the variance of the two variables, do not overlap. Knowing a person's self-rated adjustment provides no information about his memory. One could not predict his adjustment from knowledge of his memory.

THE CORRELATION MATRIX

So far the discussion has centered on the relationship between pairs of variables, or *bivariate correlations*. In published research, one seldom encounters a report of one bivariate correlation. More often the researcher reports a collection of bivariate relationships between all pairs of several variables in a **correlation matrix**. Examine the correlation matrix in Table 9–2. It exhibits two alternative forms of a matrix in which five variables are intercorrelated. Such a matrix is generated by selecting a sample of individuals (in this case, the units are classes rather than persons) and obtaining measures of all five variables in each of the classrooms. Bivariate product-moment correlation coefficients are computed between all pairs of variables, based on Formula 3–3 (p. 62), yielding ten correlations. In the first matrix, the cells, or entries in the table that represent the correlation of a variable with itself (e.g., time on task correlated with time on task), have only dashes in them. The dashes replace what would have been $r = 1.00$ in each cell *on the diagonal* of the matrix. This is done to ease visual inspection of the table. The same purpose is served by leaving blank the cells below the diagonal, which would otherwise contain information redundant with that above the diagonal. That is, the correlation of time on task with class size is the same as the correlation of class size with time on task and need not be repeated.

In the second matrix in Table 9–2 are the same statistics with one exception. Instead of dashes or correlations of 1.00 on the diagonal, the

TABLE 9–2 Two Forms of Correlation Matrix (Hypothetical Data)

	TIME ON TASK	CLASS SIZE	PUPIL SELF- DIRECTION	TEACHER CONTROL	READING ACHIEVE- MENT
Time on Task	—	−0.31	−0.47	0.52	0.37
Class Size		—	0.28	−0.19	−0.12
Pupil Self- Direction			—	−0.56	0.40
Teacher Control				—	0.24
Reading Achievement					—

Correlations above 0.296 are significant at or beyond the $p = 0.05$ level.

	TIME ON TASK	CLASS SIZE	PUPIL SELF- DIRECTION	TEACHER CONTROL	READING ACHIEVE- MENT
Time on Task	0.70	−0.31*	−0.47*	0.52*	0.37*
Class Size		0.97	0.28	−0.19	−0.12
Pupil Self- Direction			0.65	−0.56*	0.40*
Teacher Control				0.72	0.24
Reading Achievement					0.92

$p < 0.05$, $n = 45$ classrooms

researcher has placed the reliabilities of the measured variables. The cell representing the correlation of time on task with itself contains the correlation of $r = 0.70$, the interobserver reliability for that variable. The $r = 0.92$ is the test-retest reliability for the measure of reading achievement. The reason for this, other than convenience of reporting, is to alert the reader to the fact that the correlation of any two variables is constrained by the reliability of measurement of each one. Time on task, as an example, can correlate no higher with another variable than the square root of its reliability ($\sqrt{r} = \sqrt{.70} = 0.84$).

MULTIPLE REGRESSION

Regression analysis uses the correlation between two variables to predict one from the other. This is most easily understood by reference to the use of admission tests to predict success in higher education. The test developer measures aptitude in a large sample of applicants, then correlates these scores with first-year performance in school. In the next year's applicant pool, the aptitude test is administered. Based on the correlation computed the previous year, an individual's test score can predict his or her subsequent performance. The test score is called the **predictor variable**, and the performance is called the **criterion variable**. Some authors refer to these as the independent and dependent variables, respectively. We prefer predictor and criterion so that it will be clear that no causation is being inferred. Rather, the purpose is to forecast the performance of individuals based on their status on the predictor variable and the already established correlation between the two variables. One can safely say that college performance can be forecast with scholastic aptitude test scores, even though aptitude may not be the cause of performance. It is also possible to exchange the role of predictor and criterion and ask, "Based on this person's college performance, what was his scholastic aptitude score likely to have been?" A "prediction" or, more accurately, "estimation," is still possible, even though the temporal sequence rules out college performance as a plausible cause of scholastic aptitude test scores.

Besides the prediction of individual's scores on the criterion, regression analysis is also used in a more general way to ask how much change in the criterion can be expected from each increase in the score on the predictor variable. A regression analysis might be used to predict success in speech therapy from therapist experience. The question would be, "How does therapeutic success increase as therapists increase their level of experience from three to four years?" Correlation and regression would be computed simultaneously on a set of data.

Suppose that one wanted to predict success in foreign language training school for Peace Corps volunteers from a measure of their auditory memory. A sample of 20 volunteers is measured on auditory memory (the predictor variable), given the training, then tested on language performance. The scattergram in Figure 9–3 depicts the shape (linear), direction (positive), and magnitude (moderate) of the relationship of the variables. The correlation is $r = 0.61$. The criterion variable is always plotted on the vertical axis and is symbolized as Y. The predictor is plotted on the horizontal axis and symbolized as X. The diagonal line cutting through the scatterplot is the **regression line**, or line of least squares, or best fit. It is the straight line that best describes the relationship between the two variables and the "regression of language performance on auditory memory." The line in the graph is a special case of the general formula for a straight line:

Formula 9–2 $\hat{Y}_i = bX_i + c$

The formula can be read this way: $\hat{Y}_i$ is the predicted value of language performance for any chosen value of auditory memory. It equals the prod-

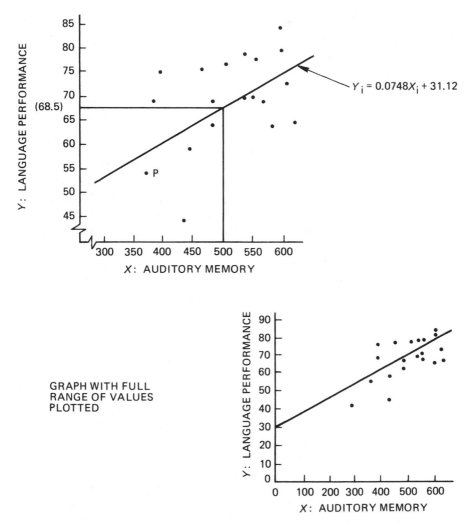

FIGURE 9–3 Scatterplot Showing the Regression of Language Performance on Auditory Memory

uct of that chosen value of auditory memory (X_i) and the **regression coefficient** (b), plus a constant (c). The constant refers to the value of language performance at which the regression line intersects the vertical axis. In this example the value of c is about 31, as you can see from the equation in Figure 9–3. The regression coefficient describes the steepness of the slope of the regression line. In this example, $b = 0.0748$, which can be interpreted this way: for every increase of one unit of auditory memory, one would expect an increase of 0.0748 of a unit of language performance. One can also predict a new student's language performance by finding the student's score on the horizontal axis (e.g., 500), drawing a straight vertical line from it to the regression line, then from that point drawing a horizontal line that intersects the vertical axis. Where that line intersects the vertical axis is the student's predicted language performance (e.g., 68.5).

The regression coefficients or regression weights are determined by the principle of **least squares**. Computation of these weights is beyond the scope of this book (see Glass and Hopkins, 1984, pp. 114 ff.) but rests on the idea that the regression line should minimize the squared distances between the predicted scores and the scores on the criterion that were actually achieved by the sample. Look at person P. His auditory memory score was 370, and the predicted language score for that level of auditory memory was determined by the regression equation to be 0.0748 (370) + 31.12 = 58.8. His obtained score on language performance was 54, however. The difference between the obtained score of 54 and the predicted language performance score of 58.8 is called **residual**, or **error of estimate**, for that person. For some individuals the errors are positive, and for others, like person P, the errors are negative (his obtained score is lower than his predicted score.) For the sample as a whole, the squared errors are minimized by the statistical procedures employed. The **standard error of estimate** is a statistic used to represent how discrepant are the obtained scores from the regression line.

In addition to the regression equation and standard error of estimate, another commonly reported feature in regression analyses is the **proportion of variance accounted for**. The components of the analysis yield an r^2, an index of the proportion of the criterion variable variance that is predictable from the predictor variable (recall Figure 9–2.) The r^2 is 0.369. About 37 percent of the variance of language performance can be accounted for by knowledge of a person's auditory memory. This is a measure of the magnitude of the relationship between the two variables. Therefore, 63 percent of the variance in language performance is *unique variance*; that is, unpredictable from auditory memory.

Still another form of reporting in regression analysis is the test of statistical significance of the regression coefficients (b). Tests such as these are made when the intent of the researcher is to generalize beyond the sample at hand to some larger population. Does auditory memory predict language performance in the population, or just in this limited sample of 20? An F-test is computed to test the null hypothesis that the predictability of language performance from auditory memory is zero. If the probability value for the obtained F-test is equal to or smaller than the researcher's chosen alpha (0.05, for example), then the null hypothesis is rejected.

Multiple regression analysis involves the prediction of a criterion variable from two or more predictor variables. The statistical procedure optimally weights each predictor, so that *together* they combine to yield a regression prediction that minimizes the squared residuals (the difference between obtained scores and scores predicted by the combination of predictors). Consider the simplest case of two predictor variables—auditory memory (X_1) and number of languages already known (X_2) predicting the language performance (Y) of Peace Corps volunteers. The equation in Formula 9–3 can be seen as an extension of Formula 9–2.

Formula 9–3 $$\hat{Y}_i = b_1X_1 + b_2X_2 + b_0$$

Translated into words, the formula reads "an individual's predicted language performance (Y_i) is equal to the sum of the constant (b_0), plus the product of that individual's score on auditory memory and the regression weight for auditory memory (b_1X_1) plus the product of number of languages known and the regression weight for that variable (b_2X_2)." The regression weights are statistically determined by the principle of least squares. In multiple regression, the regression weights are more properly called **partial regression coefficients** because their computation takes into account the correlation of the two predictor variables with each other. If auditory memory and number of languages already known are independent, then the best prediction of the criterion could be made simply by adding together the separate regression weights of each predictor. But auditory memory is likely to correlate with number of languages already known. Those who have already mastered several languages are also apt to have high levels of auditory memory. Information about language performance gained by these is redundant. In fact, if the predictors are strongly correlated with each other (either positively or negatively), the predictability of the criterion by the two variables is not improved over the predictability of the criterion by either one of the predictor variables.

The partial regression coefficient for any predictor takes into account the regression weights for the other predictors in the equation. The question becomes, "What is the predictability of language performance from number of languages already known, once auditory memory is controlled?" Or, "Once we have predicted all we can about language performance from knowledge of how many languages a person has already mastered, what more about language performance can we predict from that person's auditory memory?" The technical terms used by regression analysts are *residualizing*, *holding constant*, or *partialing* when they discuss controlling the redundancy of predictor variables.

The products of a multiple regression analysis include a multiple correlation (R, the correlation between the criterion variable and a weighted combination of predictors), the proportion of variance accounted for by the combination of predictors (R^2), errors of estimate for individual scores, a standard error of estimate, statistical significance tests for the multiple correlation and for the contribution of each predictor variable. To illustrate these features we turn to a study by Pascarella, Walberg, Haertel, and Junker (1981) on the prediction of educational aspirations from nine predictor variables. A large and representative sample of 13-and 17-year-olds

(n = 2,944) was selected from the files of the National Assessment of Educational Progress. The criterion variable, educational aspiration, was measured with the questionnaire item, "Do you expect to graduate from college?" which was coded 3 if answered "yes," 2 if "don't know," and 1 if answered "no." The bivariate correlations are presented in the top portion of Table 9–3. In the bottom portion of the panel are excerpts from the multiple regression analysis. There is a line in the table for each predictor

TABLE 9–3 Correlations and Regression Analysis

CORRELATIONS, MEANS AND STANDARD DEVIATIONS

	1	2	3	4	5	6	7	8	9	10	M	SD
1. *Educational Aspiration*	1.00	0.20	−0.11	0.26	0.24	0.28	0.14	0.01	−0.11	0.26	2.30	0.84
2. *Motivation*		1.00	−0.40	0.55	0.09	0.12	0.12	−0.18	−0.05	0.26	17.67	4.99
3. *Quality of Instruction*			1.00	−0.51	0.01	0.01	−0.04	0.01	0.12	−0.07	47.82	8.65
4. *Class Morale*				1.00	0.10	0.08	0.12	−0.09	−0.06	0.31	72.61	10.66
5. *Mother's Education*					1.00	0.51	0.25	0.05	0.15	0.27	4.16	1.24
6. *Father's Education*						1.00	0.25	−0.03	0.16	0.28	4.18	1.48
7. *Home Environment*							1.00	0.01	0.23	0.34	3.47	0.83
8. *Gender*								1.00	0.01	−0.14	1.50	0.50
9. *Ethnicity*									1.00	0.35	0.84	0.37
10. *Science Achievement*										1.00	41.76	7.87

Correlations above r = 0.08 are significant at the 0.01 level

Source: Pascarella, Walberg, Haertel, and Junker (1981).

MULTIPLE REGRESSION ANALYSIS PREDICTING EDUCATIONAL ASPIRATION

PREDICTOR VARIABLE	b	BETA	F
Motivation	0.007	0.039	1.78
Quality of Instruction	0.002	0.016	0.33
Class Morale	0.012	0.151	23.37*
Mother's Education	0.074	0.109	15.56*
Father's Education	0.106	0.186	44.83*
Home Environment	0.025	0.024	0.91
Gender	0.112	0.066	7.70*
Ethnicity	−0.511	−0.224	75.33*
Science Achievement	0.021	0.198	48.03*

Constant: −0.216
R^2 = 0.204, $p < 0.001$ (R = 0.452)
*$p < 0.01$

variable plus the constant in the regression equation. To the immediate right of the predictor variable name is the column headed "*b*" for the beta weight, or *unstandardized regression coefficient*. The next column, headed "Beta," consists of the *standardized regression coefficient* for each variable (where the variable has been converted to standard scores with a mean of zero and a standard deviation of one). In the right-hand column are the F-test values for the partial regression coefficients of each variable. The F-test for the "motivation" predictor is $F = 1.78$, which has a probability greater than alpha $= 0.01$ and therefore is not statistically significant. One would interpret this finding to mean that motivation does not reliably contribute to the prediction of educational aspirations when all other variables are "partialed out" or "controlled." The variable "class morale" has an F-test value of 23.37. As indicated by the asterisk, this is significant at the 0.001 level. There is less than one chance in a thousand that "class morale" fails to contribute to the multiple prediction of educational aspirations in the population sampled, even with the eight other variables controlled. In the population, educational aspiration can be accounted for by class morale. Each F-test is an assessment of how much of educational aspiration is predicted by the associated predictor variable or how much that predictor variable *adds to* the predictability of the criterion. The value of R^2 is 0.204. This is a measure of the variance in educational aspiration that is accounted for by the optimally weighted combination of the nine predictors. Of the variance 20 percent is common, leaving 80 percent "unaccounted for," or *unique variance*. In other words, most of the individual differences in whether a pupil expects to attend college is not explained by the nine variables used as predictors in this study. The strength of the association of all predictors with the criterion is relatively low.

Notice how certain predictor variables performed. In the correlation matrix the correlation between educational aspiration and motivation is $r = 0.20$. Because of the size of the sample this correlation is significantly greater than zero, indicating that a nonzero relationship between these two variables exists in the population. Yet in the regression analysis the partial regression coefficient did not add significantly to the prediction (the probability value of F was greater than 0.01). One can see from the correlation that there is substantial redundancy between motivation and class morale. Therefore, motivation did not add to the predictability of educational aspiration after class morale was figured into the equation. Gender seems to perform in this analysis as a **suppressor variable**. Although it fails to correlate with educational aspiration ($r = 0.01$), the partial regression coefficient for gender adds significantly to the explained variance of the criterion ($p < 0.01$). The real relationship between educational aspiration and gender is hidden in, or "suppressed," by the relationship between gender and some other variable in the matrix. When the latter relationship is partialed out, then the effect of gender on the predictability of educational aspiration emerges.

The interpretation of regression coefficients, even with the assistance of significance tests, is not always as clear-cut as one would like. The determination of which variables turn out to contribute significantly to prediction (and which do not) does not always make good sense from a theoretical standpoint. The mathematics in the equation determine the composite of those predictors whose combined correlation with the criterion results in the smallest sum of squared residuals. A statistical criterion rather than a theoretical one is satisfied by this procedure. It might be that in the Pascarella et al. data that a variable like motivation ought, in theory, to be associated with educational aspiration. Yet statistically, it is not a significant predictor in this analysis. Multiple regression is blind, as it were, to theoretical significance. Motivation is statistically redundant with class morale. In other words, the same portion of the variance of educational aspiration that is accounted for by motivation is also accounted for by class morale. Figure 9–4 depicts this phenomenon, known as **multiple collinearity** among the three variables. Attaching theoretical meaning to regression weights when multiple collinearity exists, particularly when sample sizes are small, is likely to be misleading (Cohen and Cohen, 1983). One would be taking an unreasonable risk in concluding from the Pascarella data that motivation was of no importance in understanding educational aspiration. Figure 9–5 depicts the hypothetical (and unusual, for social research) case where two predictors (X_1 and X_2) account for unique variance in the criterion variable (Y)—that is, no collinearity.

The presentation so far has centered on **simultaneous multiple regression**, where all predictor variables are included in the regression equation at once as a package. Another variety of multiple regression is **step-wise multiple regression** (Nie, Hull, Jenkins, Steinbrenner, and Bent, 1975). The analysis proceeds in incremental steps. In step 1, the single best predictor of the criterion is chosen, and R is computed. In step 2, the next most powerful predictor is chosen. The choice is based on the relationship between the predictor and the criterion, statistically controlling for the

FIGURE 9–4   Multiple Correlation as Shared Variance (Multiple Collinearity of Predictors)

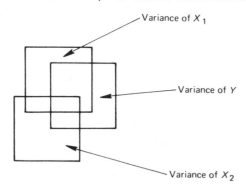

Variance of X_1

Variance of Y

Variance of X_2

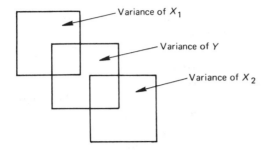

Variance of X_1

Variance of Y

Variance of X_2

FIGURE 9-5   Multiple Correlation as Shared Variance (No Collinearity)

relationship between the criterion and the predictor chosen at step 1. Step 3 selects the third best predictor after the previous two variables are partialed out or controlled. These steps continue until all predictor variables are considered. At each step an **incremental R^2** is computed. This statistic tells whether the variable entered at that step added to the predictable variance of the criterion over and above the predictors entered in previous steps. A significance test is performed on each cumulative or incremental R^2 to help interpret whether, in the population, that variable is likely to contribute to the predictability of the criterion. The cautions against interpreting individual regression coefficients, stated above, also apply to assigning meaning to the incremental R^2 for each predictor entered into the equation. The statistical procedures merely enhance the overall predictability of the criterion and do not reflect the theoretical significance of the separate predictors. An alternative design, known as **hierarchical multiple regression**, allows the researcher to specify, according to the theoretical significance of the set of predictors, which variable enters the regression equation at step 1 (Cohen and Cohen, 1983). For example, if Pascarella and his colleagues had good theoretical justification for proposing that motivation best explains educational aspiration, they could have used hierarchical multiple regression and specified that motivation was the predictor variable to enter the equation first. At subsequent steps in the analysis, predictors are selected statistically based on the amount of predictable variance they add, after motivation is partialed out. Hierarchical regression analysis is first cousin to path analysis (see Chapter 8). The techniques are similar except that the purpose of the path analyst is to assess the cause and effect relationships between predictors and criterion variables (Kenny, 1979).

Several drawbacks to regression analysis have already been alluded to, primarily the misleading interpretation of regression coefficients. A serious problem is known as "capitalization on chance," which is a by-product of the statistical procedures used to select and combine predictors to reach the optimal prediction of the criterion variable. These procedures rest on the assumption that the correlations of the variables are determined without error. The multiple correlation (R) of the criterion and the combination of predictors, as well as the proportion of the variance of the criterion that is accounted for by the predictors (R^2) is larger than it ought to be. Biased and inflated R values present problems of generalization. An inflated R is unlikely to be replicated in another sample.

Several circumstances exacerbate capitalization on chance. The first is small sample size. As the ratio of the number of predictors to the size of the sample rises, the results grow more misleading. To avoid this problem, some methodologists recommend having at least 30 subjects for each predictor variable in the equation. Others recommend that, for estimates of R^2 to be stable and generalizable, as many as 300 subjects are needed for each predictor (Kerlinger and Pedhauzur, 1973). The second problem occurs when the researcher "goes fishing" in a large pool of predictors for a subset to be entered into the regression equation. Having data on, say, 100 potential predictors, the researcher conducts a preliminary analysis by computing the correlation matrix of all these variables with the criterion. Because he knows that using too many predictor variables will distort the results, he wants to pick only five (his sample size being 200). He selects five predictors based on their high correlations with the criterion and moderate to low correlations with each other. These he uses in the final regression analysis. Unfortunately, this procedure also capitalizes on chance and produces overinflated (and nongeneralizable) values for R^2. To offset this problem, an even larger sample size is needed if a preliminary fishing expedition has been made.

Two procedures correct for inflated values of R^2 and misleading interpretation of regression coefficients. The first is a **shrinkage correction** for R^2, which reduces the magnitude of R^2 in accordance with the sample size and ratio of predictors to sample size. Analyses with small samples and large ratios of predictors to sample sizes will have relatively greater shrinkage (e.g., one would expect little shrinkage of R^2 in the Pascarella et al. data where the ratio of predictors to sample size is 9 to 2,944). The second procedure is **cross validation**. The researcher uses two samples rather than one. The regression equation and R^2 are computed in the first sample. The obtained regression coefficients are then applied to individuals in the second sample. A correlation coefficient is computed between the predicted values of the criterion variable (as determined in the first analysis) and the actual scores on the criterion variable attained by the member of the second sample. High correlations reflect good stability. Low correlations reflect capitalization on chance. The amount of overinflation of R^2 based on capitalization on chance is estimated by the size of the difference between the two values of R^2 computed in the two samples. When shrinkage is small, the two samples may be combined for the most stable estimates of R^2 and the regression coefficients for predictors (Kerlinger and Pedhauzur, 1973).

Multiple collinearity has already been cited as a problem in regression analysis. The final problem is when the relationships among variables are curvilinear rather than linear. Transformation (e.g., X^2 or log X) is often required for curvilinear data.

DISCRIMINANT ANALYSIS

Discriminant analysis is a relative of regression analysis that is used when the criterion variable is the classification of the sample into two or more discrete groups (schizophrenic versus neurotic versus normal individuals; successful versus unsuccessful managers; effective versus ineffective schools). The categories have already been defined and each subject categorized into a group. The discriminant analysis equation determines the contributions of the predictors to correct classification of the individuals into the groups. The researcher can conclude whether the collection of predictors correctly classifies individuals into groups and which of the variables contribute significantly to the prediction of group membership. All the cautions named in reference to regression analysis apply to discriminant analysis as well (Tatsuoka, 1971).

PARTIAL CORRELATION

Partial correlation is used to elucidate the relationship between two variables by holding a third variable constant, or controlling for it. Look back to the correlation matrix in Table 9–2. The bivariate correlations are called **zero-order correlations** to distinguish them from higher-order, residualized, or partial correlations. Zero-order correlations depict the relationship between two variables with the influence of all other variables mixed in. For example, the zero-order correlation between time on task and reading achievement is $r = 0.37$. This is an index of the association between these two variables no matter what the size of the class is, no matter what levels of pupil self-direction and teacher control are represented. The relationship is unconditional. But what if, say, class-size is held constant? Would the relationship between time on task and reading achievement still be apparent? Or does the relationship between these two variables depend on how big the class is? Partial correlation is a form of statistical control that can inform the researcher whether time on task and reading achievement are associated *at all levels of class size* or *only at a certain class size*. In Formula 9–4, time on task is denoted by X_1, reading achievement by X_2, and class size by X_3, the correlation between time on task and reading achievement by r_{12}, and so on.

Formula 9–4
$$r_{12 \cdot 3} = \frac{r_{12} - r_{13}r_{23}}{\sqrt{(1 - r_{13}^2)(1 - r_{23}^2)}}$$

The symbol $r_{12\cdot3}$ may be read as "the correlation between time on task and reading achievement, with class size held constant." Its value is calculated to be $r_{12\cdot3} = 0.35$. Compare this **first-order partial correlation** with the zero-order correlation between time on task and reading achievement ($r_{12} = 0.37$). That the difference is so small and the partial correlation is still significantly different from zero ($p < 0.05$) means that the relationship between time on task and reading achievement still exists even when class size is controlled; that is, one would expect to see a correlation of 0.35 between time on task and class size even if only classes of 25 students were observed. The association exists in small classes as well as large.

Now imagine a different set of results. Suppose that, contrary to the facts in Table 9–2, the first-order partial correlation was $r_{12\cdot3} = 0.12$. The substantial difference in magnitude between the zero-order correlation, $r_{12} = 0.37$, and the first-order partial correlation, 0.12, and the fact that the partial is not significantly different from zero means that the relationship between time on task and reading achievement is *conditional on class size*; that is, for classes of one fixed size—say, 30 pupils—one would *not* find a correlation between class size and time on task. If the zero-order r of time on task and class size was 0.35, but the partial r controlling for class size was near zero, it might suggest that time on task and achievement are related because both are related to class size (e.g., larger classes may suffer more disruption and confusion, lowering time on task, and also allow for less individual attention to pupils, lowering reading achievement).

The idea of partial correlation can be extended to include second-order partial correlations (the correlation of X_1 and X_2 with X_3 and X_4 controlled) and so on. You should note that partial correlation is closely related to multiple regression. One could redesign the analysis of the data in Table 9–2 into a regression analysis with reading achievement as the criterion. The regression coefficients for each predictor would be the same as the third-order partial correlation between that predictor and the criterion, with the relationships between the criterion and the other three predictors partialed out or statistically controlled.

FACTOR ANALYSIS

Factor analysis is an advanced variety of correlational study. In Table 9–2, five variables were intercorrelated, yielding ten unique bivariate correlations. With this number of correlations, it is easily possible to keep track mentally of the pattern of relationships. But what if the number of correlations was 105 (for 15 variables) or 780 (for 40 variables)? The human mind cannot efficiently process so many disparate pieces of information. Factor analysis is a way of simplifying and reducing a large number of bivariate correlations into a more parsimonious set of *factors*. The statistical technique involves the notion of the common variance in the collection of variables.

The researcher begins with a sample of individuals (or units), each of whom is measured on every variable. These measurements are converted to bivarate correlations for each pair of variables. The matrix of correlations is the material for the factor analysis. Table 9–4 contains the correlation matrix of eight political variables measured in 146 election areas in Chicago in the 1930s (reliabilities in the diagonal). These data and analysis are from Harman (1960).

The first step of the factor analysis is called *factor extraction*. The correlation matrix is searched (statistically, not literally) for sets of variables that intercorrelate, or share common variance, with each other. Each set is a factor, a mathematical combination of the variables that hang together. A second kind of correlation is computed, which is an index of the relationship between each variable in the original matrix and each of the factors extracted. This index is known as a *factor loading*. Ideally, each variable should have high factor loadings with one factor and moderate or low factor loadings with the other factors. This indicates that a variable shares variance with other variables in its factor, but its variance is distinct from that of variables loaded heavily on other factors. The researcher names each factor based on the apparent similarities of the variables that load on it. Table 9–5 contains the factor matrix. Notice that two factors have been extracted and named, traditional democratic voting (TDV) and home permanancy (HP). The percentage of an election district voting for Roosevelt correlated 0.88 with TDV and −0.48 with HP. The table also contains a line for *communality*, the variance of a variable that is shared with (or in

TABLE 9–4 Intercorrelations of Eight Political Variables for 147 Election Areas

VARIABLE	1	2	3	4	5	6	7	8
1. Percent voting for Lewis	(0.52)*							
2. Percent voting for Roosevelt	0.84	(1.00)						
3. Percent of straight party votes	0.62	0.84	(0.78)					
4. Median rental	−0.53	−0.68	−0.76	(0.82)				
5. Homeownership	0.03	−0.05	0.08	−0.25	(0.36)			
6. Unemployment	0.57	0.76	0.81	0.80	0.25	(0.80)		
7. Mobility	−0.03	−0.35	−0.51	0.62	−0.72	−0.58	(0.63)	
8. Education	−0.63	−0.78	−0.81	0.88	−0.36	−0.84	0.68	(0.97)

* Diagonal entries are reliabilities of the variables rather than 1.00s.

Source: Harman, 1960, p. 178.

TABLE 9–5   Unrotated Factor Matrix (Principal Factor Pattern) for Eight Political Variables

VARIABLE	COMMON FACTORS		COMMUNALITY
	TDV	HP	
1. Percent voting for Lewis	0.69	−0.28	0.52
2. Percent voting for Roosevelt	0.88	−0.48	1.00
3. Straight party voting	0.87	−0.17	0.78
4. Median rental	−0.88	−0.09	0.82
5. Homeownership	−0.28	0.65	0.36
6. Unemployment	0.89	0.01	0.80
7. Mobility	−0.66	−0.56	0.63
8. Education	−0.96	−0.15	0.97
Percent of total original communality	85.2%	18.8%	

Source: Harman, 1960, p. 178.

common with) all the other variables in the set of variables being analyzed as well as the percent of the total communality accounted for by each of the two factors.

The next step is *factor rotation*—the factors are manipulated mathematically to reduce the ambiguity of factor loadings. The goal is to enhance the correlation of variables with the factors they load most highly on and reduce the correlation of the variable with the other factors. In the example of the matrix of factor loadings (Table 9–5), the variable of mobility loads negatively on both factors. This is the kind of ambiguity (is mobility part of traditional Democratic voting or home permanency?) that factor rotation is designed to reduce. Table 9–6 contains the final rotated factor matrix. The ambiguity regarding mobility has been overcome, as it correlates −0.15 with TDV and 0.68 with HP.

TABLE 9–6   Rotated Factor Structure (Quartimin Solution) of Eight Political Variables

VARIABLE	FACTORS	
	TDV	HP
1. Percent voting for Lewis	0.71	0.14
2. Percent voting for Roosevelt	0.98	0.30
3. Straight party voting	0.78	−0.01
4. Median rental	−0.62	0.26
5. Homeownership	−0.20	−0.69
6. Unemployment	0.68	−0.19
7. Mobility	−0.15	0.68
8. Education	0.64	0.34

Correlation between the factors: $r_{TDV,HP} = -0.47$

Source: Harmon, 1960, p. 332.

Factor analysis is a popular and powerful tool in social research. It is particularly appropriate in three areas: First, factor analysis is used in test development to enhance the internal consistency of tests. It is a form of item analysis that checks whether all of the items on a scale are measuring the same trait. Test items are treated as variables in a correlation matrix. The factor analysis method is used to identify those items that do not share common variance with the others. Those that measure something unique are deleted. If several factors are extracted and they make good conceptual sense as subconstructs or components of a trait, subtests are constructed that are based on the separate factors.

The second application is in the theoretical understanding and validation of constructs. For example, is intelligence a single trait or is it a composite of relatively independent traits such as memory, perceptual acuity, and problem-solving skill? Factor analysis helps to clarify questions such as these. It detects whether all the variables share common variance (all individuals tend to be high or low on all of them), or whether the variance is unique from trait to trait (e.g., individuals high on problem solving are equally likely to be high or low on memory).

The third application is the selection of composite variables from very large collections of variables. If the researcher has a large number of possible predictors for regression analysis, he could perform a factor analysis. Factors—composites of variables—then can be used as predictor variables in the regression equation. Instead of scores on each of, say, 100 variables, the individuals are assigned factor scores on the five factors that were extracted and refined in the factor analysis. Factor scores can also be used as dependent variables in experiments or path analyses or may play any other role generally played by the score on a measured variable. The statistics of factor analysis are beyond the scope of this book (for more information, see Child, 1970; Harman, 1960).

CRITERIA FOR JUDGING THE MERITS OF CORRELATIONAL STUDIES

When reading correlational studies you should consider the following questions:

1. Has the sample been chosen to represent a defined population? Or have the characteristics of the sample been described sufficiently so that a judgment of generalization can be made?

2. Is the sample large enough not only to yield stable bivariate correlations but to offset problems of capitalization on chance? Is there sufficient variability in the sample?

3. Have the variables been measured with adequate reliability and validity?

4. Have scatterplots been examined to rule out curvilinear relationships between variables?

5. Have the correct correlational statistics been chosen?

6. In multiple regression studies, has a shrinkage correction been applied or cross validation performed?

7. Has the author inappropriately interpreted the meaning of significant and nonsignificant regression coefficients?

8. Has the author committed the correlation-causation fallacy in interpreting the results?

SUGGESTED READINGS

CHILD, D. *The Essentials of factor analysis.* London: Holt, Rinehart & Winston, 1970.

COHEN, J., and COHEN, P. *Applied multiple regression/correlation analysis for the behavioral sciences* (2nd ed.). Hillsdale, N.J.: Lawrence Erlbaum, 1983.

COOLEY, W.W., and LOHNES, P.R. *Multivariate data analysis.* New York: John Wiley, 1971.

DARLINGTON, R.B. Multiple regression in psychological research and practice. *Psychological Bulletin*, 1972, 77, 446–452.

GLASS, G.V., and HOPKINS, K.D. *Statistical methods in education and psychology* (2nd ed.). Englewood Cliffs, N.J.: Prentice-Hall, 1984.

GUILFORD, J.P. The structure of intellect. *Psychological Bulletin*, 1956, 53, 267–293.

HARMAN, H.H. *Modern factor analysis.* Chicago: University of Chicago Press, 1960.

KENNY, D.A. *Correlation and causality.* New York: Wiley-Interscience, 1979.

KERLINGER, F.N. and PEDHAZUR, E.J. *Multiple regression in behavioral research.* New York: Holt, Reinhart & Winston, 1973.

TATSUOKA, M.M. *Multivariate analysis: Techniques for educational and psychological research.* New York: John Wiley, 1971.

TERMS INTRODUCED IN THIS CHAPTER

direction of relationship
magnitude
linear relationship
curvilinear relationship
correction for attenuation
correction for range restriction
variance in common
unique variance
correlation matrix
predictor variable
criterion variable
regression line
regression coefficient
residual
error of estimate
standard error of estimate

proportion of variance accounted for
multiple regression analysis
partial regression coefficient
suppressor variable
multiple collinearity
simultaneous multiple regression
step-wise multiple regression
incremental R^2
hierarchial multiple regression
shrinkage correction
cross validation
discriminant analysis
partial correlation
zero-order correlation
first-order partial correlation
factor analysis

QUESTIONS AND EXERCISES FOR FURTHER STUDY

1. In your own words, state the difference in purpose between correlational and causal-comparative studies. Can they always be distinguished from each other by their methods?

2. In a sample of 50 married women, a correlation of $r = 0.40$ was found between a measure of marital satisfaction and an index of shared responsibility for housework. Interpret this correlation in terms of direction, magnitude, and shared variance. Given this correlation, what do we know about a person's marital satisfaction when we know her score on the index of shared housework?

3. A fitness researcher finds a Pearson product-moment correlation of $r = 0.11$ between amount of weight lost and self-reported fidelity to a prescribed diet among 40 obese males. The correlation coefficient was not significantly different from zero. Is the researcher's task complete, or is there some other procedure that you would recommend to understand the relationship between these two variables?

4. A researcher finds a value of $R^2 = 0.15$ resulting from a multiple regression analysis predicting college attrition from five predictor variables: sex, age of entrance, SAT, self-concept, and religiosity. Because of the large sample size, the R^2 is significant. What do you believe is the best interpretation of the result?

5. A zero-order correlation between city density and crime is $r = 0.60$ ($p < 0.01$). The first-order partial correlation between density and crime with poverty held constant is $r = 0.10$ (not significant). Interpret the partial correlation. What is the zero-order correlation between poverty and density likely to be? What is the special term used to describe the relationship between variables such as density and poverty when they are used jointly to predict crime?

6. The following table represents output from a hypothetical multiple regression analysis predicting girls' twelfth-grade math achievement from IQ, ninth-grade math achievement, and number of elective math courses taken (all predictors are entered simultaneously).

MULTIPLE REGRESSION ANALYSIS OF TWELFTH-GRADE MATH ACHIEVEMENT

ANOVA	df	SS	MS	F
Regression	3	33.26	11.02	16.88*
Residual	187	103.33	0.52	

Multiple $R = 0.49$*
$R^2 = 0.24$

PREDICTORS IN EQUATION	b_B	STANDARD ERROR	BETA	F
1. IQ	0.2503	0.07	0.26	16.95*
2. Ninth Grade Math Achievement	0.1261	0.12	0.08	1.20
3. Number of Elective Math Courses Taken	0.0635	0.04	0.10	2.65*
Constant				

*significant $p \leqslant 0.05$

    a.   Identify the criterion variable.

    b.   Identify the predictor variables.

    c.   What percentage of the variance of the criterion is predictable with this set of predictors?

    d.   Is the criterion predictable at greater than chance levels?

    e.   The column labeled Beta is the partial correlation coefficient for each predictor. Interpret Beta for the predictor IQ.

    f.   Does the nonsignificant Beta for ninth-grade math achievement mean that it is theoretically unrelated to twelfth-grade math achievement? Explain your answer.

    g.   Use this example to explain multiple collinearity and suggest some solutions to that problem.

7. A researcher wants to determine whether a set of predictors (IQ, teacher judgment, pediatrician's recommendation, and prenatal history) can explain whether or not pupils are placed in special education. What is the name of the procedure that would answer this question?

8. A researcher wants to know whether all subtests and items in a multifactorial battery of mechanical aptitude tests are really measuring a single construct or trait. What is the name of the procedure that would answer this question?

9. List four or five conditions in multiple regression that should be satisfied for the results to be credible.

10

SURVEY METHODS IN RESEARCH AND EVALUATION

The goal of all research is to produce generalizable knowledge. By that we mean that when a correlation between achievement and self-esteem is found in a sample of tenth graders, the real purpose is to know the relationship of those variables in the population. The sample is interesting only to the extent that it allows us to make inferences about some broader population of tenth graders. Survey methods provide ways to describe the variables in populations and to test the relationships among variables in populations.

Although survey methods have a venerable tradition in the scholarly disciplines of sociology and political science, their application to educational research has been somewhat less admirable. The bulk of doctoral dissertations in education are based on surveys. But in too many cases the candidates have thoughtlessly thrown together a few questionnaire items, sent the questionnaire out to poorly selected samples of poorly defined populations, accepted whatever results came back, and let the canned computer program spew out endless tables. Little mental activity was apparent. In a study of dissertations in educational administration, Haller (1979) showed that survey techniques were chosen when the doctoral candidate viewed the dissertation simply as a hurdle to be gotten over in the simplest way possible.

Yet it does not have to be this way. There are outstanding examples of survey research in education and applied social science. Studies such as that of Coleman (Coleman et al., 1966), Weiss (1978), and the National Assessment of Educational Progress (1978) follow the best traditions of survey research. By acquainting yourself with these models of good practice, you can gain a new appreciation for the value of survey methods and improve the quality of your survey efforts.

DESCRIPTIVE SURVEY DESIGNS

The fundamental purpose of survey research is to describe the characteristics or variables in populations by directly examining samples. Therefore, the most basic survey design is a **single-group, single-observation design**. Here are some typical research questions that can be addressed by this design:

1. How many certified social workers in the state of Wyoming have advanced degrees?
2. What is the attitude of school board members in the United States about educating the children of illegal aliens?
3. What is the degree of sex-role stereotyping in science textbooks?
4. What do pediatric ward nurses believe to be true about infants' sensitivity to pain?

Notice that in all four questions, the status of one characteristic defines the object of the study. In question 4, the characteristic or variable of interest is "beliefs about infants' pain sensitivity." The goal is to describe the range of such beliefs in some interesting population—namely, the population of nurses who work in pediatric wards. This might be as simple as noting the percentage of the population who believe (and the corresponding percentage who do not believe) that infants feel pain.

We might decide to answer this research question by developing a questionnaire that measures this belief and administering it to every member of the population of nurses in pediatric wards. Obviously, that would be an expensive and difficult undertaking. It also turns out to be unnecessary provided we employ particular strategies for sampling from the population. The accuracy with which the question can be answered depends on the adequacy of the **sampling design**.

A sampling design consists of the following steps:

1. Careful definition of the population
2. Selection of a sample from the population
3. Observation or measurement of the variable in the sample
4. Estimation of the variable in the population based on measurements taken in the sample
5. Statement of the accuracy of the estimates

Population definition   Despite its common meaning, in a research context the word population does not imply "all the citizens of a country." The technical meaning is "the entire collection or set of individuals to which the findings of the study apply." Depending on the purpose of the study, its population may be defined broadly (e.g., "all members in good standing of the Association of Hospital Nurses of America") or narrowly (e.g., "any employee of Pittsburgh Memoral Hospital whom its personnel office designates as a nurse"). The definition of the population is the responsibility of the researcher.

If one were to decide to measure the variable in every member (also called **sample element**) of the population, that activity would be referred to as a **census**. The elements, members, or individuals are usually persons, but they do not have to be. For example, to answer the question, "What is the ratio of nurses to hospital beds?" one could define the population as all hospitals in the state of Iowa. The elements of the population would be hospitals rather than persons. Populations can also be entire collections of schools, school districts, households, communities, curriculum units, or minutes in a school day.

Selection of the sample.   The *sample* is any subset of elements from the population that are chosen from it to be observed directly. Based on the observed characteristics of the sample, the researcher makes inferences about the characteristics of the population, which is not itself directly observed.

A sample is any subset of the population, but the way the sample is chosen determines the validity of the inference drawn from the observed characteristics of the sample to the unobserved characteristics of the population. In our study of nurses' beliefs about infants' sensitivity to pain, we could select the sample from a list of nurses at Des Moines General Hospital. Such a sample is known as a **convenience sample** because its members are chosen for their proximity to the researchers. Or we could place an advertisement in the newsletter of the Association of Hospital Nurses of America asking for volunteers to complete the questionnaire; that would give us a **volunteer sample**. Or we might determine that we want to make sure that the sample includes members from each of a set of categories such as registered nurses and licensed practical nurses, so we seek accessible volunteers from each of these groups. The resulting group is referred to as a **quota sample**. Or from an initial set of volunteers we ask for the names of additional members of the population that might be interested in the topic. This is called a **snowball sample**.

The four kinds of samples described above are examples of **nonprobability samples**. Although such samples have their uses, the individuals that are selected by nonprobability sampling methods are seldom representative of the population. We could not statistically infer that the characteristics of the sample are close approximations of the characteristics of the population as a whole. Why is this so? If the researchers chose the sample elements because of their accessibility and convenience, they might inject some bias into the selection. Consciously or unintentionally, they might choose nurses whom they know to have an opinion on the subject, perhaps even the opinion that would confirm their hypothesis. Nurses at Des Moines General might be more highly educated than nurses in general, so that estimating the characteristics of the population as a whole from this sample would be biased. Volunteers who answer an ad may be more motivated and knowledgeable about the topic and therefore give information that would be atypical of the wider population of nurses. Any generalization from a nonprobability sample to its population must be made on the basis of a reasoned comparison of the sample with the population. That is, the inference is judgmental rather than statistical.

The method of choosing a sample from a population to yield data of known representativeness and a statistical generalization is called **probability sampling**. A probability sample is selected in such a way that each element of the population has a known, positive chance of being selected into the sample. For each member of the population we can specify its probability of being selected into the sample.

The simplest and most familiar case of a probability sampling design is the **simple random sample**, or **SRS**, wherein each member of the population has the same chance of being selected in the sample as every other member of the population. To conduct the SRS design, the researcher must have a complete and accurate list of every member of the population. This list is called the **sampling frame**. In Figure 10–1 is an excerpt from an imaginary sampling frame for the population we have defined: all members in good standing of the Association of Hospital Nurses of America. There are 50,000 elements in this population, from which we have decided to select a sample of 1,000. With this ratio of the number in the sample

FIGURE 10–1 Excerpt from Sampling Frame of a Hypothetical Population

Aaholm, A.G.
Aaker, N.T.
Aaron, M.C.
Abby, C.
Abeyta, M.L.
Abbot, M.M.
. . .
Zwisler, R.A.
Zygmunt, Z.B.

00001	Aaholm, A. G.
00002	Aaker, N. T
00003	Aaron, M. C.
00004	Abby, C.
00005	Abeyta, M. L.
00006	Abbot, M. M.
. . .	. . .
49999	Zwisler, R. A.
50000	Zygmunt, Z. B.

FIGURE 10–2 Excerpt from a Sampling Frame after Enumeration

relative to the number in the population, one can say that each element of the population has a 1 in 50 chance of being part of the sample.

We next attach consecutive identification numbers to the list of names. We need the number of digits in our number system that covers the 50,000 elements in the population, or five digits. We attach the number 00001 to the first element in the sampling frame, 00002 to the second element, and so on until each element has its own unique number. The finished process is illustrated in Figure 10–2.

The next step is to use a table of random numbers; an excerpt from such a table is shown in Table 10–1. Such a table consists of strings of digits that have no relationship to each other. If you looked at, say, the first 20 digits in the table, you could not predict the twenty-first digit by any known procedure.

The task is now to pick 1,000 five-digit numbers from this table of random numbers. Notice that this table is already arranged in blocks of

TABLE 10–1   Excerpt from a Table of Random Digits

03991	10461	93716	16894	66083	24653	84609	58232	88618	19161
38555	95554	32886	59780	08355	60860	29735	47762	71299	23853
17546	73704	92052	46215	55121	29281	59076	07936	27954	58909
32643	52861	95819	06831	00911	98936	76355	93779	80863	00514
69572	68777	39510	35905	14060	40619	29549	69616	33564	60780
24122	66591	27699	06494	14845	46672	61958	77100	90899	75754
61196	30231	92962	61773	41839	55382	17267	70943	78038	70267
30532	21704	10274	12202	39685	23309	10061	68829	55986	66485
03788	97599	75867	20717	74416	53166	35208	33374	87539	08823
48228	63379	85783	47619	53152	67433	35663	52972	16818	60311
60365	94653	35075	33949	42614	29297	01918	28316	98953	73231
83799	42402	56623	34442	34994	41374	70071	14736	09958	18065
32960	07405	36409	83232	99385	41600	11133	07586	15917	06253
19322	53845	57620	52606	66497	68646	78138	66559	19640	99413
11220	94747	07399	37408	48509	23929	27482	45476	85244	35159

TABLE 10–1   (Cont.)

31751	57260	68980	05339	15470	48355	88651	22596	03152	19121
88492	99382	14454	04504	20094	98977	74843	93413	22109	78508
30934	47744	07481	83828	73788	06533	28597	20405	94205	20380
22888	48893	27499	98748	60530	45128	74022	84617	82037	10268
78212	16993	35902	91386	44372	15486	65741	14014	87481	37220
41849	84547	46850	52326	34677	58300	74910	64345	19325	81549
46352	33049	69248	93460	45305	07521	61318	31855	14413	70951
11087	96294	14013	31792	59747	67277	76503	34513	39663	77544
52701	08337	56303	87315	16520	69676	11654	99893	02181	68161
57275	36898	81304	48585	68652	27376	92852	55866	88448	03584
20857	73156	70284	24326	79375	95220	01159	63267	10622	48391
15633	84924	90415	93614	33521	26665	55823	47641	86225	31704
92694	48297	39904	02115	59589	49067	66821	41575	49767	04037
77613	19019	88152	00080	20554	91409	96277	48257	50816	97616
38688	32486	45134	63545	59404	72059	43947	51680	43852	59693
25163	01889	70014	15021	41290	67312	71857	15957	68971	11403
65251	07629	37239	33295	05870	01119	92784	26340	18477	65622
36815	43625	18637	37509	82444	99005	04921	73701	14707	93997
64397	11692	05327	82162	20247	81759	45197	25332	83745	22567
04515	25624	95096	67946	48460	85558	15191	18782	16930	33361
83761	60873	43253	84145	60833	25983	01291	41349	20368	07126
14387	06345	80854	09279	43529	06318	38384	74761	41196	37480
51321	92246	80088	77074	88722	56736	66164	49431	66919	31678
72472	00008	80890	18002	94813	31900	54155	83436	35352	54131
05466	55306	93128	18464	74457	90561	72848	11834	79982	68416
39528	72484	82474	25593	48545	35247	18619	13674	18611	19241
81616	18711	53342	44276	75122	11724	74627	73707	58319	15997
07586	16120	82641	22820	92904	13141	32392	19763	61199	67940
90767	04235	13754	17200	69902	63742	78464	22501	18627	90872
40188	28193	29593	88627	94972	11598	62095	36787	00441	58997
34414	82157	86887	55087	19152	00023	12302	80783	32624	68691
63439	75363	44989	16822	36024	00867	76378	41605	65961	73488
67049	09070	93399	45547	94458	74284	05041	49807	20288	34060
79495	04146	52162	90286	54158	34243	46978	35482	59362	95938
91704	30552	04737	21031	75051	93029	47665	64382	99782	93478

Source: Rand Corporation, *A Million Random Digits*, 1955, p. 3.

five digits. We decide to take successive blocks of five-digit numbers, starting at a random spot—in this case the second block in the second column. Our plan is to go down the rows beginning from that starting place (we could just as well have started at a different place on the table and proceeded across the columns or diagonally). The first number is 66591, and we ask ourselves, "Does this number correspond to any numbered element on the sampling frame?" Since the answer is no, we look at the next number, 30231, and ask the same question. Since the number 32960 does correspond to a numbered element, we find the name of the nurse with that number and include the name in the sample. The next number is 21704, and the person with that number is also in the sample. Skipping over numbers in the table that are higher than 50,000, we continue this process until we have 1,000 names in the sample.

The beauty of this method is that there are now 1,000 nurses in our sample who are not systematically different in any respect from the ones who were not selected. To illustrate, we could have chosen different persons in our sample by starting at a different place in the table of random numbers or by moving through it by an alternate route. For example, if we had blocked off five-digit numbers starting in the column second from the left, the initial number would have been 03659, the second, 37994, and so on. The sample so selected would have different individuals in it from the first sample, but the two subsets would differ from each other only randomly on the variable of interest. The two groups would be randomly equivalent to each other. No human biases determined who was selected for study. Instead, the basis for selection was chance. Probability theory and statistics can inform us about how far off our sample characteristics are from the characteristics of the population as a whole, but we can be fairly certain that the sample is not systematically more or less likely to believe infants feel pain than is the population as a whole.

Measurement of sample characteristics   Having selected the individuals that make up the sample, we can send them a questionnaire, observe their behavior, or use any method that provides valid assessment of the characteristic or variable specified in the research problem. The results of the measurement are quantified. Consider the simplest case. In an interview with the members of the sample, each is asked, "According to your best judgment, does a 2-day-old infant feel pain? Answer yes or no."

Estimation of population characteristics   The data from measurement of the sample yield an estimate of population characteristics. In this example the data yield a **binomial variable** (a variable with only two values, such as yes or no, male or female). The statistics that describe a binomial variable are as follows:

p is the proportion of the sample answering yes

q is the proportion of the sample answering no

$p + q = 1.00$ or 100 percent of the sample

$p \times q$ is the variance of the sample

The product of p and q is a measure of the variance, or degree of heterogeneity, of the sample. Samples with 95 percent answering yes and 5 percent answering no are quite homogeneous; most of their members think alike ($p \times q = 0.95 \times 0.05 = 0.0475$). In the hypothetical sample of nurses, however, 50 percent answered yes to the question of whether infants feel pain, and 50 percent answered no. This is a sample high in heterogeneity. Its variance is correspondingly larger ($p \times q = 0.50 \times 0.50 = 0.25$).

Based on the sample statistics (50 percent said yes and 50 percent said no) and on the size of the sample (1,000), one can compute a statistical measure of how far off our sample characteristics are likely to be from the population characteristics. This statistic is the **standard error**, and it is a measure of the precision of our estimate of the proportion of the population of nurses who believe infants feel pain. The formula for calculating the standard error and the calculation for the present example is given in Formula 10–1:

$$\text{Formula 10-1} \quad \text{Standard error} = \sqrt{\frac{pq}{n}} = \sqrt{\frac{0.5(0.5)}{1000}} = 0.016$$

Stating the accuracy of the estimates   Based on the standard error just calculated, a **confidence interval** can be constructed. It is the region above and below our sample statistic wherein the population value is likely to be. A rough-and-ready method consists of multiplying the standard error by 2 (for the exact multiplier, see Jaeger, 1984, p. 44), adding this value to the sample statistic to find the upper limit and subtracting it from the sample statistic to find the lower limit. In the present example the standard error is 0.016. Multiplying the standard error by 2 gives the value, 0.032 (or roughly 3 percentage points). Adding the latter figure to, and subtracting it from, the sample proportion of 0.50 gives a confidence interval that extends from 47 percent to 53 percent. Thus we can say that the population value for the percentage of nurses who believe infants feel pain lies somewhere between 47 percent and 53 percent. We would be correct 95 percent of the time in making statements by this method.

The confidence interval is a kind of region of uncertainty. The larger the confidence interval, the less informative are the results. One can know with 95 percent assurance that the population value is somewhere within the confidence interval, but cannot know exactly where in the interval it is. One way to decrease the size of the confidence interval is to employ a larger sample size. Another way is to decrease the variability within the sample, something that ordinarily is not under the researcher's control.

A third way of increasing the precision of the sample estimates (decreasing the size of the standard error and confidence interval) is by using a **stratified sample design**, an alternative to SRS. Like SRS, the stratified sample design requires an adequate sampling frame. This list of names must also include information on the status of each individual on the **strat-**

ifying variable. In the example of nurses' beliefs about infant pain sensitivity, one might hypothesize a relationship between the type of training a nurse received (registered nurse versus licensed practical nurse, perhaps) and the variable of interest. Type of training may be used as a stratifying variable, assuming such information is available to the researcher. If the stratifying variable and the variable of interest are correlated, precision is increased over SRS.

The procedure for selecting the sample is as follows. One determines the proportion of the population that is listed as registered nurse and chooses that same proportion in the sample. Suppose that the sample size is 1,000. According to the information on the sampling frame, 70 percent of its members are registered nurses and 30 percent are licensed practical nurses. To maintain proportionality, we would want 700 RNs and 300 LPNs in the sample. The table of random numbers would be used to sample from within the two strata. The sample is selected and interviewed, and the sample statistics are computed. An alternative formula (see Jaeger, 1984, Chapter 4) is used to calculate the standard error. Given the standard error, the confidence interval is computed. It will be smaller than the confidence interval that was based on the SRS design (provided there was a relationship between type of training and belief that infants feel pain), so the results are more informative.

The design described above is a *proportionate stratified sample design*. A *disproportionate stratified sample design* is used when the researcher wants to ensure that small strata or subcategories within a population are adequately represented in the sample. For some reason it might be important, for example, to obtain separate estimates of the stratum of male nurses' beliefs about infant pain sensitivity. The National Assessment of Educational Progress makes use of disproportionate stratified sample designs so that the achievement of ethnic minorities can be separately estimated along with that of the population as a whole.

Cluster sample designs are used to stretch the researcher's resources. When a population is spread out over a large geographical area or when no sampling frame exists, the researcher may resort to a cluster, or **multistage sample design**. Suppose that the population is defined as all currently employed pediatric nurses in the 50 states. No sampling frame exists for this population, and developing one would require as much effort as the entire study. In a cluster sampling design, we first select a random sample of 20 states (the **primary sampling unit** is states). From the states so selected, we then select a random sample of 20 counties (counties is the *secondary sampling unit*). From the selected counties, we survey all the hospitals and ask the administrators to provide a list of pediatric nurses employed there. From those lists we select a random sample of nurses. Interviewers are sent to the sample elements, who are concentrated in a few selected but representative locations. If the sample had been chosen by

SRS, the interviewers would have been sent to disparate places throughout the country, one sample element located in Last Chance, Nevada; one in Bald Knob, Arkansas; two in Manhattan; and so on.

The trade-off between the obvious savings realized by using the cluster sample design is the lower precision of estimates of the population values. Suppose that Nebraska is among the states selected at random from the 50 states, and Cass county is selected at random from Nebraska counties. Chances are great that the nurses working in hospitals in Cass county are more like each other than they are like nurses selected at random from the nation as a whole, or like nurses working in large urban counties (although such counties would have had a fair chance of being selected at an earlier stage). By using the cluster sample design and taking several nurses from Cass County, pockets of homogeneity have been created in the sample. This problem is accounted for in the method of calculating the standard error for sample statistics. The method is based on the degree of homogeneity within the clusters and the variation among individuals. Even with this alternative means of calculating standard errors, we expect less precision with the cluster sample design than with SRS. See Jaeger (1984, Chap. 7), and Kish (1965) for an advanced treatment of this topic.

Many large-scale surveys make use of complex designs with several stratifying variables and several stages of clustering to save money and obtain more accurate estimates.

The Problem of Nonresponse

The probability sampling designs are all aimed at estimating population characteristics based on data from representative samples. This goal is often thwarted, however, by the problem of nonresponse. Every researcher worries that once the sample is drawn and the questionnaires mailed, the success of the venture is in the hands of the individuals in the sample. This is a legitimate worry because the recipients of the questionnaire either complete it or discard it. There is a good deal of evidence to suggest that responders are a different animal from nonrespondents (Rosenthal and Rosnow, 1975). Responders tend to be brighter, better workers, more motivated, more highly educated, and more interested in the topic of the study. A sample consists of persons of all levels of education, intelligence, motivation, and so on—*not just those with high levels* of these characteristics. Thus, what started out as a representative sample of a defined population (consisting of all sorts of people) has produced data that are unrepresentative of the populations as originally defined. The data are only representative of the subpopulation of responders; that is, a **nonresponse bias** exists. Cochran (1977) showed that even nonresponse rates as low as 20 percent can decrease the precision of sample estimates and increase the size of confidence intervals to an unacceptable degree. Cochran's analysis showed that nonresponse is an extremely serious problem in surveys. Facile advice by some textbook writers that, say, a 60 percent response rate is typical and adequate, is incorrect, for the estimates of population characteristics from statistics computed on only the voluntary respondents are likely to be imprecise and biased.

Compensating for an expected high percentage of nonresponse by initially selecting an extra large sample is a popular but inadequate strategy. The responders, even though they are a larger number, are still unrepresentative of the population as originally defined. A better strategy calls for initially selecting an adequate sized sample and reserving enough resources to follow up nonresponders and persuade them to participate in the study. When response rates are less than 90 percent even after follow-up, the researcher should perform **nonrespondent bias checks.** For example, responders can be compared with nonresponders on demographic variables as well as any documentary data available. In the study of nurses' beliefs about infant pain sensitivity, for example, one would compare responders and nonresponders on gender, type of training, whether they worked in rural or urban settings, and the like. When differences between the two groups on these variables fail to reach statistical significance, then the argument is strengthened that *in this case* responders are not different from nonresponders. In the absence of nonrespondent bias checks, the reader has no way of knowing whether data from responders also adequately represents the characteristics of nonresponders, and consequently, the population as a whole.

There is no simple answer to the question of how high a response rate must be to insure a valid survey. Some surveys with response rates below 50 percent are valid because nonrespondent bias checks show no systematic differences between responders and nonresponders. Some surveys with 90 percent response rates contain serious biases. No rules of thumb will substitute for intelligent judgment applied to specific cases.

Sample Size

In the example already presented the sample size was arbitrarily determined. In real cases the researcher must consider several criteria in answering the question, "How big a sample do I need?"

Homogeneity of the population.   Precision of estimates of population characteristics is partly a function of the degree of homogeneity of the population. The more homogeneous the population is with respect to the variable being estimated, the smaller the sample needs to be. If one were to estimate the proportion who favored Ted Kennedy over Ronald Reagan as a presidential candidate, and the population consisted of the members of the Republican National Committee, a very small sample would be needed to estimate the characteristic in that population. A variable such as nurses' beliefs about infant pain sensitivity, on which the population is (hypothetically) sharply divided, requires a relatively larger sample.

Precision of estimates.   Precision of estimates, as reflected in the standard error, is partly a function of the sample size. The researcher must decide in advance about the degree of precision needed. Is a standard error of 10 percent enough, or does the research problem necessitate more precise estimates? Polls of preference for presidential candidates require estimates of great precision. When the difference between the votes received by two candidates on election day is 1 or 2 percentage points, then estimates of preference need to have standard errors smaller than that difference to predict the outcome of the election. Estimates of the beliefs about infant pain sensitivity in the population of nurses can be less precise, since no decision rests on the accuracy of those estimates.

Sampling design.   Stratified sampling designs increase the precision of estimates when the stratifying variable correlates with the variable to be estimated. Other things being equal, the researcher can achieve the same precision with a smaller sample size when a stratified sample design is used.

Number of subpopulations estimated.   If the researcher needs to make separate estimates about the characteristics of subpopulations as well as for the population as a whole, sample size must be increased. If the researcher had wanted to estimate separately the beliefs of RNs and LPNs, a larger sample would be needed than if he only wanted to estimate the variable in the population of nurses generally. If the research problem also required that he estimate beliefs about infant pain sensitivity in the subpopulations of male RNs, male LPNs, female RNs, and female LPNs, the sample size would have to be increased.

Cost.   The amount of money and time available to the researcher constrain sample size and sometimes compromise the other four criteria.

Notice that this list does not include the size of the population or the **sampling fraction** (ratio of sample size to population size). Those who advocate a sampling fraction of 10 percent regardless of the five criteria listed above do their readers no favors. Most public opinion polls estimate (with great precision) the opinion of the U.S. population with samples of about 2,000, a very small percentage of the population. It is a counterintuitive principle of statistics that the accuracy of estimates depends primarily on the absolute size of the sample and not on the size of the sample relative to the population size. A random sample of 1,000 is approximately as accurate for estimating the characteristics of a population of 20,000 as it is for a population of 200,000,000. As we indicated, this principle is counterintuitive.

LONGITUDINAL SURVEY DESIGNS

So far in this chapter the simplest survey design, the single-group, single-observation design, has been considered. Data from this design describe the status of one or more variables in the population, measured at only one time, like a snapshot. A second category of designs (Warwick and Lininger, 1975), called **longitudinal**, provides answers to questions about the changing status of variables in the population studied. Here are some exemplary questions:

> How does drug use change as adolescents progress through high school?
>
> Is achievement in science declining?
>
> Do symptoms of senility become more severe the longer a person remains in a nursing home?

Notice that each of these questions concerns a single characteristic and whether that characteristic alters over time. Like the single-group, single-observation design, the purpose of longitudinal designs is descriptive and the same concerns about sampling design, response rates, and sample size apply. There are various longitudinal designs, among them the trend survey, cohort survey, and panel survey.

Trend Survey Design

In the **trend survey design** a population is defined and a representative sample selected from it. That population, as originally defined, is sampled again at a later time (or at several times) so that trends or changes in the variables can be charted. The National Assessment of Educational Progress (NAEP) employs a trend survey design. NAEP (1978) defined one of their populations as all 17-year-olds in schools in the 50 states and the District of Columbia. In year 01 (1970) of their study they sampled that population, using a multistage cluster sampling design with several stratifying variables, and collected data on achievement in science. During year 04 (1973) they again sampled the contemporary population of 17-year-olds and measured their achievement in science. In year 09 (1978) they again sampled the population of 17-year-olds and measured their achievement in science. Thus the question was answered, "What is the science achievement of 17-year-olds and how has that achievement changed over an eight-year period?" The three measurements showed a downward trend in science achievement. From 1969 to 1977, the percent of the assessment items answered correctly declined. The sample statistic that was estimated for the population was the mean change from one measurement to the next. The standard error for that mean change provided a measure of the precision of the estimate.

Cohort Survey Design

In the **cohort survey design**, variables are measured on more than one occasion. Unlike the trend study, however, the members of the population as originally defined are followed through time. In the NAEP study the people who were 17 years old in 1970 had become 20 years old by 1973 and so were no longer relevant to the research problem as stated. If a cohort design were used, the researcher would define the population as all those who were 17 in 1970 and measure their achievement. In 1973 another sample of individuals would be taken from the same sampling frame used before (those who had been 17 years old in 1970), even though this population of individuals had become 20 years old, and their achievement would again be measured. These steps would be repeated as many times as desired. The research question would be different from that of the trend survey design, in this case, "How has science achievement developed in the population of persons who were 17 years old in 1970?"

Panel Survey Design

A third kind of longitudinal design is the panel study. In the **panel survey design** the population is defined, a representative sample selected, and the variable measured in the sample. In subsequent stages, the *same individuals* who made up the original sample are repeatedly measured. With this design the researchers are able not only to track changes in the status of the variables but to discover why the changes took place. This advantage is partially offset by problems of sample mortality, that is, the loss of the members of the sample through lack of interest, mobility, or death. In addition, members of the sample become accustomed to repeated measurements (recall the pretest sensitization threat to external validity presented in Chapter 6) or come to think of themselves as singled out for special attention. Thus, the data they provide may become somewhat less representative of the population as originally defined.

An outstanding example of a panel study was conducted by Jessor and Jessor (1977). They studied problem behavior such as alcohol and drug use and general deviant behavior and how those characteristics change as young people progress through college. The population was defined as freshmen who had matriculated at a particular university in 1969. A random sample was selected, and the elements of the sample were invited to participate in the four-year study. Those who volunteered were given questionnaires in the spring of 1970 and again in the spring of 1971, 1972, and

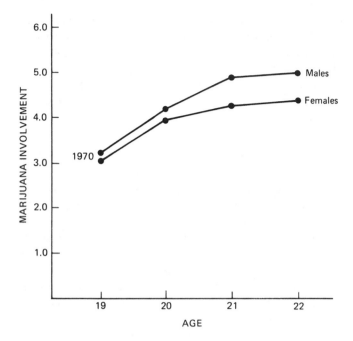

FIGURE 10-3 Panel Study on Marijuana Use During College *(Source: Jessor and Jessor, 1977, p. 158.)*

1973. Thus the same individuals were measured repeatedly throughout their college years, and the researchers were able to track the incidence of and changes in their problem behavior. Nonrespondent bias checks were performed to determine the effect of attrition from the sample on the generalization of the findings. Figure 10-3 contains a graph from the many in Jessor and Jessor's book, showing marijuana use increasing from the freshman to junior years and leveling off in the senior year of college.

EXPLANATORY SURVEYS

Another category of survey designs is the explanatory survey. In all the survey designs considered so far, the primary concern was for an adequate description of the distribution of the variables in the defined population. The **explanatory survey** deemphasizes description in favor of testing hypotheses about the relationship among variables in the population. The greater concern is for deriving a hypothesis from theory and carefully constructing measures of the variables. The measurements are made in samples that may not be statistically representative of a defined population. The basis for generalizing the results in the sample to some hypothetical, target population is not probabilistic. Rather, the conclusions are generalized much as conclusions of experiments are generalized, that is, by careful logical arguments based on the descriptive features of the sample and their comparison with what is known about the target population. The choices of design in explanatory surveys are many, and it is sometimes difficult to tell the difference between an explanatory survey and what we have called correlational, causal-comparative, and quasi-experimental studies.

Single Cross-Section, Single-Observation Design

The simplest case of an explanatory survey is the **single cross-section design**, in which the variable of interest is compared between two or more subpopulations or categories within the population. Subpopulations that might be compared are males and females; blacks, whites, and Hispanics; upper, middle, and lower socioeconomic strata, and the like. The objective of this design is to test a hypothesis about a relationship between the variable of interest and the classification variable (gender, ethnic group, or socioeconomic status, respectively). The data used to test such a hypothesis are in one of three forms: (1) mean differences on the variable of interest between the two or more categories; (2) correlation of the two variables; or (3) contingency, or cross-classification, analysis.

Table 10–2 is a bivariate contingency, or cross-classification, analysis of the relationship between participation in elective math courses and the classification variable, father's support for career. The hypothetical data consist of a sample of 259 high school girls who have been sorted into four groups based on these two variables. Thirty-four of the 259 girls partici-

TABLE 10–2   Example of a Single Cross-Section Design

HIGH SCHOOL GIRLS CLASSIFIED BY PARTICIPATION IN ELECTIVE MATH AND FATHERS' SUPPORT OF THEIR DAUGHTERS' CAREER ASPIRATIONS (PERCENTS BY ROWS)

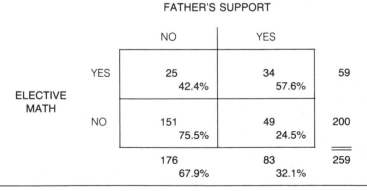

FATHER'S SUPPORT

		NO	YES	
ELECTIVE MATH	YES	25 42.4%	34 57.6%	59
	NO	151 75.5%	49 24.5%	200
		176 67.9%	83 32.1%	259

Chi square = 22.96 $p < 0.001$

pated in elective math courses and had fathers who supported careers for their daughters (the top right-hand quadrant in the table). The chi square statistic is significant at the $p = 0.001$ level, indicating that the two variables are related to each other in the population.

Multiple Cross-Section Designs

The single cross-section design can be extended to include more than one categorical variable, in which case it is called a **multiple cross-section design**. For example, the researcher might want to study the relationship of race, education, and income. The data used to examine such a relationship would take the form of either (1) mean differences of income compared among categories such as blacks with high school or less, blacks with some college, blacks with college degrees, whites with high school or less, and so on; (2) multiple regression analysis with income as the criterion variable and race and education as predictor variables (see Chapter 9); or (3) multiple (in this case trivariate) contingency table analysis. Table 10–3 shows how such a table is constructed but contains no data.

The multiple cross-section design has also been used by researchers as a way of inferring causal relationships among variables (see Chapter 8). Hirschi and Selvin (1973, pp. 42–43) presented data to illustrate this procedure. They asked that the reader consider the hypothesis, "Inadequate supervision is the cause of delinquency." In their bivariate table (reproduced in Table 10–4), their contingency analysis showed a moderate statistical relationship between delinquency and supervision.

TABLE 10–3 Example of a Multiple Cross-Section Design

PERSONS CLASSIFIED BY RACE, INCOME AND HIGH SCHOOL GRADUATION

EDUCATION (HIGH SCHOOL GRADUATION OR NOT)

GRADUATED   NOT GRADUATED

INCOME (ABOVE OR BELOW AVERAGE)

TABLE 10–4   The Relationship Between Delinquency and Supervision

DELINQUENCY BY SUITABILITY OF SUPERVISION

	SUPERVISION	
	SUITABLE	UNSUITABLE
Percent delinquent	30%	83%
Number of cases	(607)	(382)

Source: Hirschi and Selvin, 1973, p. 42.

To demonstrate causality, the researcher not only must demonstrate a statistical relationship but must also make sure the independent variable occurred prior to the dependent variable and that the relationship is not *spurious* (that is, not influenced by an antecedent variable, or third variable). An alternative antecedent variable in the relationship between supervision and delinquency is whether the mother is employed and thus outside the home. Table 10–5 contains Hirschi and Selvin's data in which the relationship between supervision and delinquency is controlled by introducing into the analysis the third, or antecedent, variable—mothers' employment status. According to the authors:

> [Table 10–5] permits reexamination of the relationship between suitability of supervision and delinquency, with mother's employment held constant. In this case, the proposed antecedent variable, mother's employment, does not affect the relation between suitability of supervision and delinquency: The relation is as strong within categories of mother's employment as it is when

TABLE 10–5   Relationship of Supervision and Delinquency with Mother's Employment Controlled

DELINQUENCY AND SUITABILITY OF SUPERVISION BY MOTHER'S EMPLOYMENT

	MOTHER'S EMPLOYMENT					
	HOUSEWIFE		REGULARLY EMPLOYED		OCCASIONALLY EMPLOYED	
SUITABLE SUPERVISION:	SUITABLE	UNSUIT-ABLE	SUITABLE	UNSUIT-ABLE	SUITABLE	UNSUIT-ABLE
Percent delinquent	31%	85%	20%	77%	33%	89%
Number of cases	(442)	(149)	(80)	(110)	(85)	(116)

Source: Hirschi and Selvin, 1973, p. 43.

mother's employment is left free to vary (see Table [10–4]). The analyst can thus conclude that the observed relationship is not spurious, at least with respect to mother's employment. (Hirschi and Selvin, 1973, p. 43)

Other Designs in Explanatory Surveys

One can readily imagine many combinations of the designs described above, such as multiple cross-section with trend, single cross-section with panel, and so on. Explanatory surveys may also combine their analytic purpose with carefully constructed probability sampling designs. In that case they provide data that are not only statistically representative of the population but also the basis for testing hypotheses about the relationships among variables in the population. Studies such as these are known as **descriptive-explanatory surveys**. The possibilities for high-quality surveys in research and evaluation in education and the social sciences are extensive.

INSTRUMENTATION

Many people mistakenly equate surveys with questionnaires. In fact, questionnaires are only one of many ways the variables can be measured in surveys. The choice of methods of measurement depends on the objectives of the study and on the definition of variables. All of the principles in Chapters 4 and 5 about definition of constructs, operational definition of variables, variety of measurement methods, and criteria for judging instrumentation in a study (particularly reliability and validity) apply in choosing instruments for a survey. The following measures are frequently used in survey research and evaluation studies and will be described in this section: content analysis schedules, structured observation schedules, questionnaires, interviews (face-to-face or by phone), and attitude scales.

Content Analysis Schedules

Persons are not the only things to be studied in surveys. An investigator might study, for example, the incidence and distribution of statements about environmental protection in the population of laws enacted by state legislatures. The sampling elements are the laws and the statements in them. A **content analysis schedule**, or coding form, that includes the categories or variables of interest is prepared. (One such category might be "specification of criminal penalties for instances of environmental offence: yes—, no—, or no mention—.") The investigator defines the population and selects a sample of the laws. Trained coders read each of the sampled laws and fill out a coding form for it, almost like filling out a questionnaire. The coded data would then be quantified and statistically analyzed.

Content analysis schedules are not without some disadvantages. Documents always have some official function; they were prepared and recorded to fulfill some purpose. Suppose the researcher wanted to do a content analysis of letters of employee dismissal as a way of studying racial discrimination in a corporation. Such letters may constitute institutional fronts reflecting the need of the organization to protect itself from lawsuits rather than containing the true reasons for dismissal. The researcher would have to be aware of the effect of this slant on the validity of the conclusions. Furthermore, the content of the documents and the organization of the content may not conform to the research questions. The document may not have sufficient detail to allow the raters to respond to all the categories of interest. Nevertheless, the analysis of content through structured schedules is an important source of instrumentation in survey research and evaluation.

Structured Observation Schedules

To study classroom processes, therapist-client interactions, or relationships between doctors and nurses, **structured observation schedules** are sometimes used. Such schedules are used in studies when a relevant population of interactions can be defined and sampled. Time can be sampled as well. For example, a classroom researcher may record instances of on-task behavior observed in every tenth minute in a three-hour observation period. Just as with questionnaires and content analysis schedules, the researcher defines the variables of interest and prepares a structured observation schedule consisting of those variables. The schedule may be a checklist of behaviors, a questionnaire that the observer completes, or a rating grid that a trained rater completes based on what is observed. The categories on the schedule are quantified so the results can be statistically analyzed. Observation may be direct, as when the observer sits in the back of the classroom or behind a one-way mirror. Or observation can be mediated by audio or video recordings, with the coding performed on the taped material.

The Flanders Interaction Analysis Category System is a popular classroom observation schedule. The variables, which are coded every third second by trained raters, include Teacher Talk (teacher accepts feelings, praises, encourages, accepts or uses ideas of students, asks questions, lectures, gives directions, criticizes, or justifies authority), Pupil Talk (pupil responds, or initiates), and Silence. Jackson and Cosca (1974) used the Flanders schedule to study differences in teacher-pupil interaction between Anglo and Mexican-American pupils. A probability sample of classrooms in schools throughout the Southwest was chosen. The authors found that teachers (both Anglo and Hispanic) gave more praise, questioned more, accepted ideas more, and talked more to Anglo pupils than to Mexican-American pupils.

Some drawbacks of structured observation systems are these: (1) the problem of density—some behavior does not occur in sufficient quantity to be reliably observed; (2) reactivity—the presence of the observer or recording device may alter the behavior of the people observed; and (3) attribution of intention—some observation schedules, called "high inference schedules," require the observer to infer the intentions of the people observed, creating problems of interobserver reliability and validity. Despite these deficiencies, structured observation schedules are another important kind of instrumentation in survey research. Simon and Boyer (1974) have developed a catalog of such systems.

Questionnaires

The questionnaire is a familiar item. Hardly a month goes by without a questionnaire arriving on the desk of an educator or social services professional. Their widespread use and apparent simplicity notwithstanding, questionnaires are difficult to construct and can go wrong in countless ways. According to Dillman (1978), three decisions must be made in constructing a questionnaire: What kind of information is required by the survey's objectives? In what format should the items by written? What words should be chosen to motivate response and measure the variables reliably and validly?

The information sought can be sorted roughly into four categories: *attitudes* (how people feel about an attitude object such as a person, idea, or institution), *beliefs* (what people believe to be true), *behavior* (what people actually do or have done), and *attributes* (characteristics such as sex, age, and income). According to Dillman (1978) item format is of four types, which are displayed in Figure 10–4. *Open-ended items* are questions or statements to which the subjects must respond with their own words. No response options are provided. *Closed-ended items with ordered choices* provide a question or statement and more than one response option. The subject is supposed to select the option that best fits his own attitude, belief, behavior, or attribute. The response options are arranged on a continuum to represent a dimension such as degree of agreement. *Closed-ended items with unordered response choices* are questions or statements with response options, but the response options are independent of each other and do not form a continuum. Since the person must choose one of the responses given, the options must cover all reasonable possibilities. *Partially closed-ended items* are questions or statements with a set of response options and an "other" category that subjects may choose if their situation does not match any of the response options. Any questionnaire may employ a variety of these formats as well as scales, checklists, and the like. Each format has certain strengths and weaknesses and may be more or less suited to individual survey objectives.

The problem of question wording is an old and persistent one. The classic text on the subject is *The Art of Asking Questions* by Stanley Payne (1951). In that book is a "Concise Check List of 100 Considerations" on

FIGURE 10–4 Examples of Four Item Formats   *(Source: Adapted from Dillman, 1978.)*

OPEN-ENDED ITEMS

A. (attitude)   What were the most important reasons you had for voting against the nuclear freeze amendment?

_____

_____

B. (belief)   According to your best recollections, what were the major accomplishments of Henry Kissinger?

_____

_____

C. (behavior)   About how many hours per week do you spend reading newspapers? _____

_____

D. (attribute)   How many years of education have you completed counting high school and college? _____

CLOSED-ENDED WITH ORDERED CHOICES

E. (attitude)   Voting is the only way ordinary people can have a say about how the government runs.
   1. Strongly agree
   2. Agree
   3. Neither agree nor disagree
   4. Disagree
   5. Strongly disagree

F. (belief)   According to your information, what percent of adult Americans are functionally illiterate (cannot read the directions on a medicine bottle)?
   1. 0% to 5%
   2. 6% to 15%
   3. 16% to 25%
   4. 26% to 35%
   5. 36% to 50%
   6. More than 50%

G. (behavior)   How many times last month did you attend church services?
   1. Two times or less
   2. Three, four, or five times
   3. Six, seven, or eight times
   4. Nine times or more

FIGURE 10-4   (cont.)

CLOSED-ENDED WITH UNORDERED CHOICES

H. (attitude)   Which of the following four things would you most prefer in a job?
1. Work that pays well
2. Work that gives a feeling of accomplishment
3. Work where there is not too much supervision
4. Work that is pleasant and where coworkers are pleasant

I. (belief)   Compared to nonadopted children, are adopted children more likely to have problems with psychological adjustment?
1. Yes
2. No
3. Don't know

J. (behavior)   What sources of information do you most often use to find out about sports events?
1. Television
2. Radio
3. Newspaper
4. Magazine

K. (attribute) Which of the following best describes your political affiliation?
1. Republican
2. Democrat
3. Independent
4. No affiliation

PARTIALLY CLOSED-ENDED

L. (attitude)   Which of the following would you most prefer in a job?
1. Work that pays well
2. Work that gives a feeling of accomplishment
3. Work with not too much supervision
4. Work that is pleasant
5. Other (explain) _____

M. (behavior)   What sources of information do you most often use to find out about sports events?
1. Television
2. Radio
3. Magazines
4. Newspaper
5. Other _____

question wording. Payne also presented a rather disconcerting case history of the refinement of a single question that went through 41 revisions. Dillman's questions about the wording of items (1978, pp. 97–116) are somewhat less formidable and are listed here.

> Will the words be uniformly understood?
>
> Do the questions contain abbreviations or unconventional phrases?
>
> Are the questions too vague?
>
> Is the question biased?
>
> Is the question objectionable?
>
> Is the question too demanding?
>
> Is it a double question?
>
> Does the question contain a double negative?
>
> Are the answer choices mutually exclusive?
>
> Have you assumed too much knowledge (on the respondent's part)?

Like all forms of instrumentation, questionnaires have disadvantages, even when properly worded. The principal problem with questionnaires is their potential reactivity, or the tendency of respondents to alter their responses to conform to the implicit purposes of the study, to portray themselves as better adjusted or a better citizen, parent, or student than they really are. The respondents may also be unable to recall the information sought, thus biasing the results of the survey. Thus a question such as, "How does your agency comply with regulations on serving the handicapped?" is not very likely to produce the truth. Its intent is obvious, its wording is loaded. If the response is negative, respondents are incriminating themselves and making themselves appear to be prejudiced against a class of individuals that is protected by the government. Although such problems can be partially alleviated by the researcher's promising anonymity and professing neutrality about the outcomes of the study, they are unlikely to be completely overcome and are frequently overlooked. The best survey involves cross-checking any self-report data with data from other sources, such as documents and observations.

Interview Protocols

An alternative to the self-administered questionnaire is the interview conducted in person or by telephone. A questionnaire is prepared with the same considerations of the kind of information sought, item format, and wording. The questionnaire, however, is completed by a trained interviewer based on the oral responses of the interviewee. The interviewer can prompt and probe when the interviewee responds inadequately, but must do so only in a controlled and standardized way (Cannell, Lawson, and Hauser,

1975). More information can be gleaned from the subjects than if they completed a self-administered questionnaire. Furthermore, response rates from both personal and telephone interviews tend to be higher than response rates of self-administered, mailed questionnaires. Unfortunately, the dynamics of the interview (Kahn and Cannell, 1957) may bias the interviewee's response, particularly when questions are not adequately presented, probes are improper, or the interviewer fails to maintain neutrality and interviewee motivation.

Attitude Scales

The final kind of instrumentation to be considered is that of attitude scales. Scales are composite measures of attitudes, meaning that they are the result of combining responses to several items that measure the same dimension or variable. Scales have some advantages over separate questionnaire items, the most important being increased reliability. The errors of measurement associated with single items are averaged out over the set of items on a scale. Furthermore, it is simpler to perform more sophisticated analysis with scales than with separate items. For example, to test the relationship between sex and attitude about school, we would only need to compare the mean of the scale for males with the mean of the scale for females. This would be more efficient than examining the mean differences between the sexes on each of the separate items. There are numerous sources of information on different methods of constructing attitude scales (e.g., Likert, Guttman, Thurstone scales, semantic differential). Edwards (1957) and Fishbein (1967) are recommended.

CRITERIA FOR JUDGING SURVEY STUDIES

As you examine research and evaluation studies that used surveys, you should ask the following questions:

1. Does the study have logical validity? Do the conclusions follow logically from findings, the findings from the methods, and the methods from the problem and hypotheses?
2. If the survey was descriptive in purpose, was the population adequately defined? How adequate was the sampling frame?
3. How representative was the sample? If the survey was descriptive in purpose, were proper probability sampling methods used? If the purpose of the study was explanatory, was the sample described and compared with the target population?
4. Was the instrumentation adequate? Were the reliability and validity of the measures determined and were they adequate? Was attention paid to problems of reactivity of the measures? Was there any attempt to cross-check findings with alternative sources of data?

5. Was an adequate rate of response achieved to eliminate nonresponse bias? Was a nonrespondent bias check performed?

6. Did the method of analysis provide adequate support for the conclusions reached?

SUGGESTED READINGS

BABBIE, E. *Survey research methods.* Belmont, Calif.: Wadsworth, 1973.
COCHRAN, W. *Sampling techniques* (3rd ed.). New York: John Wiley, 1977.
DILLMAN, D.A. *Mail and telephone surveys: The total design method.* New York: John Wiley, 1978.
EDWARDS, A. *Techniques of attitude scale construction.* New York: Appleton-Century Crofts, 1957.
FISHBEIN, M. (Ed.). *Readings in theory and measurement of attitudes.* New York: John Wiley, 1967.
HIRSCHI, T., and SELVIN, H.C. *Principles of survey analysis.* New York: Free Press, 1973.
HYMAN, H.H. *Survey design and analysis.* New York: Free Press, 1955.
HYMAN, H.H. *Interviewing in social research.* Chicago: University of Chicago Press, 1957.
JAEGER, M. *Sampling in education and the social sciences.* New York: Longman, 1984.
KISH, L. *Survey sampling.* New York: John Wiley, 1965.
PAYNE, S.L. *The art of asking questions.* Princeton, N.J.: Princeton University Press, 1951.
WARWICK, D., and LININGER, C. *The sample survey: Theory and practice.* New York: McGraw-Hill, 1975.

TERMS INTRODUCED IN THIS CHAPTER

single-group, single-observation design
sampling design
sampling element
census
convenience sample
volunteer sample
quota sample
snowball sample
nonprobability sample
probability sample
simple random sample (SRS)
sampling frame
binomial variable
standard error
confidence interval
stratified sample design
stratifying variable

cluster sample design
multistage sample design
primary sampling unit
nonresponse bias
nonrespondent bias check
sampling fraction
longitudinal survey design
trend survey design
cohort survey design
panel survey design
explanatory survey
single cross-section design
multiple cross-section design
descriptive-explanatory survey
content analysis schedule
structured observation schedule

QUESTIONS AND EXERCISES FOR FURTHER STUDY

1. What are the differences between analytic and descriptive surveys?

2. What is the difference between a nonprobability and a probability sample?

3. What is the difference between a survey and a census?

4. List and describe four kinds of nonprobability samples and state how one can generalize from them.

5. In your own words, explain what is meant by a random process. Provide three examples of techniques that follow random processes. Show how individuals selected by a random process can constitute an unbiased sample.

6. On the evening news it was reported that national polls finding a 60 percent approval rate for the president were accurate to "plus or minus 2 percentage points." Explain this statement in terms of standard errors and confidence intervals. Is any level of confidence stated or implied?

7. Suppose that in the poll described above, 20 percent of the subjects contacted had refused to respond to the question. Describe in a general way the effect of that nonresponse on one's interpretation of the results.

8. List several ways of dealing with nonrespondent bias in surveys.

9. A prominent professional organization of teachers recommends that the size of a sample should be 10 percent of the population. Is this bad advice?

10. Look up the study by Shepard, Smith, and Vojir entitled "Characteristics of pupils identified as learning disabled" (*American Educational Research Journal*, 1983, Vol. 20, pp. 309–332). Read the article and answer the following questions:
    a. What is the research problem?
    b. How was the population defined?
    c. Describe the sampling design in your own words. How were stratification and multistage sampling procedures used. What was the sampling frame?
    d. What was the method of measurement used?
    e. How was reliability established?
    f. Was nonresponse bias a problem? Why or why not?
    g. What method of analysis was used?
    h. What is the basis for inferring that the characteristics of the sample are similar to those of the population?
    i. Look at Table IV and interpret percentage of the sample that was characterized as Educable Mentally Retarded (EMR) and the standard error of the estimate.
    j. Is there a target population larger than the accessible population from which the sample was drawn? if so, what is it?

11

NATURALISTIC STUDIES

Two black boys in the back of the room jumped over chairs which they used as track horses. Keith jumped over the back of his chair to the seat and jumped up and down on it. Chris tried this feat, but was less agile. Otis also tried. Keith performed his skillful feat three times. The spelling lesson began. A white girl seated between Keith and Chris called out: "I want to move! Keith wants to cut my hair!" The spelling lesson continued. Keith jumped from his seat over the desk to the floor. He ate some of his lunch, walked about, went to the wall, and played with the clock. Chris walked about the room and played with some blocks. Keith and Chris then drummed on table tops. Turning his chair upside down, Keith sat on it. Spinning his chair around in a circle, he used the legs like a submachine gun. Chris hit Aaron, a white boy, who pushed a black girl. Keith hit Chris on the back twice. A black girl called out, "Dummy! dummy!" A black boy pulled a black girl's leg while she sat in her seat. Otis took his shoe off. A black girl was talking loudly. In response to the teacher's question, "Would you like to go out?" she got up from her seat and stood in the aisle, feet apart and knees bent. She brought her knees together and apart four times while crossing her hands together and apart in unison with the knees in a Charleston step. Then she sat down. Moments later she skipped to the door, opened it, picked up a book outside, and ran back to her seat. Then she got up on her seat and performed what in ballet is called an "arabesque." Standing on the ball of one foot, she lifted the other leg backward as high as she could, one arm held diagonally up and forward, the other diagonally down. From this position she lost her balance and fell to the floor. The teacher picked her up and carried her out of the classroom. (Hanna, 1982, pp. 328–329)

The above excerpt presents a startling contrast to the tables of statistics and significance levels that festoon the findings of experiments and surveys. The results of naturalistic studies such as Hanna's on aggression among pupils in a desegregated classroom are usually presented in ordinary language rather than in the language of theory or statistical models typical of most research reports. The form of the report is only one of several differences between naturalistic studies and studies using experimental, survey, or correlational methods.

WHAT IS NATURALISTIC RESEARCH?

Naturalistic studies can be contrasted with "traditional" studies such as experiments. For example, traditional studies are guided by hypotheses deduced from theories; naturalistic studies typically rely less on fixed, formally stated, prior hypotheses, but instead derive hypotheses or explanations from the data that are collected. Naturalistic researchers do not select or operationally define the constructs to be studied. Rather, they assume that constructs have many possible definitions that may vary from place to place, and it is their job to discover the definitions that are important in the place studied. Nor is there a standard research design that researchers bring to the site to be studied. Finally, naturalistic researchers do not intervene in the existing flow of events, but study them as they are, as they exist in nature, in a sense.

Naturalistic research typically involves the long-term study of a case (a person, social institution such as a welfare agency or a school, or a system of events such as the decision-making practices of a triage team) through first-hand contact between the researcher and the subjects of the research. The aim of naturalistic research is to understand the persons involved, their behavior and perceptions, and the influence of the physical, social, and psychological environment or **context** on them. The researcher attempts to describe them and interpret their actions for persons who have not been there and seen them directly—that is, for the readers.

The term *naturalistic* is a useful rubric for several more familiar labels. Perhaps you are familiar with **ethnography** as the kind of research that Margaret Mead did in Samoa. What anthropologists such as Mead were doing was the analysis of culture by means of extensive and long-term studies of individual cultural groups. They lived with the natives, described and analyzed their activities and language, and tried to learn how to think like a native. More recently, ethnographers have attempted to shed light on American culture by using the same techniques to study the actions of people in American institutions, such as schools, hospitals, and agencies. One of the best known educational ethnographers is Harry Wolcott. Having studied the education of the Kwakiutl Indians of the Northwest, he turned his attention to mainstream American schools. In his study, *Teachers vs.*

Technocrats (1977), he spent three years studying a school district that was implementing a new management and accountability system. The evidence gathered was analyzed according to anthropological theory. What he learned about schools permitted a greater understanding of American culture as a whole.

Another term that falls under the rubric of naturalistic research is **participant observation**. Van Maanen's (1973) participant observation of police work began with his full participation as a recruit in the police academy and stretched over many years, addressing various research topics. As the term implies, the researcher occupies dual roles: He or she acts as an investigator and performs some other role within the organization.

The **case study** is another type of naturalistic research. Case Studies in Science Education (Stake and Easley, 1978) is a collection of naturalistic case studies depicting the status of science, math, and social studies in American schools during the 1970s. Stake and Easley defined a case study as the complete study of a bounded system. The case was the science program of a high school and the junior highs and elementary schools that eventually send pupils to that particular high school. The topics of study involved describing how much science is being taught, how it is being taught, the resources available for teaching science, and the constraints on the science program.

Field study and *qualitative research* are two other terms that have been used to characterize the methods we have chosen to call naturalistic. The term **field study** suggests that data are collected in the native habitats of the subjects rather than in the academic environment of the laboratory scientist (Schatzman and Strauss, 1973). The term **qualitative research** refers to the usual (but not inevitable) form of the data—words, pictures, and graphs rather than numbers and statistics. According to Dabbs, "Quality is the essential character or nature of something; quantity is the amount. Quality is the what; quantity is the how much; Qualitative refers to the meaning, the definition or analogy or model or metaphor characterizing something, while quantitative assumes the meaning and refers to the measure of it" (1982, p. 32).

Not all naturalistic researchers work in exactly the same way. Some variability exists among them in the extent to which they quantify, pre-specify definitions and hypotheses, use words to the exclusion of numbers, and intervene in the setting (Goetz and LeCompte, 1984). Yet two characteristics are reasonably common and permit us to distinguish what we are calling naturalistic (including ethnography, participant observation, and case studies) from traditional studies (such as experiments and surveys). First, the researcher's logic is primarily (but not exclusively) inductive. In Chapter 1 we described the inductive researcher as one who proceeds from concrete data to hypotheses and theory (rather than in the other direction, as the hypothetico-deductive researcher does). Second, field methods are used to gather data. That is, the researcher directly observes the actions of the subjects in their environment, interviews them, and in general tries to understand them from their own point of view. Denzin, a sociologist, used the term *naturalistic* to refer to the researcher's "studied commitment to actively enter the worlds of native people and to render those worlds understandable" (1971, p. 166), using ethnographic descriptions and intensive interviews as the primary sources of data.

Science educator and philosopher Jack Easley used the term *naturalistic* in a slightly different way, to show that careful description is the foundation of science:

> "The term 'naturalistic' is intended to suggest that all sciences go through a natural history phase in which one learns about the underlying structure of the phenomena and how they are organized and then, from that knowledge, one can proceed to a more quantitative or formal type of methodology.... [If] we approach educational research in a naturalistic way, it will be ... more scientific in the sense that it emulates the natural sciences." (1978, p. 7)

More scientific? Easley's quotation suggests that some controversy may exist about the scientific respectability of naturalistic research; otherwise, why the need to defend it? Although naturalistic methods became more acceptable in the late 1970s, many feel that they lack reliability, validity, and the controls that are built into, say, experimental and quantitative methods. The critics are likely to be those committed to the logic of the hypothetico-deductive methods and the philosophy of logical positivism and neopositivism. Herein is the crux of the debate among various methodological schools of thought.

Traditional methods are based on a set of beliefs about how reliable knowledge is attained. Traditional methods attach great value to objectivity, making sure that if a thing such as "prejudice" exists, that more than one person will be able to observe, name, or count it in the same way. Pencil-and-paper tests are valued because they yield an unequivocal score that represents the person's status on the variable measured, regardless of who administers the test. A machine can score the test; hence, there is nothing subjective about how the numbers are assigned. Randomization to experimental and control groups ensures against any unconscious tendency of the experimenter to put the more able and enthusiastic persons in the experimental group. Every control is aimed at leaching the subjectivity out of the research process and increasing its reliability.

Traditional methods aim at reductionism; a phenomenon is to be broken into its elementary, constituent units. The hypothetico-deductive methods that have been so successful in uncovering the secrets of the physical world are believed to be equally appropriate for studying human social behavior, since all reality is explicable in the same physical terms (Meehl, 1958). The goal of research is believed to be *nomothetic*—the discovery of laws about behavior. In other words, it is assumed that scientists will eventually establish explanations for human behavior that do not vary from context to context (such as "self-esteem is a consequence of adequate maternal gratification of feeding demands"). Variations that do exist will be explained by conditional propositions (such as "self-esteem is a function of maternal gratification of adequate feeding demands for males but not for females").

Methodologists who advocate naturalistic research base their arguments on the principle that social action is context-dependent. Many of them regard the search for generalizable laws of human behavior as futile. Understanding behavior removed from its context is impossible. Therefore, to understand the teacher's behavior today, one must consider what occurred in the classroom the day before, policies for instruction being argued in the principal's office, and how much television the teacher's pupils watched the night before. The relationships among these categories or variables are "holistic" and mutually influential, so that sometimes the "causes" are the "effects," and vice versa. Methodologists who advocate naturalistic research argue that all the controls that are designed to increase objectivity and reliability do so at the expense of validity. The experimenters' imposition of controls often works against the validity of what they claim to find. Subjects in experiments may react to the artificial arrangements or to the survey instruments in ways that do not reflect their typical behavior, their deeper feelings, or their reactions to events not contrived by experimenters.

Following the philosophy of **Verstehen** (from German, "to understand"), naturalistic researchers deny that social reality is reducible in the same manner as is physical reality. If the realities differ, then so must the methods of studying them. Moreover, the only techniques we have for studying human actions are fundamentally subjective, not objective. One can objectively record the overt behaviors of another person, but the meanings, emotions, and cognitions of that person can never be known by means of objective methods. To know these private states, researchers must rely on inference by analogy from their own (that is, the researchers') meanings and emotions (hence, the term Verstehen, or sympathetic understanding). By being in direct contact with that person for an extended period, understanding the effects of the environment on him, developing empathic understanding of him, the researcher can infer, "This is how I would feel and what I would believe under these circumstances." Of course, this inference is subject to error, but it is one of the most significant ways that one person can know another. Control over error comes not from techniques such as randomization but from the amount of time the researchers spend and the quality of the empathic relationship they build with the subjects. Control is enhanced by gathering data using several different do methods and several different observers, so the researchers can look for confirmation from these different perspectives.

Naturalistic researchers conceive of generalization differently than do traditional researchers. The latter believe that when an experimenter rejects a null hypothesis at a particular level of statistical significance, the effect may be generalized to the population of subjects and to the theoretical construct from which the experimental measures were derived. Other methodologists such as Cronbach (1982), Campbell (1969) and Meehl (1978) have pointed out that this generalization is unwarranted. Samples for experiments are rarely chosen to be statistically representative of defined populations (Reichardt and Cook, 1979); hence, the observed effect could be due to the idiosyncratic sample or the way the researcher chose to measure the dependent variable and therefore would not generalize to other measures of the same construct. The only safe basis of generalizing is by careful logical analysis about the similarities and differences between the sample in the study and some other group. In this way the basis for generalizing from a case study is the same as the basis for generalizing from an experiment. Knowledge builds up gradually, and theories based on data are judged to be adequate only to the extent to which they can account for the data at hand.

STAGES IN NATURALISTIC RESEARCH

We stated earlier that naturalistic research does not always follow a prespecified design. Studies of this type are quite idiosyncratic in form and procedures (e.g., how long a case will be observed, which persons will be interviewed, what questions will be asked). Nevertheless, there are recognizable stages in naturalistic research: (1) problem formulation, (2) entree and access, (3) data collection, (4) data analysis, (5) confirmation, (6) report, and (7) exit.

Problem Formulation

Although they seldom are derived from theory, naturalistic studies do begin with research questions or topics and use a case, or bounded social system, as a way of answering that question. For example, a sociologist interested in how decision making changes as a business develops might select a business that is just getting started and document patterns of its decision making through several years of its existence. Some research problems originate from holes or discrepancies in the body of knowledge in the disciplines of psychology, sociology, and the like. For example, the need to pin down how teachers use information to plan instruction for pupils led to a series of ethnographic investigations by the Institute for Research on Teaching. Sometimes funding agencies present research problems to researchers, as the National Science Foundation did for Stake and Easley.

Some problems present themselves unbidden by the researcher. The task of evaluating the dissemination of an administration planning package eventually led to Wolcott's work, *Teachers vs. Technocrats*. An anthropologist's taking notice of the aggression among children in her daughter's classroom led to Hanna's ethnographic investigation, with which this chapter opened. Goetz and LeCompte (1984) described various sources of research problems and presented a series of questions to aid the researcher in judging the purpose of a study.

The research problem must be one appropriately suited to naturalistic methods. The researcher must be allowed to study the case first-hand and over many months. Ethnographers recommend that the researcher be on-site, collecting data throughout an entire cycle of the group's activities. Although this advice had to do with the need to observe the native group through its migration cycle or the planting and harvesting of crops, the advice is still good for all naturalistic studies, even those in which no "cycle" is easily recognized. Research on how a teacher establishes and maintains control in an elementary classroom would be incomplete unless it covers the opening day of school, the intervening ceremonies, and closing up in the spring.

The research problem must be answerable with qualitative, narrative data and yield description and interpretation of the phenomenon rather than a quantitative analysis of causes and effects. Questions such as "How many grade-equivalent units can be gained by a Chapter I pupil in one year?" or "What is the effect of systematic desensitization on snake anxiety?" would probably not be appropriate topics (although understanding the reactive nature of experiments is more appropriate for a naturalistic research study).

During the problem formulation stage, the researcher must attend to the "unit of analysis," or particular focus of the study. Much naturalistic research is focused on small, face-to-face groups such as classrooms (e.g., "What role is played by interruptions in the elementary school classroom?"), hospital wards (e.g., "Does the response of nurses to patients' requests for assistance vary among types of patient?"), or a workplace ("What is the function of humorous communication in the office?"). But naturalistic research can also be focused on smaller or larger units. An example of a smaller unit is the study of individuals. Life history methods (Bertaux, 1981; Erikson, 1975) describe and interpret the course of an individual's life. Clinical case studies are recommended as a way of analyzing how individuals learn and comprehend mathematical and scientific concepts (Easley, 1978). The clinical case study method has been used extensively and effectively by Robert Coles (1964), who analyzed children's personality to shed light on social problems such as racial segregation. Similarly, the focus of inquiry can be on dyads, such as a mother and child, nurse and patient, probation officer and offender. The unit of analysis can be episodes or events as well as persons or bounded sites; e.g., the first day of school, initial application for unemployment benefits. The unit of analysis can be larger—a hospital, a school district, a neighborhood, a corporation. Or the object of study may be a social system that consists of a specified set of activities rather than a fixed set of individuals or a locale. For example, the researcher may study the decision-making practices of child welfare teams, participatory democracy as displayed in department meetings at universities, or use of prior arrest records by judges in juvenile courts. Clearly, the unit of analysis has implications for the research design. In general, the larger and more complex the unit, the longer the researcher must collect data, or the more research assistants will have to be relied on, or the more emphasis will have to be given to "elicited" data such as interviews and documents as opposed to direct observation.

Working Design Remember from earlier chapters that the research design was the blueprint for the researcher's activities. If the study was experimental, the design specified how the subjects would be selected and allocated to treatments, the definition of the treatment, including its duration and when the dependent variable would be observed. Once written, this design does not vary, and the researcher knows in advance how everything will proceed during each day of the study. Not surprisingly, design is a different matter in naturalistic research. Many naturalistic researchers have no prespecified design at all, preferring to feel their way into the site, discovering as they go along what data are important to gather, which people are likely to be productive sources of information, and the like. Other researchers have a **working design**, or preliminary plan for what ground they want to cover. Included in this plan is likely to be the length of time they want to stay on site to collect data, what events they plan to observe, and what kinds of people they want to interview. The working design will be tentative, because the social institution is always more complex than can be anticipated. Unforeseen opportunities will present themselves in the form of informants or documents, some people will decline to provide data, parts of the institution will be closed to the researcher, the nature of the research problem itself is likely to change. Still, the working design is important, for it provides the researcher with a substantial tool for negotiating access to the site and gaining cooperation from respondents. For example, the researcher may include a copy of the working design in his proposal to do a naturalistic study in a school district.

The working design includes the researcher's idea of the units to be selected for the study and the rationale for selecting them. If the study is to be focused on a single case (one school, for example), what are the characteristics of that case compared to others in the same category? Is it to be selected because it is typical of those in the category or does it represent some extreme? For example, in a study of school policies about retaining children for a second year in kindergarten, the researcher may decide to choose one school that has a rate of retention that is average for the metropolitan area, or to choose a school with a particularly high or low rate of retention. Rather than focusing on a single case, the researcher may decide that the research questions can best be answered by selecting two cases that contrast on some dimension, for example, two schools differing on retention rate, or one previously judged to be effective and one ineffective. Or the design might call for several sites to be studied, each by a member of a team of observers (Herriott and Firestone, 1983; Stake and Easley, 1978), and all of whom have some more or less standard plan for gathering data. Sites are selected to typify certain features of the population, such as geographic region, socioeconomic status, reputation of programs, characteristics of the clientele, and the like. The design should specify the possible implications of the choice of units on the data to be gathered and inferences to be made. Similarly, the design should describe any sampling procedures within the units of study when their number is too large to collect data from each one. Persons, events, and observation times may be sampled randomly or purposively (Goetz and LeCompte, 1984).

One of us conducted naturalistic research on how school committees make decisions concerning the identification of learning disabled pupils (Smith, 1982). The working design called for observing and recording all the staffing conferences (where the decisions are made) held in eight schools of a single school district over a six-month period. In addition, four children would be followed through the decision-making process from referral to placement. Each participant in the decision-making process would be interviewed and documents such as test scores and official forms would be intensively analyzed. This was to be followed by interviews with district, state, and federal administrators of special and regular education. Although most parts of the working design were carried out, one child selected for intensive analysis simply disappeared from the district. Also, the district suspended staffing conferences during the final month of the observation period, so that data from interviews and documents had to be increased to make up for the lost opportunity for direct observation.

Working hypotheses   The inductive paradigm is based on the idea that researchers begin collecting data with the "tabula rasa"—a mind free of theories about the phenomenon. Critics have rightly charged that the tabula rasa does not exist. When researchers select and record events, they are influenced by what they already know. Many years of education have filled their heads with theories. Personal experiences have predisposed them to see certain things and neglect others. Each of them has some intellectual and political commitments, and naturalistic research is particularly susceptible to the charge that, for example, a Marxist researcher will always see social class conflicts and a psychoanalytic researcher will always see Oedipal conflicts. Naturalistic researchers are obliged to engage in self-analysis and impose controls so that the data gathered are not simply a confirmation of their initial biases. It is also true, however, as Rosenthal (1966) has repeatedly demonstrated, that researcher predispositions affect experiments.

Rather than ignoring their constructs and predispositions, naturalistic researchers must formalize them, write them down as **working hypotheses**, or potential and tentative explanations for what is likely to be observed in the course of the study. Some writers on naturalistic research have referred to these constructs as "foreshadowed problems" or issues. In the *Case Studies in Science Education* (Stake and Easley, 1978), the researchers were directed to describe the status of science, math, and social science education in selected schools, and they were armed with a long list of issues as a kind of background knowledge. These included questions such as (1) Do pupils read, write, and calculate well enough to profit from instruction in science? (2) Has the "back-to-the-basics movement" affected science instruction? (3) Is there evidence that the curriculum reform movement has affected social studies teaching? (4) What is the effect of hand-held calculators on math instruction?

The roles of questions, issues, and hypotheses such as these are quite different in naturalistic research and traditional research. In the latter there is one or a small number of hypotheses that guide the inquiry, and they are fixed for the life of the study. Testing them is really a climactic moment in the study. In naturalistic research, there may be a long list of hypotheses, new ones may be added to the list as data are gathered and analyzed, old ones may disappear or change. In many instances, hypotheses—abstract explanations for observed data—are derived from the data themselves (Glaser and Strauss, 1967); this process will be illustrated in the section on analysis in this chapter.

Entree and Access

No researcher can simply walk into an institution and start collecting data. Each must gain access in some way. The process of gaining access involves taking on a role (which social psychologists have defined as a position in a social group that is occupied by an individual and that imposes behaviors and expectations on the individual as an occupant of that role). How researchers gain access and the roles that they take on will have an impact on what data will become available to them.

If the authors of this text were to study the intellectual life of the faculty club at Arizona State University or the extent of participatory decision making in their own College of Education, they would be participating directly in the activities of their own institution and (unknown to their colleagues) recording those activities for the purpose of research. In this case they would have ready-made and official roles other than as re-

searchers in this institution. Other examples of research wherein the researcher assumes the role of "observer as participant" might be the accounts
of life in a mental hospital as written by patients or the memoirs of a
Watergate burglar.

Some researchers have joined organizations or entered institutions
ostensibly to participate but actually to conduct research. "Employee-fore-
man relationships on the assembly line" or "social exchange at the corner
tavern" are two topics that might be studied this way. The researcher takes
on an existing role in the organization and conducts the study from the
perspective of an insider with access to the specialized language and rituals
that are infrequently revealed to outsiders.

Neither of these two arrangements requires any negotiation for permission to perform the research. The researchers are already on-site and
playing a participative role in the organization. However, these arrangements are not very common in naturalistic research and pose some difficult
ethical questions because the members are not informed that they are being
studied. More typically, the researcher is an outsider, someone who plays
none of the usual roles in the organization, such as employee, supervisor,
teacher, pupil, patient, or client. The role taken by the researcher is that
of observer, researcher, or author. As such, the researcher must ask to
study the institution and the people in it. First the researcher must seek
official approval from the legitimate authority in the organization. For
public schools this is the superintendent or person designated by the superintendent. The researcher must meet this person, explain the purpose
of the study, the reason that site was chosen, the amount of time the
researcher expects to be there, the general kinds of data that are to be
collected, and the form of the report. The researcher must explain the
procedures that will be used to protect the anonymity of the site and the
persons studied. Permission to do the study must be requested, and in
almost all cases, written requests must be evaluated and approved by committees or administrators.

Once official approval is granted, the naturalistic researcher still must
gain access to the persons who will be studied as well as various levels and
factions in the institution that could either hinder or facilitate the work.
Therefore, it is important to meet with, explain the research to, and solicit
cooperation from representatives of groups such as assistant superintend-
ents and directors, parents' organizations, teachers' unions, professional
associations, student or patient councils, and the like. During meetings with
these individuals and groups, the researcher needs to establish a "persona"
that conveys an acceptance of the respondents as individuals, a noneval-
uative stance, neutrality or disinterestedness with respect to the data to be
gathered and the questions to be answered, confidentiality, and the like.
The researcher's success in projecting this persona will have a powerful

impact on the quality of data that will become accessible. Respondents who are convinced of the researcher's trustworthiness and integrity will reveal more about themselves and will behave more naturally in the presence of the researcher. Some individuals will even become "informants" in the sense that they will identify with the researcher or have more than ordinary interest in the research topic. Informants help researchers gain access to an insider's perspective on the organization and steer them to others who can provide information about the research topic. Of course, the researcher must deliver on these implicit promises of integrity and confidentiality. It is not enough to posture. Gaining rapport and establishing relationships with respondents are the topics of two interesting books, *People Studying People* (Georges and Jones, 1980) and *Fieldwork Experience* (Sheffir, Stebbins, and Turowetz, 1980).

A good example of negotiating access and role taking is Batcher's study of the function of emotions in classroom life (1981). A preliminary set of observations led to the identification of a classroom "where emotion was visible" and the teacher, Mr. Bell, was "hard-working and caring" (p. 25). Access was gained through discussions with Mr. Bell and the school principal and vice-principal. "Mr. Bell wished to receive assurances that his professional and public image would not be harmed in any way" (p. 27), so a contract was prepared and signed. The contract provided that Mr. Bell could read the finished manuscript and edit material he considered damaging or offensive. Although there is no evidence whether or not he changed anything written about him, Mr. Bell wrote a response to the study that was included in the book.

Batcher described her role in the research as rather detached from the teacher and closely aligned with the pupils, never in a supervisory, teacherlike role toward them. "My behavior was such as to give the impression that I was simply another child in class" (p. 32). Her dress, her working at children's desks, her use of their oral idioms, her informal contact with them were all part of taking on the role of participant observer and gaining access to their emotional lives.

Researcher roles are sometimes described as lying on a continuum from full participant to full observer (Gold, 1969). At one extreme is the study done by a person actually occupying an existing role in the organization. At the other is the study by the nonparticipant observer (e.g., Mehan, 1979), where no interaction takes place between researcher and subject, and the researcher studies videotapes, transcripts, or behavior viewed through a one-way mirror. The role a researcher assumes becomes a kind of social and psychological vantage point that permits access to certain data and not others. For example, the full participant role allows researchers to know what life is really like for persons occupying the same or similar roles, but denies them access to life in other parts of the organization. Researchers in the full observer role can never know the meanings held by the persons being observed, yet their knowledge is not contaminated by insider's biases.

Data Collection

It has been said that in naturalistic research, the researcher is the instrument. Certainly, researchers make decisions about what data to gather, gather them, store and process them, usually without any standardized questionnaires or observation schedules. Three primary modes of data collection characterize most naturalistic research: *observation, interview,* and *document collection.* The researcher chooses the relative emphasis to be placed on each.

Observation   Direct observation of the case is the heart of naturalistic data collection, for it is the most natural, and hence, has **ecological validity**. That is, observation provides a permanent record of the stream of ordinary behavior that would have existed if the researcher had not been in the room. Although observer effects are probably inevitable, the researcher becomes less obvious and fades into the background simply by virtue of being in the same place for a long time. The longer the researchers are present, the more the subjects take them for granted and the harder it is to maintain the facade that is typically shown to strangers.

Observing means recording, so the researcher must record the events, usually by writing a narrative account on the spot, sometimes by audio or video recording or by photographing the actions (e.g., Becker, 1978). There is a trade-off between the intrusiveness of the recording equipment or procedures (the subjects may react unnaturally in response to them) and the value of having a permanent record of behavior on tape (for reliability checks).

Suppose that the case was a classroom and the research problem was how teachers' expectations for pupil competence affect pupil achievement. The researcher would record in detail the physical appearance of the room and the arrangements of the objects in it: desks, work spaces, teacher's area, reference books, study carrels, and so on. Maps and photographs of the classroom would probably supplement the verbal description in the researcher's notes. A physical description of the persons would be provided. On any given day of observation, the researcher would describe how the teacher and pupils arranged themselves and moved among the material objects. Teaching materials, methods, textbooks, worksheets, curriculum guides, and discipline policies would be described.

An account of the actual words spoken by the indivuduals and their gestures would be kept. To obtain a complete accounting, one needs to document the interactions between teachers and pupils as well as pupils among each other. Not all of this can be done at the same sitting, but the attention of the researcher can be centered on one group or child or location in the classroom at a time, eventually covering the whole. In addition to observing overt behaviors, the researcher also interprets the emotions and intentions of the behavior and speech of teachers, pupils, and others in the class. A catalog of the events from the outside that impinge on the setting is particularly important. In studies of schools this would include intrusions of principals, evaluators, and parents, announcements over public address systems, fire drills, and the comings and goings of pupils and adults to music, special education, and remedial programs. Besides providing an accurate document of the actions and surroundings, the researcher must keep track of the time sequence of these events, to show what events preceded what other events.

The idea of context—the physical, social, and material environment in which human action takes place—is central to naturalistic methodology. Human action such as a teacher's expectations for different pupils is shaped by, among other things, the physical aspects of the classroom, the number of people in the room, the social interactions among pupils, the demands imposed on the teacher, the resources available, the system of rules laid down, the history of the teacher's relationships with pupils, the characteristics and responses of the pupils, and much more. The events occurring immediately before the behavior of interest to the researcher have bearing on that behavior, according to this methodology. People in social groups create a system of shared symbols and meanings that may be unique to that group. The fact that, for example, children in a class label those pupils assigned to the least advanced reading group as "turtles" and exclude them from friendship groups illustrates this point and shows how context may influence the relationship between teacher expectation and pupil behavior. It follows that an adequate depiction of the behavior of interest to the researcher must include contextual elements such as those described here (McDermott, Gospodinoff, and Aron, 1978).

Contrast this orientation with that of a traditional researcher studying the effect of teacher expectations on pupil behavior. This researcher decides in advance what four or five pupil behaviors are important, selects two pupils for whom the teacher holds different expectations, counts the frequency of targeted behaviors on the part of targeted pupils, and computes mean differences. The observation in such a correlational study ignores the surrounding events and treats the targeted behavior as if it occurred in a vacuum. It assumes that the relationship is caused only by the individual, psychological characteristics of the targeted persons. In naturalistic research on the same topic, the researcher casts a wide net, recording events and features of the environment that may have a bearing on teacher expectations and pupil behavior. Working hypotheses are used to decide what to record, but the researcher is also open to unanticipated influences.

In addition to recording the human action in its context, the researchers also note their own immediate perceptions and emotions relative to what is being observed. These are carefully bracketed as "observer comments," "interpretive asides," or simply "reactions." This self-description on the part of the researcher provides a check on the researcher's outlook as the study progresses and on observer effects (i.e., how the researcher's presence may have altered the natural behavior of people in the case). Another benefit of the researcher's reactions is to suggest possible patterns and explanations for subsequent analysis.

Bogdan and Biklen (1982) provided important advice about avoiding summarization, evaluations, abstractions, and generalizations, all of which are pitfalls in observation:

> Rather than saying "The child looked a mess," you might choose something like, "The child, who was seven or eight years old, wore faded muddy dungarees with both knees ripped. His nose was running . . ., and his face was streaked clean where he had rubbed it with his wet fingers." . . . Replace words like *disciplining, playing, tutoring, practicing, nice person, good student, doing nothing* with detailed renderings of exactly what people are doing, saying, and what they look like. (pp. 84–85).

In summary, observation is the heart of naturalistic research, for it ideally provides a source of evidence of human action in its most natural state—that is, as near to that which would have occurred if the researcher had not been present. Spradley's book *Participant Observation* (1980) is a valuable resource on what to observe and how to record.

Interviews Interviews produce "elicited data" because the researcher prompts the subject with a series of questions, constituting an intervention or interruption in the natural stream of behavior. Still, these interruptions are often necessary to obtain subjects' perspectives on what events mean to them.

Interviews fulfill several functions in naturalistic research, and their form differs depending on their particular function. Spradley's book *The Ethnographic Interview* (1979) provides a useful taxonomy, as do Goetz and Lecompte (1984). Some interviews serve a "gatekeeping" function; researchers introduce themselves and the purpose of the research in general terms, tell what will be expected of the subject, and explain their policy of confidentiality. In a second type of interview, the "story-telling" interview, the interviewees react to an open-ended question in their own words and in their own way. The interviewer provides few leads and uses nondirective prompts to elicit more information. Tom Cottle's research on busing (1976) and Studs Terkel's research on working life (1972) were based on this technique.

Another type of interview is semistructured, employing lists of questions and probes derived from working hypotheses. Such questions are not necessarily standardized from respondent to respondent; their purpose is to uncover the facts about the case as well as the meanings these facts have for the respondents. Kahn and Cannell's book *The Dynamics of Interviewing* (1957) and Sullivan's book *The Psychiatric Interview* (1954) provide particularly helpful advice about the techniques of interviewing.

Yet another kind of interview is the informal, *in situ* interview in which the researcher asks a question in conjunction with observation. For example, a researcher studying classroom processes might observe the teacher calling on each child in turn to recite the answers to homework problems. After class the researcher asks the teacher what function such recitation serves and how common such processes are. Informal interviews also take place in casual settings such as lounges, hallways, on the street, and in chance encounters between researcher and subject. Information gained in such interactions can be quite revealing because the subject has less chance to adopt a "research subject role" and give the socially desirable response. In all cases the researcher must document the actual words spoken by the interviewees, sometimes with the aid of audiotape recording. Researchers differ in their use of audiotape and videotape recording. Someone who studies a fine-grained problem like "the relationship of mothers' utterances and infants' development" or "what children say to themselves when they solve arithmetic problems" will probably prefer the accuracy of mechanical recording and transcriptions. Other researchers, who are interested in portraying human action in a less detailed way, have less need for exact transcriptions or choose to avoid the reactivity that may be caused by recording devices.

In her study of classroom emotions, Batcher described her interviews this way:

> I began interviews to get at certain events and attitudes through their eyes but expanded the original conception when it became obvious that every child had something original to tell. Interviews were conducted at recess, lunch, or during class time with the permission of the teacher. There was no set pattern, but there were some questions I asked just about everyone at some point, such as where they were born, where their parents came from, who was in their family, the number of their brothers and sisters, what they thought of school, who their friends were, and what they thought of the teacher. One of the least useful questions, I found, was How do you (or did you) *feel* when . . . . The children invariably used one of three descriptors, happy, sad, or mad, and that was the end of the thought. The questions Tell me about . . . or What were you thinking . . . were more likely to yield rich information because then children were free to interpret the question any way they wanted and could talk about anything they wished. Even the way children clarified these questions was an indication of the direction of their thought and how they conceptualized their experience. (1981, p. 34)

An example of one of Batcher's interviews was reproduced in the report:

Oralia, who is a good friend of Janie's, has told Mr. Bell that it was Janie who took Mariana's reading notes. . . .
   E.B.: "Why do you think she'd do that?"
   O.R.: "I don't know."
   "Remember the time you told Mr. Bell that Janie was not at the dentist, as she was supposed to be?"
   "Yeah, she was playing outside. Baseball with Natalie."
   "So, you were sure of that, eh?"
   "Mhm."
   "And what did Mr. Bell say?"
   "He didn't say nothing."
   "Why do you suppose that's the case?"
   Faintly, "I dunno."
   "Did he believe you or did he believe her?"
   "He believed her."
   "Why?"
   Pauses, then laughs. "I dunno. Like—she probably has her work up to date. She's better than me."
   "She's a better student?"
   "Yeah."
   "So because she's a better student, he believed her?"
   "Mhm."
   "But you're sure you're right."
   "Mhm. Because after, me and Cesar and Vito were walking down and we went running and we saw her go inside with all her things (baseball equipment). It was about 4:15."
   "Interesting. So there's nothing else you'd do about that, eh?"
   "No. It doesn't matter, really, to me." Faintly, "It doesn't matter."
   "Why did you tell Mr. Bell?"
   "Cause, it's no fair for other people to have to stay in and she doesn't have to stay in."
   "Even if she does have her work up to date, it's no fair."
   "Yeah. People have to suffer for her."
   "Yeah? So how did you feel when he didn't believe you?"
   "Angry."
   "And what did you think?"
   "I dunno." Faintly, "That he probably liked Janie better than me."
   "So, d'you think that's still the case?"
   "Yeah, it doesn't matter really to me."
   "Yeah, I'm sure it doesn't, but it's interesting to know how you feel, for my work, for my studies. And you think that's still the case, he likes her?"
   "Mhm."
   "How else would you know if he does?"
   "He hardly ever screams at her."
   "Hardly ever. Does he scream at most everyone else?"
   "Yeah. All the boys especially."
   "Yeah. Not too much at the girls. Or somewhat?"
   "Yeah."
   "But of all the people he screams even less at her?"

"Yeah."

"How does she feel about him?"

"I dunno. Sometimes she hates him. Sometimes she likes him."

"How do you feel about him?"

"I like him. He's nice."

"You like him, eh? What d'you like about him?"

"He gives us work to do, he's kind. But he doesn't scream that much, at boys he screams a lot, but he doesn't really scream that much at me. But he does scream sometimes."

"Do you remember the last time he screamed at you?"

"Yeah. I was talking to Natalie. He broke the ruler." Laughs and recalls animatedly, "I was talking to Natalie, and he looked at me a couple of times and told me to be quiet, and I didn't do what he said so he came up to me and screamed at me and he broke the ruler."

Laughs. "How did you feel when he broke the ruler?"

"Scared!"

"Yeah. I jumped too. Why do you suppose he did that?"

"So I wouldn't talk."

"Did you talk after?"

"No."

"What was going through your mind?"

"To be quiet so he wouldn't break another one." We both laugh. (1981, pp. 49–50)

Document collection   Thanks in part to the accountability movement, social institutions have become paper mills. Organizations produce written budgets, interoffice memos, market surveys, transcripts of meetings, personnel files, statements of policy or philosophy, and newsletters. Schools produce these and more: pupil case files, curriculum guides, test score reports, needs assessments, disciplinary codes, teachers' planning books, grade books, pupil essays, and student newspapers. Every piece of paper represents a potential source of data for the naturalistic researcher. Added to the official records and archives of the organization are the writings of individuals—letters, diaries, autobiographies, and the like. Collection of documents is the equivalent of collection of artifacts in ethnography.

There are several reasons for collecting and analyzing documents. They can be the sole source of data. Thomas and Znaniecki (1927), for example, used personal diaries as a way of studying the lives of Polish immigrants. Documents may also be used to cross-check and confirm data from other sources. Henry (1963) used pupils' essays to corroborate interview data about their attitudes toward their parents. McCleary (1977) contrasted official crime reports with data gleaned from observation and interviews. Historians rely heavily on official and personal documents. Journalists depend heavily on documents such as bank transactions, airline reservation lists, hotel registers, records of real estate transactions, and the like to confirm the facts behind a story.

These written products can be incorporated into the researcher's data record and should be evaluated according to their source (where they came from and how they were acquired) and purpose (Guba and Lincoln, 1981). For example, if a diary were used, one would want to know the individual's motives for keeping the diary. Was it meant to be found and be a source of justification for the person? Was it kept at the request of the researcher? Other documents should be similarly scrutinized. Was an evaluation report meant to convey an impartial analysis of the worth of a program, or was it a public relations device done to impress the voters? Were the crime statistics an accurate measure of crime or, as McCleary (1977, 1978) suggested, a function of the politics of the police force to increase appropriations or satisfy city hall?

Just because documents and written records were generated with ulterior motives does not reduce their importance. Many are not meant to be "objective truth" and should not be considered as such. Instead, they should be viewed as one perspective on the truth, balancing data from alternative perspectives and methods, such as participant observing or interviewing.

The data record   The documents assembled by the researcher, the interview protocols, and observation protocols mount up fast and must be stored so that they can be easily accessed. Accumulating a **data record** of a thousand pages in a naturalistic study would not be unusual. Some methodologists (Lofland and Lofland, 1984) recommend that several copies of each page of data be kept. One copy goes into a chronological notebook based on the date the data were gathered. Another copy goes into a file system organized by the topics or locations covered. Another can be cut up and used for data analysis. Bogdan and Biklen (1982) also recommend that researchers keep written accounts of their own thinking about what is being observed and what it could mean, their decisions about methods used and departures from the working design, their feelings about the subjects, any ethical problems that arise, personal preconceptions, and pet hypotheses. Since, according to some methodologists, "the researcher is the instrument," an evaluation of that instrument should be grist for the study. The researcher's self-reflection and self-criticism involve answering questions such as, "Why did I choose to observe A but not B?" "How did my antagonism to this principal alter my working design that specified interviewing all principals in the district?" or "Why did I overlook x as a possible explanation for the pattern I observed?" Such analysis is a central element in the idea of rigor or control in naturalistic research.

Qualitative Data Analysis

To speak of data analysis as a step following data collection is misleading. Analysis begins in small measure almost at the beginning of data collection as the researcher reflects on the meaning of the data and the original and evolving working hypotheses. As the study progresses, more time will be spent analyzing data and less will be spent collecting it. What is analysis, then, and what is its function?

Qualitative data analysis involves reduction of the amount of information to a smaller set of categories, themes, or propositions. One can see the similarity to quantitative analysis, which seeks to transform many scores or data points into a measure of central tendency and a measure of variability. The trick with both kinds of analysis is to reduce the volume of data without losing its essential characteristics and meaning. In naturalistic research there are several methods of data analysis (but none as routine as computing, say, an arithmetic mean). The first is the **constant comparative method**, or **grounded theory method**, developed by Glaser and Strauss (1967). Using this purely inductive method, the researcher combs through the data record, looking for possible categories or topics that mark off or characterize the data. A list of such categories is derived. Then each piece of data is coded according to the category or categories into which it falls; it may fall into several categories. Coding data is an ongoing process that occurs simultaneously with further collection of data.

As the data falling into a category begin to make conceptual sense, the researcher provides a definition for the category and begins to look for patterns of relationships between it and other categories. Essays or "analytic memos" are written about the meaning of the category and its causes and effects as well as the conditions under which the category exists (Charmaz, 1983). The researcher writes propositional statements or hypotheses that explain the data and contribute to *grounded theory* about the phenomenon. For example, a study on teacher expectations and pupil behavior might yield a category of "pupil labeling" and a proposition that "only those pupils in the most advanced reading group who use the term 'turtle' to characterize children in the least advanced reading group are those who exclude the latter from their teams during recess." Analytic memos are written to elaborate this proposition and suggest its causes and consequences. The next step in this method of analysis is called **theoretical sampling**, which in the example just stated would send the researcher back to the classroom to collect data that would support, disconfirm, or further elaborate the proposition. The final step in the *constant comparative*, or *grounded theory* method of analysis, involves writing the theory of the phenomenon.

In *Case Studies of Science Education* (Stake and Easley, 1978), Louis Smith's attempt to understand the science program in "Alte School District" uncovered the category of "teacher staleness" from recurring instances in the data record. After going through the steps described above, he presented his analysis of this category in the form of a flow chart (reprinted in Figure 11–1). Staleness in teaching was hypothesized to be the result of aging, personal or professional midlife crises, and too many years teaching

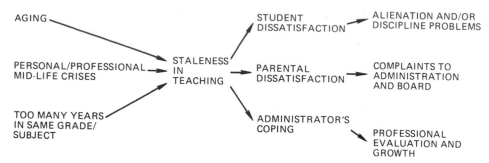

FIGURE 11-1 "Staleness in Teaching": Example of Qualitative Analysis *(Source: Smith, 1978, p. 3-85.)*

the same grade or subject, and the cause of student and parent dissatisfaction and "administrator's coping." These outcomes, in turn, contribute to alienation and discipline problems, complaints to administration and school board, and occasionally, to professional reevaluation and growth. According to Smith's self-assessment:

> In some of the early observing, a sense of particulars coalesced into a pattern labeled "teachers who have gone stale." The mix was a flatness, a lack of vitality (physically, personally, and interpersonally), a seeming lack of interest in the curriculum (science, math, and social studies) by both the teacher and the children, a lack of creativity and curricular risk-taking, a negativism toward the children—they're spoiled, they don't care, they don't try—and sometimes a negativism toward colleagues, administrators, and the college and university programs (often decades ago). Age seemed to correlate; gender did not.
>
> After this had been identified tentatively, it was explored in the latter part of a number of exit interviews with teachers, administrators, board members, and citizens. Invariably, it blew the interviews wide open; that is, the interviewees agreed that the phenomenon (or their own conceptualization of it) existed, that it was *the* problem in the district generally. Some of the individuals went on to explore the issue for upwards of an hour . . . .
>
> The major ideas that developed were these:
>
> 1. It was not just a problem in science education.
>
> 2. Some saw it as not a problem of "going stale," but a problem of some teachers who were "average/adequate" but not "good/excellent" from the start. Most interviewees eventually came down to the tenability of both hypotheses.
>
> 3. Most argued that Alte had many fewer teachers in this category than other school districts, both absolutely and in terms of percentages.
>
> 4. Many talked in detail of Alte's complex approach as to resolving the problems at both the level of the individual schools and at the level of the district. These approaches were felt by them to be the most comprehensive and sophisticated in the metropolitan area. (Smith, 1978, pp. 3-83–84)

Hanna's study (1982), a part of which introduced this chapter, also made use of categories in organizing and analyzing data on aggression among pupils in a model desegregated school. These topical categories included the characteristics of the construct she called "meddlin' " (the children's term for aggressive behavior), the arenas of meddlin', the styles of meddlin', the causes of meddlin' (e.g., racism, peer hierarchy rank, "equality" through compensation, uncontrolled anger, getting a friend, sexual competition), responses to meddlin', and consequences of meddlin'.

A partial list of categories Batcher used to organize data on classroom emotion were anger, acceptance of researcher, alien power, aggravation, apple polishing, approval, approach-avoidance, aims and objectives, appreciation, battered child, belonging, boredom, born again, bad child, Bell (the teacher) as isolate, Bell on women, control, confrontation, classroom order, caring teacher, cat's away (1981, p. 178).

In contrast to the purely inductive method of grounded theory, the second kind of qualitative analysis may follow either an inductive or deductive process of deriving categories, coding data, and developing hypotheses. The most comprehensive treatment of qualitative analysis is Miles and Huberman (1984). Although the procedures recommended by Miles and Huberman are flexible enough to be adapted by researchers with different purposes, the methods generally assume that data collection is complete. The object to be analyzed is the polished data record rather than the case itself. The task is approached with the aid of a prespecified and defined list of categories, which are themselves the result of a theoretical framework. The researcher uses this system of categories to comb through the data record. Each segment of the data is coded with a mnemonic abbreviation of the name of the category (e.g., "LAB-PUPIL" is placed in the margin of the data record next to any datum that suggests that pupils have expectations and labels for their fellow pupils). The category system acts both as an index to the location of categorized data in the data record and as an indication of potential relationships among categories (e.g., when the same set of data is regularly coded both as "LAB-PUPIL" and "AB-GROUP," for ability group).

Although a prespecified list of categories is used initially, the researcher may also discover new categories while coding the data. A second researcher may recode a segment of data, and intercoder agreement is calculated. Once coding is completed, the researcher looks for patterns among the categories, using visual displays that portray time sequences, covariation of categories, cross classifications, and the like. Propositions and hypotheses are stated, and they are progressively refined as the researcher searches the data record for disconfirming evidence.

The third kind of analysis does not look like analysis at all. The researcher proceeds artistically and intuitively to search for themes in the data to use in developing a story. Analysis consists of selecting data from the data record that best represent the researcher's understanding and interpretation of the phenomenon. That material is then translated into a narrative account. This story employs images, metaphors, and a logical dramatic structure to provide an aesthetic and affecting experience for the reader. The report is a narrative portrayal of the case and its context, often without any formal statements of findings or hypotheses. Rob Walker's case study in the *Case Studies in Science Education: Pine City* (1978) resulted in an "analysis" of this type.

> A glance at the daily schedules and the faculty list shows that science plays an important part in the curriculum of the high schools. Compared to schools in other places the emphasis is not unusual, certainly not startling, and the context of the courses seems orthodox. For the casual visitor to the school, examining the actual curriculum, science plays a lesser role than it does on paper. In junior and senior high school alike, there is only one room equipped as a laboratory. In one school it is only distinguished by a demonstration bench; in the other, by table space for perhaps twelve students to work. There is nothing like purpose-built laboratories or computer terminals. In the time I was in the high school I did not see microscopes, circuit boards or bunsen burners in use (though no doubt some of these things could be found in cupboards).
>
> The one science teaching resource that seems in abundance is the textbook. The books look new and expensive, in marked contrast to the laboratory equipment and the classroom furniture. The libraries have interesting selections of science and science-related books, and schools receive regular copies of the magazine *Current Science*. . . . (Walker, 1978, pp. 6–14)

> Miss Green teaches chemistry as well as general science. She also teaches physics, but this year there were too few students to constitute a class. This is her first regular teaching job and she has been at the school two years. . . . (Walker, 1978, p. 6–18)
>
> Miss Green clearly has a good relationship with her students. She spends time talking to them out of class and in many ways feels close to them. She shares their background. . . . .
>
> Thirty students arrive for the general science class, but again there seem more because the room is quite small. . . . This class, too, is studying the atmosphere, and Miss Green has had them collecting barometric pressures from radio weather broadcasts. They are trying to discover how to predict rain. So far it looks like you get rain when the pressure rises, but the class decides it's hard to tell with just two days and only five sets of readings recorded on the blackboard.
>
> Up in front of the class is a mobile lab bench (which also doesn't work). Miss Green has managed to find a vacuum pump so that she can demonstrate some experiments on air pressure, but as she explains to the class, they tried it yesterday in another class and discovered that one of the valves was faulty, making it difficult to get the experiments to work. In addition, one of the most dramatic of all the demonstrations—the silent alarm clock ringing in a vacuum—had to be aborted because the clock was too big to fit inside the bell jar. (Walker, 1978, pp. 6–19).

Confirmation

Naturalistic researchers frequently seek to confirm the hypotheses derived and the categories defined. They do this in several ways. An *internal check* involves the search for consistent evidence in the data record to confirm the proposition, conclusion, or hypothesis. In addition, the researcher seeks any evidence that disconfirms the propositions stated. In many cases, such disconfirming evidence results in a revision of the propositions and more refined understanding of the phenomenon. For example, the researcher might find evidence that a particular proposition is true only under some special conditions.

Triangulation is the process of converging on a conclusion from different points. For example, when evidence gleaned from interviews corroborates other evidence obtained by direct observation, or documents with interviews, documents with informant interviews, and the like, greater confidence can be placed in the conclusion. The spirit of the multioperations paradigm (see Chapter 1) is apparent here. Every method has a particular kind of error. Every perspective has a certain bias. Only by looking across methods and perspectives can one ascertain the true state of things.

External checks, another form of triangulation, involve inviting another researcher to observe the case directly or read and categorize the data record to see if convergent propositions could be reached by a second observer. In *theoretical triangulation* (Denzin, 1978) an explanation *other* than the one proposed by the researcher is introduced to see which one better accounts for the data.

Another form of external check involves the collection of data to test the hypotheses derived from naturalistic studies. The researcher may construct a questionnaire or observation schedule, sample units, and collect data to help confirm a hypothesis. For example, one of the hypotheses derived from naturalistic research on identification of learning disabilities (Smith, 1982) was that many children who did not match official definitions of learning disabilities were identified as such merely because they were behind their classmates and needed remedial help. This hypothesis was tested and corroborated in a representative survey in Colorado (Shepard, Smith and Vojir, 1983). Triangulation of all varieties is another aspect of control and rigor in naturalistic studies.

Report

The report of naturalistic research is usually written in ordinary, not technical, language and emphasizes portrayal of the case and its context. In reports such as that of Walker (excerpted earlier), narrative form is followed, excluding formal statements of conclusions. Other reports are discursive, having formal statements of conclusions logically argued from the data and illustrated with descriptive material from the data record. The excerpt from Smith's study shows how hypotheses are interwoven with descriptions, in that case to depict teacher staleness. The report should also include a description of the methods used to collect and analyze the data and to gain access to the site as well as self-analysis of the researcher.

Including these elements in the report allows the reader to examine the researcher's argument and evaluate the validity of the study's conclusions. The reader should be able to judge what the methods were and whether they were appropriate for the research problem, whether the phenomenon was adequately described, whether the researcher's predispositions might have influenced the conclusions, and whether alternative hypotheses were tested. The report should be well written, so that it provides a vicarious experience to the reader. In other words, the researcher should write well enough to convey a sense of what life in the case is like as well as the understandings the researcher came to as a result of the research.

Exit

The final stage of the study finds the researchers extricating themselves from the site and making sure their obligations have been fulfilled. Naturalistic research places heavy ethical obligations on the researcher to protect the anonymity of the site and the subjects. Parts of the final report may be submitted to the people who provided the data as a final check on how the researcher maintained confidentiality. Reports should be provided to those who requested them. Today's researchers are also responsible to the next generation of researchers, and their sites should not become inaccessible due to mistakes in exit procedures.

NATURALISTIC METHODS IN EVALUATION

We made the point in Chapter 1 that every method used in research can be used in evaluation. The purpose of judging the worth of a program or product (the goal of evaluation) can be served by evidence gained from observation, interviews, and document collection, and analyzed and reported qualitatively. Indeed, some evaluation models are based on assumptions compatible with naturalistic research: Stake's "Responsive Evaluation" (1975), Parlett and Hamilton's "Illuminative Evaluation" (1976), and Eisner's "Connoisseurship Evaluation" (1979). Parlett and Hamilton, for example, recommended that the evaluator assemble evidence from the perspective of the participants of the program: Ask what the program means to them and what difference it has made. Compare this information with data collected by alternative methods, including narrative portrayals, rich in context, of actual (not idealized) program activities. Instead of letting the evaluator or client make the judgment of program worth, submit the evidence to various stakeholders, asking them to make the judgments. For a school program, the judgments of teachers, pupils, administrators, school board members, citizens, and relevant special interest groups would be collected.

Bogdan and Biklen (1982) reported the following story about the use of naturalistic methods in a contracted evaluation. The program evaluated was a federal government mandate to increase the number of handicapped pupils served by local Head Start agencies. On the basis of an independent, survey-based evaluation, it was determined that the agencies were in compliance, having increased by 10 percent the proportion of handicapped children served. But. . .

> Using an open-ended design, [the qualitative evaluation team] went to the projects, observing and talking to parents and staff. The initial observations consisted of data collection around a number of general questions such as, "How was the mandate experienced by Head Start staff and parents?" and "What had changed, if anything, as a result?". . . The qualitative team concluded that the number of handicapped children recruited had not notably increased; rather, there had been a change in how the children were defined. They suggested that the conclusion that Head Start now served 10.1 percent was misleading. The report took the form of a narrative which discussed a number of propositons concerning the mandate's effect. These included an account of the confusion generated by the term "handicap," how staff perceived the mandate in light of their general view of "orders from Washington," programmatic variations in compliance (from "paper compliance" to "active recruitment efforts"), as well as the unanticipated consequences of the mandate (from the labeling of children who previously were not labeled, to a general improvement in individualization in programming for all children).
>
> The funding agency was unhappy with the qualitative report. They wanted to know the facts: "What was the percentage of handicapped youngsters being served by Head Start?" The funders wanted the report to Congress to be clear and unambiguous, and, as the researchers also learned, they wanted the findings to be complimentary to Head Start. (Bogdan and Biklen (1982, pp. 195–196)

Bogdan and Biklen apparently felt that the qualitative results were more valid than those of the survey. Like Patton (1980), Guba and Lincoln (1981), and Fetterman (1984), they believe that naturalistic methods can serve well the goals of evaluation. Wolcott (1982), however, expressed the need for caution, in that the aims of evaluation are antithetical to the roles, methods, and purposes of ethnographic research. The ethnographer attempts to get close enough to the research subjects to understand them from their own point of view. The naturalistic researcher studies them for an extended time, and as Wolcott noted, defers judgment in terms of any external standards of worth. The evaluator, on the other hand, is in business only to make judgments or facilitate the judgments of administrators and clients. The work of the evaluator is governed by the standard of timeliness (among other things; see Chapter 2). The evidence must be gathered quickly and in time to support a decision, a decision that probably will affect the lives of the people whom the ethnographic evaluator studied. This paradox reminds us that naturalistic methods, although contributing essential context-based description and interpretation and multi-perspective, multi-method data, should not be applied to evaluation in a wholesale or thought-less manner (see Fetterman, 1984).

HOW TO CRITIQUE A NATURALISTIC STUDY

Because of their idiosyncracies, applying uniform standards to naturalistic studies may be inappropriate. Nevertheless, studies do vary in quality. Here are some, if not standards, at least issues to be raised about the qualities of naturalistic studies:

1. *Time spent collecting data.* One of the primary controls in naturalistic research is the length of time the researcher spent in collecting data and the amount of data collected. Length of time should be assessed in light of the size and complexity of the case and the phenomenon studied. When circumstances restrict the time available, the researcher should compensate by collecting more data from alternative sources and informants.

2. *Access to data.* The quality of relationships the researcher forms with inform-ants and subjects provides access to information on the insider's perspectives. If the relationships are not adequate, the researcher will be denied access to parts of the case and the data will suffer. The report should detail the role the researcher played, which doors were open and closed as a result of the role chosen, and the impact on the data.

3. *"Naturalness" of the data.* The ideal study is one that portrays the case in its natural state, that is, without the reactivity and artificiality that can be intro-duced by a researcher. Possible observer effects should be noted.

4. *Researcher self-criticism.* The researcher's preconceptions and biases can influ-ence and perhaps distort the data. There should be evidence that these were acknowledged and controlled. If prior hypotheses or biases were evident, were they compensated for by the introduction of alternative hypotheses, multiple sources of evidence and observers, and a disciplined search for disconfirming evidence?

5. *Logical validity.* If conclusions are stated, they should have a convincing and carefully reasoned connection with the descriptive data.

6. *Confirmation.* Systematic efforts to check hypotheses and alternative hy-potheses with alternative methods, perspectives, and observers should be evident.

7. *Descriptive adequacy.* The researcher should have provided precise, specific details about the case and its context in a way that creates verisimilitude and a vicarious experience for the reader. The perspective and meanings of the subjects should be extensively illustrated. Methods of the study should be described. Reliability, validity, and generalizability are enhanced by specifi-cation of methods, roles, selection, and sampling of units, and analytic tech-niques (Goetz and LeCompte, 1984).

8. *Significance.* The study should have addressed theoretically important ques-tions and have been designed in such a way that the questions could be answered.

SUGGESTED READINGS

DOUGLAS, J.D. *Investigative social research.* Beverly Hills, Calif.: SAGE, 1976.

ERICKSON, F. Qualitative methods in research on teaching. In Wittrock, M.C. (Ed.), *Handbook of research on teaching* (3rd Ed.). New York: Macmillan, 1986.

GLASER, B.G., and STRAUSS, A.L. *The discovery of grounded theory.* Chicago: Aldine, 1967.

GOETZ, J.P., and LeCOMPTE, M.D. *Ethnography and qualitative design in educational research.* Orlando, Fla.: Academic Press, 1984.

LOFLAND, J., and LOFLAND, L.H. *Analyzing social situations.* Belmont, Calif.: Wadsworth, 1984.

MILES, M.B., and HUBERMAN, A.M. *Analyzing qualitative data; A sourcebook of new methods.* Beverly Hills, Calif.: SAGE, 1984.

SPINDLER, G. *Doing the ethnography of schooling.* New York: Holt, Rinehart & Winston, 1982.

SPRADLEY, J.P. *The ethnographic interview.* New York: Holt, Rinehart & Winston, 1979.

SPRADLEY, J.P. *Participant observation.* New York: Holt, Rinehart & Winston, 1980.

TAYLOR, S.J., and BOGDAN, R. *Introduction to qualitative research methods.* New York: John Wiley, 1984.

TERMS INTRODUCED IN THIS CHAPTER

context
ethnography
participant observation
case study
field study
qualitative research
Verstehen
working design
working hypothesis

researcher role
ecological validity
data record
qualitative data analysis
constant comparative method
grounded theory method
theoretical sampling
triangulation

QUESTIONS AND EXERCISES FOR FURTHER STUDY

1. Explain the importance of context in naturalistic research.

2. Select a case with which you are familiar—for example, a classroom, dormitory, hospital ward, community center, faculty lounge. List 10 features of the context that might impinge on a typical event in that case.

3. How does a hypothesis in naturalistic research differ from a hypothesis in traditional research following the hypothetico-deductive paradigm?

4. A methodologist stated at a scholarly conference that a good naturalistic research study is more generalizable than a good experiment. What are the arguments to support such a statement?

5. Compare the effects of reactivity and experimenter effects in an experiment and in naturalistic research study.

6. How does the rigor, or control, achieved in naturalistic research compare to that achieved in a survey? In an experiment?

7. What is triangulation?

8. Suppose that a naturalistic researcher concluded that "mental health technicians prefer working with less severely disturbed inpatients in the Boulder Mental Health Center." List five procedures that would contribute to triangulation of this proposition.

9. If you were to study the socialization of freshmen college students in a dormitory, what are some considerations you should give to a working design, access, time and methods of collecting data, and ethical treatment of subjects?

12

LOCATING AND USING REPORTS OF STUDIES

In the first 11 chapters of this book we have presented concepts and principles of research and evaluation along with many examples of different methods and types of study. Having mastered this material, the student should be ready to apply it to actual studies, effectively critique them and, perhaps, begin to consider adding to the existing literature. Reports of studies must first be located, however. Two conditions make finding the studies a daunting task. First, there is the sheer number of studies. Literally tens of thousands of reports of studies in education and the social sciences exist, and the body of work grows daily. Some studies are relevant to the reader's topic of interest, and some are not, so systematic search procedures must be undertaken. Second, the scholarly literature is spread across numerous disciplines, each with its own code words, sources, and systems of access. Knowing how to find studies becomes as important as understanding the concepts of statistical significance, for example, or reliability of measurement.

Science, in its ideal conception, is supposed to be cumulative. No investigator starts with the idea that his or her topic has never before been studied. Nor can one afford to reinvent the wheel or make the same mistakes that other researchers have made. Each study is novel in one sense (in that no complete replication is possible in social science) and cumulative in another sense (in that it builds on the existing base of knowledge of the topic). The context for any one study is the accumulated knowledge from reports of earlier studies. Therefore, the investigator must be able to catalog the studies on the topic, break them into their elements and judge their merits, synthesize the information in them, and then build on that knowledge by designing a new study. To catalog studies the investigator or reader must first find them. This chapter is designed to assist you in the search.

First, some terminology: Sources of study reports fall into two categories: **archival** and **fugitive**. Archival sources are those located in books or journals and are available from most academic libraries. Fugitive sources are located elsewhere, such as proceedings of professional meetings, unpublished papers, technical reports, and theses. Sources may also be categorized as either **primary** or **secondary**. Primary sources are the actual reports of investigations written by the investigator. Secondary sources are collections of studies, such as reviews of research, commentaries on research (e.g., when an investigator summarizes the results of several of his own studies), bibliographies of studies on a topic, textbooks, handbooks, encyclopedias, and meta-analyses (the statistical summary and integration of a number of separate studies on a topic).

The principal source of primary research in education is the archival journal literature. There is a huge number of periodical publications in English alone that publish scholarly works on education; three hundred periodical titles would barely capture the majority of all work published in journals. But the most prominent and influential journals number a few dozen. One way in which the importance or impact of a journal is measured is by counting how often the articles it publishes are cited by other scholars. Table 12-1 lists those journals with the highest "citations per article" in 1978. All articles published by these journals in 1976 and 1977 were followed into 1978, and the frequency with which each article was referenced in other journal articles in that year was calculated (Smart and Elton, 1981). There are many reasons why this measure is a less than ideal indication of the intellectual importance of a journal or a particular piece of research. Nonetheless, the tabulation of these results gives at least a rough notion of which journals are visible and influential and which are more obscure.

The sources themselves—that is, the primary studies and the secondary summaries, reviews, and so on—must be distinguished from **access systems**. Access systems comprise sets of procedures for organizing the sources and indexing them so that the searcher can find them easily. *Psychological Abstracts* is such a system of access, as is *Educational Resources Information Center* (ERIC).

SENSIBLE SEARCH STRATEGY

I. Consult Secondary Sources

If a student or new researcher has a preliminary topic, such as the characteristics of effective therapists, it would be inefficient to look directly

TABLE 12–1 Thirty Most Frequently Cited Education Journals Per Article in 1978

TITLE	CITATIONS PER ARTICLE[a]
(1) *Review of Educational Research*	3.681
(2) *Harvard Educational Review*	2.564
(3) *Monograph of the Society for Research in Child Development*	2.000
(4) *Educational Research*	1.956[b]
(5) *Journal of Applied Behavioral Analysis*	1.854
(6) *Journal of Child Psychology and Psychiatry and Allied Disciplines*	1.688
(7) *Journal of Counseling Psychology*	1.401
(8) *American Educational Research Journal*	1.245
(9) *Child Development*	1.194
(10) *Journal of Experimental Child Psychology*	1.149
(11) *Developmental Psychology*	1.128
(12) *Journal of Educational Psychology*	1.089
(13) *Journal of Learning Disabilities*	1.084
(14) *Measurement and Evaluation in Guidance*	1.033[b]
(15) *Journal of Applied Behavioral Sciences*	0.986
(16) *Human Development*	0.882
(17) *American Journal of Mental Deficiency*	0.881
(18) *British Journal of Educational Psychology*	0.818
(19) *Journal of Educational Measurement*	0.789[b]
(20) *AAUP Bulletin*	0.781[b]
(21) *Language Learning*	0.727[b]
(22) *Exceptional Children*	0.726
(23) *Reading Research Quarterly*	0.694[b]
(24) *American Annals of the Deaf*	0.679[b]
(25) *Teachers College Record*	0.657[b]
(26) *Instructional Science*	0.655[b]
(27) *Journal of School Psychology*	0.638
(28) *School Review*	0.597[b]
(29) *Journal of Curriculum Studies*	0.594[b]
(30) *Personnel and Guidance Journal*	0.593

[a] Calculated by dividing (a) the total number of 1978 citations to articles published by each journal in 1976 and 1977 by (b) the number of articles each journal published in 1976 and 1977 (Institute for Scientific Information, 1979).
[b] Not listed in Table III.
Source: Smart and Elton, 1981, p. 408.

for primary studies on that topic. Even knowing the name of one journal that might contain relevant studies does not overcome the difficulty of looking at the index or table of contents of individual issues of the journal and perhaps finding nothing relevant in several volumes of the publication. A more sensible procedure would be to start by consulting secondary sources. Secondary sources are particularly helpful to a student new to a topic because they provide a map and a framework for organizing the separate primary studies, and they eliminate the need to track down each one. They provide information about the quantity of primary sources on the topic (how many studies have been done on this and related questions—i.e., whether the field has been lightly or heavily mined). They also provide some insight into the philosophical perspectives that guide research on that topic. For example, research on therapeutic effectiveness might be divided into philosophical "camps" (behavioristic versus psychodynamic, perhaps). The reader is more likely to be informed about this division by reading a chapter in a handbook than an individual study. Whenever experts write entries in an encyclopedia or chapters in a handbook, they are synthesizing the material, going beyond the separate studies to provide a coherent picture of the collected findings of the studies. Such sources also alert the reader, in a way that primary sources cannot, of weaknesses and problems in the methods of sampling, design, measurement, and analysis, as well as the conceptualization of ideas that characterize the studies in the field. As readers consult secondary sources, they often find themselves narrowing or redefining their preliminary topics. They begin to modify the terms and concepts from their own definitions to ones more commonly used in the literature. What seems to be a clerical exercise becomes a learning experience. What follows is a listing of frequently used secondary sources. These are usually to be found in reference rooms of academic libraries or in specialty sections of libraries (e.g., education libraries; social science, medical, or psychology libraries).

The *Encyclopedia of Educational Research* is a good place to start for topics related to education. Currently in its fifth edition, it consists of four volumes, covering 164 topics, arranged alphabetically from "Academic Freedom and Tenure" to "Writing, Composition, and Rhetoric." Each topic or section was written by an expert in that field and is in the form of an essay that summarizes the status of empirical research and theory related to the topic. It includes a bibliography (though usually not an exhaustive one) of the existing studies.

The *Handbook of Research on Teaching*, issued about ten years apart in three editions (Gage, 1963; Travers, 1973; Wittrock, 1986) that cover selected topics, consists of longer essays and more comprehensive bibliographies than does the *Encyclopedia*. Not as many topics are covered, however. Experts on the topics selected by the editors of the *Handbook* are asked to contribute chapters that summarize and integrate empirical and theoretical work. In the second edition (Travers, 1973), the topics include: "History of the Impact of Research on Teaching," "Contemporary Models of Teaching," "Theory Construction for Research on Teaching," "Social and Political Influences on Educational Research," "Use of Direct Observation to Study Teaching," "Techniques of Observing Teaching in Early Childhood and Outcomes of Particular Procedures," "Assessment of Teacher Competence," and 35 others.

The *Handbook of General Psychology* consists of nearly 50 chapters written by subject matter experts who summarize the methods and findings of research studies on the topic of the chapter. *Review of Research in Education* provides critical reviews of research on about 10 topics each year. The topics are chosen by the editor and written by authorities in the field. *Annual Review of Psychology* is made up of critical essays and review of research on topics in psychology. *NSSE Yearbooks* consist of summaries of research on selected topics published by the National Society for the Study of Education. *Mental Measurements Yearbooks*, described in Chapter 5, are an important secondary source. They include review essays of published tests in psychology and education. Along with the reviews are bibliographies of studies that used the test as a dependent or predictor variable or that contributed to construct validation.

The following is a list of the names of handbooks and encyclopedias that serve as secondary sources and may be found in most academic libraries or ordered through interlibrary loan services.

Annual Review of Anthropology
Alcoholism Treatment Research
Current Theory and Research in Motivation, a Symposium
Encyclopedia of Crime and Justice
Encyclopedia of Education
Encyclopedia of Psychology
International Dictionary of Education
International Encyclopedia of Educational Research
International Encyclopedia of Higher Education
International Encyclopedia of the Social Sciences
Handbook of Adult Education
Handbook of Aging and the Individual
Handbook of Aging and the Social Sciences
Handbook of Applied Psychology
Handbook of Applied Sociology
Handbook of Bilingual Education
Handbook of Child Psychology
Handbook of Child Psychopathology
Handbook of Clinical Psychology
Handbook of Community Mental Health
Handbook of Counseling in Higher Education
Handbook of Criminal Justice Evaluation
Handbook of Criminology
Handbook of Developmental Psychology
Handbook of Family Therapy
Handbook of Human Intelligence
Handbook of Infant Development
Handbook of Industrial and Organizational Psychology
Handbook of Leadership
Handbook of Learning and Cognitive Processes
Handbook of Marketing Research
Handbook of Measurement and Evaluation in Rehabilitation
Handbook of Medical Sociology

Handbook of Mental Deficiency
Handbook of Methods for the Study of Adolescent Children
Handbook of Methods in Nonverbal Behavior Research
Handbook of Minimal Brain Dysfunctions
Handbook of Organization Management
Handbook of Personality Theory and Research
Handbook of Political Psychology
Handbook of Political Science
Handbook of Political Science Methods
Handbook of Psychiatry
Handbook of Psychology and Health
Handbook of Psychotherapy and Behavior Change
Handbook of School Psychology
Handbook of Small Group Research
Handbook of Social Intervention
Handbook of Social Psychology
Handbook of Speech Pathology and Audiology
Handbook of Teaching and Policy
Handbook of Vocational Education Evaluation
Handbook on Drug and Alcohol Abuse
Handbook on Learning Disabilities
Political Science Annual
Psychology of Learning and Motivation
Public Administration Review

In addition to the references listed above, several periodicals contain important secondary sources of studies. The *Review of Educational Research* is published four times a year by the American Educational Research Association (which also publishes the *Encyclopedia of Educational Research*, *Handbook of Research on Teaching*, and *Review of Research in Education*). The articles in it are submitted by authors who select the topics and review and synthesize research. *Psychological Bulletin* follows the same format. *Contemporary Psychology* and *Contemporary Education Review* publish critical reviews of books, some of which are the primary sources of research.

II. Select Terms for a Search

Access systems are entered via what are called **key-word descriptors**, or concepts that characterize the contents and methods of the research. But getting from the words that people ordinarily use to talk about education to the descriptors that open the door to access systems can be a problem in itself. Take the question, "What characteristics of teachers are associated with effective clinical teaching?" This is the topic as the individual researcher thinks about it. Perhaps his professors have defined the term *clinical teaching* as the method of tailoring instruction to the needs of individual learners. But *clinical teaching* is not a term recognized by the access system for this area of research. If the searcher looked for studies of clinical teaching, he might falsely conclude that no previous research had been done on that topic. Some adjustments must be made between the way the searcher defines the important constructs and the way the access systems do so. Each of two access systems, the ERIC system and *Psychological Abstracts*, has a *Thesaurus* so that these connections can be made.

The ERIC system is part of the federal government's National Institute of Education. It was developed in the 1960s to deal with the information explosion in educational research. It consists of 16 clearinghouses, each devoted to a different branch of educational research (e.g., Clearinghouse on Languages and Linguistics, Clearinghouse on Urban Education). At each clearinghouse experts review each study and document in the domain of interest. These documents are submitted to ERIC by authors or sponsoring agencies. The experts categorize a study according to several key-word descriptors. For example, a study entitled "Allocated time and context covered in mathematics classrooms" (Romberg, 1983) was categorized (by the Clearinghouse on Science, Mathematics, and Environmental Education at the Ohio State University) under the following key-word descriptors: *educational research, elementary education, elementary school mathematics, mathematics curriculum, mathematics instruction in primary education, teaching methods, time factors in learning,* and *time on task.* The key-word descriptors become the basis of the ERIC indexing system. If a reader happened to be looking in ERIC for studies of *time on task*, Romberg's study would be one of the ones listed. A different searcher, looking for studies of elementary school math, would also find this study.

The ERIC *Thesaurus* bridges the gap between the way a searcher defines topics of interest and the way the ERIC access system defines and indexes them. It is an alphabetical list of terms and concepts. Some of the terms listed are key-word descriptors and some of them are not. A page from the ERIC *Thesaurus* is reproduced in Figure 12–1. The terms printed in capital letters are designated as key-word descriptors. Those in lowercase letters are not key-word descriptors but are entries under which a searcher might look. One of these is the term *clinical teaching (individualized instruction),*" the topic of one of the searchers described above. Under the term is the message, "USE INDIVIDUALIZED INSTRUCTION," which indicates that *clinical teaching* is not a key-word descriptor used by ERIC, but *individualized instruction* is a likely synonym that is used. Figure 12–2 shows the *Thesaurus* listing under the term INDIVIDUALIZED INSTRUCTION. The date refers to the first time this key-word descriptor was used by ERIC. The number next to CIJE indicates that 3,444 studies have been indexed under this key-word descriptor in the *Current Index to Journals in Education,* which is the access system for published or archival sources. In *Resources in Education* (RIE), the access system for fugitive sources, 4,621 documents have been indexed under this key-word descriptor. The GC stands for group code, which is a higher-order classification within which individualized instruction falls. The initials SN stand for Scope Notes, the definition of the key-term indicator according to the ERIC system. It is the primary means that searchers have for understanding ERIC's definitions and adjusting for differences between their own definitions and those in ERIC. For example, a searcher might have in mind an entirely different meaning than "adapting instruction to individual needs within the group," in which case he must search further in the *Thesaurus* for key-word descriptors that do fit his meaning. The initials UF are short for "Use for," which means that *individualized instruction* is the key-word descriptor that should be used for such non-key-word descriptors as *personalized instruction*. *Teaching methods* is a broader term (indicated as BT) than individualized instruction; no narrower term (NT) is listed. Related terms (RT) are other key-word descriptors that the searcher might employ.

FIGURE 12–1　Excerpt from ERIC *Thesaurus*　(*Source:* ERIC Thesaurus (*9th Ed.*), 1982, p. 39.)

CLINICAL PSYCHOLOGY　　*Oct. 1977*	**CLUSTER ANALYSIS**　　*Mar. 1971*
CIJE: 142　　RIE: 26　　GC: 230	CIJE: 162　　RIE: 125　　GC: 820
SN　Branch of psychology devoted to psychological methods of diagnosing and treating mental and emotional disorders, as well as research into the causes of these disorders and the effects of therapy	SN　Systematic method of grouping measures or variables together according to their degree of similarity in a correlation matrix or table
BT　Psychology	BT　Multivariate Analysis
RT　Behavior Problems	RT　Classification
Clinical Diagnosis	Cluster Grouping
Emotional Disturbances	Correlation
Experimental Psychology	Factor Analysis
Mental Disorders	Multidimensional Scaling
Personality Problems	
Psychiatry	**CLUSTER COLLEGES**　　*Feb. 1971*
Psychological Evaluation	CIJE: 17　　RIE: 43　　GC: 340
Psychological Studies	SN　Colleges, in close physical proximity, that constitute a single institution, share facilities and services, and usually have a centralized administration—generally each college in the cluster focuses on one area of study (note: do not confuse with "consortia"—prior to mar80, this term was not restricted by a scope note)
Psychological Testing	
Psychometrics	
Psychopathology	
Psychophysiology	
Psychotherapy	
Social Psychology	BT　Colleges
	RT　Consortia
Clinical Services	Educational Complexes
USE　CLINICS	Experimental Colleges
	House Plan
CLINICAL TEACHING (HEALTH	Shared Facilities
PROFESSIONS)　　*Sep. 1981*	**CLUSTER GROUPING**　　*Jul. 1966*
CIJE: 7　　RIE: 0　　GC: 210	CIJE: 237　　RIE: 216　　GC: 820
SN　Instruction in the clinical setting where actual symptoms are studied and treatment is given	SN　Classifying or selecting the items within a collection (of people, ideas, objects, etc.) on the basis of specified similarities (note: use a more precise term if possible)
BT　Teaching Methods	BT　Classification
RT　Allied Health Occupations Education	RT　Bibliographic Coupling
Clinical Experience	Class Organization
Medical Education	Cluster Analysis
Medical School Faculty	

Practicums
Practicum Supervision
Teaching Hospitals

Clinical Teaching (Individualized Instruction)
USE INDIVIDUALIZED INSTRUCTION

CLINICS *Jul. 1966*
    CIJE: 220   RIE: 168   GC: 920
UF Clinical Services
    Preschool Clinics (1966 1980) #
    Rural Clinics (1966 1980) #
    Treatment Centers
NT Dental Clinics
    Mental Health Clinics
    Mobile Clinics
    Psychoeducational Clinics
    Speech And Hearing Clinics
RT Clinical Experience
    Facilities
    Health
    Health Facilities
    Hospitals
    Medical Services
    Meetings
    Services

Clockmakers
USE WATCHMAKERS

Closed Schools
USE SCHOOL CLOSING

CLOTHING *Jul. 1966*
    CIJE: 84   RIE: 138   GC: 210
UF Fashions (Clothing)
RT Clothing Design
    Clothing Instruction
    Fashion Industry
    Laundry Drycleaning Occupations
    Needle Trades
    Patternmaking
    Self Care Skills
    Sewing Instruction
    Sewing Machine Operators
    Textiles Instruction

CLOTHING DESIGN *Jul. 1966*
    CIJE: 39   RIE: 47   GC: 420
UF Costume Design
    Dress Design
BT Design
RT Clothing
    Clothing Instruction

Group Structure
Homogeneous Grouping
Occupational Clusters

Cmi
USE COMPUTER MANAGED
      INSTRUCTION

Co Op Programs
USE COOPERATIVE PROGRAMS

Coaching Teachers (1966 1974)
USE TUTORS

Coast Guard Air Stations
USE MILITARY AIR FACILITIES

COCOUNSELING *May. 1970*
    CIJE: 38   RIE: 16   GC: 240
SN Two or more counselors working as a
    team with a single client or group of clients,
    usually at the same time but sometimes
    consecutively
UF Conjoint Counseling
    Team Counseling
BT Counseling
RT Teamwork

Cocurricular Activities (1966 1980)
USE EXTRACURRICULAR ACTIVITIES
      Language Patterns
      Language Usage
      Language Variation
      Linguistic Borrowing
      Linguistic Performance
      Morphology (Language)
      Multilingualism
      Phonology
      Sociolinguistics
      Syntax
      Vocabulary

CODES OF ETHICS *Jan. 1978*
    CIJE: 102   RIE: 77   GC: 520
SN Standards of ethical conduct, violation of
    which may subject individuals to discipli-
    nary action
UF Honor Codes
BT Behavior Standards
RT Accountability
    Cheating
    Codification
    Discipline
    Discipline Policy
    Ethics
    Faculty College Relationship
    Loyalty Oaths
    Malpractice

Design Crafts
Fashion Industry
Needle Trades
Patternmaking

Clothing Industry
USE   FASHION INDUSTRY

CLOTHING INSTRUCTION   *Jul. 1966*
      CIJE: 21   RIE: 106   GC: 400
BT   Instruction
RT   Clothing
      Clothing Design
      Consumer Science
      Fashion Industry
      Home Economics
      Laundry Drycleaning Occupations
      Needle Trades
      Patternmaking
      Sewing Instruction
      Sewing Machine Operators
      Textiles Instruction

CLOZE PROCEDURE   *Jul. 1966*
      CIJE: 261   RIE: 375   GC: 460
SN   Completion exercises requiring the reader
      to insert missing words with the aid of
      surrounding context
UF   Cloze Techniques
BT   Methods
RT   Context Clues
      Informal Reading Inventories
      Language Skills
      Language Tests
      Readability
      Reading
      Reading Comprehension
      Reading Skills
      Reading Tests
      Substitution Drills
      Teaching Methods

Moral Development
Moral Values
Plagiarism
Stealing
Student College Relationship

CODIFICATION   *Jul. 1966*
      CIJE: 105   RIE: 177   GC: 710
SN   Process of collecting and arranging laws
      and standards according to a system
BT   Classification
RT   Codes Of Ethics
      Documentation
      Laws
      Standards

COEDUCATION   *May. 1969*
      CIJE: 130   RIE: 75   GC: 330
BT   Education
RT   Heterogeneous Grouping
      Single Sex Colleges
      Single Sex Schools
      Women's Education

COGNITIVE ABILITY   *Jul. 1966*
      CIJE: 643   RIE: 554   GC: 120
SN   (note: prior to apr80, the instruction
      "mental ability, use intelligence" was car-
      ried in the thesaurus)
UF   Mental Ability
BT   Ability
RT   Academic Ability
      Aptitude
      Cognitive Development
      Cognitive Measurement
      Cognitive Tests
      Epistemology
      Intelligence
      Metacognition
      Productive Thinking
      Social Cognition
      Spatial Ability

The *Thesaurus of Psychological Index Terms*, a publication of the American Psychological Association, works the same way for the *Psychological Abstracts* system as the *Thesaurus* does for the ERIC system. In place of keyword descriptors is the "controlled vocabulary." Terms in the controlled vocabulary are listed alphabetically in the Relationship section, which uses the same format of Scope Notes (SN), Use for (UF), and so on.

Not all access systems provide a thesaurus and a program of experts to categorize studies by the key words in the document. For example, the *Dissertation Abstracts* access system is based on terms taken from the titles of dissertations. Many access systems have been created in the last 20 years; many remain to be created. Some of the more prominent systems of interest to educational researchers and social scientists are:

Abstracts in Anthropology
Abstracts on Criminology
Anthropological Literature: An Index to Periodical Articles
Books in Print
Child Development Abstracts
College Student Personnel Abstracts
Communication Abstracts
Criminal Justice Abstracts
Cumulative Book Index
Education Index
Educational Administration Abstracts
Environment Abstracts
Exceptional Child Education Resources
Government Reports Announcements and Index
Human Resources Abstracts
Humanities Index
Index Medicus
Index of Economic Articles
International Bibliography of Economics
International Bibliography of Political Science
International Bibliography of Sociology
Journal of Economic Literature
Language Teaching Abstracts
Library of Congress Catalog
National Institute for Mental Health Grants and Contracts Information System
National Technical Information Service
Public Administration Abstracts
Smithsonian Science Information Exchange
Social Sciences Index
Sociological Abstracts
Sociology Reviews
Statistical References Index
Women Studies Abstracts

III. Choose Manual or Computer Search Method

After the access systems are selected, the titles of studies that are indexed according to key-word descriptors or controlled vocabulary must be located. This may be accomplished either by hand or by computer. The DIALOG system (a branch of the Lockheed Corporation) is an on-line computer storage and retrieval system that makes available the following access systems: ERIC, *Psychological Abstracts, Sociological Abstracts, Social Science Citation Index, Exceptional Child Education Resources, Family Resources Database, Drug Information/Alcohol Use and Abuse, Comprehensive Dissertation Index, Government Printing Office Catalogue, National Library of Medicine,* and others.

INDIVIDUALIZED INSTRUCTION

Jan. 1969

CIJE: 3,444   RIE: 4,621   GC: 310

SN   Adapting instruction to individual needs within the group (note: do not confuse with "independent study" or "individual instruction")

UF   Clinical Teaching (Individualized Instruction)
Individualized Curriculum (1966 1980)
Individualized Education
Personalized Instruction

BT   Teaching Methods

RT   Adapted Physical Education
Autoinstructional Aids
Competency Based Education
Competency Based Teacher Education
Computer Assisted Instruction
Diagnostic Teaching
Group Instruction
Humanistic Education
Individual Instruction
Individualized Education Programs
Individualized Programs
Individualized Reading
Individual Needs
Learning Centers (Classroom)
Learning Laboratories
Learning Modules
Mass Instruction
Pacing
Programmed Instruction
Small Group Instruction
Special Education

FIGURE 12–2   Another Excerpt from ERIC *Thesaurus*   (*Source:* ERIC Thesaurus (*9th Ed.*), 1982, p. 117.)

"Profilers"—librarians and others who are familiar with DIALOG and with particular access systems—interact with the system based on the key words supplied by the user. The system provides a printout with either the number of documents in the system that are indexed under the key words specified, a list of references of studies so indexed, or the abstracts of the studies. A fee is charged (although it is not always billed to the user) based on the amount of computer time taken in the retrieval and the amount of information provided. In addition to saving time and labor, the computer search allows combinations of descriptors to be specified. For example, the searcher might narrow his topic to individualized instruction for secondary schools only. The profiler may accommodate this plan by restricting the computer search to those studies that are indexed under both individualized instruction *and* secondary schools. Studies of individualized instruction among elementary schools and colleges would not be listed on the printout. Or the searcher might specify studies of individualized instruction published after a certain date (which is handy for up-dating bibliographies). Computer searches are particularly effective in locating and listing studies that are indexed by author or in using the *Social Science Citation Index*. The computer system is not foolproof, however. Unless the profiler is particularly skillful, it is likely that the searcher will have many false positives (studies on the computer printout that are not relevant to the topic) and may miss false negatives (relevant studies that are not on the printout). The issue of cost must be weighed against the time required for a manual search. The reader is referred to Geahigan and Geahigan (1982) for a "primer" on methods of computer search and to the reference staff of most academic libraries.

IV. Using Terms in Index

The manual search method proceeds in three steps (from index to abstract to the report of the study itself) through each access system (CIJE, RIE, *Psychological Abstracts*, *Dissertation Abstracts*, etc.) that is relevant to the topic. Taking the *Current Index to Journals in Education* (archival sources) as an example, the searcher takes the list of key-word descriptors to the subject index where key-word descriptors are listed alphabetically. Under each key-word descriptor appear the titles of studies, as one can see in the reproduction of the Subject Index of CIJE in Figure 12–3. The searcher judges the relevance of each title to his own study and lists the EJ number of those that fit. Notice that several titles on the page seem tangential to the searcher's interest ("What Schooling for the Gifted?") or appear not to be primary sources or reports of original research ("Standing Close to the Door at the Computer Celebration") or deal with special rather than regular education or pertain to an age group beyond the searcher's scope of interest. These can be safely culled (and would turn up as false positives on a computer search). From the page, the searcher may note the EJ numbers of perhaps a dozen potentially fruitful titles. In one case—"Individualized Systems of Instruction in Secondary Schools"—the searcher would know immediately that the article should be located, since it is published in the *Review of Educational Research*, one of the most important secondary sources in education.

V. From Index to Abstract

With the list of EJ numbers the searcher goes to the next section of the CIJE volume, the Main Entry section. This section is listed, not alphabetically, but numerically by EJ number. Figure 12–4 contains a reproduction of this section with entry number EJ 283 173. The entry includes

Individualized Instruction

Relationship of Individualized Teaching Strategies to Academic Learning Time for Mainstreamed Handicapped and Non-handicapped Students. *Journal of Special Education;* v16 n4 p449–56 Win 1982   EJ 278 055

A Reading Project in Barking. *Special Education: Forward Trends;* v9 n4 p6–9 Dec 1982
                                                       EJ 278 090

A Model for Advising in an Individualized Undergraduate College. *NACADA Journal;* v2 n2 p90-96 Nov 1982   EJ 278 190

Keller's Personalized System of Instruction: The Search for a Basic Distance Learning Paradigm. *Distance Education;* v3 n1 p51-71 Mar 1982   EJ 278 314

Nutrition and Fitness Course for Junior High Students. *Journal of Nutrition Education;* v15 n1 p22 Mar 1983   EJ 278 513

Individualized Science Packets for Gifted Students. *School Science and Mathematics;* v83 n4 p326-32 Apr 1983   EJ 278 621

Effects of Individualized Assignments on Biology Achievement. *Journal of Research in Science Teaching;* v20 n2 p105-15 Feb 1983   EJ 278 627

Evaluating Individualized Educational Programs: A Recommendation and Some Programmatic Implications. *Urban Review;* v14 n2 p73-81 Sum 1982   EJ 278 943

The Learning Styles of Students Related to Individualized Typewriting Instruction. *Delta Pi Epsilon Journal;* v25 n2 p41-51 Apr 1983   EJ 279 109

Self-Directed Learning of the Basic Skills. *Clearing House;* v56 n8 p372-73 Apr 1983
                                                       EJ 279 416

Receiving and Individualizing Inservice Education. *Education;* v103 n3 p274-77 Spr 1983
                                                       EJ 279 884

A Note on Independent Study in Introductory Microeconomics. *Journal of Economic Education;* v14 n2 p69-73 Spr 1983   EJ 280 068

Student Achievement as a Function of Person-Environment Fit: A Regression Surface Analysis. *British Journal of Educational Psychology;* v53 Pt1 p89-99 Feb 1983   EJ 280 412

Computers: Tools for Thinking. *Childhood Education;* v59 n4 p251-54 Mar-Apr 1983
                                                       EJ 281 622

Computer Enhanced Collaborative Learning: A New Technology for Education. *Technological Horizons in Education;* v10 n7 p96-101 May 1983   EJ 281 687

Standing Close to the Door at the Computer Celebration. *Training;* v20 n6 p44-45,51 Jun 1983
                                                       EJ 282 347

Interactive Effects of Source of Direction, Allocated Time, Reading Ability, and Study Orientation on Achievement in High School Science. *Science Education;* v67 n4 p509-22 Jul 1983
                                                       EJ 283 173

Geographical Inquiry and Learning Reinforcement Theory. *Journal of Geography;* v82 n3 p121-22 May-Jun 1983   EJ 283 272

A Generalized Learner-Controlled Education System. *Journal of Educational Technology Systems;* v11 n1 p3-21 1982-83   EJ 284 244

The 4MAT System: An Experiment. *Journal of Developmental & Remedial Education;* v6 spec iss p4-7 1983   EJ 284 270

Using Microcomputers in the Classroom. *European Journal of Teacher Education;* v6 n2 p157–60 1983   EJ 284 813

Individualized Systems of Instruction in Secondary Schools. *Review of Educational Research;* v53 n2 p143-58 Sum 1983   EJ 284 878

Self-Directed Learning and Lifespan Development. *International Journal of Lifelong Education;* v2 n1 p29-46 1983   EJ 284 973

What Schooling for the Gifted. *Gifted Child Quarterly;* v27 n2 p51-56 Spr 1983   EJ 285 516

Effects of Individualised Feedback and Instruction on Effort Attributions, Ability Attributions and Spelling Achievement. *Educational Studies;* v9 n2 p105-13 1983   EJ 285 956

FIGURE 12–3   Excerpt from CIJE Subject Index   (*Source:* ERIC Current Index to Journals in Education, *Semi-Annual Cumulation, July–September, 1983, p. 672.*)

the name of the document, its authors, bibliographic reference, the key-word descriptors under which this document is indexed by ERIC, and a brief abstract or summary of the article. The searcher reads it, judges whether it is relevant to his topic, and if so, notes the reference.

FIGURE 12–4 Excerpt from CIJE Main Entry Section (*Source:* ERIC Current Index to Journals in Education, *Semi-Annual Cumulation, July–December, 1983, p. 313.*)

MAIN ENTRY SECTION

Descriptors: *Biology; Educational Trends; Mathematics Teachers; *Physical Sciences;
  Science Education; *Science Teachers; Secondary Education; *Secondary School Science;
  *Teacher Responsibility; *Teacher Shortage
Identifiers: *North Carolina

In North Carolina, reports are being generated and publicized about the science/mathematics teacher shortage. Findings are cited from several of these reports as examples of how concerned persons might initiate similar campaigns to generate the publicity and support that must precede change. Teacher shortage facts/myths and implications of same are considered. (JN)

EJ 283 172   SE 533 820
Learning Science: A Generative Process. Osborne, R.J.; Wittrock, M.C. *Science Education;*
v67 n4 p489–508 Jul 1983 (Reprint: UMI)
Descriptors: Cognitive Processes; *Concept Formation; Elementary School Science;
  Elementary Secondary Education; Higher Education; Learning; *Learning Theories; Memory;
  *Science Education; *Science Instruction; Secondary School Science; *Teacher Education
Identifiers: *Generative Learning Model; *Science Education Research

The generative learning model is explored and linked to recent science education research findings. The implications of the model for the teaching and learning of science, the training of science teachers, and science educational research are discussed. (JN)

EJ 283 173   SE 533 821
**Interactive Effects of Source of Direction, Allocated Time, Reading Ability, and Study Orien-
tation on Achievement in High School Science.** Tate, Richard; Burkman, Ernest *Science
Education;* v67 n4 p509–22 Jul 1983 (Reprint: UMI)
Descriptors: *Academic Achievement; High Schools; *Individualized Instruction; *Reading Ability;
  Science Course Improvement Projects; Science Education; *Science Instruction;
  *Secondary School Science; Study; Teaching Methods; *Time Factors (Learning)
Identifiers: Individualized Science Instruction System; Science Education Research

Examined interactive effects of direction source (teacher, student, or group direction), allocated time, reading ability, and study orientation on student achievement (N = 1108) on three Individualized Science Instructional System (ISIS) minicourses. Results (among others) indicate superiority of student-directed approach over teacher/group-directed approach. (JN)

EJ 283 174   SE 533 822
Student Problem Solving in High School Genetics. Stewart, James *Science Education;* v67
n4 p523–40 Jul 1983 (Reprint: UMI)
Descriptors: *Biology; *Genetics; High Schools; *Problem Solving; Science Education;
  *Science Instruction; *Secondary School Science
Identifiers: National Science Foundation; Science Education Research

Describes set of specific steps (procedural knowledge) used when solving monohybrid/dihybrid cross problems and extent to which students could justify execution of each step in terms of their conceptual knowledge of genetics and meiosis. Implications for genetics instruction are discussed. (JN)

VI. Locate The Study

The report of the study itself is then located in the periodical or books where it appeared. Books and periodicals not available in the college library can usually be traced and acquired temporarily by the interlibrary loan service.

Steps IV, V, and VI are repeated for each access system. For ERIC Resources in Education (RIE—fugitive sources in education), the searcher takes his list of relevant key-word descriptors to the RIE Subject Index, where descriptors are listed alphabetically. The searcher judges the relevance of each title to his project and notes the ED numbers of the relevant documents (see Figure 12–5). These are taken to RIE Document Resumes, a section of which is reproduced in Figure 12–6. Each entry contains the title, authors, reference, abstract, price of the document, and so on. If the abstract appears relevant, the searcher may obtain the document from ERIC Document Reproduction Service. In addition, many academic libraries subscribe to a service that provides these documents on microfiche. Both CIJE and RIE are published monthly and accumulated in biannual volumes. They also contain indexes for authors, titles, and journals.

Searching *Psychological Abstracts* involves the same sequence of steps. Terms from the *Thesaurus* are used in the Subject Index, which lists the entry numbers of relevant studies. The numbers refer to brief abstracts.

FIGURE 12–5 Excerpt from RIE Index   (*Source: ERIC* Resources in Education, *Index, July–December, 1983, p. 221.*)

Guidelines for Development and Implementation of Quality I.E.P.s.
ED 231 140

The Illinois State Study of the Impact of PL 94-142 on the Families of Children with Different Handicapping Conditions. Revised Annual Report, Second Year.
ED 226 534

Individualized Educational Programming. Revised.
ED 226 554

Individually Prescribed Education: A Case Study.
ED 228 218

Mainstreaming: From Intent to Implementation.
ED 232 322

Measuring Pupil Progress in Special Education.
ED 232 412

Observed Changes in Instruction and Student Responding as a Function of Referral and Special Education Placement.
ED 228 825

tional Education Through Correspondence. A Combined Report on Dual Projects Begun June 1977 and Continuing to Date. Revised.
ED 230 359

Fundamental Vocational Skills for Disadvantaged Learners. Final Report. September 15, 1978-July 30, 1979.
ED 232 008

Individualized Study by Technology (IST).
ED 229 004

Individualized Study by Technology (IST) for Alaska, A Model for the Future?
ED 229 005

An Individualized Teaching Approach: "Audio-Tutorial." College Teaching Monograph.
ED 226 656

Innovative Inservice: Excellence through Diversity.
ED 231 804

Labor Market Experiences of Handicapped Youth.

Plan Instruction for Exceptional Students. Module L-3 of Category L—Serving Students with Special/Exceptional Needs. Professional Teacher Education Module Series.

ED 227 256

Providing for Individual Learner Needs. Instructor Training Module #7.

ED 227 299

Record Exchange Process. A Set of Records for Handicapped Students in Vocational Education. Vocational Investigation and Placement Demonstration Project.

ED 231 961

Reintegrating Behaviorally Disordered Students into General Education Classrooms: Monograph 4. Monograph Series in Behavior Disorders.

ED 231 113

Resource Specialist Training Resources. Volume III.

ED 228 776

Serving the Learning Disabled Child in New York State. [Updated Version].

ED 226 548

Teaching Structure and Student Achievement Effects of Curriculum-Based Measurement: A Causal (Structural) Analysis.

ED 227 127

Transition to Non-Categorical Vocational Training That Utilizes Computer Assisted Educational Intervention and Nontraditional Child Study Team Functions.

ED 226 121

Using the Apple II Microcomputer to Facilitate the Development of the Individualized Education Plan.

ED 227 822

VEEAP Procedures and Training Handbook. Vocational Education Evaluation and Assessment Process for Special Needs/Handicapped Students.

ED 228 404

Individualized Instruction

Bronx Multidiscipline Special Education Bilingual Program. E.S.E.A Title VII Annual Evaluation Report, 1980-81.

ED 231 913

Combining Student Teams and Individualized Instruction in Mathematics: An Extended Evaluation.

ED 231 619

Creating Classroom Options: A Handbook for Teachers.

ED 227 189

Developing Instructional Materials for Apprentices. Instructor Training Module #4.

ED 228 445

Learning Unlimited: A Model for Options Education.

ED 227 188

A Manual for the Individualized Instruction Inventory (III).

ED 226 795

Matching Instructional Tasks to Students' Abilities and Learning Styles.

ED 229 916

The Preschool Program: Adaptation to the Individual Child.

ED 226 862

Process and Product in Higher Education: Student-Directed Learning.

ED 232 429

Relationships among Student Ability, School Performance, and Fleet Supervisor Ratings for Navy "A" School Graduates.

ED 230 782

The Strategy Selection Matrix—A Guide for Individualizing Instruction.

ED 229 910

Team-Assisted Individualization: A Cooperative Learning Solution for Adaptive Instruction in Mathematics.

ED 232 852

The Use of Keller's Personalized System of Instruction.

ED 231 295

The Validation of Learning Hierarchies.

ED 227 163

Water Fit to Drink.

ED 226 994

Why, How To, and This & That from Howell School.

ED 231 796

Individualized Programs

Evaluating Individualized Programs.

ED 229 408

Individualized Reading

The Case for the Language Experience Approach and Individualized Reading.

ED 232 124

Individualized Study by Technology

Evaluation of IST Courses. FY81 Pilot Study. Part I and Part II. Final Report.

ED 229 003

Individualized Study by Technology (IST).

ED 229 004

Individualized Study by Technology (IST) for Alaska, A Model for the Future?

ED 229 005

ED 231 619   SE 041 905
Slavin, Robert E. And Others
Combining Student Teams and Individualized Instruction in Mathematics: An Extended Evaluation.
Johns Hopkins Univ., Baltimore, Md. Center for the Study of Social Organization of Schools.
Spons Agency—National Inst. of Education (ED), Washington, DC.

Report No.—JHU-CSOS-336
Pub Date—May 83
Grant—NIE-G-83-0002
Note—20p.
Pub Type—Reports–Evaluative (142)
EDRS Price–MF01/PC01 Plus Postage.
Descriptors—Educational Research, Elementary Education, *Elementary School Mathematics, *Individualized Instruction, *Mathematics Instruction, *Teaching Methods, *Teamwork
Identifiers—Mathematics Education Research, *Student Teams
    This study evaluated the achievement effects of the Team-Assisted Individualization (TAI) mathematics program over a 24-week period. Involved were 1,317 students in grades 3, 4, and 5, with 700 students in 31 classes receiving TAI instruction and a control group of 617 students in 30 classes receiving other mathematics instruction on the same objectives. Analysis of covariance was used to analyze the data, with achievement measured by the Mathematics Concepts and Applications and the Mathematics Computation subtests of the Comprehensive Test of Basic Skills. TAI classes gained more than control classes on each test at each grade level. The differences were statistically significant for grades 3 and 5 on the Computation subtest. On the Concepts and Applications subtest, differences were statistically significant for grade 4 and marginally significant for grade 5. In overall analyses, the TAI classes significantly exceeded control classes on both tests. (Author/MNS)

FIGURE 12–6   Excerpt from RIE Main Entry Section   (*Source: ERIC* Resources in Education, *Abstracts, July–December, 1983, pp. 154–155. (Washington: DC. U.S. Government Printing Office).*)

(For additional instruction in searching the psychological literature, see Reed and Baxter, 1983.)

Dissertations are accessed by author or subject index. The subject index is arranged alphabetically by key words in titles. The searcher judges the relevance of the title to his project and finds the abstracts in *Dissertation Abstracts International.* If the abstract looks promising, the entire study may be ordered from University Microfilms International in Ann Arbor, Michigan. Some university libraries loan dissertations that have been completed at that university. Figure 12–7 contains a portion of the Education section

FIGURE 12–7   Excerpt from *Dissertation Abstracts* System   (*Source:* Comprehensive Dissertation Index, *Ten Year Cumulation, 1973–1982, Vol. 22, Education I-N, 1984, p. 75.*)

INDIVIDUALIZED
A STUDY OF PERFORMANCE CHARACTERISTICS OF POST-SECONDARY VOCATIONAL STUDENTS ENROLLING IN A FLORIDA VOCATIONAL-TECHNICAL CENTER PROVIDING THE INDIVIDUALIZED MANPOWER TRAINING SYSTEM (IMTS)—CONRAD, HAROLD NIXON, JR. (ED.D. 1982 AUBURN UNIVERSITY) 82p. 43/06A, p.1948 **DEO82–25466**
A COMPARISON OF SPECIALIST-BASED TEAMS AND PRACTITIONER-BASED TEAMS FOR THE ASSESSMENT, WRITING, AND IMPLEMENTATION OF SPECIAL EDUCATION **INDIVIDUALIZED** EDUCATION PROGRAMS.—WELTON, JOHNNY W. (ED.D. 1982 UNIVERSITY OF CALIFORNIA, SAN FRANCISCO) 235p. 43/05A, p.1415 **DEO82–18074**

AN ETHNOGRAPHY OF STUDENTS' CONCEPTUALIZATIONS OF **INDIVIDUALIZED** LEARNING ENVIRONMENTS.—RUDOLPH, ANN PATRICK (PH.D. 1982 THE UNIVERSITY OF CONNECTICUT) 157p. 43/05A, p.1413 **DEO82–24547**

A STUDY OF **INDIVIDUALIZED** AND TRADITIONAL INSTRUCTION IN AN INTERMEDIATE SECONDARY GERMAN PROGRAM.—HOWELL, HARRY KLINE, JR. (ED.D. 1982 UNIVERSITY OF GEORGIA) 183p. 43/01A, p.99 **DEO82–14289**

AN **INDIVIDUALIZED** TEACHER-DIRECTED SPELLING PROGRAM COMPARED WITH A COMPUTER-BASED SPELLING PROGRAM.—GUSTAFSON, BRIAN (PH.D. 1982 IOWA STATE UNIVERSITY) 119p. 43/04A, p.991 **DEO82–21191**

A COMPARISON OF TWO APPROACHES TO THE TEACHING OF MATHEMATICS: TEAM-TEACHING VERSUS **INDIVIDUALIZED**-LABORATORY INSTRUCTION.—DONG, ARCHER WAH (ED.D. 1982 UNIVERSITY OF MASSACHUSETTS) 131p. 43/03A, p.710 **DEO82–10316**

USE AND FEASIBILITY OF VIDEOCASSETTES FOR **INDIVIDUALIZED** INSTRUCTION BY HOME ECONOMICS EXTENSION AGENTS WITH RESPONSIBILITY IN HOUSING AND HOME FURNISHINGS.—HAMMETT, WILMA SCOTT (PH.D. 1982 THE UNIVERSITY OF NORTH CAROLINA AT GREENSBORO) 220p. 43/03A, p.699 **DEO82–18666**

AN **INDIVIDUALIZED** LEARNING PACKAGE PROGRAM IN BEGINNING COLLEGE JAPANESE: A MULTI-MEDIA APPROACH.—HIRAMATSU, MICHIKO (ED.D. 1982 UNIVERSITY OF SAN FRANCISCO) 204p. 43/02A, p.386 **DEO82–16717**

INDIVIDUALIZED INSTRUCTION IN THE COMMUNITY COLLEGE.—FRANK, SHERRILL JOAN (ED.D. 1982 UNIVERSITY OF SOUTHERN CALIFORNIA) 43/03A, p.641 **DEO05–37717**

A STUDY OF FACTORS ASSOCIATED WITH THE IMPLEMENTATION AND CONTINUANCE OF AN **INDIVIDUALIZED** INSTRUCTIONAL PROGRAM IN ASSOCIATE DEGREE NURSING PROGRAMS IN CALIFORNIA.—MISCHLER, JANET KATHRYN (ED.D. 1982 UNIVERSITY OF SOUTHERN CALIFORNIA) 43/05A, p.1403 **DEO05–50407**

THE EFFECTS OF A "PRESCRIPTIVE **INDIVIDUALIZED** PROGRAM" AND A "NONPRESCRIPTIVE GROUP TASK PROGRAM" ON FUNDAMENTAL MOTOR PATTERN AND ABILITY ACQUISITION, SELF-CONCEPT, AND SOCIALIZATION SKILLS OF KINDERGARTEN CHILDREN.—MOYER, STEVE WILLIAM (ED.D. 1982 TEMPLE UNIVERSITY) 106p. 42/12A, p.5056 **DEO82–10536**

SURVEY ANALYSIS OF SPECIAL EDUCATION TEACHERS' REACTIONS TO AND EXPERIENCES WITH **INDIVIDUALIZED** EDUCATION PROGRAMS.—CAVANAGH, GRACE ROSEMARY (ED.D. 1981 COLUMBIA UNIVERSITY TEACHERS COLLEGE) 175p. 42/10A, p.4217 **DEO82–07306**

THE RELATION OF PERSONALITY FACTORS AND LEARNING STYLE PREFERENCES TO ACHIEVEMENT OF SEVENTH GRADE **INDIVIDUALIZED** MATHEMATICS STUDENTS.—JENKINS, OLGA CULMER (ED.D. 1981 COLUMBIA UNIVERSITY TEACHERS COLLEGE) 135p. 42/10A, p.4342 **DEO82–07322**

TRAINING UNDERGRADUATE SPECIAL EDUCATION STUDENTS TO WRITE CLEAR, COMPLETE, AND REASONABLE GOALS AND OBJECTIVES FOR **INDIVIDUALIZED** EDUCATIONAL PROGRAMS.—PIAZZA, ROBERT LOUIS (ED.D. 1981 COLUMBIA UNIVERSITY TEACHERS COLLEGE) 186p. 43/01A, p.141 **DEO82–07335**

A COMPARISON OF THE ACHIEVEMENT OF UNIVERSITY STUDENTS TAUGHT BY AN **INDIVIDUALIZED** INSTRUCTIONAL APPROACH VS. THE TRADITIONAL INSTRUCTIONAL APPROACH IN A COMBINED BUSINESS MATH/BUSINESS MACHINES COURSE.—WELLS, PEGGY LARUE (ED.D. 1981 UNIVERSITY OF HOUSTON) 142p. 42/11A, p.4697 **DEO82–10438**

THE IMPACT UPON THE ROLE OF THE ELEMENTARY PRINCIPAL DUE TO THE DEVELOPMENT AND ADMINISTRATION OF **INDIVIDUALIZED** EDUCATION PLANS IN COMPLIANCE WITH PUBLIC LAW 94-142, THE EDUCATION FOR ALL HANDICAPPED ACT OF 1975.—GIANGRECO, MARIANNE RANSON (PH.D. 1981 IOWA STATE UNIVERSITY) 211p. 42/11A, p.4666 **DEO82–09120**

of the subject index of *Comprehensive Dissertation Index—1982 Supplement* on the topic of individualized instruction. The entries include the name of the dissertation, author's name, degree, name of the college that granted the degree, the location of the study's abstract in *Dissertation Abstracts*, and the number that can be used to order the study.

VII. Branching Bibliographies

Studies that have been obtained in Step VI also serve as secondary sources in the sense that they contain a list of references to related studies.

VIII. Citation Search

The *Science Citation Index* (SCI) and the *Social Science Citation Index* (SSCI) offer another way to track down studies on a topic. Suppose that the searcher knows of one landmark study on a particular topic, its author and year it was published. One example, if the searcher was interested in the topic of teacher expectations, is Robert Rosenthal's book *Pygmalion in the Classroom* (Rosenthal and Jacobson, 1968). The author's name can be found in the *Social Science Citation Index.* Figure 12–8 reproduces the relevant section from the 1983 Annual, Part 3, which displays only a portion of Rosenthal's citations for 1983. Under the author's name are listed his publications that have been cited in someone's study during 1983. In other words, some other author who published a research study during 1983 had included *Pygmalion in the Classroom* in his or her list of references. This author, therefore, probably was writing about or researching some aspect of the topic of teacher expectation, or critiquing Rosenthal's study. Rosenthal's publications are printed in boldface, and *Pygmalion* is the sixteenth study listed. Under that title and date are 36 instances of documents that referenced the study. The last instance was authored by R.E. Young and published in *The Australia Journal of Education*, Volume 27, pages 3 and following, 1983. This "forward tracking" feature of the SCI and SSCI is a unique and valuable aide in collecting literature on a topic and is known as a **citation search**.

FIGURE 12–8 Excerpt from *Social Sciences Citation Index* (*Source:* Social Science Citation Index, Citation Index, 1983, column 1195.)

ROSENTHAL R					
** **ESSENTIALS BEHAVIORA**					
ROSNOW RL	J MIND BEH		4	319	83
** **J CONSULT CLIN PSYCH**					
MULLEN B	BEHAV RES M	N	15	392	83
** **J EDUC PSYCHOL**					
STRUBE MJ	J CONS CLIN		51	14	83
62 PERCEPT MOTOR SKILL 15 73					
SHAPIRO DH	J TRANSPERS		15	61	83
"	PERSP BIOL		26	568	83
63 AM SCI 51 1					
VANDERMO HH	ERGONOMICS		26	535	83
63 AM PSYCHOL 51 268					
SEE SCI FOR 1 ADDITIONAL CITATION					
WHITNEY JC	J MARKET C		20	167	83
63 J PROJ TECH PERS ASS 27 324					
MISHRA SP	J CLIN PSYC		39	603	83

63 J PSYCHOL 55 33					
SAWYER AG	J MARKET C		20	122	83
63 PSYCHOL REP 12 491					
LEBUFFE JR	AM ANN DEAF	E	128	795	83
64 PROGR EXPT PERSONALI 80					
MISHRA SP	J CLIN PSYC		39	603	83
64 PSYCHOL BULL 61 405					
FEINSTEI AD	CLIN PSYCH		3	1	83
65 HUM RELAT 18 389					
BRADLEY CF	WOMEN HEAL		8	35	83
66 EXPERIMENTER EFFECTS					
FREEMAN FE	J SOC PSYCH		119	119	83
GREENBER RP	PSYCHOL REP		53	355	83
66 EXPT EFFECTS BEHAVIO					
SEE SCI FOR 2 ADDITIONAL CITATIONS					
ADAIR JG	TEACH PSYCH		10	159	83
BALPH DF	AUK	E	100	755	83
EDINGER JA	PSYCHOL B	R	93	30	83
FALK G	HUMAN RELAT		35	1123	82
FORGAS JP	ADV EXP SOC		15	59	82
FUCHS D	J PSYCHOL		114	37	83
GOLDMAN L	COUNS PSYCH		10	87	82
GREENWOO JD	EUR J SOC P	R	13	235	83
KOTSES H	BIOL PSYCH		17	97	83
LEBUFFE JR	AM ANN DEAF	E	128	795	83
LEW MB	CHILD ST J		12	223	82
MEERMANN R	INT J EAT D		2	91	83
MESSING K	INT J HE SE		13	635	83
READING AE	J BEHAV AS		5	11	83
RICHERT A	PSYCHOTH/TR		20	321	83
ROSNOW RL	J MIND BEH		4	319	83
SCHACHT TE	PSYCHOTH/TR		20	359	83
SMITH K	AM J ORTHOP		53	315	83
WINEFIEL AH	MOTIV EMOT		7	145	83
66 EXPT EFFECTS BEHAVIO 324					
KARGER HJ	SOCIAL WORK		28	200	83
66 PYGMALION CLASSROOM					
FINE M	PERS SOC PS		8	637	82
66 PSYCHOL REP 19 115					
HARGROVE EC	PEABODY J E		60	1	83
SCHEIN JD	J VIS IMP B		77	152	83
SERBIN LA	AM J MENT D		88	86	83
67 PSYCHOL BULL 67 356					
GREENBER RP	PSYCHOL REP		53	355	83
68 PYGAMALION CLASSROOM					
HOLDAWAY SL	PSYCHOL SCH		20	388	83
68 PYGMALIAN CLASSROOM					
HARGROVE EC	PEABODY J E		60	1	83
NOVAK M	INT J AGING		16	231	83
68 PYGMALION CLASSROOM					
AVORN J	J AM GER SO		31	137	83
BLEASE D	EDUC STUD		9	123	83
BONDY AS	CHILD CARE		11	312	82
BROPHY J	J EDUC PSYC		75	544	83
BROPHY JE	"		75	631	83
COHN T	INT J POL E		6	1	83
CZAJKOSK EH	JUVEN FAM C		33	49	82
DARLEY JM	J PERS SOC		44	20	83

DUSEK JB	CONT PSYCHO	B	28	840	83
"	J EDUC PSYC		75	327	83
FELDMAN RS	"		75	27	83
FREEMAN J	PSYCHOL ERZ		30	67	83
GERARD HB	AM PSYCHOL		38	869	83
GRAY SW	PEABODY J E		60	70	83
HAMILTON SF	ELEM SCH J		83	313	83
HASKINS R	J EDUC PSYC		75	865	83
KIRSCHEN DS	PROF PSYCH		14	159	83
KNOWLES CJ	J SPEC EDUC		16	449	82
LACY WB	J NEGRO ED		52	130	83
LEBUFFE JR	AM ANN DEAF	E	128	795	83
LORANGER M	PSYCHOL REP		51	915	82
LORENZI NM	B MED LIB A		71	410	83
MAHONY P	WOMEN ST IN		6	107	83
MARTIN DS	J REHABIL		49	51	83
MCKINNEY JD	J LEARN DI	R	16	360	83
MILLER LC	PERS SOC PS		8	748	82
MISKEL C	EDUC ADMIN		19	49	83
POMEROY R	EDUC REV		35	51	83
RIGGS JM	PERS SOC PS		9	253	83
SERBIN LA	AM J MENT D		88	86	83
STEWART RAC	SOC BEH PER		10	221	82
STGEORGE A	BR J ED PSY		53	48	83
STRAYHOR JM	AM J ORTHOP		53	677	83
TUDGE J	CORNELL J S		16	84	82
VERTINSK P	BR J EDUC S		31	229	83
YOUNG RE	AUST J EDUC		27	3	83
69 ARTEFACT BEHAVIORAL					
SANDERS D	PSYCHOS MED		45	487	83
69 ARTIFACT BEHAVIORAL					
EMRICK CD	AM PSYCHOL		38	1078	83
FISCHHOF B	J SOC ISSUE		39	133	83
HOUSE AE	BEHAV ASSES		5	83	83
JOBE JB	J PERSONAL		51	95	83
LEITKO TA	J APPL BEH		18	447	82
LEVIN IP	ORGAN BEH H		31	173	83
MILLER AG	CONT PSYCHO	B	28	827	83
NEDERHOF AJ	EUR J SOC P		13	255	83
NEIMEYER G	COUNS PSYCH		10	75	82
ROSNOW RL	J MIND BEH		4	319	83
TRICE AD	PSYCHOL REP		53	898	83
TURNER RM	AM J COMM P		11	593	83
WHITE KD	AUST PSYCHL	E	18	261	83
WHITNEY JC	J MARKET C		20	167	83
69 ARTIFACTS BEHAVIORAL					
HORNKE LF	PSYCHOL ERZ		30	54	83
LYMAN RD	PSYCHOL REP		52	43	83
69 ARTIFACT BEHAVIORAL		181			
BALPH DF	AUK	E	100	755	83
SAWYER AG	J MARKET C		20	122	83
71 ET CETERA 34 252					
HETHERIN NS	NATURE	E	306	727	83
71 PYGMALION UNTERRICHT					
MULLER RGE	HEILPAD FOR	B	10	366	83
72 AM J PSYCHIAT 128 1363					
BENNUM I	SUICIDE LIF		13	71	83
72 BRIT J PSYCHIAT 121 259					
ARIEL RN	ARCH G PSYC		40	258	83

BIGELOW LB	BR J PSYCHI		142	284	83
DAVISON K	PSYCHIAT D	R	1	1	83
NASRALLA HA	PSYCHIAT R		8	251	83
RANDALL PL	MED HYPOTH		10	247	83
SEIDMAN LJ	PSYCHOL B	R	94	195	83
TRESS KH	BR J PSYCHI		143	156	83

CONCLUSIONS

The preceding sections have shown how a searcher may gain access to extant studies. Using the information in them, however, is a separate skill. The searcher must be able to summarize the methods and substance of the separate studies. He must be able to apply the relevant criteria to them to identify any critical weakness and understand what deficiencies characterize the studies as a whole. Then some synthesis must take place so that the searcher can acquire an overall picture of accumulated literature and its message. Several techniques can be used. The traditional review of research includes a narrative summation of the findings of the studies. The vote-counting method involves the creation of statistical tables showing the frequency or percentage of studies that show positive and negative effects relative to the researcher's hypothesis. **Meta-analysis** is the statistical summary of the results of all the studies on a topic. Our book, *Meta-analysis in Social Research* (Glass, McGaw, and Smith, 1981), describes these three methods. Each is designed to serve the same purpose, however—to create a context for future research by describing where it fits in with the already accumulated knowledge on the topic. *Summing Up* by Light and Pillemer (1984) provides an excellent treatment of all methods of reviewing and synthesizing studies.

SUGGESTED READINGS

GEAHIGAN, G., and GEAHIGAN, P.C. Using computers to search the educational literature. *Contemporary Education*, 1982, *1*, 179–193.

GLASS, G.V., McGAW, B., and SMITH, M.L. *Meta-analysis of social research*. Beverly Hills, Calif.: SAGE, 1981.

LIGHT, R.J., and PILLEMER, D.B. *Summing up*. Cambridge: Harvard University Press, 1984.

REED, J.G., and BAXTER, P.M. *Library use: A handbook for psychology*. Washington, D.C.: American Psychological Association, 1983.

TERMS INTRODUCED IN THIS CHAPTER

archival sources
fugitive sources
primary sources
secondary sources

access systems
key-word descriptors
citation search
meta-analysis

QUESTIONS AND EXERCISES FOR FURTHER STUDY

1. Classify the following papers according to whether they are archival or fugitive, primary or secondary.
   a. A review and synthesis of research studies on sex differences in delinquency published by the University's Bureau of Sociological Research.
   b. A study of the prediction of marital satisfaction published in the *Journal of Marriage and the Family.*
   c. The report of the evaluation of early kindergarten screening programs, published by the school district's evaluation department.
   d. A meta-analysis of research on the effects of various methods of reducing performance anxiety published in *Psychological Bulletin.*
   e. A paper delivered at the Annual Meeting of the American Educational Research Association on methods of predicting enrollment in junior college.

2. Assuming that each paper listed in question 1 is indexed in ERIC, indicate which would be indexed in *Resources in Education* and which in *Current Index of Journals in Education.*

3. What is the first step in a literature search on the topic, "What is the effect of advanced organizers on comprehension of a passage in a social studies text?"

4. For each item on the left, indicate in what source (from the list on the right) one would most likely find it.

Bibliography of studies that used the California Test of Personality	*Handbook of General Psychology*
An article in which research on the relationship between teacher clarity and pupil performance is reviewed and synthesized	*Dissertation Abstracts International* *Review of Educational Research*
An essay on the status of research literature on the measurement of aptitude for college	*Contemporary Psychology* *American Educational Research Journal*
The report of a study about time on task and its relationship to achievement	*Encyclopedia of Educational Research*
Alphabetically arranged titles of Ph.D. theses	*Mental Measurements Yearbook*
References to research studies that have been included in the bibliographies of other studies	*Dissertation Index*
Indexed key words and their definitions to use for literature searches	*ERIC Thesaurus*
A critical review of the book, *The Mismeasure of Man*	*Social Sciences Citation Index*

5. List four reasons for consulting secondary sources.

6. Explain why the ERIC system is more efficient than the *Dissertation Index* system if one is searching for research on a topic such as alternative schools.

7. What must be considered when deciding whether to use a manual or a computer system to conduct a search?

8. Conduct a modified literature search on the topic of drug abuse. Limit your check of secondary sources to the *Encyclopedia of Educational Research* and the *Handbook on Drug and Alcohol Abuse* (check the reference section of your university library).

    a. Check these secondary sources for bibliographies. Take a note on the number of references cited and the general points made.
    b. Use the ERIC *Thesaurus* to pick out relevant key-word descriptors.
    c. With the descriptors listed in item b, consult the most recent issue of *CIJE* and estimate number of entries related to the topic that are listed in the Subject Index.
    d. Take one title gleaned from the Subject Index and trace it to its abstract in the Main Entry section.
    e. Consult the most recent issue of *RIE* and estimate the number of relevant entries in the index. Estimate how many entries appear to be research studies as opposed to other kinds of papers.
    f. Find one title from item e in *Document Resumes*.
    g. If your library maintains these documents on microfiche, find the document from item f.
    h. Use the *Thesaurus of Psychological Index Terms* and find the relevant terms.
    i. Use the most recent issue of *Psychological Abstracts* and locate the title and brief abstract of one relevant study.
    j. Find where the relevant journals are located in your library.
    k. Note whether any other indexing system might be appropriate.

REFERENCES

ALKIN, M.C. Evaluation theory development. *Evaluation Comment*, 1969, *2*, 2–7.

American Psychological Association. *Standards for educational and psychological tests*. Washington, D.C.: APA, 1974 and 1983.

BABBIE, E. *Survey research methods*. Belmont, Calif.: Wadsworth, 1973.

BARBER, T.X. Pitfalls in research: Nine investigator and experimenter effects. In R.M.W. Travers (Ed.), *Second handbook of research on teaching*. Chicago: Rand McNally, 1973.

BATCHER, E. *Emotion in the classroom*. New York: Praeger, 1981.

BECKER, H.S. Arts and crafts. *American Journal of Scoiology*, 1978, *2*, 485–500.

BEERE, C.A. *Women and women's issues: A handbook of measures*. San Francisco: Jossey-Bass, 1979.

BERTAUX, D. (Ed.). *Biography and society: The life history approach in the social sciences*. Beverly Hills, Calif.: SAGE, 1981.

BLALOCK, Jr., H.M. *Causal models in the social sciences*. Chicago: Aldine, 1971.

BLALOCK, Jr., H.M. *Conceptualization and measurement in the social sciences*. Beverly Hills, Calif.: SAGE, 1982.

BOGDAN, R., and BIKLEN, S. *Qualitative research for education*. Boston: Allyn & Bacon, 1982.

BOGDAN, R., and TAYLOR, S.J. *Introduction to qualitative research methods*. New York: John Wiley, 1975.

BONJEAN, C.M., HILL, R.J., and McLEMORE, S.D. *Sociological measurement: An inventory of scales and indices*. San Francisco: Chandler, 1967.

BORICH, G.D., & MADDEN, S.K. *Evaluating classroom instruction: A sourcebook of instruments*. Reading, Mass.: Addison-Wesley, 1977.

BORUCH, R.F., and CORDRAY, D.S. (Eds.). *An appraisal of educational program evaluations: Federal, state, and local agencies, report to Congress*. Evanston, Ill.: Northwestern University, 1980.

BRACHT, G.H., and GLASS, G.V. The external validity of experiments. *American Educational Research Journal*, 1968, *5*, 437–444.

BREWER, M.B., and COLLINS, B.E. (Eds.). *Scientific inquiry and the social sciences*. San Francisco: Jossey-Bass, 1981.

BRODBECK, M. *Readings in the philosophy of social science*. New York: Macmillan, 1968.

BUROS, O.K. (Ed.) *Personality tests and reviews*. Highland Park, N.J.: Gryphon Press, 1970.

BUROS, O.K. (Ed.). *Mental measurements yearbook (7th and 8th ed.)*. Highland Park, N.J.: Gryphon Press, 1972; 1978.

BUROS, O.K. (Ed.). *Tests in print* (Vols. I, II, and III). Highland Park, N.J.: Gryphon Press, 1961, 1974, and 1983.

CAMPBELL, D.T. Reforms as experiments. *American Psychologist*, 1969, *24*, 409–429.

CAMPBELL, D.T., and FISKE, D.W. Convergent and discriminant validation by the multitrait-multimethod matrix. *Psychological Bulletin*, 1959, *56*, 81–105.

CAMPBELL, D.T., and STANLEY. J.C. *Experimental and quasi-experimental designs for research.* Chicago: Rand McNally, 1966. Also in N.L. GAGE (Ed.). *Handbook of research on teaching.* Chicago: Rand McNally, 1963.

CANNELL, C.F., LAWSON, S.A., and HAUSER, D.L. *A technique for evaluating interviewer performance.* Ann Arbor, Mich.: Institute for Social Research, University of Michigan, 1975.

CHAMBERS, A.C., HOPKINS, K.D., and HOPKINS, B.R. Anxiety, physiologically and psychologically measured: Its effects on mental test performance. *Psychology in the Schools*, 1972, 9, 198–206.

CHARMAZ, K. The grounded theory method: An explication and interpretation. In R.M. EMERSON (Ed.), *Contemporary field research.* Boston: Little, Brown, 1983.

CHILD, D. *The essentials of factor analysis.* London: Holt, Rinehard & Winston, 1970.

CHUN, K.T., COBB, S., and FRENCH, J.R. *Measures for psychological assessment: A guide to 3,000 original sources and their application.* Ann Arbor: Institute for Social Research, University of Michigan, 1974.

COCHRAN, W. *Sampling techniques (3rd ed.).* New York: John Wiley, 1977.

COHEN, J., and COHEN, P. *Applied multiple regression/correlation analysis for the behavioral sciences* (2nd ed.). Hillsdale, N.J.: Lawrence Erlbaum, 1983.

COLEMAN, J.S., CAMPBELL, E.Q., HOBSON, C.J., McPARTLAND, J., MOOD, A.M., WEINFELD, F.D., and YORK, R.L., *Equality of educational opportunity.* Washington, D.C.: U.S. Government Printing Office, 1966.

COLES, R. *Children of crisis.* Boston: Little, Brown, 1964.

COLLINS, B.E. Hyperactivity: Myth and entity. In M.B. BREWER and B.E. COLLINS (Eds.), *Scientific inquiry and the social sciences.* San Francisco: Jossey-Bass, 1981.

COMREY, A.L., BACKER, T.E., and GLASER, E.M. *A sourcebook for mental health measures.* Los Angeles: Human Interaction Research Institute, 1973.

CONNORS, C.K. Rating scales for youth in drug studies with children. *Psychopharmacology Bulletin* (Special issue, *The pharmacotherapy of children*, 1973, 24–84.

COOK, T.D., and CAMPBELL, D.T. *Quasi-experimentation: Design and analysis issues for field studies.* Chicago: Rand McNally, 1979.

COOLEY, W.W., and LOHNES, P.R. *Multivariate data analysis.* New York: John Wiley, 1971.

COTTLE, T.J. *Busing.* Boston: Beacon, 1976.

CRONBACH, L.J. *Essentials of psychological testing (3rd ed).* New York: Harper & Row, 1970.

CRONBACH, L.J. Beyond the two disciplines of scientific psychology. *American Psychologist*, 1975, *30*, 116–127.

CRONBACH, L.J. *Designing evaluations of educational and social programs.* San Francisco: Jossey-Bass, 1982.

CRONBACH, L.J. and ASSOCIATES. *Toward reform of program evaluation.* San Francisco: Jossey-Bass, 1980.

CRONBACH, L.J., GLESER, G.C., NANDA, H., and RAJARATNAM, N. *The dependability of behavioral measurements: Theory of generalizability for scales and profiles.* New York: John Wiley, 1972.

CRONBACH, L.J. and MEEHL, P.E. Construct validity in psychological tests. *Psychological Bulletin*, 1955, *52*, 281–302.

CRONBACH, L.J. and SUPPES, P. *Research for tomorrow's schools.* New York: Macmillan, 1969.

DABBS, J.M. Making things visible. In VAN MAANEN, J., DABBS, J.M., and FAULKNER, R.R. (Eds.), *Varieties of qualitative research.* Beverly Hills, Calif.; SAGE, 1982.

DARLINGTON, R.B. Multiple regression in psychological research and practice. *Psychological Bulletin*, 1972, *77*, 446–452.

DENZIN, N.K. The logic of naturalistic inquiry. *Social Forces*, 1971, *50*, 166–182.

DENZIN, N.K. *The research act.* New York: McGraw-Hill, 1978.

DEWEY, J. *How we think.* Boston: Heath, 1933.

DILLMAN, D.A. *Mail and telephone surveys; The total design method.* New York: John Wiley, 1978.

DOUGLAS, J.D. *Investigative research methods.* Beverly Hills, Calif. SAGE, 1976.

DREGER, R.M. Review of the State-Trait Anxiety Inventory. In O.K. BUROS (Ed.), *Mental measurement yearbook (8th ed.).* Highland Park, N.J.: Gryphon Press, 1978.

EASLEY, J.A. Some methodological issues in research oriented toward problems of teachers. Paper presented to the Committee on Culture and Cognition, University of Illinois, Urbana, Illinois, October 1978.

EDWARDS, A. *Techniques of attitude scale construction.* New York: Appleton-Century Crofts, 1957.

EISNER, E. *The educational imagination.* New York: Macmillan, 1979.

ELLIOT, D.S., AGETON, S.S., and CANTER, R.J. An integrated theoretical perspective on delinquent behavior. *Research in Criminology and Delinquency*, 1979, *16*, 3–27.

ELLIOT, D.S., AGETON, S.S., HUNTER, M., and KNOWLES, B.S. Self-reported delinquency instrument. *Research handbook for community planning and feedback instruments (rev. ed.).* Boulder, Colo.: Behavioral Research Institute, 1976.

ENGLISH, H.B. and ENGLISH, A.C. *Comprehensive dictionary of psychological and psychoanalytic terms.* New York: David McKay, 1958.

ERICKSON, E.H. *Life history and the historical moment.* New York: W.W. Norton & Co., 1975.

ERICKSON, F. Qualitative methods in research on teaching. In Wittrock, M.C. (Ed.), *Handbook of Research on teaching (3rd ed.).* New York: Macmillan, 1986.

Evaluative Criteria. Washington, D.C.: National Study of Secondary School Evaluation, 1969.

FETTERMAN, D.M. *Ethnography and educational evaluation.* Beverly Hills, Calif.: SAGE, 1984.

FISHBEIN, M. (Ed.). *Readings in attitude theory and measurement.* New York: John Wiley, 1967.

FISKE, D.W. *Measuring the concepts of personality.* Chicago: Aldine, 1971.

GAGE, N.L. (Ed.). *Handbook of research on teaching.* Chicago: Rand-McNally, 1963.

GEAHIGAN, G., and GEAHIGAN, P.C. Using computers to search the educational literature. *Contemporary Education Review*, 1982, *1*, 179–193.

GEORGES, R.A., and JONES, M.O. *People studying people.* Berkeley: University of California Press, 1980.

GLASER, B.G., and STRAUSS, A.L. *Discovery of grounded theory.* Chicago: Aldine, 1967.

GLASS, G.V, and ELLETT, F.S. Evaluation research. *Annual Review of Psychology*, 1980, *31*, 211–228.

GLASS, G.V, and HOPKINS, K.D. *Statistical Methods in Education and Psychology (2nd ed.).* Englewood Cliffs, N.J.: Prentice-Hall, 1984.

GLASS, G.V, McGAW, B., and SMITH, M.L. *Meta-analysis in social research.* Beverly Hills, Calif.: SAGE, 1981.

GLASS, G.V, WILLSON, V.L, and GOTTMAN, J.M. *Design and analysis of time-series experiments.* Boulder: Colorado Associated University Press, 1975.

GOETZ, J.P., and LeCOMPTE, M.D. *Ethnography and qualitative design in educational research.* Orlando, Fl.: Academic Press, 1984.

GOLD, R.L. Roles in sociological field observation. In G.J. McCALL and J.L. SIMMONS (Eds.), *Issues in participant observation.* Reading, Mass.: Addison-Wesley, 1969.

GOLDMAN, B.A., and BUSCH, J.C. *Directory of unpublished experimental mental measures, Vol. II.* New York: Human Sciences Press, 1978.

GOODWIN, W., and DRISCOLL, L. *Handbook for measurement and evaluation in early childhood education.* San Francisco: Jossey-Bass, 1980.

GUBA, E.G., and LINCOLN, Y.S. *Effective evaluation.* San Francisco: Jossey-Bass, 1981.

GUILFORD, J.P. The structure of the intellect. *Psychological Bulletin*, 1956, *53*, 267–293.

GUTHRIE, P.D. *Measures of social skills: An annotated bibliography.* Princeton. N.J.: Educational Testing Service, 1971. (ERIC Document No. ED 056 085)

HABERMAS, J. *Knowledge and human interests.* Boston: Beacon Press, 1971.

HALLER, E. Questionnaires and the dissertation in educational administration. *Educational Administration Quarterly*, 1979, *15*, 47–66.

HANNA, J.L. Public social policy and the children's world: Implications of ethnographic research for desegregated schools. In G. SPINDLER (Ed.), *Doing the ethnography of schooling.* New York: Holt, Rinehart & Winston, 1982.

HARMAN, H.H. *Modern factor analysis.* Chicago: University of Chicago Press, 1960.

HARTLEY, H.J. PPBS and an analysis of cost effectiveness. *Educational Administration Quarterly*, 1969, *5*, 65–80.

HAYS, W.R. *Statistics for the social sciences.* New York: Holt, Rinehart & Winston, 1973.

HENRY, J. *Culture against man.* New York: Random House, 1963.

HERRIOTT, R.E., and FIRESTONE, W.A. Multisite qualitative policy research: Optimizing description and generalizability. *Educational Researcher*, 1983, *12*, 14–19.

HIRSCHI, T., and SELVIN, H.C. *Principles of survey analysis.* New York: Free Press, 1973.

HOEFNER, R., and others (Eds.). *CSE elementary school test evaluations.* Los Angeles: Center for the Study of Evaluation, University of California, 1976.

HOPKINS, K.D. Regression and the matching fallacy in quasi-experimental research. *Journal of Special Education*, 1969, *3*, 329–336.

HOPKINS, K.D. and GLASS, G.V *Basic statistics for the behavioral sciences (2nd ed.).* Englewood Cliffs, N.J.: Prentice-Hall, 1986.

HOPKINS, K.D. and STANLEY, J.C. *Educational and psychological measurement (6th ed.).* Englewood Cliffs, N.J.: Prentice-Hall, 1981.

HOUSE, E.R. *School evaluation: The politics and the process.* Berkeley, Calif.: McCutchan, 1973.

HOUSE, E.R. The objectivity, fairness, and justice of federal evaluation policy as reflected in the Follow-Through evaluation. *Educational Evaluation and Policy Analysis*, 1979, *1*, 28–42.

HOUSE, E.R. *Evaluating with validity.* Beverly Hills, Calif.: SAGE, 1980.

HYMAN, H. *Survey design and analysis.* New York: Free Press, 1955.

HYMAN, H. *Interviewing in Social Research.* University of Chicago Press, 1957.

JACKSON, G., and COSCA, C. The inequality of educational opportunity in the Southwest: An observational study of ethnically mixed classrooms. *American Educational Research Journal*, 1974, *11*, 219–230.

JAEGER, R.M. *Sampling in education and the social sciences.* New York: Longman, 1984.

JESSOR, R., and JESSOR, L.J. *Problem behavior and psychosocial development.* New York: Academic Press, 1977.

JOHNSON, O.G. *Tests and measurements in child development: Handbook II.* San Francisco: Jossey-Bass, 1976.

Joint Committee on Standards for Educational Evaluation. *Standards for evaluation of educational programs, projects, and materials.* New York: McGraw-Hill, 1981.

JUDD, C.M., and KENNY, D.A. *Estimating the effects of social interventions.* Cambridge: Cambridge University Press, 1981.

JURS, S.G., and GLASS, G.V The effect of experimental mortality on the internal and external validity of the randomized comparative experiment. *American Educational Research Journal*, 1971, *40*, 62–66.

KAHN, R.L., and CANNELL, C.F. *The dynamics of interviewing.* New York: John Wiley, 1957.

KAPLAN, A. *The conduct of inquiry.* San Francisco: Chandler, 1964.

KENNY, D.A. *Correlation and causation.* New York: Wiley-Interscience, 1979.

KEPPEL, G. *Design and analysis: A researcher's handbook.* Englewood Cliffs, N.J.: Prentice Hall, 1982.

KERLINGER, F.N., and PEDHAUZER, E.J. *Multiple regression in behavioral research.* New York: Holt, Rinehart & Winston, 1973.

KISH, L. *Survey sampling.* New York: John Wiley, 1965.

KRIPPENDORF, K. *Content analysis: An introduction to its methodology.* Beverly Hills, Calif.: SAGE, 1980.

KUHN, T.S. *The structure of scientific revolution.* Chicago: University of Chicago Press, 1962.

LAKE, D.G., MILES, M.B., and EARLE, R.B. *Measuring human behavior: Tools for the assessment of social functioning.* New York: Teachers College Press, 1973.

LEVIN, H.L. *Cost-effectiveness: A primer.* Beverly Hills, Calif.: SAGE, 1983.

LIGHT, R.J., and PILLEMER, D.G. *Summing up.* Cambridge: Harvard University Press, 1984.

LINN, R.L. (Ed.). Educational measurement *(3rd ed.).* Washington, D.C.: American Council on Education and Macmillan, 1986.

LOFLAND, J., and LOFLAND, L.H. *Analyzing social situations.* Belmont, Calif.: Wadsworth, 1984.

LORD, F.M., and NOVICK, M.R. *Statistical theories of mental test scores.* Reading, Mass.: Addison-Wesley, 1968.

MacDONALD, B. Evaluation and the control of education. Norwich, England: Centre for Applied Research in Education, University of East Anglia, 1974.

MACKENZIE, A.A., and WHITE, R.T. Fieldwork in geography and long-term memory structures. *American Educational Research Journal*, 1982, *19*, 623–632.

MARASCUILO, L.A., and McSWEENY, M. *Nonparametric and distribution-free methods for the social sciences.* Monterey, Calif.: Brooks/Cole, 1977.

McCLEARY, R. How parole officers use records. *Social Problems*, 1977, *24*, 576–589.

McCLEARY, R. *Dangerous men: The sociology of parole.* Beverly Hills, Calif.: SAGE, 1978.

McCLEARY, R., and HAYS, R.A. *Applied time-series analysis.* Beverly Hills, Calif.: SAGE, 1980.

MCDERMOTT, R.P., GOSPODINOFF, K., and ARON, J. Criteria for an ethnographically adequate description of concerted activities and their contexts. *Semiotica*, 1978, *24*, 245–275.

MCLAUGHLIN, M.W. *Evaluation and reform.* Cambridge, Mass.: Ballinger, 1975.

MCNEMAR, Q. Lost: Our intelligence. Why? *American Psychologist*, 1964, *19*, 871–882.

MEEHAN, E.J. *Reasoned argument in social science.* Westport, Conn.: Greenwood Press, 1981.

MEEHL, P. Philosophical predispositions of psychologists. In M.H. SCHARLEMANN (Ed.), *What, then, is man?* St. Louis: Concordia, 1958.

MEEHL, P.E. Theoretical risks and tabular asterisks. Sir Karl, Sir Ronald, and the slow progress of soft psychology. *Journal of Consulting and Clinical Psychology*, 1978, *46*, 806–834.

MEHAN, H. *Learning lessons: Social organization in the classroom.* Cambridge, Mass.: Harvard University Press, 1979.

MERTON, R. *Social theory and social structure.* New York: Free Press, 1949.

MERWIN, J.C. Review of the "Wide Range Achievement Test." In O.K. BUROS (Ed.), *Mental measurements yearbook (7th ed.).* Highland Park, N.J.: Gryphon Press, 1972.

MEVARECH, Z.R., and RICH, Y. Effects of computer-assisted mathematics instruction on disadvantaged pupils' cognitive and affective development. *Journal of Educational Research,* 1985, *79*, 5–11.

MILES, M.B., and HUBERMAN, A.M. *Analyzing qualitative data: A sourcebook of methods.* Beverly Hills, Calif.: SAGE, 1984.

MILLER, D.C. *Handbook of research design and social measurement (4th ed.).* New York: Longman, 1983.

MORRIS, L.L., FITZ-GIBBON, C.T., and HENERSON, M.E. *Program evaluation kit.* Beverly Hills, Calif.: SAGE, 1978.

National Assessment of Educational Progress. *Three national assessments of science changes in achievement, 1969–1977.* Denver: Education Commission of the States, 1978.

NIE, H., HULL, C., JENKINS, J., STEINBRENNER, K., and BENT, D. *SPSS: Statistical package for the social sciences.* New York: McGraw-Hill, 1975.

NUNNALY, J. *Psychometric theory (2nd ed.).* New York: McGraw-Hill, 1978.

ORNE, M.T. Demand characteristics and the concept of quasi-controls. In R. ROSENTHAL and R.L. ROSNOW (Eds.), *Artifact in behavioral research.* New York: Academic Press, 1969.

OWENS, L., and BARNES, J. The relationship between cooperative, competitive, and individualized learning preferences and students' perceptions of classroom learning atmosphere. *American Educational Research Journal*, 1982, *19*, 182–200.

OWENS, L., BARNES, J., and STRATON, R. *Classroom Learning Atmosphere Scale—Secondary, Form B.* Sydney: University of Sydney, Department of Education, 1978.

OWENS, L., and STRATON, R. The development of a cooperative, competitive, and individualized learning preference scale for students. *British Journal of Educational Psychology.* 1980, *50*, 147–161.

PARLETT, M., and HAMILTON, D. Evaluation as illumination: A new approach to the study of innovative programs. In G.V GLASS (Ed.), *Evaluation studies review annual, Vol. I.* Beverly Hills, Calif.: SAGE, 1976.

PASCARELLA, E.T., WALBERG, H.J., HAERTEL, G.D. and JUNKER, L.K. Individual and school-level correlates of the educational aspirations of older adolescents. *Journal of Educational Research*, 1981, *75*, 30–43.

PATTON, M.Q. *Utilization-focused evaluation.* Beverly Hills, Calif.: SAGE, 1978.

PATTON, M.Q. *Qualitative evaluation methods.* Beverly Hills, Calif.: SAGE, 1980.

PAYNE, S. *The art of asking questions.* Princeton, N.J.: Princeton University Press, 1951.

PRICE, J.L. *Handbook of organizational management.* Lexington, Mass.: Heath, 1972.

PROVUS, M. *Discrepancy evaluation.* Berkeley, Calif.: McCutchan, 1971.

QUINN, B., VON MONDFRANS, A., and WORTHEN, B.R. Cost-effectiveness of two math programs as moderated by pupil SES. *Educational Evaluation and Policy Analysis*, 1984, *6*, 39–52.

RAIZEN, S., and ROSSI, P.H. *Program evaluation in education: When? How? To what ends?* Washington, D.C.: National Academy Press, 1981.

REED, J.G., and BAXTER, P.M. *Library use.* Washington, D.C.: American Psychological Association, 1983.

REEDER, L.G., RAMACHER, L., and GORELNIK, S. *Handbook of scales and indices of health behavior.* Pacific Palisades, Calif.: Goodyear, 1976.

REICHARDT, C.S., and COOK, T.D. Beyond qualitative *versus* quantitative. In T.D. COOK and

C.S. REICHARDT (Eds.), *Qualitative and quantitative methods in evaluation research*. Beverly Hills, Calif.: SAGE, 1979.

RIECKEN, H.W. Introduction: Experiments for program development and evaluation. In R. F. BORUCH and H.W. RIECKEN (Eds.), *Experimental testing of public policy*. Boulder, Colo.: Westview, 1975.

RIPPEY, R.M. (Ed.). *Studies in transactional evaluation*. Berkeley, Calif.: McCutchan, 1973.

ROBINSON, J.P., ATHANASION, R., and HEAD, K.B. *Measures of occupational attitudes and occupational characteristics*. Ann Arbor, Mich.: Institute for Social Research, 1969.

ROBINSON, J.P., RUSK, J.G., and HEAD, K.P. *Measures of political attitudes*. Ann Arbor, Mich.: Institute for Social Research, 1968.

ROBINSON, J.P., and SHAVER, P.R. *Measures of social psychological attitudes*. Ann Arbor, Mich.: Institute for Social Research, 1973.

ROBINSON, S.D., KEITH, T.Z., and PAGE, E.B. Now who aspires to teach? *Educational Researcher*, 1983, *12*, 13–21.

ROMBERG, T.A. Allocated time and context covered in mathematics classroom. Madison, Wisc.: Wisconsin Center for Educational Research, 1983. (ERIC Document No. 231 616).

ROSEN, P. *Self-concept measures: Head Start collection*. Princeton, N.J.: Educational Testing Service, 1973.

ROSENFELD, P., LAMBERT, N.M., and BLACK, A. Desk arrangement effects on pupil classroom behavior. *Journal of Educational Psychology*, 1985, *77*, 101–108.

ROSENTHAL, R. *Experimenter effects in behavioral research*. New York: Appleton-Century-Crofts, 1966.

ROSENTHAL, R., and JACOBSON, L. *Pygmalion in the classroom*. New York: Holt, Rinehart & Winston, 1968.

ROSENTHAL, R., and ROSNOW, R.L. (Eds.), *Artifact in behavioral research*. New York: Academic Press, 1969.

ROSENTHAL, R., and ROSNOW, R.L. *The volunteer subject*. New York: John Wiley, 1975.

ROSNOW, R.L., and DAVIS, D.J. Demand characteristics and the psychological experiment. *Et Cetera*, 1977, *34*, 301–313.

ROSS, H.L., CAMPBELL, D.T., and GLASS, G.V Determining the social effects of a legal reform: The British "breathalyzer" crackdown of 1967. *American Behavioral Scientist*, 1970, *13*, 493–509.

ROSSI, P.H., FREEMAN, H.E., and WRIGHT, S.R. *Evaluation: A systematic approach*. Beverly Hills, Calif.: SAGE, 1979.

ROUTH, D.K. *Bibliography on the psychological assessment of the child*. Washington, D.C.: American Psychological Association, 1976.

SARACHO, O.N. The effects of a computer-assisted instruction program on basic skills achievement and attitudes toward instruction of Spanish-speaking migrant children. *American Educational Research Journal*, 1982, *19*, 201–219.

SCHATZMAN, L., and STRAUSS, A.L. *Field research: Strategies for a natural sociology*. Englewood Cliffs, N.J.: Prentice-Hall, 1973.

SCHRAG, P., and DIVOKY, D. *The myth of the hyperactive child and other means of child control*. New York: Pantheon Press, 1975.

SCRIVEN, M. Evaluation bias and its control. In G.V Glass (Ed.), *Evaluation studies review annual, Vol. 1*. Beverly Hills, Calif.: SAGE, 1976.

SCRIVEN, M. Methods of inquiry in philosophy of education. In R.M. JAEGER (Ed.), *Alternative methodologies in educational research*. Washington, D.C.: American Educational Research Association, 1986.

SHAFFIR, W.B., STEBBINS, R.A., and TUROWETZ, A. *Fieldwork experience*. New York: St. Martin's Press, 1980.

SHAVELSON, R.J. *Statistical reasoning for the behavioral sciences*. Boston: Allyn & Bacon, 1981.

SHAW, M.E., and WRIGHT, J.M. *Scales for the measurement of attitudes*. New York: McGraw-Hill, 1967.

SHEPARD, L.A., SMITH, M.L., and VOJIR, C.P. Characteristics of pupils identified as learning disabled. *American Educational Research Journal*, 1983, *20*, 309–332.

SHOHAM-SALOMON, V., and JANCOURT, A. Differential effectiveness of paradoxical interventions for more versus less stress-prone individuals. *Journal of Counseling Psychology*, 1985, *32*, 449–453.

SIEGEL, S. *Nonparametric statistics for the behavioral sciences*. New York: McGraw-Hill, 1956.

SIMON, A., and BOYER, E.G. *Mirrors for behavior, III: An anthology of observation instruments*. Wyncote, Pa.: Communications Materials Center, 1974.

SIMONS, R.L., MILLER, M.G. and AIGNER, S.M. Contemporary theories of deviance and female delinquency: An empirical test. *Journal of Research in Crime and Delinquency*, 1980, *17*, 42–57.

SKINNER, B.F. The operational analysis of psychological terms. In H. FEIGL and M. BRODBECK (Eds.), *Readings in the philosophy of science*. New York: Appleton, 1953.

SMART, J.C., and ELTON, C.F. Structural characteristics and citation rates of education journals. *American Educational Research Journal*, 1981, *18*, 399–414.

SMART, L.M. Science education in the Alte schools. In R.E. STAKE and J.A. EASLEY (Eds.), *Case studies in science education*. Urbana, Ill.: School of Education, University of Illinois, 1978.

SMITH, M.L. *How educators decide who is learning disabled*. Springfield, Ill.: Charles C Thomas, 1982.

SMITH, M.L., GABRIEL, R., SCHOTT, J., and PADIA, W.L. Evaluation of the effects of Outward Bound. Boulder, Colo.: School of Education, University of Colorado, 1975. Reprinted in G.V GLASS (Ed.), *Evaluation studies review annual, Vol. I*. Beverly Hills, Calif.: SAGE, 1976.

SMITH, M.L., GLASS, G.V, and MILLER, T.I. *Benefits of psychotherapy*. Baltimore: Johns Hopkins University Press, 1980.

SPINDLER, G. *Doing the ethnography of schooling*. New York: Holt, Rinehart & Winston, 1982.

SPRADLEY, J.P. *The ethnographic interview*. New York: Holt, Rinehart & Winston, 1979.

SPRADLEY, J.P. *Participant observation*. New York: Holt, Rinehart & Winston, 1980.

STAKE, R.E. *Evaluating the arts in education: A responsive approach*. Columbus, Ohio: Charles E. Merrill, 1975.

STAKE, R.E., and EASLEY, J.A. *Final Report: Case studies in science education*. National Science Foundation Contract C7621134. Urbana: School of Education, University of Illinois, 1978.

Standards for educational and psychological testing. Washington, D.C.: American Psychological Association, 1985.

STRAUS, M.A., and BROWN, B.W. *Family measurement techniques: Abstracts of published instruments*. Minneapolis: University of Minnesota Press, 1978.

STUFFLEBEAM, D.L., FOLEY, W.J., GEPHART, W.J., GUBA, E.G, HAMMOND, R.L., MERRIMAN, H.O. and PROVUS, M. *Educational evaluation and decision-making*. Itasca, Ill.: Peacock, 1971.

SULLIVAN, H.S. *The psychiatric interview*. New York: W.W. Norton & Co., 1954.

SUTTCLIFFE, J.P. A probability model for errors of classification. I: General conditions. *Psychometrica*, 1965, *30*, 73–96.

SWEETLAND, R.C., and KEYSER, D.J. (Eds.). *Tests: A comprehensive reference for assessments in psychology, education, and business*. Kansas City, Mo.: Test Corporation of America, 1983.

TATSUOKA, M.M. *Multivariate analysis: Techniques for educational and psychological research*. New York: John Wiley, 1971.

TAYLOR, S.J., and BOGDAN, R. *Introduction to qualitative research methods*. (2nd ed.). New York: John Wiley, 1984.

TERKEL, S. *Working*. New York: Pantheon Books, 1972.

THOMAS, W.I. and ZNANIECKI, F. *The Polish peasants in Europe and America*. New York: Knopf, 1927.

THORNDIKE, R.L. Review of the Wide Range Achievement Test. In O.K. BUROS (Ed.), *Mental Measurements Yearbook (7th ed.)*. Highland Park, N.J.: Gryphon Press, 1972.

THORNDIKE, R.L., and HAGEN, E.P. *Measurement and evaluation in psychology and education (4th ed.)*. New York: John Wiley, 1977.

TRAVERS, R.M.W. *Second handbook of research on teaching*. Chicago: Rand McNally, 1973.

TROCHIM, W.M.K. *Research design for program evaluation: The regression discontinuity approach*. Beverly Hills, Calif.: SAGE, 1984.

TYLER, R.W. *Basic principles of curriculum and instruction*. Chicago: University of Chicago Press, 1950.

VAN HOUTEN, R., MALENFANT, L., and ROLIDER, A. Increasing driver yielding and pedestrian signaling with prompting, feedback, and enforcement. *Journal of Applied Behavior Analysis*, 1985, *18*, 103–110.

VAN MAANEN, J. Observations on the making of policemen. *Human Organization*, 1973, *32*, 407–418.

WALKER, M.J., and FETLER, M.E. *Instruments for use in nursing education research*. Boulder, Colo.: Western Interstate Commission on Higher Education, 1979.

WALKER, R. Case studies in science education: Pine City. In R.E. STAKE and J.A. EASLEY (Eds.), *Final report: Case studies in science education*. Urbana: School of Education, University of Illinois, 1978.

WARWICK, D.P. and LININGER, C. *The sample survey: Theory and practice*. New York: McGraw-Hill, 1975.

WEBB, E.J., CAMPBELL, D.T., SCHWARTZ, R.D., SECREST, L., and GROVE, J. *Nonreactive measures in the social sciences*. Boston: Houghton Mifflin, 1981.

WEISS, I. *Reports of the 1977 National Survey of Science, Mathematics, and Social Sciences Education*, National Science Foundation SE-78-72. Washington, D.C.: U.S. Government Printing Office, 1978,

WHALEN, C.K., and DENKER, B. *Hyperactive children: The social ecology of identification and treatment*. New York: Academic Press, 1980.

WILLSON, V.L., and PUTNAM, R.R. A meta-analysis of pretest sensitization effects in experimental design. *American Educational Research Journal*, 1982, *19*, 249–258.

WITTROCK, M.C. (Ed.). *Handbook of research on teaching (3rd ed.)*. New York: Macmillan Publishing Company, 1986.

WOLCOTT, H.F. *Teachers vs. technocrats*. Eugene: Center for Educational Policy and Management, University of Oregon, 1977.

WOLCOTT, H.F. Mirrors, models, and monitors: Educator adaptations of the ethnographic innovation. In G. Spindler (Ed.), *Doing the ethnography of schooling*. New York: Holt, Rinehart & Winston, 1982.

WORTHEN, B.R., and SANDERS, J.R. *Educational evaluation: Theory and practice*. Worthington, Ohio: Charles A. Jones, 1973.

INDEX

AUTHOR